POLITICS and

CATHOLIC FREEDOM

POLITICS
and
CATHOLIC FREEDOM

by
GARRY WILLS

foreword by
WILL HERBERG

HENRY REGNERY COMPANY *Publishers*
CHICAGO 4, ILLINOIS

To
AMERICAN CATHOLICS
for being both

Knowledge has a freedom in the Catholic Church which you will find in no other religion, though there, as elsewhere, freedom degenerates unless it has to struggle in its own defence.

LORD ACTON

FOREWORD

THE encyclical *Mater et Magistra*, issued by Pope John XXIII in 1961, captivated world opinion by the breadth and generosity of its appeal. It also raised some questions, and initiated a controversy, that, in the long run, may prove as significant as the substantive content of the message. The questions raised related to the nature and extent of the assent required of believing Catholics to a Papal encyclical and its various parts. The controversy over these questions flared up for a brief moment, and then appears to have subsided. But the appearance is surely deceptive. For the time being, the élan of *aggiornamento* seems to have swept everything else out of the way; but even *aggiornamento* cannot simply conjure fundamental questions out of existence. And the questions raised by *Mater et Magistra* were surely fundamental, for they touched the question of the *magisterium,* i.e., the teaching authority of the Church. Such questions concern not only the Catholic people, naturally always alive to the proper authority of the Church and its magisterium; they concern the non-Catholic world as well, for reasons that every Catholic should try to understand and take seriously.

I myself had a small part in the controversy over *Mater et Magistra*; and perhaps a brief account of how I, a non-Catholic, came to be involved may help to suggest the full range of the problem. For some years, I had been studying, as carefully as I could, the mind and work of the Church in this country and in Western Europe; and I had come to the conclusion that religiously and culturally, socially and even politically, the Roman Catholic Church was the most significant positive force in the West. Of course, as a Jew, I still had—and still have—my basic theological differences with the Church; but I could not help admiring the way the Church had held out against the secularizing, "liberalizing," and "progressivizing" madness of the nineteenth century, and had defied the *Zeitgeist* in order to preserve the fundamental truths about the spirituality, dignity, and destiny of the human person and of mankind as a whole in the emerging mass society of the industrial age. Because, for decades, it had not feared to be denounced as reactionary, the Church was now once more in the van in the struggle for humanity against the demonic forces of totalitarian dehumanization. It was definitely—and, I must say, for many of us, rather unexpectedly—on "our" side.

It became all the more important, therefore, to re-examine realistically the scope of thought and action vouchsafed the believing Catholic by his Church. And here, once more, we were in for a most welcome surprise. Instead of the monolithic uniformity we had been taught to expect, we found, in the Catholic community throughout the world, an astounding diversity of opinion, and a most fruitful freedom of thought—within the well-defined dogmas of faith, of course. And we found, too, eminent Catholic spokesmen who not only acknowledged this diversity and freedom, but gloried in it, seeing it as the condition (though by no means the only condition) of a vital spiritual and cultural life. In my case at least, the enthusiasm engendered by these discoveries ran high; and I became, as I have often been pointedly reminded, a kind of volunteer "apologist" of the Catholic Church *in partibus infidelium*. And I still am.

Imagine, then, the shock I experienced when, some three years ago, I was confronted with the admonitions to a rigorous conformity appearing in certain sections of the American Catholic press in connection with *Mater et Magistra*. And these stern admonitions stemmed, curiously enough, not so much from the so-called "closed mind" organs of Catholic "integralism," but from those that, until very recently, had been very "open minded" indeed. It was most disconcerting to find journals that had been eagerly promoting freedom of Catholic thought and inquiry suddenly insisting that *all* pronouncements of the magisterium were alike entitled not only to respectful and docile attention, but to "inward assent" as well—without bothering to explain the kinds and degrees of inward assent involved. Everything in *Mater et Magistra,* and, two years later, everything in *Pacem in Terris,* had to be assented to and approved of simply as a matter of Papal authority. So fragile did the "openness" of the "open minded" prove itself once they thought they were in possession of encyclicals that seemed so much theirs, so unequivocally "liberal" and "progressive"! It was indeed awe-inspiring to watch Father A and Mr. B donning the robes of Monsignor X and sternly warning the Catholic faithful that not the least little deviation could be permitted from so authoritative a teaching of the magisterium as an encyclical!

Awe-inspiring, indeed; but not exactly convincing. It just could not be the way the "liberals" turned conformists insisted it should. How much "inward assent," for example, can the faithful Catholic give to the Papal Bull *Rex Gloriae* of the year 1311, in which Clement V (formerly the Archbishop of Bordeaux) in effect exalted France to the position once occupied by Israel as God's Chosen People? How much agreement is required to the corporative system outlined as the proper organization of society in Pius XI's encyclical of 1931, *Quadragesimo Anno*? But to come closer to our own day, does everything in *Mater et Magistra* (1961) and *Pacem in Terris* (1963) really demand a uniform degree of assent? Granted that where an encyclical contains doctrinal teaching, Catholics are bound to give it "interior as well as exterior assent and obedience"; the question remains, however, just what part of an encyclical does constitute *doctrinal* teaching on faith and morals. It certainly belongs to the doctrine of the Church that man is a spiritual being divinely endowed with certain natural rights; it certainly belongs to the doctrine of the Church that economic policy ought to be subordinated to morality so far as ends and the evaluation of means are concerned. But is it also, and in a like manner, part of the doctrine of the Church to which interior as well as exterior assent is required that the common good can best be attained by governmental intervention and control instead of through the operation of the free market, as so many contemporary economists contend? In other words, is Keynesian economics to be canonized as Catholic teaching, but the "neo-liberal" economics of von Mises, Roepke, and Milton Friedman outlawed? It is Catholic doctrine that all human beings are bound together by a "solidarity which . . . makes them members, in a sense . . . of the same family" (*Mater et Magistra*); and no one who denies this can claim to be in line with the age-old teaching of the Church. But does one, in the same way (again referring to *Mater et Magistra*), have to acclaim the ILO and the FAO just because the Pope in his encyclical expresses his "warm approval" of their work? One must recognize the obligation of universal charity as an obligation imposed by faith; but does that mean that one cannot, in good Catholic conscience, advocate a foreign aid policy geared primarily to an over-all strategy for the defense of our country and mankind against Soviet totalitarian tyranny? In a careful and balanced comment on *Pacem in Terris* ("Things Old and New in *Pacem in Terris*," *America*, April 27, 1963), Father John Courtney Murray, S.J., raised the possibility that "there may be some warrant for the thought that the spirit of confident hope which the Pontiff [John XXIII] courageously embraces fails to take realistic account of the fundamental schism in the world today," so that "there will be those who think as I do [i.e., as Father Murray does] that we have been given limited guidance." Are these doubts to be interpreted as a faltering, or a failure, of the "interior as well as exterior assent and obedience" required for the teaching of a Papal encyclical?

These are real questions, and the problem they point to is a real problem. It is, of course, an aspect of the perennial problem of authority and freedom within the Roman Catholic Church; but though perennial through the centuries, it confronts us with particular urgency today, at a time when the Catholic Church bids fair to retrieve a position of spiritual and intellectual prestige it has not enjoyed for centuries. That is what makes the present work of Garry Wills so very important. Mr. Wills is deeply disturbed at the attempts being made in certain Catholic quarters to cast a mantle of quasi-infallibility over certain ideologies and policies; he is even more deeply disturbed lest these obscurantist tactics, however unnoticed at first, redound to the discredit of the Church in time to come. His concern is the concern of a man who loves truth and is committed to his Church; he is therefore angered by statements and attitudes that seem to him calculated to injure either or both. His anger leads to polemic; but it is one of the singular merits of this work that the author proves able to get beyond polemic to the high ground of a fundamental inquiry into the problem itself. Mr. Wills approaches his task with the passion of a believer and the conscience of a scholar; and the measure of his achievement is the penetration with which he opens up the problem to its depths and the clarity with which he pursues the analysis. I have myself read the book twice in manuscript; and I do not hesitate to say that I have not laid down a chapter without a sense of new insight and understanding gained.

It is no wonder, then, that I heartily recommend this work to every Catholic and non-Catholic alike who is concerned with a problem—that of authority and freedom—that is of universal significance, and of particular importance in our time because of the pre-eminent position of the Roman Catholic Church in the life of the West. Mr. Wills does not answer all questions, and some of the answers he gives will not prove acceptable to every reader, any more than they have proved to me. But no reader, I am sure, will fail to profit greatly from Mr. Wills in his polemics, in his historical investigations, and in his philosophical analyses. Mr. Wills' book may yet become a powerful factor in bringing reason and clarity to the situation with which he is so deeply concerned.

Will Herberg

Drew University
January 1, 1964

Contents

INTRODUCTION

A GENTLEMAN, in the quaint etiquette now happily fallen into disuse, does not debate political or religious differences with his friends. We have, by now, modified this code of courteous inarticulateness; so that discussion of religion, or discussion of politics, each taken separately, is permitted, even (cautiously) encouraged. But it is still bad form to talk about them *at the same time.* The last presidential campaign was enough to remind us that open discussion of religion as a force in politics embarrasses most Americans. It is *there,* but it is unrefined to advert to its presence. By the ground rules of American political debate, one is supposed to act and speak as if it were *not* there. Perhaps some of the lunatic appeal in religious attacks on Mr. Kennedy, during his campaign, arose from an obviously hollow ring in the assurance that "there is no religious issue in American politics."

It is no accident that reality was forced some distance toward the surface by a Catholic's campaign for the Presidency. The Catholic Church is a challenge to the fiction that religious and political views coexist, but with an intervening distance that precludes fraternization, within the mind of the American voter. That Church has a history antedating the polite convenience that defines religion as "a private affair," a fact without influence, a thin ghost that may still haunt private life but fades instantly in the sunlight of public affairs. Before the intransigent facts of Catholic history this illusion cannot be maintained. The Church has not only had "entangling alliances" with political regimes, but with regimes Roman, mediaeval, monarchical, military. To the American, the presence of the Church of Constantine and Charlemagne, of Gregory VII and Boniface VIII, is a disconcerting part of the modern scene. He cannot reduce this religion to a private matter in certain individuals' lives; yet he cannot treat it as *more* than this without abandoning his primary conviction and rule of action in this matter, which asserts that *all* religion is a private matter. Caught in this dilemma, the American remains, for the most part, elaborately tolerant toward the Catholic Church, not "suspicious" in any malevolent way, but uncertain of his conduct toward it, because its very proximity has a solvent effect on his presuppositions.

Catholics are in much the same condition, themselves. They are Americans, and share much of the American bewilderment about certain aspects of their Church. The world of Boniface VIII is as remote from them as from their non-Catholic fellows in this country. Although they do not suspect that Rome is biding its time, ready to reinstate the mediaeval order of politics, they too wonder at the Church's checkered history. They are so willing to believe that there is no incongruity between the Church's possession of thirteenth-century ideas in the thirteenth century, and of twentieth-century concepts in the twentieth, that they often jump to this view without bothering to make the historical analysis that establishes it. And so they are not anxious to debate difficulties in a view they hold as eminently reasonable, but have not investigated with rigor. All this simply means that American Catholics *are* Americans, that they share the specifically American virtues and shortcomings in the area of conscious political wisdom.

I do not mean to say that Catholics feel any conflict in principle between their allegiance to Rome and to the American Constitution. It is true that these are not one and the same allegiance, and therefore an adjustment of competing claims may sometimes be necessary. But this is true of the moral life lived at all levels of commitment. Conscience necessarily involves a choice between conflicting claims—what one owes to one's neighbor, what to one's self; what to Caesar, what to God. This conflict is inherent in the nature of human activity, and any principle that denied its possibility would itself be defective. The same conflict is apparent in non-Catholic moral life. As D. W. Brogan put it, "Christians have always thought that holding civil office had its special moral dangers. The Catholic politician is no worse off than the deeply believing Protestant Christian."

But certain ways of formulating a conflict between Rome and Washington can mislead the Catholic conscience, or direct debate into sterile channels. Foremost among these polemic structurings of the divided allegiance problem is the treatment, in some quarters, of Papal encyclicals. Are these marching orders, a political platform to be injected—the complete package, self-enclosed—into the formative processes of American life? If not, are they general moralizings with no practical aim at all? If the Papal letters are *neither* a platform nor an exercise in platitude, then what precise middle ground do they occupy, and how are we to fortify that proper location against the encroachments of simplifiers who would make the letters partisan, on the one hand, or irrelevant, on the other?

Here is a real problem, often encountered in the electric atmosphere of politics, not only by Catholics but by those non-Catholics who have, increasingly, been impressed by the political wisdom of recent encyclicals but puzzled by the conflicting attitudes of Catholics themselves towards these Catholic documents. This is not the only point of dubious accord or undefined irritation among Catholics, but it is a key one; understanding achieved at this point would prevent misunderstanding in many tangential areas.

The cloudiness or lack of consensus on this subject is certainly not the result of any failure in interest or discussion. But the discussion has become stratified, moving on layers of awareness which rarely intersect, and then by way of simple collision: encyclicals are treated in the juridical niceties of the theological handbooks, needing interpretation in practical terms for the layman, or, alternatively, in the hasty rhetoric of politics, where a reduction of the controversial temperature is necessary if there is to be mutual understanding and agreement.

It is in the gap caused by the failure of these two approaches to "mesh" that I see the place of this book. I do not mean to duplicate any of the work done on the two levels where thought has progressed in a useful way, but without mutual effect. I do not mean to proceed toward sociological generalizations, or to write a theological work on the nature of Papal authority; and that for three reasons. First, and most important by far, I do not have the professional knowledge of a sociologist or a theologian. Besides, these are the areas in which work has been and is being accomplished. Finally, these specialists' very skills, geared to the demands of their discipline, can make their conclusions relatively inaccessible to the laymen who actually have the problems. My aim is far more modest.

Rather than generalize on "Catholic debate" across a large spectrum of sociological sources for ascertaining the nature of this debate, I begin with one clear, sharp dispute and study it with some thoroughness. The usefulness of the effort will depend, not on the internal merits of this first debate, or of any proposition advanced in the course of it, but on its *paradigmatic* character—on the fact that later examples I shall cite of Papalist "intimidation" on all kinds of subjects operate implicitly on the ideas and principles made embarrassingly explicit in the clear, articulated stages of this first controversy.

In dealing with such controversies I do not attempt, what is beyond me anyway, to derive from them or impose on them a complete theology of Papal encyclicals. Rather, I go to the theological guides available to a layman, to see what can be said about the *mode* of Catholic debate in these specific instances—looking to the norms of adjudication rather than to the substantive matters that are *sub judice*; testing the resources at hand for fruitful continuance of discussion; and offering the theologians (whose right of professional competence it is to treat the subject systematically) a case book of trial-and-error, in the arena of actual conflict, to be of service to them in their better equipped if less frequented laboratories. By giving the dispute I have chosen a "guinea-pig" treatment, I make myself a guinea pig for the observation of men qualified by their collegiate discipline to draw larger conclusions from our performance. In all this I adhere to Father Yves Congar's reminder that the theologian cannot adequately fulfill his office unless the layman presents questions and problems in a frank and pointed way.

Perhaps a cautionary note should be sounded, to prevent a misunderstanding that would cripple this kind of "laboratory approach" from the outset. If Americans have a prejudice against the serious discussion of the role of religion in politics, there is good reason for such an attitude. Religious matters are of such deep importance, they so thoroughly possess the soul, that acrimony in this area, if not guarded against, can reach a pitch of intensity that is terrifying. Although this book begins by renewing the memory of an argument that became heated at times, what is reprinted is part of the public record, and has not disturbed the good order either of religion or politics. The grounds of agreement between Father Thurston N. Davis, S.J., and Mr. William F. Buckley, Jr. (to take the two most deeply engaged participants in this opening dispute) are so deep and broad that they would not dream of considering each other primarily as antagonists. Before taking up more general aspects of the question of Catholic freedom in politics, I deal with a specific controversy which is, among other things, a clear picture of that freedom in operation. This controversy is part of that large, exciting, and (in the strict, the etymological sense) *edifying* process that is endemic to Catholic thought. This authentic tradition of the Faith was presented by Newman in the following terms:

It is the custom with Protestant writers to consider that, whereas there are two great principles in action in the history of religion, Authority and Private Judgment, they have all the Private Judgment to themselves, and we have the full inheritance and superincumbent oppression of Authority. But this is not so; it is the vast Catholic body itself, and it only, which affords an arena for both combatants in that awful, never-dying duel. It is necessary for the very life of religion, viewed in its large operations and its history, that the warfare should be incessantly carried on. Every exercise of Infallibility is brought out into act by an intense and varied operation of the Reason, from within and without, and provokes again a reaction of Reason against it; and, as in a civil polity the State exists and endures by means of the rivalry and collision, the encroachments and defeats of its constituent parts, so in like manner Catholic Christendom is no simple exhibition of religious absolutism, but it presents a continuous picture of Authority and Private Judgment alternately advancing and retreating as the ebb and flow of the tide;—it is a vast assemblage of human beings with wilful intellects and wild passions, brought together into one by the beauty and majesty of a Superhuman Power—into what may be called a large reformatory or training-school, not to be sent to bed, not to be buried alive, but for the melting, refining, and moulding, as in some moral factory, by an incessant noisy process, (if I may proceed to another metaphor), the raw material of human nature, so excellent, so dangerous, so capable of divine purposes (*Apologia*, p. 328).

Entirely aside from misunderstandings about the scope of Catholic debate, criticism may be directed against the book's method, which is to proceed from a locally and temporally confined controversy, scrutinized up close, to discussion of the points raised by it. I may seem, at first, to devote an unnecessary amount of attention to what was, after all, a small scuffle. But I hope the usefulness of this approach will establish itself in the results, as the analysis proceeds. Therefore, a certain suspension of judgment concerning these results may be necessary in the first steps of the process. I cannot pretend to a lack of bias with regard to the political views held by disputants here—or, for that matter, to a freedom from even deeper kinds of bias or inclination (e.g., some of the participants in it are my friends)—but I can, and do, attempt the observance of priorities in the hierarchy of questions at issue. Though I have opinions, more defined on some subjects, less on others, about most of the specific political questions that are raised in these disputes, I do not mean to express any of my opinions, or defend them as such. If I have inadvertently lapsed from this good resolve, the reader should try to ignore my failure, that we may both attend to the matter immediately at issue: What is the general relation of papal teaching to such political disagreements? I do not explicate that papal teaching on any question. I am concerned only with the preparatory stages of such an investigation, the rules to be observed in embarking on it. When I say, as I shall, that specific arguments have no moral force—for instance, quoted examples of "papal teaching" as endorsing the United Nations Organization or opposing "right-to-work" laws—I am not saying that other arguments could not arrive at the same conclusion by valid routes of inference. My interest is solely procedural: what *kind* of things do the encyclicals say, and mean, in such areas?

If most of the examples of faulty procedure treated here are those in favor of "Liberal" legislation, this is because Catholic Liberals have been more interested in encyclicals, have tried to use them more extensively (and so have failed in a proportionately larger and clearer number of instances), than have Catholic Conservatives. I have no illusions that Catholic Conservatives, put in the position, journalistic and academic, of Catholic Liberals, would have any more acumen or success in their efforts at interpretation of these documents. There are already cases of haphazard citation in Conservative polemic, and it is safe to say that, if Liberals should read encyclicals more carefully, Conservatives should read them more carefully *and read them more.* Furthermore: though the Liberal treatment of encyclicals is the one that comes to hand for assessment, I know that many shortcomings in this treatment were caused by the fact that there has been little give-and-take of informed debate: Liberals begin to think their interpretation of encyclicals *must* be correct since it is not effectively challenged by spokesmen of another point of view.

That is not the challenge I mean to make. A discussion of contemporary American Conservative thought in the light of papal teaching is badly needed, but this is not it by any means. Let all the points made by Liberal spokesmen be objectively correct—I would still maintain that the arguments criticized in this book are invalid. Because invalid, they spread confusion over the subject of the encyclicals' intent, making the moral call of the Pope less effective, puzzling the conscience of those who, not predisposed to the Catholic Liberal's conclusions from papal premises, wonder how on earth he got from the one to the other. This book will try to trace, for them, the voyage. It is hoped that it will promote the effort at drawing improved maps of the moral world, both on the Liberal and the Conservative side of American debate. But I offer no such maps myself; only some fundamentals of cartography.

G. W.

PART ONE

THE
CONTROVERSY

O_N August 13, 1961, the *New York Times* ran a story with the headline, "Jesuits Attack Buckley on Encyclical." Two items in the journal *National Review*, edited by Mr. William F. Buckley, Jr., had touched off this minor explosion. One was a brief paragraph preceding the magazine's titled editorials. It appeared in the issue of July 29, 1961, and one phrase from it was to become notorious. This is the paragraph:

The large sprawling document released by the Vatican last week on the seventeenth anniversary of Leo XIII's famous encyclical *Rerum Novarum* will be studied and argued over for years to come. It may, in the years to come, be considered central to the social teachings of the Catholic Church; or, like Pius IX's *Syllabus of Errors,* it may become the source of embarrassed explanations. Whatever its final effect, it must strike many as a venture in triviality coming at this particular time in history. The most obtrusive social phenomena of the moment are surely the continuing and demonic successes of the Communists, of which there is scant mention; the extraordinary material well-being that such free economic systems as Japan's, West Germany's, and our own are generating, of which, it would seem, insufficient notice is taken; and the dehumanization, under technology-*cum*-statism, of the individual's role in life, to which there are allusions, but without the rhetorical emphasis given to other matters. There are, of course, eloquent passages stressing the spiritual side of man, as one would expect there should be. But it is not unlikely that, in the years ahead, *Mater et Magistra* will suffer from comparison with the American Catholic Bishops' hierarchy of emphases, in their notable annual message of November 1960.

Another phrase that would achieve notoriety appeared two weeks later in the same magazine's collection of miscellaneous items under the heading "For the Record":

Going the rounds in Catholic conservative circles: "Mater, sí; Magistra, no."

There was an instant response from the Jesuit-edited weekly, *America,* which ran the following among its editorial paragraphs for August 12, 1961:

Affront to Conservatives

The following item appears in the *National Review* for August 12, 1961:

> Going the rounds in Catholic conservative circles: *"Mater, sí; Magistra, no."*

Although the editors of the *National Review* possibly have more intercourse with Catholic "conservatives" than we do, we question the veracity of that report and resent the insult to fellow Catholics. We consider the statement slanderous.

So-called Catholic conservatives, like the rest of us, may be honestly mistaken in their judgments of modern trends; they may even be confused about this or that principle of Catholic social teaching; but they are not disloyal. However embarrassing it may be for some of them to discover from *Mater et Magistra* that their brand of conservative thinking can in some respects scarcely be reconciled with Pope John's teaching, they will accept it with filial respect. We have no doubt whatsoever that they are Catholics first, last and all the time—even if this means saying a good word for the International Labor Organization and the UN Food and Agriculture Organization. The *National Review* owes its Catholic readers and journalistic allies an apology.

In the same issue, Rev. Thurston N. Davis, S.J., editor of *America,* discussed both the passages that had appeared in *National Review* as examples of the misguided wit of Mr. Buckley, and reminded his fellow-editor that *Qui mange du Pape, en meurt.* The middle paragraph of his feature column made the phrase "venture in triviality" famous:

Mr. Buckley is no ordinary person. It takes an appalling amount of self-assurance for a Catholic writer to brush off an encyclical of John XXIII as though it had been written by John Cogley. Mr. Buckley was equal to the challenge. It takes a daring young man to characterize a papal document as "a venture in triviality." From long practice on the high wire, Mr. Buckley possesses that kind of daring. Moreover, to have coined the comment that the Church may one day be as embarrassed by *Mater et Magistra* as she is by the Syllabus of Errors of Pope Pius IX reveals the sophistication and the wit that once made Mr. Buckley the lion of Yale's common rooms. Finally, as to his sprightly play on the opening words of the encyclical—*Mater, sí; Magistra, no*: "conservative Catholic circles" accept the Church as Mother but not as Teacher—well, the editor of the *National Review* just couldn't resist it.

It will be noticed that "Mater, sí" is no longer a quip "going the rounds in conservative Catholic circles," but a witticism of Mr. Buckley's meant to announce that these circles do not accept the Church as Teacher. Whence the demand that Mr. Buckley apologize to these circles, whose faith he had gravely impugned.

It was this version of the matter that was presented in the secular press (the *Times, Time* magazine, etc.) and stimulated diocesan editorialists to indignation. The tenor of this reaction can be sampled in excerpts from syndicated columnists who appear in the diocesan papers. The first is from the column of Rev. William J. Smith, S.J.:

A venture in triviality! Where will one find so insulting, so stupid a statement as that? . . . When a spiritual intellectual giant of the stature of Pope John XXIII is ridiculed by a hypercritical pigmy, the shout of protest should be loud and lasting. . . . This is the kind of stuff from which seedling schisms sprout. . . . According to report, it [*National Review*] has a good many Catholics among its subscribers. It also has a considerable following of easily aroused, emotionally charged admirers. If they find a conflict of loyalties between the encyclical *Mater et Magistra* and the sad little commentary of the *National Review,* for the health of their own souls they should make up their mind and make it up quickly on which side their loyalty stands.

The second example is from Mr. Donald McDonald's column:

If any Catholic is really uncertain concerning the comparative qualifications of Pope John on the one hand and William Buckley on the other to speak out on the great social problems of our age, no argument from me is likely to have much effect. . . . True conservatives must stand aghast at this latest display of anti-intellectual temper tantrums by the men at *National Review.*

And Msgr. George G. Higgins wrote in his column:

The only really nasty comment I have seen appeared in the *National Review*. . . . This snide comment is disgraceful but it will not have been written in vain if it serves to open the eyes of those Catholics who have hitherto looked to the *National Review* for guidance.

The Providence *Journal* ran a cartoon of Mr. Buckley nailing the slogan "Mater, sí" to the door of St. Peter's in Rome.

The issue had now become the Catholicism of Mr. Buckley, and of any Catholics who wander so far from the fold as to read *National Review*. Many were warning the faithful that *National Review* is not a Catholic magazine; to which Mr. Buckley replied that indeed it is not, and therefore it should be allowed to comment on the political and historical effect of encyclicals without being accused of rebellion from a faith it does not represent:

I gently remind the editors of *America* that *National Review* is no more a Catholic magazine because its editor is a Catholic, than the present Administration is a Catholic Administration because its head is a Catholic. The editorial in question represented the position of the editorial board of *National Review*, on which the three major religious faiths are represented, Catholic, Protestant, and Jew.

> —from "The Strange Behavior of *America*,"
> *National Review*, August 26, 1961

On the grounds that specifically Catholic controversy is best carried on in the Catholic press, Mr. Buckley asked Father Davis to print a letter on the subject of this controversy. This request was turned down. Not only that, *America* informed *National Review* that it would accept no further advertisements. Mr. Buckley then ran his letter in *National Review*, with an explanatory preface:

During the past few weeks, several editors of Catholic magazines and diocesan newspapers have gleefully seized upon NATIONAL RE-VIEW'*s references (July 29) to Pope John's recent encyclical,* Mater et Magistra, *as excellent grounds for a good hanging party. I am not myself particularly surprised, as I have grown used to humorless polemical opportunism, which goes on among American ideologues irrespective of race, color or creed. But I care very much*

that those readers of NATIONAL REVIEW *who are Catholics, and live*
within the firing range of the aforementioned press, should not feel
cowed by the local zealotry.

    For that reason I wrote three weeks ago an open letter to Father
Thurston Davis, editor of America, *the Mourner-in-Chief, discuss-*
ing the nature of the resentment over NATIONAL REVIEW'S *commen-*
tary. I sent copies of that letter to all bereaved editors, hoping to
staunch their grief by a reasoned analysis. But America *has declined*
to publish my soothing words, as have the other editorial ululators,
who appear to resent any interruption of their tribulation, even in
the high cause of free speech.

    I therefore publish the letter below, for the benefit of our Cath-
olic readers. And I beg the pardon of our non-Catholic readers,
who are of course interested in any general commentary involving
political trends within the Catholic Church, for devoting so much
space to what must strike many of them as a venture in triviality.

—W. F. B. Jr.

Dear Father Davis:

Let us begin by distinguishing between NATIONAL REVIEW's editorial treatment of *Mater et Magistra,* and the lighthearted quip
about it which we published in our periscopic gossip column, "For
the Record." To deal first with the latter, let me say plainly what I
thought we'd never be called upon to say: the crack *Mater Si Magistra No,* which originated with a Catholic scholar and journalist in
Virginia, was a flippancy, pure and simple. It was hardly a hammer-
blow driving articles of defiance into the Vatican's churchdoor.
I am absolutely astonished that any serious man, endowed or not
with a sense of humor, should so have construed it. If—God forbid
—I should ever be tempted to defy the teaching authority of the
Church, whose cause I have taken seriously ever since I was in my
teens (Dwight MacDonald referred to me in the *Reporter* as a Sav-
onarola-type when I was 23 years old), I shall not announce my
apostasy in doggerel.

    I take no objection to your denouncing the flippancy as having
been in imperfect taste: I am quite prepared to subject myself to
the criticism of my elders on such matters. I very much object,
however, to the solemn construction you and other critics, equating orthodoxy with an arch solemnity, gave to what was merely a
jeu d'esprit. I ask myself: What on earth seized Father Davis—
and Father Smith, and Monsignor Higgins, and Mr. Donald Mc-
Donald—to strike out on so reckless a tack? Do they sincerely *believe* that I have decided to reject the *depositum fidei* because
along came an encyclical whose rhetorical emphases disappointed

me? I cannot bring myself to entertain so condescending a version of your intelligence and wit. I chose, and choose even now, to believe rather that we have before us an act of opportunism, which you should search your conscience to justify. You know what is NATIONAL REVIEW's mode. It matters not whether you approve of it: you know it is our mode, and you must understand what we do in context of that knowledge. Proceed, if you like, publicly to despair over our insouciance or frivolity—but to edge us over into infidelity is more than uncharitable; it is irrational, and, in the true sense, scandalous.

Last summer a business executive, who probably once had heard one of Bishop Sheen's speeches on the place of humor in Catholic life, or read a volume by Chesterton, gave way to an impulse of political exuberance, and titillated a rally of local Republicans by announcing that the Democratic prayer had, at the Los Angeles convention, been amended to read, "Hail Mary, you all." The next day the wretched man, a vice-president of General Motors, was almost drowned by cries of Intolerance and anti-Catholicism. He managed, before going down for the third time, to thrust forward his scapulars and announce to the press that a) he was, far from being anti-Catholic, a Catholic himself; that b) he had devoted much of his spare time to raising money for Catholic charities; that c) he had been awarded any number of Catholic honors and decorations. . . . His critics, finally satisfied, left, though it is reported he was still numbly professing his faith one hour later, having brought in a certified public accountant to tally the number of indulgences he had earned over the preceding decade.

On that occasion, NATIONAL REVIEW remarked on the terrible dangers of a prurient search for sacrilege in the hugger-mugger of secular exchanges. Jonathan Swift wrote a modest proposal that eighteenth-century Ireland solve its social problems by eating supernumerary babies. Things were pretty grim in eighteenth-century Ireland, but God was good to have spared Dr. Swift coexistence with *America,* and *Commonweal,* and Mr. Donald McDonald.

Let me say it again, I do not object to your saying this flippancy, or that, is tasteless, or even—provided you say it carefully—subversive in objective effect. A friend of mine heard a priest say from the altar last January 21, "Hail Mary, full of grace/ The Masons are in second place." Now, if I were cornered and had to express myself on the taste of this jest—entered under the putative rubric of the Holy Ghost—I confess I would deplore its gracelessness, though I think I would not search out a public opportunity for doing so. It would not occur to me to suggest that here was evidence that the priest's partisan political fervor had displaced his sublimer commitments to charity, understanding and love.

You raise the question of our response to the Encyclical itself. You commit the error, if my understanding is correct, of confusing

decorum and fidelity. In exclusively Catholic circles, Catholic decorum must—and should—prevail. You are no doubt aware that
Senator John Kennedy, upon greeting Cardinal Cushing when the
two came together on a public platform before thousands of alumni,
to receive honorary degrees from Harvard, declined to kiss his
Ordinary's ring: on the grounds, presumably, that the semi-litur-
gical obeisance, in such surroundings, would have been inappropriate; more, that its memorialization coast-to-coast by the AP pho-
toservice might have caused a lamentable dissension in a Protestant
community ever eager to find confirming evidence of the kind of
servility which is athwart traditional American notions of the
proper relationship between Church and State. I am not so sure
Mr. Kennedy's conspicuous departure from Catholic etiquette was
clearly justified, but neither I, a political opponent of Mr. Kennedy, nor you, a political ally, transmuted his act into a gesture of
defiance of the prerogatives of a prince of the Holy Roman Catholic Church.

Mater et Magistra was released as a very public document. It
entered into the bustle of political controversy and demanded attention as a political document. NATIONAL REVIEW wrote the plain
truth when it said that parts of it "must strike some"—of course
they so struck some!—"as a venture in triviality." I consider that
the body of papal literature—and I have often said this, in public
platforms across the land—is the most important literature, in be-
half of the highest claims of humankind, that has been generated
out of any single modern source. In no way is that generality con-
travened by the specific criticisms NATIONAL REVIEW made of the
order of emphasis of a single encyclical. Indeed, the editorial in
question spoke not one word of criticism of the intrinsic merit of
Mater et Magistra. Our disappointment was confined to the matter
of emphasis, and timing, and by implication, to the document's
exploitability by the enemies of Christendom, a premonition rapidly confirmed by the Encyclical's obscene cooption by such declared enemies of the spiritual order as the *New Statesman* and the
Manchester Guardian, which hailed the conversion of the Pope to
Socialism!

What on earth would you expect an ecumenical Christian journal to do under the circumstances! Curtsey and go away? You are
infinitely patient with the dogged materialism and secularism of
the United Nations. Yet you seem to be denying to a Christian
journal of opinion the expression of its opinions on the tactical
or strategical uses of a single encyclical and, in the process, calling
into question the traditionally exercised right of Catholics generally, to analyze and discuss and weigh, in context of their abiding
faith, the meaning of papal encyclicals. I am as a Christian journalist dismayed by your position. And as a fervent Catholic I am ap-
palled by your methods. You publicly announce yourself, with im-

perial presumption, as "*The* National Catholic Weekly Review";
I explicitly deny your claim. If you are indeed *the* voice of the
Catholic Church in America, then your words are to some extent
solemnized. But can seemingly invincible ignorance be solemnized?
One of your staff declared (*America,* November 28, 1959) that
NATIONAL REVIEW's editor argues a case for a society ". . . in which
. . . individuals of every rank would be equally and absolutely free
to rummage in garbage pails for their dinner and to use park
benches for their bedding." Your haughty dismissal of the painstaking efforts of the writers and staff of NATIONAL REVIEW to further the course of truth and freedom and love and Christianity
represents a lapse into an ideological sectarianism which is a continuing affront upon the transcendent imperatives of an engaged
Catholicism. Why does not the censorious National Catholic
Weekly try to comprehend the efforts of that great body of American Catholic opinion which has found a truer political expression
of the faith of our fathers in NATIONAL REVIEW than in your own
journal?

A final word. In refusing to accept any further advertisements,
you have levelled against us your ultimate sanction—one which
NATIONAL REVIEW uses only against Fascists and Communists and
racists. Five years ago, you announced that you would refuse to
accept manuscripts from any writer whose name appeared on the
masthead of NATIONAL REVIEW, specifically rejecting articles you
had months before accepted from Drs. Russell Kirk and Erik von
Kuehnelt-Leddihn. Granted, in due course prudence prevailed,
and you relaxed the embargo. But your record of animosity has
been consistent. During these five years, NATIONAL REVIEW has
entered into the public record as distinguished a series of analyses,
and exhortations, and criticisms, and belletrisms as any journal in
the land—enough to commend us to a legion of Catholic readers,
of humble and exalted standing. I hope you will, from time to time,
review the grounds of your new anathema. When we stand together, as well we may, in that final foxhole, you will discover, as
we pass each other the ammunition, that all along we had the same
enemy; and that if we had acted in concert, we might have spared
ourselves that final encounter, under such desperate circumstances.

Yours faithfully,
Wm. F. Buckley, Jr.

A non-Catholic editor of *National Review,* Mr. Frank Meyer,
had meanwhile addressed a letter to *America,* asking a) why the
editors of *America* had assumed that he must live under specifically
Catholic discipline, an assumption they acted on when they censured in terms of that discipline an editorial for which he and his
non-Catholic colleagues were responsible, and b) whether, if he

became a Catholic, he would be embracing not only a faith but a political "line" dictated from Rome. The editors answered, in an editorial called "Magistra, Sí" (*America*, September 30, 1961), that Mr. Meyer's is "the characteristically neo-secularist viewpoint —which it must now be clear to everyone is the viewpoint of *National Review*":

To those who approach a papal social statement with this attitude of mind, it appears quite logical to accept or reject the message of an encyclical to the degree that it squares or does not square with personal political or economic opinions. This, it is now obvious, is the explanation of what happened at *National Review* headquarters, where the encyclical was weighed, found wanting and dismissed as a "triviality."

National Review should have accepted the encyclical in its entirety, not treated it as if men could "accept or reject." In other words, Mr. Meyer *is* to be treated as subject to Catholic discipline. *National Review* is therefore a Catholic magazine? No. Reversing themselves, the editors repeated what was becoming one of the most popular warnings in the Catholic press: in its final words, the editorial not only reassured Catholics that *National Review* is not "an authentic voice of Catholic conservatism," but concluded with dramatic, Beethovian insistence: "It is *not*. We repeat: it most certainly is not."

The theme of "neo-secularism" was treated, later that same fall, by Rev. Philip S. Land, S.J., whose "Pope John XXIII: Teacher" appeared in *America* on November 4, 1961. Lamenting a growth of laicism in America, Father Land devoted his final paragraph to what, apparently, he considers the primary organ of this laicism:

Moreover, as one whose life work has been the assimilation and the teaching of Catholic social doctrine, I can say with absolute certainty that no collaborators Pope John might have turned to—European or American or other—could have or would have prepared an encyclical that would be acceptable to the editors of *National Review*.

The religion editor of *National Review* is not a Catholic, and he obviously was not satisfied by the answers *America* had given to Mr. Meyer's questions. In his column for November 4, 1961,

Mr. Will Herberg weighed the controversy to that date. On the one side, he found no evidence that Mr. Buckley was impugning the teaching authority of the Church, though he did feel the magazine had been tasteless in its treatment of the encyclical:

Mater, si, Magistra, no! may be very clever, but it is a kind of cleverness which one ought not to permit oneself, because it is so susceptible to misunderstanding. Nor does it seem wise for anyone, Catholic or non-Catholic, to focus his first comments on a Papal encyclical in terms of its immediate context, rather than in terms of its intrinsic, long range significance. It might be true that the Pope's timing was not of the happiest, and hence the Papal statement might have struck some as "trivial"; but *National Review* would have done better by far to examine internal and intrinsic meaning, rather than the theatrical effect.

Turning to the other side of the debate, Mr. Herberg expressed again the uneasiness Mr. Meyer had voiced in his letter:

But, on the other hand, I do not think that the editors of *America* will have any particular reason to feel happy at the way they have defended the Encyclical against Mr. Buckley and his friends. In defending the Encyclical, the editors of *America* have naturally had to defend the teaching authority of the Church; but this they have done in such a way as to bring dismay to many Catholics and to numbers of non-Catholic well-wishers as well. They have virtually converted their defense of the teaching authority of the Church into a claim of blanket immunity from criticism for every part of the Encyclical alike. . . . For years, I have been arguing before Protestant, Jewish, and other non-Catholic audiences that there is no such thing as a "Catholic line," that on economic, social, cultural, and political matters, insofar as they do not touch the basic teachings of the Church on faith and morals, there is the widest diversity of opinion among Catholics permitted within the Church. Have I been wrong in so arguing? As a non-Catholic who does not have to prove his friendliness to the Church, I should like to have this question answered at this time.

America answered Mr. Herberg on November 11, 1961, saying that it did not mean to make all parts of an encyclical equally authoritative, but to emphasize that the Pope's documents have a "distinctive character," and are authoritative for Catholics. (So presumably *that* is what had been denied in the offensive editorial.)

Discussion of *Mater et Magistra* itself now fell off, but the large issues of the dispute were kept alive in the pages of *America*. On February 10, 1962, the magazine printed a statement of policy which explained its decision against running advertisements for *National Review*:

We will not publish advertisements for a journal which, in our opinion, seriously and consistently undercuts positions which we judge to be central to our faith, the natural law, or the explicit and long established social doctrines of the Church.

That is, *National Review* is *ex natura* on the *Index Librorum Prohibitorum*, and not to be read by Catholics even in the small segments an advertisement might contain. The task of containing its threat was advanced on December 2, when the "Campus Corner" feature warned college students against allowing theological security risks to appear on their platforms:

Neither can you turn a campus platform over to a pro-something-or-other and make out that it's purely a business engagement. A host has to be hospitable . . . But there are some ideas and some causes that a Catholic college cannot treat pleasantly. Not because of any personal prejudices, but because they don't contribute to the business of a Catholic college. . . . Doesn't deliberate opposition to Catholic social doctrine come close to being anti-Catholic? Can anti-labor, anti-UN, anti-foreign aid speakers be hosted and toasted on a Catholic campus?

Another threat calling for America's vigilance came from what Father Davis considered an unexpected quarter, *Ave Maria* magazine. Mr. Donald Thorman had written in that journal, on October 28, 1961:

The fact does remain that Catholic conservatives and liberals are often conducting a sometimes unhealthy, often unchristian—and totally unnecessary—internecine feud. I know I speak for many when I call upon conservatives and liberals alike to begin to think seriously now of ways in which this apparent impasse can be resolved for the sake of Church and country. . . . Is it out of the question to hope that quiet meetings between members of both camps might be held to work out Christian ground rules for debate and to decide on a basic, minimal program for a united fight against

Communism and for the promotion of justice and charity in our society?

Mr. Buckley sent to *Ave Maria* what he felt would be a contribution to this dialogue, which was accepted and printed as such (see editorial, *Ave Maria*, April 14, 1962). Mr. Buckley's article, which appeared on April 7, said that one of the misunderstandings to be resolved was the belief that a political opponent of the Communist empire's dimensions needs no direct strategic countering, that virtue will of itself disarm enmity, that working for social justice is enough to halt Communism—a variant of the belief that a truly *good* man will walk through the jungle without tempting any tiger's palate. Some Catholics, for instance, say that the best way to fight Communism is to desegregate the American South. To which Mr. Buckley replied:

The Communists could not care less whether there is segregation in the South, and the Negroes in the South have never been attracted to communism on account of segregation. If every white Southerner were to miscegenate tomorrow, the Communist Party would not be set back by five minutes. . . . To suggest that a Just Solution (instant integration, according to some) will silence the Communist carpers is naïve: The Communists would find just as much to criticize in an integrated South as in a segregated South, just as they are finding it as easy to criticize our prodigious trade union movement, as to criticize the fledgling thing of 30 years ago.

To claim a moral duty is not a sufficient strategic instrument against a determined foe is not to deny that it is a moral duty. (In fact, as a moral duty, it should not have to rely on practical advantage as its sole motive.)

Our fight against communism is not to be understood merely as a fight against sin: That is a fight in which each one of us is supremely engaged, and stands to lose his own soul. The other fight is one in which we are engaged as a civil collectivity, and the distinction is not between "just" and "unjust" acts in relation to fighting communism, but between relevant and irrelevant means of fighting communism. . . . I believe we should make justice—because it is the right thing to do to make justice; but I do not for a moment believe that every act of justice draws strength away from the Communist movement.

In presenting the defeat of Communism as a strategic problem, as well as a moral one, he drew this parallel:

Lincoln wrote to Horace Greeley in the dark days of the Civil War that his aim was to keep the union, that if he could do so by freeing every slave, he was prepared to free every slave; if he could keep the union by freeing half the slaves, he'd let the Negro population stay half slave and half free; that if he could keep the union by letting all the slaves stay slaves, why thus they would remain. Lincoln meant by that letter not, obviously, that the highest imaginary ideal was the survival of the union, but that the survival of the union was the highest ideal of which he could hope to be the instrument; the survival of the union was his highest existential responsibility; and the union having been secured, then, under its framework, civilized discourse would resume, and men with black faces would in due course become free.

At the end of his piece, he returned to Mr. Thorman's suggestion:

Let us understand one another, for God's sake; and let us not put off the day of our reconciliation. How commendable is the effort of Mr. Thorman! We must come to know one another. To prove my sincerity, I shall on the day I return to the United States (I write this from Switzerland) once again invite to lunch with me, to talk over our differences, the editor of *America*. I hope he will not, once again, refuse.

In the next issue of *America*, Father Davis wrote:

Last night, more in sorrow than in anger, I read William F. Buckley's article in the current *Ave Maria*, that ancient weekly which issues from the Golden Dome of the University of Notre Dame.

In a closing paragraph Mr. Buckley says he intends to invite me to lunch.

Parts of his long article deal with the race question. I repeat: the race question—not the question of how we are to work toward and achieve interracial justice for the Negro.

If I read this unprecedented *Ave Maria* contributor aright, we have no collective responsibilities with respect to the Negro. We need worry only about those "individual ledgers" in which we daily tot up our purely personal accounts in the field of race relations. A logical conclusion from his philosophy of individualism.

The one thing that matters, according to Mr. Buckley—the single item of business that could be said to demand collective effort —is the fight against communism. This cause is not affected, one would gather, by the interracial work of Fr. Louis Twomey (whom Mr. Buckley belabors) or by the lifetime of effort of Fr. John La-Farge (whom he does not mention).

Reading this article I recognize the Yale-trained voice of young William Buckley, but feel the rough hand of old Leander Perez (p. 41). That impression comes through clear and strong in sentences like this: "If every white Southerner were to miscegenate tomorrow, the Communist party would not be set back by five minutes."

If a fellow were to eat that one raw sentence, word by word, he might be inclined to skip lunch.

T.N.D.
"Of Many Things,"
America, April 14, 1962

The assistant editor of *Ave Maria,* Mr. Terry F. Brock, addressed the following answer to Father Davis, which appeared in *America's* correspondence column for May 5, 1962:

EDITOR: As the editors of AMERICA well know, the dangers that Catholic periodicals face when attempting to interpret the issues and crises of the day in the light of the Church's thinking are immeasurably frightening.

But even more dangerous and more frightening for what it portends was AMERICA's—specifically, Father Davis'—"sorrow" over the appearance of an article by William F. Buckley Jr. in the April 7 issue of *Ave Maria.*

First, the reader is given the impression that "that ancient weekly which issues from under the Golden Dome of the University of Notre Dame" is a Notre Dame publication—a fact which the editor of AMERICA knows to be untrue.

Second, the venerable editor (surely, "venerable" is more pleasing to the ear than "ancient") of that youngster of the Catholic press, AMERICA, leaves his readers with the impression that Mr. Buckley should be neither seen nor heard in any Catholic publication. Of course, he didn't mean to say this—or did he?

Third, by taking one example—the race problem—from the article and dwelling upon it with a gentle ferocity, the editor of AMERICA denigrates his colleague-in-scathing-rhetoric Buckley by truncating his thesis—which is, of course, that the Communists couldn't care less about racial justice, that they use racial tensions and bickering as a point of conflict, that they would, if the circumstances dictated it, use mass miscegenation to the same end.

Fourth, the editor of AMERICA orates: "I recognize the Yale-trained voice of young William Buckley, but feel the rough hand of old Leander Perez." He thus equates Mr. Buckley with an active segregationist.

I'm quite sure that Mr. Buckley would differ with him on this point. In his charity, however, I don't believe that he will bring suit for libel. (Mr. Buckley opposes the John Birch Society; the editors of AMERICA oppose the John Birch Society. Thus, under the Fordham-trained voice of AMERICA I detect the suave sophistication of William Buckley. Yes, I know—good grief!)

Fifth, AMERICA's editor fails to tell his reader that the article in question is a discourse on ways and means to battle communism— not a discourse on racial justice. The point that Mr. Buckley emphasizes is that a complete, loving acceptance of the Negro as a human being with an eternal soul destined to languish in the embrace of the Beatific Vision, as our brother in Christ, as an individual in the family of man—this unequivocal acceptance, Mr. Buckley asserts, will in no way deter Communist aggression.

Whether Mr. Buckley is right or wrong is open for debate, heated debate if you like. But nothing in the article—and, to my knowledge, in any of Buckley's writings—gives his critic just cause to imply that the gentleman is either secretly or overtly a racist or a segregationist.

Ave Maria's intent in presenting the article to our readers was to offer them the opinions of an intelligent, mature, articulate Catholic spokesman for the conservative cause. We did so because we consider our readers to be intelligent, mature and thinking Catholics, too.

I long for the day when AMERICA will show this trust in its own readership and offer its subscribers a similar opportunity. Have we reached such a state in the Catholic press that editors with fixed political opinions cannot tolerate a divergent point of view in their own publications?

> Terry F. Brock
> *Ave Maria*
> Notre Dame, Ind.

It will be remembered that in Father Davis' feature column on Mr. Buckley, there was a reference linking him with Leander Perez, the racist who defied Archbishop Rummel, in New Orleans, and was excommunicated. In the same issue that dealt with Mr. Buckley, an editorial was devoted to Perez, whose entrenched moral cretinism was treated as a symbol of mushrooming anticlericalism:

Some years back, writing in a mass-circulation weekly, Fr. John Courtney Murray dropped a remark about anticlericalism in the United States. He saw this problem then as a small cloud on the horizon, "no larger than a man's hand." But he hinted that it was growing.

Father Murray's article, which appeared in *Life* for December 26, 1955, said that anticlericalism would increase if clericalism became too repressive: "There is the kind of clericalism that would deny to the layman—in fact if not in doctrine—any real responsibilities and consequently any genuine freedom even in the fields in which the layman belongs and has competence." Father Murray then gave journalism as an example of an area in which laymen should be given more freedom than some priests would allow them. This article seems inappropriate as a tool for analyzing the rebellion against Archbishop Rummel, who is surely not a clericalist causing the kind of tension Father Murray was concerned with. But the editorial was on its way to the cultured voice *behind* Perez, to what was by now the King Charles' Head of *America,* Mr. Buckley. It was using Father Murray's warning *against* priests' suppression of the independent lay journalist precisely *in order* to suppress Mr. Buckley.

Anticlericalism of this kind is not limited to Louisiana and does not manifest itself merely with respect to the Church's stand on desegregation. In a variety of forms the same phenomenon is to be observed in the battle of many so-called "conservatives" against the social doctrine of the Church as this doctrine is propounded by the modern Popes and by the American hierarchy. People turn against Church leaders when insistence is laid on principles of social and economic import which go against the grain of individualistic prejudices. We all witnessed what happened last summer at the time of the publication of Pope John XXIII's encyclical *Mater et Magistra* (Christianity and Social Progress). This document was downgraded and dismissed as trivial in some quarters, and the assumptions on which it rests—the right and duty of the Church to pronounce on the moral aspects of economic and social life—were so vigorously disputed that Fr. Philip Land, writing in *America* at the time, declared himself shocked by what he had encountered among Catholics all over the United States. . . . It looks as though Fr. Murray's tiny cloud has blown up into a nasty little storm.

Note the progression: by subsuming everything under the catchword "anticlericalism" and using Leander Perez as the medium of transition, the editorial has Father Murray condemn Mr. Buckley. As *The Catholic Reporter* summed up the argument: "He who is segregationist is anticlerical is conservative." For even *The Catholic Reporter,* a journal that agrees with *America* politically, could not stand by and watch this "label-hanging" without protest. In its editorial for April 13, 1962, it analyzed "this lumping together of events and personalities" in a grand sweep of guilt by association, and concluded:

America's editorial, it seems to me, is the first real hint that, as many have been contending, the American Catholic consensus is hardening into a party line that won't admit of argumentation, or strong differences of opinion. Something regrettable will have happened, and something serious will be wrong under the surface, if *America* actually can silence Buckley, as it seems to want to do so badly. We could stand a lot of silence from Buckley, but we don't want it forced on him.

But Father Davis showed no signs of drawing back in his campaign to crush the new anticlericalism whose name is Buckley. In June of 1962, Msgr. John Tracy Ellis gave two commencement addresses making the same point that Father Murray had made in his *Life* article—that a repressive clericalism breeds anticlericalism. Father Davis, in a long article, did not get the connection: he described the three kinds of anticlericals he knows as a) crackpots who like to pester priests, b) others who have somewhat the same ideas but are more balanced in presenting them, and c) the real thing Father Davis has been aiming at throughout the article, the anticlericalism of *National Review*:

This is found among some of today's so-called "conservative" Catholics, once again regularly practicing members of the Church, who in many cases openly reject the very right of the Popes and bishops to instruct consciences—as they do in the social encyclicals and in national synodal declarations—on matters touching social and economic life, international responsibility or interracial justice. It is to this not-inconsiderable group that Fr. Albert J. Nevins, immediate past president of the Catholic Press Association, referred May 31 in a speech in New York in which he blamed such Catholics for permitting a situation in which "the *National Review* is more authoritative than the New Testament." My own experience with these persons unquestionably supports Fr. Nevins' judgment.

—"Anticlerical 'Virus'?"
America, June 16, 1962

In this 2,000-word exegesis of Msgr. Ellis' speech, there is no mention of its main point—the danger of repressive clericalism.

We have come a long way from the attack on misguided wit, the defence of Catholic conservatives' honor, with which the original comments on *Mater et Magistra* were received—a tortuous way, touching all the proper nerves for response among Catholics: neo-secularism, laicism, anticlericalism. It is not a journey that has much to offer us as an example of argument or rational debate; but its appeal to certain instincts, its persistent refrains *are* enlightening as an example of the functional disorders that can arise in Catholic discourse, that can impair Catholic freedom. It is time to step back from the controversy itself, and look at this single aspect of it, before we consider further examples of the process.

PART TWO

THE MECHANICS
OF REPRESSION

By a paradox that delights, exasperates, or simply confuses men, the Catholic Bishop of Rome has so much power that he is often immobilized by it. As Cardinal (then Father) Newman wrote, "There are gifts too large and too fearful to be handled freely."[1] The Papacy is not the seat of a divine despot, but a ministry to God and man, a *diaconia*, and the stewardship over a deposit of truths with their guarantee outside the person of the individual Pontiff. If we are to seek a natural analogue, the Pope's office is not that of a king but of the seer—of Teiresias, not Oedipus; of Calchas, not Agamemnon; of Cassandra, not Clytemnestra. The servant of God is constantly reminded, by the very office that gives him authority, that he is *not* God. And so, despite the apprehensions caused by its unique authority, the Catholic Church has been as much criticized for its failure to intervene in political matters (a refusal as ancient in the Christian tradition as *Titus* 2.9) as for its interference. Many, both within and outside the Catholic faith, not bearing themselves the awful burden of this authority, think that its powers should make themselves felt as a constant in all areas of human life. All discussion, they feel, should take place in the shadow of an impending Judgment from which there is to be no appeal. Monsignor Ronald Knox once compared these voices to that of the Temptor who urged Christ, on the temple's peak, to descend miraculously into the midst of men:

Often in history and not least in our own day, the Church has been rebuked for her want of spirit in allowing the world's injustices to go unchallenged, asked why she does not interfere in secular quarrels, at whatever risk to her own popularity and influence . . .

[but] because she is in a unique position, she is reluctant to take advantage of it. Because her empire over souls is so vast, she knows that she retains some kind of hold, though it be a slight one, over many whose consciences are imperfectly formed; because they are such a Babel of nationalities, she knows that wide differences of tradition and outlook will divide them. Because she retains, in spite of everything, so powerful a hold over the affections, she shrinks from setting up in their minds a conflict of loyalties— Church against class, or religion against race—to confuse them and to hurry them into acting against their private conscience. Because her powers are so terrible, as holding the keys of the kingdom of heaven, she is more afraid of the consequences—to them—of alienation from her membership than some voluntary association of Christians, calling itself a Church, would be in the same circumstances.[2]

How, then, if the essential and inestimable power of the Pope is so hedged, has "condemnation," in varying degrees and under many formal guises, become such a constant phenomenon in the Church? Everyone knows that Catholic thinkers have often been threatened with, or actually suffered, "silencing" on certain matters or for certain periods. Even young Father Angelo Roncalli (he let it be known, after becoming Pope John XXIII) lived for a while under this shadow of suspicion, when the Holy Office opened a dossier on him. Does this not give the lie to Newman's assurances that the Papacy is not repressive? Newman, too, lived under "official" suspicion. He was forced to surrender his editorial position on the controversial journal, *The Rambler*—a position he had assumed to prevent the silencing of his predecessor, Simpson, and a position in which his successor, Acton, was silenced in his turn. Does this not show—what theologians are presumed to know all too well, from Saint Paul's time to Bellarmine's and on to Karl Rahner's and Courtney Murray's—that Peter is a jealous ruler, who will not let the truth be enunciated save from his lips?

Not so; though the case histories be true, the analysis of cause is not. Yet even Catholics are not enough aware of the forces at work here; and this makes it difficult to assess the kinds of freedom and restraint a Catholic enjoys. For it is not a matter of mere intellectual demonstration. A servile attitude in Catholics will blunt the best work of theologians in presenting true Catholic principle.

Thus, for the general welfare of his Church, as well as for his own maturity and self-respect, the Catholic should be clear in his mind about the kinds of authority that exist over him, and the kinds of pressure that work on him.

Peter disagreed with Paul, but did not "silence" him; he came, in fact, to agree with him. And the Pope himself rarely silences individual Catholic teachers. As Newman said, "So little does the Pope come into this whole system of moral theology by which (as by our conscience) our lives are regulated, that the weight of his hand upon us, as private men, is absolutely inappreciable."[3] On the rare occasions when the highest power does intervene in an individual's work, the reason is usually to prevent confusion rather than to crush error. This is the kind of disciplinary action that, in the long run, promotes truth, channeling discussion along established lines, preventing chaos, allowing private motives or momentary passions to subside. The Church, Catholics believe, will endure. They do not have to risk all for a *dying* cause. Men will sift their debates; a facet of truth now hidden from the light of day will be turned toward it in time; an argument neglected will be recovered. The Church's dependence on historical transmission of the apostolic authority places on her a demand of conscious continuity, a constant reliving of the past, that is a unique pledge of relevance for all Catholic thinkers.

Furthermore, since the truths under discussion by a Catholic relate almost entirely to charity, there is an obvious contradiction in the attitude of a man who would press his own argument even at a time when this would dismay rather than comfort, cause darkness rather than light. The mark of the heretic, Newman asserted, is not error but pride. The heretic demands an instant and uniform submission to his arguments; he will not let these truths be tested in the Christian experience, be lived in the dark mystery of a human Church kept afloat, against the odds, by divine guarantee. His arguments may prove, in the end, acceptable, may bless the lives of those within the Church. But the man who urged them intemperately will have lost their capacity to bless by working against the grain and outside the human context of that divine institution he tried, and failed, to understand. To use Newman's words again, "We must be patient, and that for two reasons, first in order to get at the truth, and next in order to carry others with us. The Church moves as a whole; it is not a mere philosophy, it is a communion."[4]

It is with these truths in mind that the Catholic thinker responds to the pressures of the body he belongs to. Men rightly suspect the theologian who is careless of the Church's peace, just as they suspect a surgical theorist who is careless with the human body. The Catholic theologian knows that no continuous effort of human thought has endured as Christian theology has endured through centuries of articulation, that no Western school of philosophy has had the advantage of long adjustment and accretion that the Church has made possible to Catholic philosophers. The wise men will not miss the lesson of this history. This authority has opened doors of the mind, not closed them.

But am I merely softening the phraseology, while admitting the substance, of Gladstone's accusation in the last century or Paul Blanshard's in this? Is the Catholic afraid to stir for fear of displeasing other Catholics, and especially those further up the hierarchical ladder than he? Is the Romanist mentality so conditioned to constant discipline that initiative and originality are destroyed at their source? Is the peace of Catholics a sign that they no longer struggle against restraint, because victory has been total for the repressing force? Is the Catholic merely one who *likes* to live under discipline, a happy child who never has to grow up?

Not if we are to judge by history. The great Catholic thinkers have not been notably plastic to repressive influence in any but the essential regard for charity. The Christian theologian should not turn medicine into poison by intemperate urging of his views; but he must also realize that some medicines go down hard, even in the right doses. To say that a Catholic disturbs his fellows is not the same thing as accusing him of scandal—though there are persons all too ready to equate these two. As the scripture scholar, John L. MacKenzie, S.J., said in an article called "Intellectual Liberty Revisited,"

If the scholar is unwilling to pay the price of a degree of unpopularity and distrust, he should not attempt to carry on scholarly work. ... The scholar smiles when he hears that he is regarded as a contemporary nuisance at best, a menace at worse. "If a little man like myself can cause so much alarm," he thinks, "what would these people do if Thomas Aquinas or Jerome or Augustine were here to disturb them? Those firebrands would make the contemporary intellectual ferment look like an Altar Society picnic."[5]

Father MacKenzie's wry reaction to the charge that he might be a menace recalls the time when a Monsignor Talbot could write from Rome, warning Cardinal Manning in 1867 that "Dr. Newman is the most dangerous man in England." Perhaps no one in modern times has suffered so much as Newman at the hands of those who, not possessing Peter's power, nonetheless try to exercise it in support of their own views. It was this that prompted him to say:

While I acknowledge one Pope, *jure divino,* I acknowledge no other, and I think it is a usurpation too wicked to be comfortably dwelt upon, when individuals use their own private judgment in the discussion of religious questions, not simply *abundare in suo sensu,* but for the purpose of anathematizing the private judgment of others.[6]

The mechanism of repression in the Church is a complex thing, then, a set of reciprocal pressures from within, not a single burden imposed from above. Overt heresy has usually violated these pressures in a callous way long before any authoritative pronouncement is made against it. A man may want very much to reach a certain place; but if he becomes so intent on his goal that, traveling toward it, he does not stop to eat or sleep, he cannot complain of "suppression" if he collapses far from the desired object. In the same way, heretics have usually ignored the signs of tearing fabric and screaming nerve while they were on their way to the point of collapse. The Church's highest authority does not come, usually, to amputate a diseased limb, but to tend the body after a limb has torn itself away.

Knowing this, the Catholic thinker may be cowed by *every* sign of opposition; he may equate all disturbance with scandal; but if he yields to this temptation, he is shirking his responsibility rather than obeying legitimate authority. Father Hans Küng reminds us that the attitude of the early disciples to the world and to each other is recurrently described in Scripture by the word *parrhesia*, "out-spokenness." Charity may demand deference and consideration in the presentation of ideas; but it also demands that the ideas *be* presented, that fear of frank exchanges be assuaged and sloth energetically expelled. The Church would not, after all, be a human body if some men did not try to use the inertia of its size and stability to prevent activities that displease them. Thus, the normal way of "silencing" a Newman is not to bring Rome crashing on his head. Instead, men assured him that he would confuse and mislead his fellow Catholics; and then, to give their argument point, they created the conditions in which Newman's teaching must seem unorthodox. I do not say that this was done from malice; W. G. Ward sincerely believed that Cardinal Wiseman's *Dublin Review* had the truth for English Catholics. But instead of saying that Newman erred in this or that point, he and others said that a Catholic voice like the *Rambler*'s would weaken men's faith by weakening the hold of the *Dublin Review* on its readers. Faced with this arranged crisis, Newman realized that his opponents would not back down; and so, in charity, he did. The debate had reached a stage where discussion was clouded under suspicion of disloyalty. Those without authority (like Monsignor Talbot) had worked, with all their might, to create disfavor for Newman among those in authority. And those in authority (like Bishop Ullathorne), without using their specific powers, hinted at disfavor and the possibility of higher powers' intervention. When such tensions have been created, a Newman will not push himself (or Ward) into heresy; but he must lament the loss of energies inflicted on the Church by such careless pretensions to her power. In such an atmosphere, this great defender of Rome's authority could say of the cloudy and undefined pseudo-authority stirred, everywhere, against him:

And now, alas, I fear that in one sense the iron has entered into my soul. I mean that confidence in any superiors whatever can never blossom again within me. I never shall feel easy with them.[7]

This loss of confidence was caused by the fact that Catholic fears had been inflamed to the point where pastoral apprehension became restrictive without formal enactment. For, even when author-

ity is at last brought to bear against a Catholic, it has often been
forced to this extreme through the misuse of pressure by subordi-
nates, a pressure that, left to work by itself, would cause greater
damage to the Church than the repressive act that has now become
necessary. Knowing this, Newman did not let things reach this
pitch. He tactfully restrained his fellow editors, Simpson and Acton, and retired from the troubled areas himself.

Catholics must recognize, if they are honest, the dark side of that
bright picture created by the Church's long life of mutual deference among its members, of thought tempered by charity. Trying
to push arguments at the wrong time leads men into heresy; but a
Ward can deliberately *retard* the Church's capacity to respond.
Catholics can be silenced without recourse to explicit authority.
This is done by creating sensibilities that will be violated by the
teaching one wants to discredit. This process is a temptation naturally arising from the Catholic system, so interdependent, alive in
all its members, its parts so responsive to each other. If heresy is a
member's self-amputation, this kind of repression is an effort to
make the body so delicate that the push of healthy effort will damage its fabric, will lead to a rending that resembles or even becomes heresy. The body is deliberately made sickly, so that un-
wanted exercise is impossible.

Newman felt himself obliged to yield to a situation created by
pressure, not *authority.* The real problem for a Catholic is not that
involved in submitting to authority. If that is a problem, he is not
a Catholic. The problem is to know when, in prudence and charity,
one should submit to pressure. Father MacKenzie draws the distinction in "Intellectual Liberty Revisited." He says, on the one
hand, that "Catholic biblical scholars feel no tension whatsoever
with the teaching authority of the Church. . . ." But he adds (p. 353)
"I [do] observe tension between exegetes and some ecclesiastics
who, without any canonical mission to do so, claim to speak for the
Church. . . ." And "In summary: there is no tension which I have
observed between intellectuals and the teaching authority of the
Church. There is tension between intellectuals and some who fear
that the teaching authority of the Church is unable or unwilling
to do its duty." Such men try to prod the reluctant wielders of power

into action by agitating events in such a way that the consequences of non-intervention would be grave.

Needless to say, Newman's actions were not always above criticism. The *Rambler* article on the laity, which caused the fiercest agitation against him, was imprudently phrased and poorly timed. Cardinals Wiseman and (later) Manning were burdened with pastoral responsibilities that did not weigh upon Father Newman. But the brutal use of doctrinal suspicion put Newman under a cloud, stilled his pen for five years, and made him chary of any public action or pronouncement. This is the grim cost of repression, once its machinery is set in motion. As a recent contributor to the *Dublin Review* (Ward's own journal) said, of those who silenced Newman and *The Rambler,* "one wonders at times whether we have even now begun to recover from the consequences of their doubtless well-intentioned but uninformed opposition to Newman's great vision."[8]

Compared with the cruel treatment of Newman, the dispute recorded earlier in these pages seems—and is—minor. For all their merits, neither Father Davis nor Mr. Buckley is a Newman; the hierarchy was not involved; grave scandal did not result. But it is precisely the smaller conflicts that admit of useful, detailed analysis. When great things are at stake, men are often too committed, too intent on the large objects of the dispute, to study the mere *mechanics* of Catholic discourse. There are moments when detachment is impossible, even frivolous. It is the task of Catholics to prevent such critical stages of conflict by understanding the tendencies of their own body, the large strength and many small weaknesses of the Church's organizational bond. When the pressures are still slight, we can study them with some hope of harnessing them for good, using the dynamics of discourse to incite growth rather than repression.

What, then, were the precise points at issue in the *Mater et Magistra* controversy?

At one level, there was a clear violation of decorum on the part of *National Review.* Whatever the final verdict of history, it is absurd on the face of it to suppose that *Mater et Magistra* could come to be considered by anyone as "a venture in triviality." The phrase was usually quoted out of context; certainly anyone encountering it in the outraged reporting of the Catholic press would never have guessed that this was presented as one of several historical judgments that men might make—including the judgment that the encyclical is "central to the social teachings of the Catholic Church"; and it is perhaps imprudent to hold every journal to a strict standard of religious decorum, under pain of Catholic resentment; but, nonetheless, it was an unfortunate phrase, an example of reckless rhetoric in a very sensitive area of discourse.[9]

The quip "Mater, sí" was also a flippancy that should not have been printed. The light chaff of private conversation is often improper material for public controversy. Jesuit seminarians were saying "Veterum, sí, Sapientia, no" soon after the Apostolic Constitution *Veterum Sapientia* commanded a more extensive use of Latin in seminary courses; but *America* wisely did not print this little joke when the magazine expressed regret that the document might impede the cause of English in the liturgy.

So far, Professor Will Herberg was justified in questioning the decorum of *National Review*'s remarks. But offenses against journalistic protocol would not justify the intensity of the Catholic press's reaction. And, in fact, *National Review*'s editorial and reported comment were not treated as lapses in good taste. The "Mater, sí" quip was taken as an ingenious invention of Mr. Buckley, meant to impugn the loyalty of Catholics. The sentence "Whatever its final effect . . ." was treated as a challenge to the whole principle of papal authority. On the basis of this interpretation, the Rev. William Smith, S.J., urged Catholics, "for the health of their own souls" to "make up their mind and make it up quickly on which side their loyalty stands," with Pope John or *National Review*.[10] The Rev. Albert J. Nevins, recently president of the Catholic Press Association, accused Catholic Conservatives of holding that "the *National Review* is more authoritative than the New Testament." *America* meditated extensively on the anticlericalism, laicism, racism, and general divergence from Catholicism, to be observed among its journalistic rivals.

Here, too, taking the matter at the most superficial level, there was a breach of decorum. There is no more serious charge against a

Catholic than defiance of an authority he believes to be divine; and nothing more offensive in any controversy than the assertion that one's opponent is acting in bad conscience, feigning a loyalty he does not feel. It was such "muddying the springs" that called up Newman's masterpiece of anger, the *Apologia,* and made him answer a correspondent, who had assured him that he was outside the pale of orthodoxy, with these words:

He who addresses another in these terms in a question of faith, begins where he ought to end. He forfeits the right of remonstrance and the hope of influence.[11]

Ironically, the mobilization of the Catholic press against Mr. Buckley was *least* justified if its charges were true. Those misled into incipiently disloyal positions should be recalled by charity, gentle rhetoric, close documentation of error. An attempt should be made to distinguish between the errors of the leader and the instincts of the followers. Every latitude of interpretation should be made as to personal motive, while the doctrinal points at issue are dispassionately expounded. Yet the substance of this dispute was inaccurately or inadequately discussed; comments obviously made in a whimsical vein were reported as heinous confessions; and the motivation of Catholic conservatives generally was presented as despicable. In this respect, Mr. Buckley's admonition that rhetorical mode must be considered is not only a valid point but the *basic* rule for interpreting, before attacking, one's foe: *C'est le ton qui fait la chanson.* The tone of *National Review*'s attempted jest, the column in which it appeared, make it difficult to see how anyone could take it seriously except by the most resolute desire to exploit an occasion for arousing suspicion.

When we go below the level of decorum, seeking the substantial points of disagreement in this dispute, we find there were three criticisms made of *Mater et Magistra* by *National Review.* All three points were on the matter of emphasis and timing. The magazine editorialized that the document's historical significance might be reduced—even, in the offensive phrase, reduced to triviality—by three omissions: the omission a) of sufficient reference to Communism's continued advance, b) of praise for the free world's economic recovery as a deterrent to that advance, and c) of criticism directed at the "dehumanization" caused by technological and governmental complexities in modern society.

Such objections on the grounds of strategic emphasis would not of themselves constitute a denial of papal teaching authority, even if we concede that a non-Catholic journal has a duty to accept that authority. It is true that criticisms of this sort *might* conceivably be advanced as a veiled first stage in a campaign to undermine loyalty to the Church. But before judging the editorial as part of an operation in undermining Catholic faith, a man should be cautious enough to consider with great care the actual criticisms made; he should undertake a methodical elimination of alternative explanations for the comments. Only when no other reason can be found for the egregious words might a man, in justice and charity, make public his reasoned conclusion that disloyalty was the editorial's aim and motive.

But is it likely, from any angle of inspection, that *National Review*'s criticism had this hideous significance? Under the most unfavorable view of Mr. Buckley's intelligence and moral state, is it likely that he could think the Church's doctrine had changed on the subject of Communism? Did the magazine's criticism imply a total failure of the teaching authority of the Church? Or, from another side of the thing, is not one paying tribute to a document when he regrets the lack, in it, of emphases congenial to his own deeply held estimate of the strategic situation?

This latter is the traditional view among Catholics. Precisely *because* of the importance of papal documents, Catholics hope they will emphasize matters on which there is no real doctrinal confusion. One example of this—though examples abound—is particularly relevant, since it involves *Mater et Magistra*. In its issue for July 29, 1961, *America* magazine expressed regret that "the present text does not treat explicitly of the race question," and hoped for some future papal pronouncement that would supply an accent the magazine felt was lacking. Does this mean that *America*'s writer *doubted* the soundness of papal teaching on racial equality? Or does it mean that *America*'s editor no longer recognizes the Pope's authority, that *America*'s readers have elevated Father Davis to the position of an anti-Pope? Was *America*'s remark "nasty," "snide," "an anti-intellectual temper tantrum"? By the standards used in criticizing *National Review,* the answer to all these questions would have to be yes; and, where the controversial Mr. Buckley is no longer the victim of these standards, their injustice can be seen in an instant. (*Mater et Magistra* was, in fact, followed by *Pacem in Terris,* the third section of which was largely devoted to the issue of racial equality.)

Catholic journals in other lands criticized *Mater et Magistra*'s distribution of emphases. The London *Tablet* regretted the absence of stress on *moderation* in the discussion of that drive toward independence that is shaking Africa and the "new nations." This is a traditional mode of approaching difficult moral matters, made explicit for instance by Leo XIII in the encyclical *In Plurimis.*[12] And, so far as I know, the *Tablet*'s editorial has not been used to attack the motives of its editor, Mr. Douglas Woodruff. The English Catholic editors merely felt, on the basis of their acquaintance with political activities around them, that the modern world would do well to remember this part of the moral teaching of the Church, and that mention of it in a new encyclical would most forcibly recall the point to memory.

It can justly be urged that *National Review*'s criticisms were not presented with the thoroughness or the evidence of scholarly intent that would justify any elaborate analysis of them. But our concern here is *procedural,* with the *conduct* of Catholic debate; and it is necessary to look sharply at the actual words that blew up this flurry of accusations. This is twice necessary, because so few of *National Review*'s critics studied these words with any care. Some critics, for instance, *assumed* that the magazine made the crude mistake of equating "socialization," in the American translation, with "socialism"—a matter which did not enter into *National Review*'s remarks. Again, *America* pictured the writhings of the Conservative conscience under the Pope's praise for the International Labor Organization. This imaginative effort made it unnecessary even to mention the three points of actual criticism offered by the magazine.

The few diocesan editorialists who proved they had read *National Review*'s critique, rather than *America*'s description of it, took the stand that there is no need for the Pope to mention Communism, since that has been so often and forcefully condemned. This misses the point. *National Review* did not ask for a "new" condemnation—any more than *America* expected new doctrine on the subject of race relations. But *Mater et Magistra* put itself expressly in the great tradition of *Rerum Novarum* and *Quadragesimo Anno*. It was the third major document in a continuing analysis of economic ills, threats, cures. Surely Communism is not noticeably less a threat today than it was in 1891 or 1931. And if it is not, then the political and economic causes of this perdurance are, arguably, pertinent to a resumé of economic trends since 1931. Strictly from the standpoint of relevance, *National Review*'s criticism touches a matter more intimately related to the theme of the major encyclicals than does *America*'s suggestion on race or the London *Tablet*'s comments about gradualism in the process of decolonization. None of these Catholic critics was suggesting that the Pope's teaching needed correction, with the implication that it was erroneous; only that Catholics need more specific help in sorting out priorities in the field of social action. Men can disagree in their analysis of contingent events, on which this sense of priorities is based, without calling into question the Church's teaching, or any Catholic's allegiance to that teaching. Certainly most encyclicals would be considerably reduced in bulk if no mention were to be made of matters that had already been treated in the papal literature.

As to *National Review*'s second point, the recovery of Western Europe's economy proves that the doctrines of subsidiarity and of private ownership have not become anachronisms in the changed circumstances of our decades. This, too, is directly pertinent to the theme of the social encyclicals. It is clear that *Mater et Magistra* does not repudiate subsidiarity, which is called "the guiding principle" of the State's action in economic matters (par. 53) ; nor does it depart from the principle of private property, which is called the indispensable support of liberty (par. 109). The editors of *National Review* simply maintained that a large-scale example of these principles in action might have made them more impressive to the contemporary audience.

National Review's third point of criticism sounds a note that was characteristic of Pius XII's last years—criticism of the tendencies that work toward what he called "depersonalization" in modern society. This was made the central theme of the American Bishops' 1960 statement to their flock. It was taken up by Pope John when he discussed the rate of increase in the complexity of social relationships (*socialium rationum incrementa,* clumsily simplified to "socialization" in the Vatican translation). While not denying the points made by Pius XII—that is, that such increases in complexity "conspire to make it difficult for a person to think independently of outside influences, to act on his own initiative, exercise his responsibility and express and fulfill his own personality"[13]—the Pope says that these do not *necessarily* make freedom impossible, so long as the dangers are understood and circumvented. *National Review*'s editors apparently thought this was the time to stress the dangers rather than the point that the dangers are not necessarily fatal. They might more usefully have recognized the encyclical's clear and choice phrasing of those dangers. At any rate, the criticism was made within the context of discussion that has been advanced in papal encyclicals, and not in repudiation of the whole function of encyclicals.

Those who were shocked by *National Review*'s rhetorical lapse may feel that nothing can redeem the suggestion that a papal document might become trivial in some historical perspective. To bother with a close look at what was actually said, by way of substantive criticism and suggestion, is a courtesy that will make such men impatient. This is an impatience observably proportioned to political hostility to the magazine. It is an understandable impatience, and few men would be foolish enough to claim they are exempt from promptings of this sort. But Catholics must try to keep down its influence in the discussion of other Catholics' fidelity to the Church. What is a deplorable, but perhaps (in the mass) inescapable failing, when other matters are under consideration, becomes a grave threat to freedom where religious authority is concerned.

The Church makes a claim upon man, in his totality, that has no parallel. Because of the stringency of this claim, it shows a care that many have called excessive for the proper freedom of those who recognize the divine force of her doctrinal position. This restraint has made the Church a unique organization among the powers of the earth. This alone of earthly bodies has regularly used less power than it could, at any moment, effectively claim. Newman explains such actions thus:

So difficult a virtue is faith, even with the special grace of God, in proportion as the reason is exercised, so difficult is it to assent inwardly to propositions, verified to us neither by reason nor experience, but depending for their reception on the word of the Church as God's oracle, that she has ever shown the utmost care to contract, as far as possible, the range of truths and the sense of propositions, of which she demands this absolute reception. "The Church," says Pallavicini, "as far as may be, has ever abstained from imposing upon the minds of men that commandment, the most arduous of the Christian Law—viz., to believe obscure matters without doubting." To co-operate in this charitable duty has been one special work of her theologians, and rules are laid down by herself, by tradition, and by custom, to assist them in the task. She only speaks when it is necessary to speak; but hardly has she spoken out magisterially some great general principle, when she sets her theologians to work to explain her meaning in the concrete, by strict interpretation of its wording, by the illustration of its circumstances, and by the recognition of exceptions, in order to make it as tolerable as possible, and the least of a temptation, to self-willed, independent, or wrongly educated minds. A few years ago it was the fashion among us to call writers, who conformed to this rule of the Church, by the name of "Minimizers"; that day of tyrannous *ipse-dixits,* I trust, is over.[14]

Newman must have known, even as he wrote the words, that his hope of an end to tyrannous repression would not be fulfilled. The Church will remain an exception among the political bodies of the earth, exceptional in its powers, exceptional in the restraint with which it uses them; but some of its members will fail to exempt discussion within the context of the Faith from the controversial procedures used in other areas. Catholics individually will remain liable to that temptation which the Church as a body has so signally withstood. And the good of the Church demands that men prevent this inclination (to extend authority when it is politically convenient) from becoming a Catholic instinct in any particular group or on any particular subject.

It is in this light that the *Mater et Magistra* dispute poses a challenge. The substance of *National Review*'s "attack" on the encyclical was minor; it appeared in an organ not directly subject to Catholic discipline; it was procedurally defensible even if one argues that it was based on mistaken notions. But the substance of the critique was not clarified, not given rigorous examination, not corrected on obscure or inaccurate points, *it was not even referred to,* in most attacks on the magazine. Those attacks took the form of personal accusation. This accusation was, in turn, used to "escalate" the affair into an assault on readers as well as editors. The basic charge of disloyalty was made the center of a whole series of charges, ranging, finally, from anticlericalism to racism. John Cogley was not exaggerating when he wrote in *The Commonweal* for May 3, 1963, that *Mater et Magistra* was used "not as an inspiration and a guide for action but as a kind of loyalty oath by which various parties within the Church are tested."

The temptingly effective method for sealing off debate, retarding frank criticism, making any disagreement seem like disloyalty, is— as we saw earlier—to create tensions that will snap, sensibilities that will recoil, if discussion is continued; and then to accuse one's opponent of crass disregard for such tensions and sensibilities. What else was the attempt to summon the spectre of apostasy, of laicism, of racism, the strangely exhilarated descriptions of "the stuff from which seedling schisms sprout," or of a "nasty little storm" of anticlericalism? Mr. Buckley is a popular campus speaker; and *America* suggested that conservative Catholics should not be allowed to speak on campuses. When some Catholics were excommunicated in New Orleans, Father Davis stretched logic to link Mr. Buckley with their position (and thus cast a shadow of their estrangement across his Catholic status). One cannot escape the impression that, acting from what they consider the best of motives, certain Catholics have decided to use the machinery of repression against one American journal and its editor. No doubt they feel that the good of the Church demands this. Most men who have used this process have been sincerely convinced that they are serving their Faith. But repression is a process full of dangers, one that almost invariably backfires. Thus, Mr. Herberg's other observation on the

Mater et Magistra controversy is also justifed. He said that *America* was guilty of more than a breach of decorum; it had confused the whole question of Catholic freedom of discussion, had "tended to wipe away all distinctions," had undercut the defense Mr. Herberg makes, in American religious debate, of the Catholic Church's freedom from a "Catholic line" in national politics. This is a serious work of confusion, and can recoil as easily upon *America* as upon *National Review*. It is not an attitude Catholics can afford to ignore, especially when it shows itself over a long period of time, and becomes increasingly virulent. Thus an attentive look at the controversy here reprinted is important as a means of preventing immediate bad effects, as well as for its interest as a paradigm and starting point for the discussion of Catholic freedom and the things that threaten it.

Some Catholics viewed with composure the conduct of *America* in this dispute, on the grounds that certain men or certain groups may not have been caught in any clear violation of the faith (e.g., *National Review*, in printing the "Mater, sí" quip, may not *really* have *said* that its editor no longer considers the Church competent to teach), but that such men or groups think, and would like to say, unorthodox things if they could (e.g., Mr. Buckley *means* to challenge the Pope even when he does not expressly *do* so) . Therefore it is legitimate to *seek an occasion* for unmasking the crypto-heretics, the people of whose bad faith we are certain, forcing them to make professions of the faith, and then pointing out that they cannot really mean it. This is a form of challenge that is implicitly issued in the rhetorical ploy so often used in political commentaries on the encyclicals: "*This* passage will certainly disconcert *those* Catholics who . . ." or "There is no room in the Church *now* for those who . . ." or "How can we think they are in good conscience who say something different from *this*. . . ." The appearance of a new encyclical seems almost to occasion a frantic scramble for shibboleths to use against one's political opponents. Commentaries on them are organized around the theme of identifying precisely *whom* the Pope is attacking *here*. One would almost think, after reading some of this literature, that Catholic priests and columnists rejoice in watching others have difficulties of conscience, so gloatingly do they report that segment x or y of the population is in for a severe case of them.

This widely accepted form of inquisition came before me in a very vivid way on one occasion. I had just delivered a lecture to a Catholic group in Washington on the danger of using Catholic "loyalty tests" as instruments of political certification. Most of my time was devoted to a discussion of the *Rambler* controversy in the last century, but I had also referred to the attacks being made at that very time on Mr. Buckley and the readers of *National Review*. Afterward, an articulate and educated man came up to say how much he agreed with me; but he wished I had not mentioned Mr. Buckley as one victim of such treatment, since he was certain of this particular man's bad faith. I said that, unless he had indisputable proof of this, his position actually increased the usefulness of my example. One should not base rules of fairness on the courtesy one shows to one's friends or to revered idols, about whom there is no possible doubt or prejudice to be exploited for political advantage. The test of one's standards is established by one's dealings with the men one dislikes—and he obviously disliked Mr. Buckley intensely. He said he had no single, specific proof of bad faith in Mr. Buckley's case, but that he had a certain "feel" for such things. When I suggested that this was inadequate for concluding, or even starting, a public trial, for making the editors of *America* undertake the work of the Holy Office, he offered what he thought *was* a strong and certain piece of evidence: even though the "Mater, sí" crack did not constitute a serious statement of disloyalty in itself, he said, only a mind twisted from the faith could have invented it.

The man obviously depended heavily on his feel for style. Since he had listened to me speak for an hour, and had read and reviewed a book I wrote, I asked him whether I had betrayed in my cadences or mannerisms a taint of the heterodoxy for which he had perfected such delicate instruments of detection. "Oh, no!" So I told him that I—never suspecting my feeble jest would be passed on to the office of *National Review,* or that the magazine would be imprudent enough to give this hostage to their opponents' humorlessness by printing it—had been the one who started the "Mater, sí" remark the horrible things he says; but when an outraged Catholic is asked for some of these, he normally supplies the horrible things he thinks Buckley *meant* to say or ("mark my words") someday *will* say.

Mr. Buckley therefore offers us an instance of the pressures that can be exerted against one who is a Catholic and voices political opinions unpalatable to other Catholics. His case is illustrative, no matter what one makes of his political stand in itself; in fact, the more unpopular his views are, the more enlightening is the treatment accorded him as an index of the level of mature discourse in this country. One does not test a system of fair trial by observing a court's gentle handling of the town hero, but of a defendant whom there is some tendency to prejudge. Even if Mr. Buckley *has* put on record enormities against the faith and against reason, the attacks and insinuations that are not based on these passages, but on an idle wisecrack printed in the journal he edits, on a "feel" for orthodoxy, on the dislike he elicits, remain examples of the devices that can be used with terrible effectiveness to discredit a Catholic in the eyes of other Catholics. For the treatment accorded him is only more persistent and public, not different in kind, from the pressures that work less spectacularly on many Catholics more quenchable than he is. This applies not only to readers of *National Review* whose faith is called into doubt by the editors of *America,* but to *Commonweal* readers who are informally excommunicated, month after month, by the editors of the *American Ecclesiastical Review.* The mode of repression we are concerned with here is the same, whether it is used against a Newman or a nonentity, whether invoked on one side of the fence or the other, whether used against political or theological positions. Bigotry wears no party colors; or, rather, it wears them all. Some Catholic Conservatives—though far less prominent than their Liberal counterparts, though publishing in holes and corners, rather than from the rooftop—tried to discredit John F. Kennedy with the kind of "loyalty test" the editors of *America* used on Mr. Buckley.[16] Few have so blithely continued against the blast of these repressive efforts as Mr. Buckley, who thus occasions recurring and progressively more intense evidences of the repressive instinct.[17] The treatment is not, in its mechanics, any different from that given to various Catholics—great men and small, good men and bad—for their assumption of various stands. And wherever we encounter the treatment, it is dismaying.

One of the saddest things about it is that it is undertaken with such sincerity for the good of the Church. It is a melancholy fact of history, recorded in such volumes as Msgr. Knox's *Enthusiasm,* that sincerity and indiscretion are often united in men's attempts to further religious truths and practices. It is easy to see how this can happen. In attacking Newman, Msgr. Talbot obviously thought he was doing the Church a great service. If he became a bit careless in his charges, he could justify this by the unique importance of the cause he was serving, and the fact that Newman's plausibility and "slipperiness" made him a greater menace. He was hard to pin down in open heterodoxy, but that just made it more imperative that he be discredited. And—further along in the self-justifying process—it must be *inconceivable,* to many Catholic thinkers today (as it has been to certain kinds of churchmen through the ages), that those who share the important and terribly relevant truths of their faith could disagree on anything. Disagreement with non-Catholics is understandable, and can be separated from any other kind of disagreement by a programmatic tolerance and "dialogue." But *Catholics* cannot disagree on any significant matter without one party's putting itself outside the pale.[18] (Needless to say, this latter view, taking most issues as solved, makes the "dialogue" with non-Catholics seem condescending. *They* are given the elaborate courtesy due to children and other inescapably handicapped intellects.)

Since there are no *legitimate* intellectual grounds for difference, the kind of Catholic described begins a search for other and more sinister forces at work. He explores the possibilities, and is forced to grant the improbable—that Mr. Buckley means to impugn the loyalty of those Catholics he most agrees with, that he is deliberately fanning the blaze of anticlericalism, that he deliberately works to reduce the good that the Vatican can perform in this world which (heaven knows) needs all the help it can get.

Too often the result of such tendencies is a more or less explicit belief that there is *one* Catholic attitude, if only we can discover what it is, toward every problem. The argument takes an either-or simplicity. Either the Church can and does teach on everything moral, or it does not. And so, on any issue of politics that involves a moral choice (and what does not?), one side is bound to be closer to the Church's teaching than another. One mistake or so can be allowed in a man's political views; but *continued* disagreement with this kind of Catholic, over a *wide* area of political choices, is almost certain, sooner or later, to wear away what scruples are left him in the matter of suppressing Catholic disagreement.

The logic of this view will be considered later. Here, it is enough to consider the consequences of such an attitude, the part it plays in a belief that the Church prospers by denial of freedom. If there is *one* Catholic view on every subject, where are we to find such an attitude, stringent and authoritative in its singularity, but in Catholic authority itself, seen as a monolithic thing, exerting *all* its weight on *every* issue? And when that authority has dealt with a political issue often enough, is this not a clear indication to Catholics that this matter is closed?[19] After x number of references to the United Nations, is it not the duty of Catholics to say, as Father Robert Graham, S.J., has, that the UN is not, any longer, a debatable subject? Would not the denial of this lead to a denial that there is any discernible social teaching of the Church?[20]

The man who holds such views will grant a theoretical distinction between the matters on which the Church speaks infallibly and those on which she speaks with an authority commanding respect and deference but not *belief* of the qualitatively different kind called forth by the doctrinal indefectibility of the Church. He will however, blur this distinction so far as he is able. Papal co-operation will be stretched to mean papal endorsement, and endorsement is easily elevated, in the atmosphere such men breathe, to the status of a command. Authority and pressure will be confused, and every pressure will be interpreted as a claim upon the Catholic's allegiance.

It is this attitude that tends to make the layman superfluous for articulating informed Catholic response to any even technical challenge of the age. Laymen are to register the attitudes determined for them by those in authority. "Study" of these attitudes tends to become a psychological exercise in "group-think." Such study is not directed at the *content* of the teaching, but at psycho-

THE MECHANICS OF REPRESSION

logical means for assuming correct attitudes as rapidly and completely as possible. Only by achieving the *one* acceptable Catholic view on each question is such a man assured that he is practicing his faith. He will admit the danger of exaggeration, but thinks it comparatively unimportant since his is a *pious* generosity of *surrender.*

Such, I believe, are the assumptions held, or half-held, or acted on when not consciously held, by some American Catholics. It is this set of assumptions, and not specific animosities of specific clergymen or laymen, that has impeded the development of an informed and active laity. It is this attitude that was probably expressed, and certainly encouraged, in the course of the attack on *National Review.* And it is this attitude that Pope John XXIII expressly rejected, on the occasion of his coronation, when he said:

Some believe the Pope should busy himself in guiding the affairs of nations, that he should be a seasoned diplomat or universal genius, that he should be wise in directing the day-by-day life of man, or that he should be the sort of Pope whose spirit embraces all the advances of this modern age without exception. But, Venerable Brothers and beloved sons, they are not on the right track, since they fashion an image of the Supreme Pontiff which is not fully consistent with sound thinking or the purpose of this office.[21]

NOTES TO PART TWO

(For editions cited, see the Bibliographical Note on page 293).

1. "Letter to the Duke of Norfolk," in *Newman and Gladstone,* Notre Dame, p. 199.

2. *The Pastoral Sermons of Monsignor Ronald Knox,* edited by Philip Caraman, S. J., Sheed and Ward, 1960, pp. 38-9. For more on the temptations of Christ as those of the Church to an earthly messianism, *cf.* P. Simon, *The Human Element in the Church of Christ,* Newman, 1954, pp. 1-10, 60-71. Dostoevski's famous interpretation of the scriptural temptations, in Ivan Karamazov's "poem" on the Grand Inquisitor, moves in this direction also; and though Dostoevski held that the Roman Church succumbed to the temptation of ruling earth and giving earthly bread, smothering the mystical in the practical, the "poem" is of wider import than an indictment of "Jesuitism." Ivan knows that few, even in Rome, can have accepted the idealistic diabolism of his Grand Inquisitor—the stand the world asks the Church to take, the raising of "the banner of bread . . . uniting all in one unanimous, harmonious ant-heap."

3. "Letter," p. 115.

4. Letter to R. Whitty, April 12, 1870. *Cf. Apologia,* pp. 333-4: "In reading ecclesiastical history, when I was an Anglican, it used to be forcibly brought home to me, how the initial error of what afterwards became heresy was the urging forward some truth against the prohibition of authority at an unseasonable time. There is a time for everything, and many a man desires a reformation of an abuse, or the fuller development

of a doctrine, or the adoption of a particular policy, but forgets to ask himself whether the right time for it is come; and, knowing that there is no one who will do anything towards it in his own lifetime unless he does it himself, he will not listen to the voice of authority, and spoils a good work in his own century, that another man, as yet unborn, may not bring it happily to perfection in the next." See also the sermon on "Submission to Church Authority" in *Pastoral and Plain Sermons*, vol. 3, especially p. 199: "The whole body of Christians thus become the trustees of the truth . . . and, in fact, have thus age after age transmitted it down to ourselves. Thus, teachers have been bound to teach in one way not in another, as well as hearers to hear. As, then, we have a share in the advantage, let us not complain of sharing in the engagement; as we enjoy the truth at this day by the strictness of those who were before us, let us not shrink from undergoing that through which we inherited it. If hearers break the rule of discipline, why should not teachers break the rule of faith? and if we find fault with our teacher, even while he is restrained by the Church's rule, how much greater would be our complaint when he was not so restrained? Let us not, then, be impatient of an appointment which effects so much, on the ground that it does not effect all."

5. *The Homiletic and Pastoral Review*, January, 1961, p. 358.

6. "Letter," p. 203.

7. Journal, October 30, 1867.

8. Rev. Edward Siller, *Dublin Review*, Spring, 1963, p. 77. Newman's encouragement of Catholic freedom will continue to irritate a certain mentality. Long after the *Rambler* controversy, he was made the target of "Modernist" accusations, and, in recent years, Msgr. Fenton of the *American Ecclesiastical Review* has devoted many pages to attacking Newman on the grounds that "Newman prided himself on being a minimist in matters of doctrine. One might also say with truth that he was something of a minimist in the field of charity" (*Am. Eccles. Rev.* 138, p. 61). Newman, after all, was critical of Msgr. Fenton's appropriate hero, William Ward; he praised "the despicable writings of Acton"; he edited "a Review in which such writers as the infamous Acton sought to turn Catholics away from the Vicar of Christ"; and, by opposing the definition of papal infallibility at the Vatican Council, he made himself "a part of the campaign dominated by the venomous writings of Döllinger" (*Am. Eccles. Rev.* 113, pp. 311, 306, vol. 139, p. 121). These articles, punctuated at regular intervals with such adjectives as "venomous," are meant to correct *Newman's* bitter and harsh language.

9. The magazine again displayed this lamentable tendency to rhapsodic denunciation when, in the issue of July 31, 1962, *America* was characterized as "the proto-sanctimonious weekly of a little set of ideological schismatics within the Jesuit order," and its policy called one of intellectual lynch law, presided over by "Ku Klux clerics." Such an outburst is not only meaningless in itself, but spreads a meaninglessness over the whole debate. Argument is abandoned for insult.

10. "The Pope or X" is a formula that comes very easily to some lips. In an 1871 letter to Miss Emily Bowles, Ward praised the charms of Newman, but said that, reluctantly, he "had to choose between submitting my intellect to F. Newman on the one hand or to the Pope and Bishops on the other." And so the choice "Buckley or the Pope" is presented to much of the Catholic public as the most pressing problem they must face (*cf.* pp. 5-6). Or, as it was put in a particularly tasteless article in Baltimore's diocesan newspaper (*The Catholic Review*, May 3, 1963): "Box score at the end of one full inning: Pope, 1, *National Review*, 0."

11. Letter to Dr. Gillow, September 2, 1859.

12. "The Church has deprecated any precipitate action in securing the manumission and liberation of slaves, because that would have entailed tumults and wrought injury, as well to the slaves themselves as to the commonwealth" (par. 9, Gilson, p. 299). And Pius XII wrote, in *Summi Pontificatus* (NCWC, par. 40), "The Church hails with joy and follows with her maternal blessing every method of guidance and care which aims at a wise and orderly evolution of particular forces and tendencies having their origin in the individual character of each race, provided that they are not opposed to the duties incumbent on men from their unity of origin and common destiny." Here, as in the matter of racial equality, *Pacem in Terris* supplied the emphases that some had

thought lacking in *Mater et Magistra*. Besides some references to *Summi Pontificatus,* and enunciation of the general principle that "to proceed gradually is the law of life in all its expressions" (par. 162), we have the passage (par. 97) that says "It should be noted, however, that these minority groups, either because of a reaction to their present situation or because of their historical difficulties are often inclined to exalt beyond due measure anything proper to their own people, so as to place them even above human values, as if what is good for humanity were to be at the service of what is good for the ethnic groups themselves. Reason rather demands that these very people recognize also the advantages that accrue to them from their peculiar circumstances. For instance, no small contribution is made toward the development of their particular talents and spirit by their daily dealings with people who have grown up in a different culture."

13. *Mater et Magistra,* par. 62. Pius XII, warning against socialization and "technologization," did not deny that they can be harnessed for the service of man (*cf.* Chinigo, pp. 316-7, 291-2, Yzermans II, p. 176).

14. "Letter," pp. 183-4.

15. Appearing to debate Mr. Buckley on the subject of "The Catholic and National Affairs," Mr. William Clancy, past editor of *The Commonweal* and *Worldview,* spent part of his set speech discussing anti-Semitism, with implied relevance to his opponent, a relevance that was made explicit in the answer period. See *Public Forum,* published transcript of St. Leo's debates in East Peterson, N.J., the debate of Nov. 27, 1960, p. 12 on the past of "many of Mr. Buckley's present friends," and p. 18 on this "historic record" of "certain people who support Mr. Buckley."

16. See p. 189.

17. Some of these attacks, collected from a ten-year period, are reviewed in Mr. Buckley's "Very Personal Answer to My Critics," which appeared in *The Catholic World* for March, 1961.

18. This special intolerance Catholics save for other Catholics may explain the strange insistence with which men continue to publish the information that *National Review* is not a Catholic magazine. One wonders why this is considered such an important message. The reason usually given is that many Catholics read *National Review.* Yet many Catholics read *Time* and the *New Republic,* the Chicago *Tribune,* and the New York *Times,* without being given periodic dark reminders that these are not organs of the hierarchy. Again, it is said that some Catholics not only read the magazine but *agree* with it, approve of it, find it congenial to their principles. Yet the same could be said of Catholics who are devout readers of the *Times* or the *Tribune.* There is an implication that Catholics should not read this particular magazine at all, that the magazine is "not Catholic" in the sense that it is anti-Catholic or outside the range of permissible reading. The editor of *America* seems to take it as a personal affront when some Catholics continue to subscribe after he has interdicted it. After all, he rejected excerpts from it as actively opposed to revelation and natural law (see pp. 10, 13). Without wishing to go further in open censorship, or the creation of an informal supplement to the *Index Librorum Prohibitorum,* he and others simply give a sinister accent to the repeated "not Catholic" pronounced of *National Review.* One correspondent even went so far as to say that *National Review* was *posing* as a Catholic magazine, because some of its articles are listed in the *Catholic Periodical Index.* An editor of that index had to assure men (in *America*'s correspondence column of Sept. 9, 1961) that its policy is to list articles, from any source, the editors consider of special interest to Catholics (*e.g.,* articles appearing in *National Review,* written by Sir Arnold Lunn, Evelyn Waugh, Sir Shane Leslie, *et al.*). Since, for whatever reason, *National Review* has often been treated as a Catholic journal, or attacked for *not* being one, simply because its editor is Catholic, I append the following statistics: Of the four editors, Mr. Buckley is Catholic. The other three—Messrs. James Burnham, Frank S. Meyer, William F. Rickenbacker—are not. The religion editor (Will Herberg) is not a Catholic; neither is the publisher (William Rusher); neither is the head of the book review section (Frank Meyer). Of former editors, two were Catholics (Brent Bozell and Willmoore Kendall), three were not (Whittaker Chambers, John Chamberlain, Suzanne La Follette).

19. For an explicit proposal of this quantitative test, *cf. The American Ecclesiastical Review*, 128 (1953), pp. 213-5, discussed below (on page 220).

20. *Cf.* published transcript of May 25, 1960, debate, in the St. Leo's *Public Forum*, pp. 12-13. This debate, one of a series, should be studied closely for an insight into the workings of the either-or argument. Mr. Clancy began his prepared speech with what was obviously meant as a trap:

> A question I would anticipate here and would like to ask Mr. Buckley in our discussion period is: do you admit that the Church has any teaching functions at all in political and social areas? Because the questions we are here to consider tonight are not political questions in themselves; they are political questions as they are related to a recognizable teaching, a discernible mind, of the Church on contemporary issues. And we are to consider them from the standpoints of the "Conservative" *National Review* and the "Liberal" *Commonweal*. I think that before we do this, we must ask ourselves the question I anticipated a moment ago: is the very status of the question unreal? Will we find, if we think carefully about it that both the "Conservative" and the "Liberal" Catholic approach are equally Catholic—or perhaps equally a-Catholic or un-Catholic in the sense that we are considering here social and political questions that are morally and religiously neutral, questions where the Church has not spoken definitely and where there is no recognizable "Catholic" position, either liberal or conservative, but only equally permissible positions held by various Catholics?

The trap is carefully prepared; observe how Mr. Clancy moves from assumption to assumption, under his rhetorical questions—that a) there is a teaching function of the Church; that b) part of this teaching function is exercised in formulating a recognizable Catholic mind on social questions; that c) if one cannot prefer the Conservative or Liberal position as more expressive of this mind, one is implicitly denying b) and therefore denying a). Grant a) and you must grant c). How simple. The only thing left, now that we have established that the Church's whole teaching function is at issue in every confrontation of Liberals and Conservatives, is to decide which of the two is the *Church's* position. We are not allowed to remain long in doubt:

> The clear, over-all direction of papal teaching on political-social problems has been in the general direction of what we in this country, rather loosely, for lack of a better term, call "Liberal." (*Ibid.*, p. 18.)

And, sure enough, since Mr. Buckley suggested that things were not this easily settled, the trap was sprung:

> I deny his [Mr. Buckley's] implicit thesis that there is no discernible teaching of the Church (p. 18).

During the exchange of unprepared questions and answers, Mr. Clancy kept trying to impale his foe on one or other horn of this simplifier's dilemma:

> I would like to have your ideas, Mr. Buckley, on what is the teaching function of the Church in the temporal order . . . is there any discernible Papal teaching, or is it merely a game of shooting quotations back and forth to each other? (p. 23.)

If there is some political question the Pope has not settled, then the Pope has no teaching function. Strange to say, Mr. Clancy can advance these views before a Catholic audience, yet, at approximately the same time, draft for the New York *Times* a letter expressing the conviction of Catholic laymen that a Catholic President would not be under papal directive in coming to political decisions.

21. *The Pope Speaks*, 5.2, pp. 139-40.

PART THREE

MOTHER AND TEACHER

CHAPTER ONE

AUTHORITY

P APAL encyclicals have assumed great importance in the modern world, for non-Catholics as well as Catholics. The encyclicals that are devoted to social matters belong to the small, indispensable body of writings that have shaped the last century; and when one places them in the company they share, in their creative impact on society, a strange thing appears. The works of Darwin, Marx, Freud, and other recent figures present us with the private insights of individual genius. But encyclicals are issued by a man who speaks, expressly, as the head of a very large and very ancient body. At a time when committee reports clog today's presses and tomorrow's wastebaskets, one organized body shows a life, of intellect and imagination, that is undimmed by the age and vast size of that body. The encyclicals are another manifestation of what an historian might call the Church's unique corporate "personality"—the mystery that enables her to defy, century after century, the normal processes of rigidification and bureaucratic stultification.

Taking into consideration the importance and familiarity of the more famous encyclicals, the study groups that have devoted attention to them, the amount of secondary literature that has grown up around them, a person not familiar with theology might naturally fall in with a judgment like the following:

We regret . . . that the new encyclical so promptly became entangled in the truly elementary issue of its authority. This shouldn't have been necessary at this late date.[1]

Yet perhaps no subject is more shadowy, in the modern Catholic's mind, than the precise nature of an encyclical's authority. The popular literature on the subject is superficial, contradictory, and too vague to be helpful. There are of course exceptions, like the introduction to Anne Fremantle's *The Papal Encyclicals,* written by the Rev. Gustave Weigel, S.J. But the distinctions drawn by Father Weigel carry the layman into a set of questions which the theologians themselves are only now exploring. In fact, we cannot claim to have advanced much since 1952, when Dom Paul Nau wrote: "As to the encyclicals themselves, their true nature is not very well understood at large, and even the theologians are on occasion reluctant to determine the extent of their authority."[2]

This is not surprising. Despite their sudden emergence into prominence, encyclical letters are a comparatively recent addition to the Papacy's teaching instruments. For a formal treatment of them, one cannot turn to the Fathers of the Church or the Scholastic theologians. The first encyclical letter, as that term is presently used, was issued in 1740, by Benedict XIV.[3] Since then, the rate of appearance has accelerated; the average since the reign of Pius IX has become one letter every six months.[4] But, even when the Church's highest authority mobilizes itself to meet contemporary problems, the final theological formulae that describe her actions are not struck off over night.[5] More particularly, the social encyclicals have registered the change in relations between Church and State that has taken place in the modern world, a subject that is demanding the finest efforts of modern theologians.

With the loss of the Papal States, and the elaboration of a philosophy of "pluralistic" societies, it seemed to many that the Church's influence on politics had disappeared. The last vestiges of the mediaeval arrangement had been swept away. But it was just at this moment that the Church, relying on her own eternal tradition, saw an aspect of her role that would correspond with modern reality. The Church's essential relationship with the State was not fixed by the exigencies of mediaeval politics, when the Church had to supply many functions of the State that were dormant; when, as Otto of Freisung put it in the twelfth century, many of man's political skills and instruments were still unawak-

ened from the Dark Ages (*tamquam sopita civitate mundi*), and
the Church did the world's work when the world was unable to do
that work without her assistance. Modern theologians have bene-
fited by Leo XIII's reaffirmation of the proper autonomy of the
State; following the implications of this truth, they criticize "hiero-
cratic Christendom" because it does not express the political maturity demanded of Christians if they are to base their lives on the
natural law and Revelation.[6] Pope John XXIII made this clear in
his address at the opening of the Second Vatican Council, where
he described the Church's loss of political ties as a *liberation*: "It
has eliminated the innumerable obstacles erected by worldly men
to impede the Church's freedom of action."[7] Forced by new circumstances to go beneath the *merely* circumstantial elements in its
old relationship with the State, the modern Church has made more
precise the connecting link that exists between these autonomous
(but not entirely unrelated, and certainly not antipathetic) institutions. That link is the magisterium, or teaching office of the
Church, as it makes available to *conscience* the guiding principles
for man's exercise of a full human freedom and mature political
responsibility.[8]

The First Vatican Council began that refinement in definition
of the magisterium that has gone with the Church's maintenance
—against the expectations of those who watched the Papal States'
disappearance—of a respected teaching role before the nations of
the earth. But, unfortunately, war broke off the Council's deliber-
ations before it could consider the question of the Pope's powers in
their full context—in the set of questions *De Ecclesia* where it was
originally raised. The Council, prorogued *sine die,* was not formally adjourned until John XXIII declared it closed. Thus, for
almost a century, discussion of one subject from the schema *De
Ecclesia* assumed a prominence that was misleading. Referring to
this unbalanced emphasis on the Pope's infallibility, Jean Daniel-
Rops, in his book on Vatican II, calls the chapter on Vatican I "The
Uncompleted Council." There he describes

that lack of balance in estimating the results of this council, a lack
often remarked, and one engraven indeed on the pages of history
when, in an effort at simplest expression, the First Council of the

Vatican is described as the council of Papal Infallibility. . . . The Council of the Vatican thus brought into high relief one point of the theological doctrine, but only one; leaving most patently to its successor in the future an obligation to bring its work to a conclusion.[9]

This judgment confirms, ninety years later, the assessment Newman made of the First Vatican Council's achievement:

Future popes will explain and in one sense limit their own power. . . . Let us be patient, let us have faith, and a new Pope, and a reassembled Council may trim the boat.[10]

Most of the modern treatises *De Ecclesia* were written as part of a controversy thus sharpened to a single issue—papal infallibility, the exercise of the Pope's *extraordinary* magisterium. The importance of this question made exploration of the Church's ordinary magisterium progress at a slower rate.[11] And, for that matter, ecclesiology itself is, as Father Weigel and Father Congar have pointed out, a young branch of theology.[12] There is, for instance, very little formal consideration of the Church in St. Thomas' *Summa*.

To those familiar with Newman's statement of the concept of doctrinal development, this contemporary ferment, this slow filling in of theological opinion and insight around a new definition, will not come as a surprise. But it is a bit surprising to hear it said that the many problems connected with the Pope's exercise of his ordinary magisterium are "elementary" and should no longer be raised. The ordinary Catholic layman who looks for guidance will not feel as secure about this. There is not even an article on the word "magisterium" in the *Catholic Encyclopedia*—nor, for that matter, in the *Dictionnaire de théologie catholique* or the *Enciclopedia Cattolica*. And though there is one now in the *Lexikon für Theologie und Kirche* (Karl Rahner's, s.v. "Lehramt," cols. 884-90), it is so technical and compressed that it will not much help the layman.

Thus, despite all the attention that has been directed toward the encyclicals, few Catholics could pass a test on the fundamentals of their authoritative structure. Some popular treatments seem deliberately to discourage the further study of this subject. The impression given is that encyclicals are not infallible statements, but binding in the highest degree this side of infallibility, so that distinguishing exact grades of certitude is a sterile exercise in legalism, without practical relevance for the ordinary Catholic. For a large body of Catholics (especially, it seems, American Catholics), the distinction between, say, the doctrine of the Assumption and the teaching on profit-sharing is a fine point to be pursued only as a theological curiosity.[13] This kind of presentation is usually buttressed with quotations from authoritative sources—most often a paragraph from *Humani Generis*—expounded to mean that encyclicals are "not infallible, but almost." An example of this occurs in the introduction to Vincent A. Yzermans' two useful volumes of Pius XII's speeches. After citing the *Humani Generis* passage, with its technical distinctions about the way the Pope "closes debate" in specific areas, Father Yzermans rushes on:

This, we admit, is a theological discussion involving a moral issue. For our part, we much prefer to follow the attitude expressed some thirty years ago by Jacques Maritain when he wrote: "the papacy has never wearied of instructing, reminding, setting off for us in bold relief the essential conditions and fundamental truths without which the modern world must look in vain for the solution of its gravest problems and for the satisfaction of its most pressing needs." This attitude, we feel, will best promote apostolic activity, intellectual endeavor and moral perfection. A Catholic motivated in such a way will possess that elusive quality, *sentire cum Ecclesia,* which will bring about Pius' great desire for a "better world willed by God."[14]

One avoids moral difficulties; one prefers to take an undefined attitude of submission leading to an "elusive quality"; this is what best promotes apostolic activity, etc. Father Yzermans' motives and approach show a good heart; but the head needs a little attention in this area. Those who are certain they have this "elusive quality" seem free to brand others as apostates whenever disagreement of any sort arises. The controversy recorded in the first part of this book, and other examples of confusion that will be presented in later pages, show that the popular approach epitomized in Father Yzermans' words is no longer adequate. A number of misconceptions have arisen because of the lack of rigor in discussing papal authority. We had best begin sorting them out here:

Misconception number one: *the encyclicals are not infallible.* Thus, nakedly, the matter is usually presented. But there is no reason why this should be true, at least as a prescriptive norm. If the Pope chose to make an encyclical the vehicle of an *ex cathedra* statement, there would be no impediment to this. All the conditions of such a definition could be satisfied in an encyclical. By this I do not mean merely that the Pope can repeat essentials of Catholic doctrine in them. If this mode of transfer were valid, every Catholic who can recite his catechism would have the gift of infallibility. It goes without saying that doctrines which already have the highest degree of defined certitude are not going to lose any of that certitude by being echoed in an encyclical. One can even go further, and say that the statement, in an encyclical, of a truth that is opposed to some error formally condemned elsewhere, has a binding force related to the binding force of the condemnation.[15] The grounds for this obligation are not the encyclical itself, but the prior declaration. We are here concerned with the *direct* authority of statements made in encyclicals, and such statements *can* be infallible; that is, the Pope can, if he wishes, exercise his *extraordinary* magisterium in an encyclical.[16]

It is the general opinion of theologians that the Popes have not yet chosen to do this. Some, it is true, hold that certain pronouncements—such as that against the use of contraceptives in Pius XI's *Casti Connubii*—qualify as infallible declarations,[17] but most theologians take a very severe view of the conditions of *ex cathedra* statement, in accord with the exact terms used by the first Vatican Council in defining this power.[18] In fact, Pius XII stated the general practice in this matter when he said: "In writing [encyclicals] . . . the Popes do not exercise their teaching authority to the full."[19] But there is no reason why a Pope *cannot* define in an encyclical, if he wants to.

It may be objected that this possible occurrence would be "extraordinary" in every way, an exception to the normal degree of authority exercised in an encyclical. This response brings us to

Misconception number two: *an encyclical has a degree of author-*

ity all its own in the scale of papal statements. One hears, for instance, men discuss the comparative weight of papel utterances according to their vehicle: is a Bull more binding than an encyclical, or an encyclical more binding than a *Motu Proprio?* Does *Rerum Novarum* come higher up the scale of established instruments than the *Syllabus of Errors?*

But the obligation that divine faith places upon a Catholic is so important that every papal pronouncement imposing this obligation is specifically formulated to remind Christians of its gravity. And even when the Pope is not speaking infallibly, his every enunciation is given a specific force by its immediate formulation. Those who look at the formulations of infallible doctrine are sometimes repelled by the apparently harsh and exaggerated condemnation of views as totally reprehensible, *anathema,* to be set entirely aside, etc. This strong underlining of things that must be foresworn is actually a part of the *gradation* of warnings that allows for all legitimate freedom of opinion. As Bishop Fessler wrote, "the Church . . . precisely defines and limits its subject matter, in order to remove all occasion of giving unfounded anxieties, misapprehensions, and misapplications, which would tend to disturb the conscience."[20] By so clearly marking the things that are outside the doctrinal center of belief, the teaching authority allows for a long series of less severe admonitions, of more debatable propositions, from warnings and exhortations all the way down to suggestions, hypotheses, and illustrations.[21] Thus, in the words of Cardinal Franzelin,

It is an error in method to distinguish the teaching documents and acts of the Supreme Pontiff according to their extrinsic character —to distinguish, for instance, between the errors censured in the encyclical *Quanta Cura* or in other letters, and errors reproved in allocutions delivered orally. One should not concern oneself with the extrinsic form of a document, whether the Pope has spoken in an encyclical or in letters to particular bishops or in an allocution; one should observe the phrasing, the formulas, he has employed in these different acts. Beyond question, the Supreme Pontiff can have and act on the purpose of presenting, definitively, a rule that must be followed by all the faithful, even in an allocution (which, in our day especially, is a public document offered to the attention of the entire Church). On the other hand, he can exhort and admonish in encyclicals, without intending to define any truth.[22]

The documentary forms in which the Popes issue their teaching have varied through the ages, and will continue to do so. This is not only the result of a natural development from a less organized external apparatus to a more defined procedure. Flexibility, and response to the changing forms of human discourse, the altered needs of the faithful, make this adaptability of the teacher to his various pupils in various ages highly desirable. To contain the Pope's voice in rigid forms would lead to a legalism, a remoteness from man's real speech, that could freeze the learning experience in formalism. When, for instance, the teaching of theology was at the center of all education, there was less need for the Pope to lead and stimulate discussion of the truths of the faith. Papal documents usually took the form of *enactment,* in Bulls and Constitutions. But in the modern age, the discursive and analytic method of encyclicals has captured men's attention; and, because of the prestige these documents have come to command, a Pope might decide to present a strict definition in them. Other forms of communication may in time come to the fore, such as those made possible by radio and television. The varied strategic uses to which encyclicals are put can be seen in Pius XII's general policy of restricting them to theological matters, and publishing his social teaching in allocutions, especially in his annual Christmas message. This policy did not make his social teaching either less or more binding than, say, Leo XIII's.

But the modern interest and emphasis on *encyclicals* as such might lead men into the error being discussed here. It could, for instance, be asserted that the encyclicals, though they have no juridically fixed status, have acquired, *de facto,* a uniquely important position in the teaching economy of the Church which Popes are aware of and mean to employ. This statement is partly true; but, as related·to the argument, it is often based on:

Misconception number three: *encyclicals are homogeneous so far as their authority is concerned.* It will be seen that this is simply another aspect of the second misapprehension, and it is to be answered with much the same arguments. Papal statements are authoritative to the degree established by their own terminology in each case. A whole document is not infallible because it *contains* a solemn definition. Nor is it enough, when urging some program, to say that a mention was made of the matter at hand *in an encyclical.* One must look to the terms of each statement in its context to discover the papal intent. As we shall see, a matter need not be of great urgency merely because it was mentioned in an encyclical. Nor, when recommendations have been presented in encyclicals, is it to be assumed that they are of equal weight. It is said, for instance, that encyclicals have "come out for" subsidiarity, the corporatist state, "socialization," labor unions, and profit sharing. Each is discussed in a large doctrinal context; each has its place along a delicately calibrated range of recommendations. Four of the things mentioned are in varying degrees tolerable or desirable; only one—subsidiarity—is a constant condition of *all* political activity.[23] It would be slovenly to give them equal status merely because they have all been discussed in encyclicals.

Perhaps the most egregious embodiment of this third misapprehension is the frequent use made of paragraph twenty of Pius XII's *Humani Generis.* This paragraph is frequently cited to establish the injunctive character of any citation from any encyclical. A priest even tried to settle the controversy over *Mater et Magistra* by reminding *National Review* that this passage makes the Pope's *ordinary* magisterium infallible![24] Another misuse of the paragraph occurred in a debate in which Mr. William Clancy, former editor of *Commonweal,* had made it his express aim to clarify the question whether there is a discernible papal teaching on political matters. Asked by someone in the audience whether it was possible for a Pope to be "objectively wrong" on any point put forth in an encyclical, Mr. Clancy answered:

This is a question that was raised and answered by Pope Pius XII in *Humani Generis. I can't quote directly but I think I am quoting almost directly.* It has, wrote the Pope, been said by some Catholics that the ordinary teaching magisterium of the Church is not binding unless the Roman Pontiff declares that he is speaking ex cathedra. This is clearly a misunderstanding of the magisterium of the Church; in his ordinary pronouncements as the supreme teacher of the universal Church, when they are addressed to the universal Church in an encyclical or, by extension, certainly, in a local situation, when this is done through the bishops, then although these teachings are not binding under pain of mortal sin or excommunication, *in the words of Pius,* it shows extreme temerity for any Catholic to depart from them.[25]

Needless to say, the emphasis is added. One of the major sociological phenomena of contemporary American Catholicism is the number of men who spend a large part of their lives "defending" the papal encyclicals without acquiring the art of quoting them accurately. This is a strange way to show respect for carefully phrased documents.

More to the point, Mr. Clancy thought that a reference to the *Humani Generis* passage would settle the status of *any* sentence "addressed to the universal Church in an encyclical." This is an error that many share with him. Mr. Clancy, it is true, makes some contributions of his own: e.g., the solemn phrase "not binding under pain of mortal sin," wandering in from memories of catechism class, thoroughly confuses things, since it would definitely be sinful to depart from "the ordinary magisterium of the Church," which is not the same thing as the ordinary magisterium of the Pope, and which *is* unquestionably infallible. Such pontifications repay analysis, but are not directly relevant to the problem we are approaching.

What, in fact, does the famous twentieth paragraph in *Humani Generis* say? The passage occurs in a section of the encyclical that discusses the work of theologians as subject to the magisterium. The paragraph itself runs thus, in Monsignor Ronald A. Knox's translation, which has been praised by Gustave Weigel, S.J., for its "close adherence to the explicit text of the original":[26]

Nor is it to be supposed that a position advanced in an encyclical does not, *ipso facto,* claim assent. In writing them, it is true, the Popes do not exercise their teaching authority to the full. But such statements come under the day-to-day teaching of the Church, which is covered by the promise, "He who listens to you, listens to me" (Luke 10.16). For the most part the positions advanced, the duties inculcated, by these encyclical letters are already bound up, under some other title, with the general body of Catholic teaching. And when the Roman Pontiffs go out of their way to pronounce on some subject that has hitherto been controverted, it must be clear to everybody that, in the mind and intention of the Pontiffs concerned, this subject can no longer be regarded as a matter of free debate among theologians.

As befits a passage expressly directed to theologians, this pronouncement is made in very precise and technical wording; and we must go to the theologians for an accurate exposition of the last sentence. But up to that point, the wording is clear to any careful reader:

1) The Pope distinguishes between the extraordinary magisterium, which the Popes do not normally exercise in encyclicals,[27] and the ordinary magisterium; in Knox's translation, between the teaching authority exercised to its full extent and the "day-to-day teaching of the Church."

2) He says that the faithful have the duty to obey this day-to-day teaching also, which is covered by the general scriptural command to honor Christ in those given authority over us by Christ. But the Pope does not go further into the exact nature of that authority here; he does not even distinguish between *his* ordinary magisterium and that of the entire Church; instead, he looks to the special consideration that:

3) For the most part, the doctrinal matter of encyclicals has an authoritative character because it is expounded *elsewhere* in a binding manner, *under a different title*. (It should be remembered that, although encyclicals deal with doctrinal matters, and in an authoritative way, the primary mode of the great mass of encyclicals is exhortatory, dealing with devotion and duty, urging Catholics to live up to the faith they profess.)

4) But there are some decisions in papal encyclicals which have expressly to do with the settling of disputed theological matters; and it is these that the Pope goes on to discuss. The matter under this heading must be delayed for a moment, until expert theological opinion can be consulted.

Glance back, now, at Mr. Clancy's use of this paragraph. He is answering the question whether any error can occur in an encyclical. He says that *this* subject was expressly raised *and answered* by

Pius XII. He says that a decision has been made with regard to the nature of the Pope's ordinary magisterium. Yet under our four headings, we saw that Pope Pius says:

1) that the Popes do not normally exercise their extraordinary magisterium in encyclicals; yet

2) even the Pope's ordinary statements "claim assent" because they are part of the magisterium taken in its widest sense, and "He who listens to you, listens to me"; besides,

3) many things have the stamp of the Church's authority from another source.

So far, only the matter under the second heading deals with the subject of the ordinary magisterium, and it does not specify the *way* in which one must listen to the Pope as Christ when he is speaking across the whole range of topics covered in encyclicals, and using the whole range of injunctive formulae. There is never argument, among Catholics, that one must heed the Pope's teaching; but there are many ways of doing this, and so far in this paragraph the Holy Father has not specified a precise *kind* of authority belonging to encyclicals as such. He has only specified the kind they do *not* have, in his statement that the encyclicals are not normally organs of the extraordinary magisterium, and that much that is binding in them has its force from other sources.

But can Mr. Clancy argue, as many have, that the last sentence defines the response we must make to *any* statement issued through the ordinary magisterium of the Pope? Whenever the Pope speaks, in any way, on any subject, in any encyclical, is the topic he has considered "no longer to be regarded as a matter of free debate"? To maintain this, one would have to say that, after *departing* from the general subject of the ordinary magisterium (in the words concerned with binding statements drawn from other sources), the Pope *returns to his ordinary teaching and gives it a definition.* And the only way to maintain this is to disregard the run, and context, and terminology of the passage. The passage occurs, remember, in a section devoted to the guiding role the magisterium plays over the work of the *schola theologorum.* This whole section began with a presentation of certain exaggerated views of the freedom of theological speculation. Then, in the paragraph preceding the one quoted, the Pope begins the refutation of these exaggerated views:

Adroit reasoning, but there is a fallacy in it. It is quite true as a general principle that the Popes give theologians full liberty of speculation over questions which are variously answered by doctors of repute. But history teaches us that many propositions which were at one time freely discussed, have afterwards been settled beyond the possibility of dispute.

The Pope then goes on to specify a way in which free speculation can be limited. The matter in point 4) above, then, is the key one in the paragraph. What is said earlier is by way of general prelude, to put the settling of *this* point in its proper context. Pope Pius says that, even though no statement of the extraordinary magisterium be made in the encyclical, still it is an organ of the Pope's teaching, and must be heeded. So far, in general terms. Then Pius turns to one specific situation: "And *when* the Roman Pontiffs *go out of their way* to pronounce on some subject which has hitherto been controverted, it must be *clear to everybody* that, *in the mind and intention of the Pontiffs concerned,* this subject can no longer be regarded as *a matter of free debate among theologians.*" In the next paragraph, the Pope shows another way that free speculation (in this case, on the meaning of Scripture) can be limited by the magisterium. Then, having shown ways in which the Pope can guide the work of theologians, Pius *did* pronounce on several theological opinions; so we can confirm his meaning by observing the actual examples he gives us in this document. But before doing that, it is necessary to look at the specific terms in which the key sentence of paragraph twenty is cast.

It should be obvious, from the structure of the passage, from the exact terms of the pronouncement, and from the general character of the encyclical (which is, as Father Weigel puts it, "a direct and special message for the theologians"[28]), that the Pope was not talking about the universal assent that must be made by Catholics to encyclicals as such. Yet, since the passage has been used, by Mr. Clancy and in many popular expositions of the force of encyclicals, we must turn to the theologians for an explanation of the technical terms used here. A complete exposition of the passage, taking into account all the discussions preceding its appearance, was made by the Rev. Edmond Benard in his paper on "The Doctrinal Values of the Ordinary Teachings of the Holy Father in View of the *Humani Generis*" delivered to the Catholic Theological Society of America.[29] With its help, we can turn to the three most important phrases used in the sentence.

1) The first limiting phrase is that which describes the situation about which the Pope is speaking: "When the Roman Pontiffs go out of their way to pronounce on some subject. . . ." The word Knox translates as "go out of their way to pronounce" are *data opera sententiam ferunt*. The adverbial phrase *data opera* denotes, in Church documents, a very formal way of going about something, and of *marking* one's deliberated intention. Father Benard collects the usages which indicate that the Pope is talking about an *exceptionally emphasized decision* within encyclicals, and not about the whole text of encyclicals as such.[30]

2) The next important phrase is that which establishes *what* the Pope can do in the situation he is discussing, namely, declare "that this subject can no longer be regarded as a matter of free debate among theologians." Does this mean, as Mr. Clancy, "quoting almost directly," makes it mean, that "it shows extreme temerity for any Catholic to depart from" *any* statement that is "addressed to the universal Church in an encyclical"? Common sense would seem to indicate not. For one thing, the Pope rarely presents a truth to the whole body of the faithful in the merely procedural terms of "closing debate," and especially of closing debate "among theologians." And the theologians themselves remind us that closing debate is not the same thing as closing the question; the Pope would surely not use the former term to indicate the latter. In the former case, "debate is closed, even though the question itself be left open, either to die of inanition or to be reopened by the magisterium itself according to its norms at some possible future date."[31] In directing the service which the theologians do the Church (and this, after all, is the role chosen by them in the very nature of their

studies), the Pope can close discussion for disciplinary as well as doctrinal reasons, to prevent chaos, to sharpen theological discussion, to give shape to the *schola*'s efforts, to direct wayward ingenuity to the important issues. This explains things like the concentration, during a critical period of intense apologetic activity, on one text of the Bible, the Vulgate; and the very same considerations have led to the different approach taken by modern exegetes and approved by the magisterium. Father Weigel describes this guiding task of the magisterium in these words:

The function of the magisterium is not to develop dogma but to preserve it intact without blur. In fulfilling this office it may be necessary to interfere with the theologians who, unlike the magisterium, are primarily interested in the development of revealed truth. Such interference is not intrusion. Lines of theological research and discussion, well-intentioned and innocent enough within the enclosure of the theological brotherhood, may be dangerous and misleading when they reach the non-theological public, and such discussion does jump over the wall. The magisterium with frightening duties to the total *ecclesia discens* will have to step in, in order to fulfill its urgent and divine mission, and the theologian will have to be silent and correct his speech. Development may be delayed, but the first obligation of the magisterium must be satisfied. The faithful at large, theological and non-theological, must not be led astray from the God-given truth.[32]

The Pope, then, is not primarily addressing the faithful when he tells theologians how to act for the good of the faithful.

3) The final phrase that calls for consideration is that which establishes the way in which the Holy Father means to accomplish the closing of debate—that is, according to his stated intention ("in the mind and intention of the Pontiffs concerned"). In other words, debate can be hedged in various ways, and the limits in any one case are set by the purpose of the Pope. For instance, when Paul V closed the controversy on efficacious grace between the Jesuits and the Dominicans, he did not forbid either side to teach on grace at all; he did not even forbid them to hold their own position; he did not forbid them to teach it. He simply forbade them to cast their theories in such a way as to lead to the direct confrontation of those

mutually exclusive and presumptively all-inclusive statements on
the mystery of grace that had sharpened debate without clarifying
doctrine.[33] And every time a Pope intervenes in a technical discussion of this sort, and does so *data opera,* he will establish the precise area of controversy that must be suspended. Again, we are far
from the general teaching role of the encyclicals as they address the
whole body of the faithful.

Thus Father Benard concludes (p. 102), concerning the meaning of this passage, that:

We may recognize the intention of the Sovereign Pontiff to remove
a controverted matter from the field of debate when (1) he makes
a definite, direct statement—not an *obiter dictum;*[34] (2) which
clearly and with recognizable intention applies to a hitherto controverted matter; and (3) which does at least implicitly manifest
his will that the controversy be closed.

Under investigation, the passage from *Humani Generis* is revealed
as a striking example of the proposition that has been taken as our
necessary starting point in this discussion—that papal authority
establishes its terms in each instance.

To make the practical import of the passage clear, we need only
look at one of the examples of its use in *Humani Generis* itself. In
this encyclical, Pope Pius *does* make such theological decisions.
For instance, there is a formal ban against teaching two forms of
"polygenistic" theory. In paragraph 36, the Pope says that various
theories of material evolution, including the evolution of the
human body, can be entertained by theologians so long as there
is no denial of the immediate creation of human souls. He goes
on, in paragraph 37:

There are other conjectures, about polygenism (as it is called),
which leave the faithful no such freedom of choice. Christians cannot lend their support to a theory which involves the existence,
after Adam's time, of some earthly race of men, truly so called,
who were not descended ultimately from him, or else supposes that
Adam was the name given to some group of our primordial ancestors. It does not appear how such views can be reconciled with the
doctrine of original sin, as this is guaranteed to us by Scripture and
tradition, and proposed to us by the Church.

How does this passage qualify, under our consideration of the three key phrases from paragraph twenty, as a papal directive closing discussion?

1) It is obvious that this is a decision given *data opera,* not only from the terms of the passage itself (this theory "leaves the faithful no . . . freedom of choice," it is a theory to which "Christians cannot lend their support"), but from the fact that the Pope stated earlier in the encyclical itself the precise way in which he could (and, it turns out now, *would*) limit discussion. He stated the general obligation, then imposed it in a specific instance.

2) That this is a controverted matter is clear to most men today, and can be easily indicated by quoting a priest who described his own scientific theory in these terms: *"In the eyes of science,* which at long range can only see things in bulk, the 'first man' is, and can only be, *a crowd,* and his infancy is made up of thousands and thousands of years. . . . At those depths of time when hominisation took place, the presence and the movements of a unique couple are positively ungraspable."[35] In Pius' words, "Christians cannot lend their support to a theory which involves . . . [the supposition] that Adam was the name given to some group. . . ."

3) The precise limits within which Pope Pius meant his restriction to have force are indicated by many things—by the fact that he prefaced this paragraph with express notice that theories of evolution, insofar as they do not involve the evolution of the soul of man, are not subject to this ban; by the fact that he specifies two hypotheses as unacceptable, in terms that say nothing about other hypotheses;[36] and by the fact that he presents the dogmatically certain truth that does not fit into the currently available hypotheses of polygenism: "It does not appear how such views can be reconciled with the doctrine of original sin. . . ."

In this way the Pope exemplified the kind of pronouncement he was describing in his twentieth paragraph: every aspect of the qualified ban is made perfectly clear, in theory and practice—its origin, force, extent, and motive. The Pope clearly notes what is objectionable in the current theories of polygenism, what point of Catholic doctrine is excluded by them, the extent to which they cannot be supported—namely, so far as they conflict with the doctrine of original sin. "As Boyer puts it, the polygenism as defined by the encyclical, that is, that which cannot be reconciled with Catholic dogma, is out now and forever. That is evident from the concepts. Concerning some polygenism not being considered by the Pope, it is a banal tautology to say that he is not talking about it."[37] The limits within which the ban is operative were stated this way by Augustin Bea, S.J., formerly rector of the Biblical Institute in Rome, and now Cardinal Bea, head of the Secretariat for Christian Unity:

The encyclical does not enter into the scientific side of the question. It is content to reject as irreconcilable with dogma two recent attempts at explaining original sin. Whether there can be forms of polygenism which can be brought into resonance with constant Church-teaching, is a question that is shelved.[38] The Church has no grounds for making any statement on the point; she can rest satisfied with explaining solid doctrine, and leave it to the representatives of science to see if perhaps new forms of polygenistic theory can be found which do not contradict dogma.[39]

This one example of the loose treatment of a sentence or paragraph from an encyclical has been dealt with at length to show what enormities lax interpretation can lead to. When the authority of the magisterium must be used for the good of the faithful, it is brought to bear in the most considered, formal, carefully limited way. *Humani Generis* gives us a clear picture of this process, of the grave reasons adduced for making a specific judgment on a specific controversy. Yet, from this elaborate, carefully expressed document, men can quote, or misquote, or make up sentences for use in political controversy; they can do this to hint at a papal endorsement of their own political position, and to cast doubt upon the good faith of Catholics who disagree with them.

If discussion of encyclicals is ever to be fruitful, it must work from a scrupulous accuracy in the reading and reporting of anything that comes from so high an authority. The Holy Ghost is not to be enlisted in political campaigns. A reckless application of Pius' paragraph to every word contained in an encyclical recalls Newman's warning to W. G. Ward (who claimed that Pius IX's reign was virtually one continuous *ex cathedra* statement[40]):

You are doing your best to make a party in the Catholic Church, and in St. Paul's words are dividing Christ by exalting your opinions into dogmas.[41]

And a Pope's own words put the seal on Newman's description of the misuse of papal teaching: Leo XIII wrote, in *Immortale Dei*,

In matters merely political, as, for instance, the best form of government, and this or that system of administration, a difference of opinion is lawful. Those, therefore, whose piety is in other respects known, and whose minds are ready to accept in all obedience the decrees of the apostolic see, cannot in justice be accounted as bad men because they disagree *as to subjects We have mentioned*; and still graver wrong will be done them, if—as We have more than once perceived with regret—they are accused of violating, or of wavering in, the Catholic faith.[42]

NOTES TO CHAPTER ONE: AUTHORITY

1. *America*, Nov. 11, 1961, p. 176.

2. *Une source doctrinale: les encycliques*, Paris, 1952, p. 10.

3. Headline, New York *Times*, July 15, 1961, p. 7: "Encyclicals Issued 20 Centuries."

4. For figures on individual pontiffs, see *Lexikon für Theologie und Kirche*, s.v. "Enzyklika."

5. "Leo XIII did not compose his doctrine in the midst of academic quiet, in the leisure of a library, sealed off from the swirling struggles in the marketplace of the late nineteenth-century world. Rather, he hammered it out as the head of an embattled Church, which was under an attack more radical and total than any that the Church had encountered in history" (John Courtney Murray, S.J., "Leo XIII on Church and State," *Theological Studies* 14, 1953, p. 1).

6. *Cf.* Karl Rahner, S.J., *Free Speech in the Church*, pp. 83-84: "The mediaeval form of the Church's power over society, the State, and civilization in general, cannot by any means be regarded as something essentially demanded by the nature of the Church." The same judgment is expressed in Msgr. Charles Journet's *The Church of the Word Incarnate*, I, pp. 260-2, and Rev. Yves Congar's *Lay People in the Church*, p. 98. For an answer to the defenders of the mediaeval arrangement as a modern ideal (one is tempted to call them, as the Russians call the absolutists of *laissez-faire* economics, "the last of the Mohicans"), *cf.* John Courtney Murray's articles in the *American Ecclesiastical Review*, vols. 124 and 126, and Rev. Gustave Weigel's article in *Thought*, vol. 27.

7. *The Pope Speaks*, 8.3, p. 210. Newman's view of the Temporal Power was expressed in a letter to Mary Holmes in 1870: "There is one thing worse than open infidelity, and that is, secret, and the State of Rome such as to honeycomb the population of Italy with deep unbelief, under the outward profession of Christianity."

8. *Cf.* Pius XII's address on the anniversary of *Rerum Novarum* (Yzermans, *Major Addresses*, I, pp. 27-8): "Leo XIII . . . had no intention of laying down guiding principles on the purely practical, we might say technical side of the social structure; for he was well aware of the fact—as Our immediate predecessor of saintly memory Pius XI pointed out ten years ago in his commemorative Encyclical, *Quadragesimo Anno*—that the Church does not claim such a mission . . . but the Church, guardian of the super-

natural Christian order in which nature and grace converge, *must form the consciences even of those who are called upon to find solutions for the problems and the duties imposed by social life*" (emphasis added). *Cf.* John Courtney Murray, S.J., *Proceedings, Cath. Theol. Soc. of Am.* 3 (1948), pp. 59-60.

9. *The Second Vatican Council,* pp. 53, 55. *Cf.* Rev. Francis Dvornik's recent book *The Ecumenical Councils,* written for the Twentieth Century Encyclopedia of Catholicism (vol. 82), p. 109: "The Neo-Ultramontane opinions and suggestions found no official support, but the tendency to attribute all sorts of things to the vague formula 'the spirit of the Vatican Council' still exists and may, if pushed to extremes, prove as dangerous as the opposite excess." Peter Fransen, S.J., even notices in some quarters "a certain form of 'papolatry' due to reactions following on the Vatican Council," so that "a certain exaggerated glorification of the Papal Primacy threatens to falsify both our devotion to the Holy See and also, above all, the orthodoxy of our idea of the Church. . . . Our Western Church has developed the juridical side of the Church's life to such a degree that many theologians have become incapable of thinking of anything else" ("The Authority of the Councils," in Todd, *Problems of Authority,* pp. 53, 70, 63).

10. Quoted by Rev. Hans Küng, *The Council, Reform and Reunion,* p. 162.

11. The theological emphasis on "centralism" was strengthened by several historical accidents. For instance, Heinrich Rommen points out that there was a temporary obscuring, among Catholic theologians during the nineteenth century, of the traditional theory of the state. This was caused by a reaction to Rousseau's errors, in isolating which Catholic theorists often departed from the "translation theory" of political authority inherited from Scholasticism (*The State in Catholic Thought,* pp. 451 ff.). *Cf.* John Courtney Murray, S.J., "The Church and Totalitarian Democracy," *Theol. Stud.* 13 (1952), pp. 525-63.

12. *Cf.* Father Weigel's Taylor lecture, "Catholic Ecclesiology in Our Time," in *Catholic Theology in Dialogue.*

13. *Cf.* Rev. Norman Galloway, O.S.A., "How Binding are the Encyclicals?" *Catholic Mind,* Nov. 1956, p. 625: "The possibility of error in these documents is so utterly remote that it is practically non-existent, even as a possibility." Father Galloway is speaking of the possibility of error in technical and historical matters as well as doctrinal, since he gives as one of the pledges for his statement the Pope's ability to call on *expertise* in all fields.

14. *The Major Addresses of Pope Pius XII,* I, p. 23.

15. *Cf.* Rev. Clement Bastnagel, "The Authority of Papal Encyclicals," *Catholic Educational Review* 28 (1930), pp. 166-9. Obviously, the wording of both passages must be very carefully observed, as Newman demonstrated by his study of the explicit references made to other documents in the *Syllabus of Errors* ("Letter," pp. 155 ff.).

16. The Pope's extraordinary magisterium is exercised when he speaks *ex cathedra;* and the Vatican Council declared this magisterium infallible. The Pope's ordinary magisterium is exercised in all of his other day-to-day modes of teaching. It is usually said, in lay treatments, that this ordinary magisterium is *never* infallible; but this remains a subject of some theological debate. For a discussion of the norms on which such debate proceeds, *cf.* Rev. Edmond Benard, *Proc. Cath. Theol. Soc. of Am.* 6 (1951), pp. 78-84, 109. One must remember, throughout this discussion, that the ordinary and extraordinary magisterium of the Pope are not the same as the ordinary and extraordinary magisterium of the Church. The voice of the whole Church exercising these latter powers is discerned in a consensus of the college of Bishops teaching in their own dioceses (the *ordinary* magisterium of the *Church,* which is infallible) and by the pronouncements of that body in Council assembled (the Church's extraordinary magisterium). The relation of these powers to each other is part of that discussion of "collegiality" which Vatican II has engaged in.

17. Indisputably, the record for finding infallible definitions in encyclicals is held by Msgr. Joseph Clifford Fenton, of the *American Ecclesiastical Review,* who approved another author's opinion that "the letter *Testem Benevolentiae* [was] a real definition, despite the fact that this letter does not contain any solemn form of pronounce-

ment" (*Am. Eccles. Rev.* 128, p. 215). But, as Dom Paul Nau puts it (*Une source*, p. 61): "Though they may be preceded, in the Constitutions where they are normally promulgated, by considerations of some length, definitions themselves are regularly presented in a few lines, and have the precision of a juridical document." Thus, even documents which publish their intent of defining infallibly, are not infallible in their total text (*cf.* Newman, "Letter," pp. 187-9). It is not likely that an entire letter, in which no formal solemnity was observed, *was itself* "a real definition."

18. The stringency of these conditions does not much impress Msgr. Fenton. In seven pages of great value to the teacher of logic (*Am. Eccles. Rev.* 128, pp. 185-91), he argues that:

1) one condition is *always* fulfilled in encyclicals (that the Pope speak as ruler and teacher)—and so is not a condition at all;

2) one condition "can be and is surely verified" (that the subject of definition be a matter of faith and morals);

3) one condition "can be and, it would seem, not infrequently is, verified" (that a certain and definite judgment be rendered);

4) one condition "would seem to follow" from the "not infrequent" satisfaction of the preceding one (if a certain judgment is rendered, then all must obey it);

5) and the final condition is not a condition at all, in its own right, if the others have been fulfilled (that the Pope should consciously be using his supreme power).

Msgr. Fenton frequently depores the textual niceties of "minimists" like Newman; but he shows he can shave a point as fine as any man when dealing with the First Vatican Council's definition, where there seems a clear intent to make the conditions of *ex cathedra* statement *remain* significant conditions. For a commentary on the Council's intent written by the Council's secretary and endorsed by Pius IX, *cf.* Bishop Fessler's *The True and False Infallibility of the Popes*. The Bishop remarks that the Pope must "give a formal definition in the matter" (p. 51), points out the technical limits of the term "definition" (p. 124), and maintains that if the faithful are not given "a certainty free from all doubt as to whether, in a certain case, there is a papal utterance *ex cathedra*," then the matter must be referred back to the Pope for clarification (pp. 51-2). No theological *commentator* can impose an obligation that the Pope has not unquestionably imposed. Further, even where a definition *has* clearly been made, this gives one no warrant, "rejecting its own prescribed limitations and doing violence to its plain language and signification, to extend the definition perversely in a most unwarrantable manner to provinces with which it has nothing whatever to do, and all this to the great disturbance of men's minds, and to the injury of the Church" (p. 113). The passages cited here are from the Oratory translation of Bishop Fessler's work; Ambrose St. John took up this task of translation during his last days as a service to Newman, whose "Letter" was already being called "minimist," though it agreed with Fessler's authorized exposition of the doctrine of papal infallibility.

19. For this clause from *Humani Generis*, see pp. 60, 62, and, more especially, note 27 to this chapter.

20. *The True and False Infallibility of the Popes*, p. 131. Rev. Walter J. Ong, S.J., has recently described the protection given to men by this doctrinal stability of the Church. Movements relying on an *esprit* or "myth" or ideal, rarely controllable, are subject to sudden exaggerations or shifts in purpose. This is the random power of those "isms" and ideologies that have been unleashed on the modern world. The Church is not an "ism" but a body of men with a body of formed and stated beliefs. (*The Barbarian Within*, Macmillan, 1962, p. 141: "It might be noted that the explicitation of its dogma and, even more basically, the fact that it is, and conceives of itself as, a concrete body of persons, keep the Catholic Church as a reality essentially independent of any myth of 'Catholicism' which might develop. Significantly, the Apostles' Creed does not read, 'I believe in Catholicism,' but 'I believe in . . . the Holy Catholic Church.' ") *Cf.* Pope Pius XII's allocution of September 7, 1955 (Yzermans I, p. 357): "This term [Catholicism] is neither customary nor fully adequate for her [the Church]. She is much more than a simple, ideological system; she is a reality just as visible nature, as a people or a State, are realities."

21. These are only some of the beneficent "uses of anathema." For another important function of the formal harshness in ecclesiastical pronunciations—protection of Chistians from pious exaggerators—see notes 27 and 30 below.

22. *Études* 47 (1889), p. 356; but my source is the quotation of this passage in Kothen, *L'Enseignement social de l'église*, pp. 31-2. Kothen remarks that papal documents are not "monolithic," but form a "mosaic" of teachings, each with its own special character (*ibid.*, p. 31).

23. Discussion of these matters will be touched on at later, more appropriate points —pp. 90-1 (subsidiarity), pp. 138, 198-9 (the corporatist state), pp. 138-9 ("socialization"), pp. 194-206 (labor unions), pp. 159-82 (profit-sharing).

24. *America*, correspondence column, Dec. 2, 1961. The correspondent confuses Pius' words about the *Pope*'s ordinary magisterium with maxims, imperfectly recalled from his theology days, on the *Church*'s ordinary magisterium.

25. *Public Forum*, transcript of May 25, 1960, debate, p. 34.

26. Weigel, "Gleanings from the Commentaries on *Humani Generis*," *Theological Studies* 12 (1951), p. 528. Father Weigel prefers the Knox version to two other English ones he considers in this article. The Knox version was published in the London *Tablet* for September 2, 1950.

27. Knox translates as a separate, concessive sentence "In writing them, *it is true* . . ." what is a causal clause in the Latin (*cum* with subjunctive), giving the *insufficient* ground for thinking encyclicals can be dismissed. Msgr. Fenton, for obvious reasons, prefers to take the clause as stating an *erroneous* ground for any discussion at all—the *pretext* that the Pope does not exercise his teaching authority to the full in encyclicals (*Am. Eccles. Rev.* 128, 1953, pp. 183-4). But if the Pope meant to say *that* (namely, that encyclicals *are* exercises of the extraordinary magisterium), he would hardly have tossed off this "error" in a subordinate clause which escaped the notice of the great body of theologians in the world. Here we have one of the "uses of anathema." The Pope would not condemn a generally held opinion in an *obiter dictum*, with all the force of his condemnation arising from a grammatical ambiguity.

28. Weigel, "Gleanings," p. 526.

29. *Proceedings, Cath. Theol. Soc. of Am.* 6 (1951), pp. 78-111.

30. Msgr. Fenton (in an article that appeared in *Am. Eccles. Rev.* 134, 1956, p. 111) contends that, since the Holy Father naturally deliberates over an encyclical, and the document is itself a formal one, *data opera* "does not add any new note to a pontifical doctrinal judgment or decision." Armed with a dictionary, and not bothering to answer Father Benard's collection of texts that establish the meaning of *data opera* in ecclesiastical documents, Msgr. Fenton laments the "utterly misleading comment on the meaning of the expression *data opera*." It would be an interesting test of human ingenuity to try inventing a restrictive phrase that would remain restrictive under Msgr. Fenton's exegetical techniques.

31. Weigel, "Gleanings," p. 537.

32. *Ibid.*, p. 538.

33. A clear instance of the ban against reckless debate that does not forbid private study was given with regard to the authenticity of I John 5.7. In 1897 the Vatican forbade the open teaching that this was not authentic, but in 1917 the Holy Office expressly declared that nothing in the ban itself was meant to retard the growth of responsible knowledge through scientific investigation of the subject. (*Cf.* Francis J. Connell, C. SS. R., "Does Catholic Doctrine Change?" *Am. Eccles. Rev.*, pp. 321-31). Concerning *this* mode of closing debate, Newman wrote "We are called upon, not to profess anything, but to submit and be silent" (*Apologia*, p. 333).

34. On things said *obiter*, see Newman, "Letter," p. 190 and Fessler, *True Infallibility*, p. 54.

35. Pierre Teilhard de Chardin, *The Phenomenon of Man*, Harper and Brothers, 1959, p. 185 (emphasis is that of the original).

36. His care in formulation is indicated by the words "after Adam's time." The state of the human body, of possible pre-Adamite races, before that time, do not enter into the restricted material, since they have no bearing on the problem of original sin.

37. Weigel, "Gleanings," p. 547.

38. The words Knox translates *"It does not appear how* such views *can* be reconciled . . ."* are *cum nequaquam appareat quomodo . . . queat.* Since this sentence gives the formal reason and norm for the exclusion of erroneous theory (so that, for instance, pre-Adamite theory is not excluded), one would expect its formulation to be a careful one. Yet the Rev. Anthony C. Cotter, S.J., translated the phrase *"It is unintelligible how* such an opinion *can* be squared. . . ."* In his commentary on his complete translation of the encyclical he wrote, "Some die-hards might wish to see a loophole in the words 'for it is unintelligible' *(cum nequaquam appareat)* as if they left the door open for a different decision in the future." Father Cotter gives his game away when he admits that he translated only part of the phrase, leaving out *quomodo queat.* The Rev. Francis Connell, C. SS. R., wishing to make the same point, recasts the phrase in another way, leaving out *appareat quomodo.* The Pope has obviously not been harsh enough for these men's tastes. (The examples used are taken from Weigel's "Gleanings," p. 545.)

39. Weigel ("Gleanings," p. 546) excerpts and translates this from Cardinal Bea's article on *Humani Generis* in *Scholastik* 26 1951), pp. 36-56.

40. Ward's words are: "In a figurative sense Pius IX may be said never to have ceased from one continuous ex cathedra pronouncement" (Wilfrid Ward, *Newman,* II, p. 213). Ward's famous desire to have a Papal Bull to read every morning with his *Times* prompted Sir Shane Leslie to call him "the theocrat of the breakfast table" *(Cardinal Manning,* Kenedy, 1954, p. 95).

41. Ward, *Newman* II, p. 233.

42. *Immortale Dei,* par. 48 (Gilson, p. 183), emphasis added.

CHAPTER TWO

HISTORY

The attempt to make all the statements in an encyclical "level up to" the kind of pronouncement Pius XII described in *Humani Generis* would have a disastrous effect on the teaching strategy of the Popes in their letters. The Supreme Pontiff often explains Catholic moral principle in terms of accepted categories, or applies it to contingent circumstances. If all his sentences were to be taken as "closing discussion" for Catholics, the result would be a combination of the tragic and the absurd.

Consider, for instance, the problem of explaining concepts in practical sciences like economics and politics. Unless the teacher is to confine himself to sterile hypotheses of a completely unreal sort, he must seek useful examples in history. In discussing the Christian view of slavery, for instance, Leo XIII devoted much of his encyclical *In Plurimis* to a history of slavery in the ancient and the Christian world. In discussing the moral basis of working men's organizations, the same Pope offered the mediaeval guilds as a model for working men's organizations. And on the subject of "modern liberties" he wrote, in *Libertas Praestantissimum* (par. 2), "whatsoever is good in those liberties is as ancient as truth itself ... but whatsoever has been added as new is, to tell the plain truth, of a vitiated kind, the fruit of the disorders of the age, and of an insatiate longing after novelities." Pius IX lamented in several encyclicals the loss of the Papal States, and put among the proscribed opinions of the *Syllabus* the view that such a loss would be beneficial. More recently, Pope John XXIII wrote in *Mater et Magistra*, of the historical period immediately preceding the publication of *Rerum Novarum,* that "personal gain was considered the only valid motive for economic activity" (par. 11).

Now, in these concrete instances—and the list could be continued until almost the entirety of known or knowable history is included in it—has the Pope "closed the discussion" of whole eras in history? He has adduced matters of fact; is certitude concerning these vouchsafed by his doctrinal infallibility? Is it impossible for Catholics to take another view on the factual outlines of the history of slavery, on the objective merit of guilds, on the unforeseen advantages that the Church won from the loss of the Papal States, on the contributions made by the modern concern for liberty, or on the exact degree of perfidy registered in the last century's economic life?

The case of the guilds is a specially interesting one, because the majority of Scholastic theologians condemned them as repressive monopolies.[1] When Leo XIII wrote, a romantic view of mediaevalism was the possession of much of mankind. He chose a familiar and favored historical institution to illustrate his point; but subsequent historical research has altered much of the nineteenth century's view of the thirteenth century. In particular, a closer look has been taken at the estimate of guilds formed by the very mediaeval churchmen who, Pope Leo wrote, lifted civil society to

so excellent a life that nothing more perfect had been known before, or will come to be known in the ages that have yet to be.[2]

Were the great theologians from that age, who had the opportunities of first-hand observation, wrong in their estimate of the guilds? Perhaps. But must we take the view that they were wrong in their estimate of the facts of history because they did not possess the teaching primacy of Pope Leo XIII? The Scholastic revival encouraged by Leo himself has given us more information from the very source the Pope was praising and using, so far as it was available to him. He is like other men in his access to the facts of experience and testimony. Saint Thomas recognized this when he wrote, "In judgments concerned with particular matters of fact, as in the settlement of property, the judgment of crimes, and such matters, the judgment of the Church can be erroneous because of false witnesses *(propter falsos testes).*"[3]

There is an important principle implied in this estimate of the effect of false testimony. St. Thomas was discussing, directly, the decisions of an ecclesiastical court, where systematic investigation of narrowly limited facts is at stake. When we consider the complexity of history, of social problems, of economic and political systems interacting in various ways around the world, when we add to this the generally partial and partisan sources that must be used to gain knowledge of these events, it is obvious that there will always be room, in a judgment of the particulars of history, for error *propter falsos testes.*

To take a different position would destroy the very possibility of historical research among Catholics. The Pope would be credited with clairvoyance on matters of recondite fact; such a charisma would make his erudition more extensive than that of the entire body of laborers who, by painstaking research, slowly fill in our knowledge of the past. In fact, he would exercise in encyclicals a higher power than the inspired writers possessed in Scripture; for Catholic exegetes do not hold that inspiration made Saint Paul an infallible historian when dealing with the facts of Hebrew history, an infallible textual critic when citing the Old Law. We have escaped the fundamentalist belief that inspiration freed the scriptural writers entirely from the modes of thought, the common intellectual heritage, of their age.

The contention that the Pope is exempt from dependence on man's limited knowledge of historical fact would not only put him above the inspired authors, but would give to the encyclicals a protection not extended to definitions of the *extraordinary* magisterium. Newman described how the Third Council of the Church, establishing doctrine, quoted an heretical author under the impression that it was quoting Pope Julius. The doctrinal pronouncement was in no way vitiated by this historical error in attribution. The doctrine remains true, no matter whose phrasing of it is adopted.[4] Surely, if the Church's defining authority can err in ascribing a sentence to its author, the Pope can err on the far more intimate, obscure matter of an author's *intent* in writing the sentence. Thus,

Rev. Thomas Pègues, O.P., speaking of the condemnation of certain positions, propositions, books, says "We do not claim the Pope is infallible in attributing this book to this author, or in determining the subjective meaning of the author."[5] The fluid nature of language, the elusive and individual relation each man has with his own and other languages, make it hard for any man to formulate his exact meaning; and "Who among men knows the things of a man save the spirit of the man which is in him?" (I Cor. 2.11.) The Pope cannot penetrate the soul, reading its secrets, known only to the Holy Ghost. Thus Newman wrote, of Pope Honorius, some of whose letters were condemned by the Sixth Ecumenical Council, "we may rather hope and believe that the anathema fell, not upon him, but upon his letters in their objective sense, he not intending personally what his letters legitimately expressed."[6]

This is not a denial that there *is* an objective sense to condemned propositions; Newman goes on to say that the Church's magisterium could not be conceived as applying to thought as separate from language; an infallibility that did not extend to control over language would be a mockery.[7] With regard to the latter, every society must exact a minimal agreement on objective usage, or all oaths, legislation, and instruction would be empty. This is not the same thing as saying that language can be frozen, can escape the imperfection that is its law and the law of this fallen world. The Church's teaching role guarantees a proper control of language—which means the adequate use of its natural function, not a denial of that function. Even the Scripture must be read in terms of the concepts and words current in the authors' time, of the single writer's style, and of the particular context. When Saint Paul uses the word *sarx*, he may mean something quite different from the concept conveyed in our word "flesh." He can, for instance, use the word to describe *man* considered as *fallen* (Rom. 7.18). But it is not safe to take that meaning and apply it in every other passage where the word occurs. Sometimes he means by it "the law of sin" (Rom. 7.23-5), while in other places it means simply "the body," not the undisciplined forces that act in and on the body of fallen man. Or he can use the word to indicate the body as corruptible (I Cor. 15.50 and 39). Paul's use of the term is sometimes literal, sometimes (as in *Romans*) symbolic, sometimes (as in the second *Corinthians*) affected by imagery. It would be disastrous to generalize about the word from any one use of it.[8]

Popes are not free of the usages and concepts of their time, any more than the inspired authors were. Their statements must be read in an historical and literary context. And language not pinned down with the technical precision of doctrinal definition will contain, inevitably, a verbal dross on its surface that is part of the general flow of language through any one period in history. As Alfred de Soras, S.J., says, with regard to the difficulty of interpreting encyclicals:

A third exegetical difficulty is caused by the fact that both in doctrinal and historical pronouncements, where the pastoral magisterium clearly exercises, in different degrees, its charismata of wisdom and prudence, the pronouncements are intermixed, at certain points in encyclicals or other documents, with remarks which seem nothing but fleeting echoes, in the language of the Popes, of opinions currently accepted when they wrote, opinions which are not given a critical examination in themselves. Of this sort are the papal documents of the early nineteenth century that seem to "legitimize," without close scrutiny, the regimes of various kings and princes.[9]

Rev. Peter Fransen, S.J., has demonstrated ways in which these observations of the law of language must be applied to the interpretation of conciliar language.[10] And he remarks:

Protestants and even sometimes a certain number of Catholics are scandalized when they observe the precise analyses to which the theologians subject the conciliar texts. It seems to them legalistic logic-chopping. Surely all this is not in accordance with our Lord's will? The answer is that it is, since he willed his own Incarnation and hence the expression of the divine message in human language. When we have any text before us, we must read it correctly. We must therefore apply the rules of literary criticism, especially when we are dealing with texts in a foreign or ancient language.[11]

In connection with the nature of language, it is often asserted that the Church's Latin, precisely because it is a dead language with a high degree of artificiality, is more stable and apt for doctrinal expression than other vehicles. There is a great deal of truth in this;

but no language is perfect, and the very genius of ecclesiastical Latin for abstract statement makes it at best a clumsy vehicle for dealing with the particulars of history.

The Latin language tends of itself to put formulations in abstract and general terms. Latin's genius is more synthetic than analytic, tending to absorb the particulars of individual things into words of broadest applicability. Furthermore the solemn air of pontifical Latin aggravates this tendency.[12]

These reflections will clarify a point in Newman's "Letter to the Duke of Norfolk" that has been misunderstood. Though Newman made it clear that he considers the Church's protection of doctrine to involve, within its defining activities, a certain infallible control of language, he added that it is the job of the faithful, and especially of her theologians, to labor at the correct interpretation of the official language: "There are no words, ever so clear, but require an interpretation, at least as to their extent."[13] This interpretation goes on under the guidance of the Church, which gives a set of restraining formulations, formulations usually negative, condemning error;[14] but it would involve a denial of three things to say that the Pope can present some verbal formula to the faithful that needs no internal effort at understanding, merely instant external profession. First, this would work against the nature of language—which depends on established usage, discourse, *community* in its widest sense, and a *continuance* of discourse in community.[15] It would further deny the psychological structure of man, who must learn things by continual comparison, of one fact with another, of one proposition with another.[16] It would, third and finally, deny the task of conscience confronted with a world of trial. The Christian is not saved by parroting uncomprehended phrases. He must undertake the burden of using intellect and will, trying to understand, to draw out the consequences of doctrine in practical formulations to fit his condition. The following view, for instance, would serve as a guide for medicine men dealing in shibboleths, but not for Christians approaching the authoritative teaching of their faith:

The Holy Father has issued his encyclical as a series of statements. Apart from those which he himself stamps as manifestly merely opinative, all of these statements stand as the Holy Father's own declarations. The man who subjects these declarations to an analysis in order to distinguish the element of Catholic tradition from other sections of the content must employ some norm other than the authority of the Holy Father himself. The Holy Father's authority stands behind his own individual statements, precisely as these are found in the encyclicals. When a private theologian ventures to analyse these statements, and claims to find a Catholic principle on which the Holy Father's utterance is based and some contingent mode according to which the Sovereign Pontiff has applied this Catholic principle in his own pronouncement, the only effective doctrinal principle is the private theologian himself. According to this method of procedure, the Catholic people would be expected to accept as much of the encyclical as the theologian pronounced to be genuine Catholic teaching. . . . It is difficult to see where this process would stop.[17]

It is all or nothing, you see; all the activity takes place on the Pope's part, or on the theologians'. There is no room left, in this passage, for the effective engagement of two active minds in the teaching process. There are other oddities in the paragraph—the implication that the Pope's teaching is isolated, individual, sheer personal fiat not based on Revelation and natural law (the laws of language forming part of the latter), not explicated in terms of the Church's history and his own office,[18] not to be examined in relation to all of these. The author of these words makes it sound as if it were a matter of *personal pride,* on the Pope's part, that no one analyze his documents. But to investigate these oddities now would take us further than this preliminary point—that, *in dealing with historical particulars,* the Pope relies on certain kinds of testimony, formulated in a certain period's language, according to certain available concepts.

With these norms in mind—and operating, always, under the first principle, that papal authority establishes its own extent in its own language—turn, again, to the simple test passages proposed for consideration.

When Pope John says that economic activity was almost exclusively motivated by a conscious philosophy of materialism during the last part of the last century, is this a judgment that no historian, deeply versed in the currents of that century, can modify? There

are alternative views with some respectable testimony to present—
the Weber-Tawney view, to mention just one, a view presented in a
Catholic philosophic context by A. Fanfani.[19] This analysis finds
in aberrant religious drives (the Puritan salvation ethic), rather
than a-religious materialism, the energy that was poured into economic and industrial expansion. As the evidence is sifted, as the
testimony of every sort is re-examined and augmented by historical
research, must any Catholic come to the discussion with an *a priori*
commitment to one view of this complex historical phenomenon?

This is not simply a hypothetical question. Men do speak and
argue as if the Pope had condemned an era as well as an idea when
he condemned economic liberalism. Furthermore, it is sometimes
said or implied that anyone who engages in the techniques originated by that era is of necessity doing so for the motives described
as an economic form of naturalism. That is, the condemned laissez-
faire economic theory is treated as if it had left an historical residue
of evil contaminating any technique that was used in a certain
period, a residue to be cleansed only by renunciation of the techniques themselves, of all the things that might be historically asso-
ciated with the condemned doctrine. The phrase "Catholic capitalist" is treated by such critics as if it were a contradiction in terms,
as one might say "a Catholic atheist."[20] There is a Manichean basis
for this argument; but here it is mentioned only to show the dangerous consequences of transforming doctrinal condemnations, illustrated by historical examples, into pronouncements on the facts
of history as such. The error in this approach has been isolated and
criticized by Pope John XXIII in *Pacem in Terris* (par. 159):

It must be borne in mind, furthermore, that neither can false philosophical teachings regarding the nature, origin and destiny of the
universe and of man, be identified with historical movements that
have economic, social, cultural or political ends, not even when
these movements have originated from those teachings and have
drawn and still draw inspiration therefrom. For these teachings,
once they are drawn up and defined, remain always the same, while
the movements, working on historical situations in constant evolution, cannot but be influenced by these latter and cannot avoid,
therefore, being subject to changes, even of a profound nature. Besides, who can deny that those movements, in so far as they conform

to the dictates of right reason and are interpreters of the lawful aspirations of the human person, contain elements that are positive and deserving of approval?

Strange to say, those who make advocacy of capitalist economic techniques equivalent to philosophic naturalism are quite capable of distinguishing the papal strictures against a *philosophy* of free speech, free press, etc., as this was defined by Pius IX and others, from the *programmatic* aspect of these freedoms, when supplied with a sound philosophical substructure. Yet they are unwilling to grant that such distinctions can be made by those who analyze practical problems in a manner different from that of the anti-*capitalist* authors.[21]

Is it possible, then, for a Catholic historian to doubt that a numerical majority of guilds was beneficial in the thirteenth century, or that a numerical majority of agents in the economic life of the last century formally espoused naturalism? Is it possible for a scholar, who has no temptation toward the utopianism of Teilhard de Chardin, to doubt that the mediaeval world was so perfect that "nothing more perfect . . . will come to be known in the ages that have yet to be"? Must one hold that the modern preoccupation with liberty has produced *no* new insights into this difficult philosophical concept? Merely to formulate the question is to arrive at an answer. Historical judgments of a precise and cogent sort are not cast in such terms of wholesale praise or condemnation as the Popes have used in these instances. This language, by its departure from the clear and careful terms in which doctrinal truth is enunciated, establishes its merely illustrative character. The teacher is using accepted instances of a truth, but not in such a way as to attempt scholarly intervention in the domain of historical work. The Popes' language is different, in these cases, from the disciplined terminology of pronouncements like the *Humani Generis* paragraph considered in the last chapter. Again we see the principle verified that papal teaching is self-qualifying, self-certifying in the very terms of its presentation.

The loose form of these historical generalizations should make clear the range of language available to the Pope in the delicate task of teaching men of all nations. Pope John's description of the late nineteenth century occurs in the exordium of his letter, where he is praising his predecessor's encyclical for its influence on the world. That praise is certainly meant seriously, and is certainly justified; but the terms in which it is cast are to some degree conventional and courteous. Every statement of an "illustrious predecessor" is, by the protocol of official documents, honored. And a great letter like *Rerum Novarum* needs some distinctly imaginative superlatives. Leo XIII himself, in paragraph 34 of *Immortale Dei*, endorsed the doctrinal content of Pius IX's *Syllabus*, even while taking a different practical approach to some of the matters treated in that document. If Alexander VI were mentioned in an encyclical, he might well be the author's "illustrious predecessor." But historians can still consider him less than illustrious. Thus, when Leo XIII gives a summary history of the Church's relations with slavery, he does not mention any failure on the part of the Church, as an historical institution. But historians might discover a few!

Here is the problem, then. In order to *teach* in realistic terms, the Popes must use understandable examples, the shared concepts of historical and scientific discourse, yet without allowing the unchanging doctrine of the Church to be linked with the shifting fortunes of these human disciplines. This difficult task is achieved by the stylized and finely adjusted language that has been developed in the only body with the Church's long experience of change and of the changeless. A shift in historical estimate of the middle ages will in no way affect Pope Leo's defense of the workers' right to freedom of association. A different estimate of the nineteenth century will not invalidate the condemnation of economic liberalism. It is the moral doctrine that has been presented for belief, not the historical illustration.

For that matter it is hard to say how matters of individual historical occurrence can be presented as objects of faith (except for the special facts intimately related to the deposit of doctrine, such as historical events in the life of Christ).[22] How is one to formulate with precision a doctrine on the good intentions of guild masters? Is one to say *Credo* to the proposition that at least 51% of the economists of the nineteenth century were motivated by a conscious philosophy of naturalism?

It may seem an unnecessary refinement to insist that the historical facts referred to in encyclicals have no special warrant derived
from the Pope's office. But we shall find this a key point when we
discuss, later, the degree to which such historical judgments enter
into certain forms of papal recommendation. Furthermore, the
widely varying uses to which language is put in the historical or
formal parts of these letters reveal the care that must be used in
determining their doctrinal context. Not only do the authoritative
directives of these documents form a mosaic of prescriptions with
widely differing force. Many of the statements that go into an explanation of moral principle contain elements purely illustrative.
For this we have an analogy in the *extraordinary* teaching of the
Church. Theological explanations of a doctrine are not usually incorporated into the actual definition of the doctrine's content.[23]
The relation of doctrine to theological arguments suggests, analogously, the difference in force that exists between the Church's social teaching and historical illustrations appended to that teaching,
between the doctrine on freedom of association and the praise of
guilds, between the doctrine on slavery and the blanket praise of
the Church's historical role in eliminating this evil. The Pope is
not attempting a Bolshevik rewriting of history, to put the Church
in an unvarying good light, when he is courteous to predecessors,
pious toward good efforts of the past, general in his historical allusions. He is simply using human language for a variety of tasks.
If he cannot speak except with one degree of authority, at a single
unbroken level of solemn proclamation, he is, effectively, silenced.
His voice is far more flexible, relevant, intelligent than some of his
zealous advocates would make it. It addresses intelligence; it is not
issued by way of incantation, but in order to *teach*.

NOTES TO CHAPTER TWO: HISTORY

1. *Cf.* the collection of references in Raymond de Roover, "The Concept of the Just
Price: Theory and Economic Policy," *Journal of American History* 18 (1958).
2. *Rerum Novarum*, par. 27 (Gilson, p. 220).
3. *Quaest. Quodlibet.* 9.16. The passage is discussed by Msgr. Journet, *Church of the
Word Incarnate*, p. 334.
4. "Letter," p. 188.
5. "L'autorité des encyclique pontificales d'après Saint Thomas," *Revue thomiste*
12 (1904), p. 523.

6. "Letter," p. 181.

7. *Ibid.*, p. 191: "For the Pope's condemning the language, for instance, of Jansenius is a parallel act to the Church's receiving the word 'Consubstantial,' and if a Council and the Pope were not infallible so far in their judgment of language, neither Pope nor Council could draw up a dogmatic definition at all, for the right exercise of words is involved in the right exercise of thought." (When five propositions from the *Augustinus* of Jansenius were condemned by Innocent X, the Jansenists tried to maintain that the Pope had missed the objective meaning of Jansenius. But in "Ad sacram beati," Alexander VII declared that the objective meaning of the propositions in the *Augustinus* and in the condemnation was one and the same. Whatever the private disposition of Jansenius' soul, his *enunciated meaning* was condemned; had Jansenius been alive when the condemnation was issued, he could have proved his sound interior orthodoxy only by repudiating the doctrines in the sense in which he had formulated them and in which they had been condemned.)

8. See Newman's treatment of the range of scriptural meanings for "the World," in his sermons "The World Our Enemy" (*Parochial and Plain*, vol. 7, no. 3), "Faith and the World," "The Church and the World" (*Sermons on Subjects of the Day*, nos. 7 and 8).

9. "La facture des documents pontificaux," *Rev. de l'action pop.*, March, 1961, p. 271. These relatively unexamined concepts, the intellctual and linguistic counters of any period of history, are accurately described by Newman when, in his classification of various kinds of "assent," he discusses "the civilizational furniture of the mind" accepted on what he calls "credence": "It is the sort of assent which we give to those opinions and professed facts which are ever presenting themselves to us without any effort of ours, and which we commonly take for granted, thereby obtaining a broad foundation of thought for ourselves, and a medium of intercourse between ourselves and others. This form of notional assent comprises a great variety of subject-matters; and is, as I have implied, of an otiose and passive character, accepting whatever comes to hand, from whatever quarter, warranted or not, so that it convey nothing on the face of it to its own disadvantage" (*Grammar*, p. 60).

10. Todd, *Problems of Authority*, pp. 72-8.

11. *Ibid.*, pp. 60-1.

12. Alfred de Soras, "La facture," p. 269.

13. Letter to Miss Isy Froude, July 28, 1875.

14. "More recently it has been noted that, for the most part, Councils refuse to explain a revealed truth but content themselves with condemning obvious errors arising from all quarters. It is as though they are defining the limits within which the outlook of our faith remains orthodox, by simply excluding views which have no future" (Peter Fransen, S.J., *Problems of Authority*, p. 57). All men and institutions using words to cope with serious affairs must (like lawyers) be aware of the limits of language. But this is far more true of the Church, which deals in mysteries of the highest and most difficult order. The center of these mysteries, God, is ineffable; all terms used of him are analogous, and predication made of him must be negative or relative (St. Thomas Aquinas, *S.T.* I, q. 13, a. 4 resp., *C.G.* I, 30.4).

15. "Every human truth is acquired, elaborated and developed within a community. None of us can think without using a language, without using words. So true is this that the discovery of certain aspects of truth is sometimes impeded by the fact that some languages do not possess words or the grammatical constructions which are found in others" (Peter Fransen, S.J., *Problems of Authority*, p. 46).

16. For an excellent description of this process in Thomistic terms, *cf.* Walter J. Ong, S.J., *The Barbarian Within* (Macmillan, 1962), pp. 105 ff.

17. *Am. Eccles. Rev.* 121 (1949), p. 218. *Ibid.*, p. 220: "This tendency to consider the pronouncements of the *ecclesia docens*, and particularly the statements of Papal encyclicals, as utterances which must be interpreted for the Christian people, rather than explained to them, is definitely harmful to the Church." The distinction between interpretation and explanation is not instantly obvious; there seems to be an assumption that papal teaching can be rephrased in simpler language for the less learned

among the faithful, but without there being any possibility of disagreement on the nature, scope, consequences and large import of the teaching itself, nor any discussion of these matters that might entail such disagreement. One is reminded of the Marxist's approach to official documents, which are taken as the current expression of "historical inevitability," to which one attunes oneself by all psychological means available. The Popes obviously have something else in mind when they compose encyclicals, as Leo XIII emphasized when he said that Catholics "cannot in justice be accounted as bad men because they disagree as to subjects we have mentioned" (p. 69 above), or Pius XII when he encouraged "the clash of diverse opinions" on matters he had just discussed (p. 95). Msgr. Fenton means to defend a papal infallibility he finds everywhere threatened in the Church; but his standards make it impossible to go to that authority itself, since he rules out the careful scrutiny of each statement's exact terminology, which is precisely the point where papal authority announces its intent and exerts its force. To ignore authority's own terms by homogenizing response is to adopt norms not directly derived from the living authority. This turns a delicate mosaic of precise statements into a crushing, monolithic talisman.

18. *Cf.* Peter Fransen, S.J.'s discussion of the principle that "Since ecclesiastical authority is divine, it is never the possession of any man" as a personal attribute; the office does not serve him, but he it (*Problems of Authority*, pp. 45 ff.).

19. *Catholicism, Protestantism, and Capitalism*, Sheed and Ward, 1936.

20. The eminent Catholic economist Colin Clark, whose work has been praised in the Pastoral Letters of the Austrian Bishops, demonstrates the possibility of using certain economic processes, themselves morally indifferent, in the service of a Christian view of the world. It does not matter that some of these instruments were first developed by the Manchester school of economics, and were based, there, on a naturalist philosophy. The Church long ago clarified—during the patristic ages—the possibility of turning "pagan wisdom" to Christian uses. And the Rev. R. L. Bruckberger, O.P., in *Image of America* (Viking, 1959) has demonstrated the possibility of interpreting American capitalism in terms other than the Manchesterian. It is extraordinary that, with all the study being devoted to encyclicals, a belief should become general that the teaching of the Church, and especially of Scholasticism, on the just price is opposed to the entire idea of a free market. One of the factors in the Scholastic idea of the just price is precisely that price "which, at a given time, can be gotten from buyers, assuming common knowledge and the absence of all fraud and coercion" (Cajetan, expounding the teaching of St. Thomas at *S.T.* II-II, q. 7 a. 3 and a. 4). Both St. Albert the Great and St. Bernardine of Sienna defended negotiation according to prices set by exchange in the market *(secundum aestimationem fori)*. Number 884 of the Canon *Placuit* deals with the legality of the price that merchants can sell their goods for in the market, *quam in mercatu vendere possint*. And St. Thomas, defending the merchant who "takes the price he can get" *(vendit rem secundum pretium quod invenit)*, gives this example: A grain merchant arriving first in an area where famine has raised prices has no obligation to say that other merchants are following. To do so would be more virtuous, but not an obligation in justice *(S.T.* II-II, q. 77, a. 3 and 4). This teaching is the more remarkable when we remember the comparatively static notion mediaeval teachers had of money as the medium of trade, a notion reflected in their teaching on usury. Yet the study groups devoted to encyclicals seem as innocent of this knowledge as of the Scholastic attitude toward the guilds. *Cf.* Raymond de Roover, "The Concept of the·Just Price: Theory and Economic Policy," *Journal of Economic History* 18 (1958), pp. 418-28.

It should be noted that the Young Americans for Freedom campus chapter was suppressed at Niagara University because of the eighth tenet in its founding statement. That tenet reads: "That when government *interferes* with the work of the market economy it *tends to reduce* the moral and physical strength of the nation; that when it takes from one to bestow on another, it diminishes the incentive of the first, the integrity of the second, and the moral autonomy of both" (emphasis added). Surely it is possible to disagree with these clauses without asserting, as Rev. John Caine, C.M., did in banning the organization, that "as they are written they are in conflict with Catholic social principle." Father Caine's interpretative skills can be gauged from the fact that he says "This [eighth] tenet, as it stands, would oppose *any* legislation *affecting* the economy by Federal or State government" (emphasis added). The tenet neither says this, nor has been interpreted in this way by the organization, as its officers tried to point out to Father Caine. But it is difficult to exact close attention to language from a man who could write the following: "The YAF statement 'That liberty is indivisible and that political freedom cannot long exist without economic freedom' indicates that government has no right to interfere in the economic life of the Nation." Would Father Caine draw the same conclusion from the following sentences? "Further, history and experience testify that in those political regimes which do not recognize the rights of private ownership of goods, productive included, the exercise of freedom in almost every other direction is suppressed or stifled. This suggests, surely, that the exercise of freedom finds its guarantee and incentive in the right of ownership." Presumably not, since they come from par. 108 of *Mater et Magistra*.

21. For instance, it is enough that a man praise the advantages of free market technique for Mr. Kevin Corrigan to proclaim that such a man "is at grave variance with the social teaching of the Church" (*The Catholic World*, January, 1961.) When the victim of this conveniently quick method of total refutation answered 1) that he considered the economic devices only *as* economic devices, to be used within a framework of natural law philosophy, 2) that he did not accept, had in fact attacked, the Benthamite bases for that laissez-faire theory which the Popes condemned in the passages Mr. Corrigan had cited, and 3) that he could not find a Pope who condemned the mode in which he held certain economic opinions, Mr. Corrigan answered: "In your March issue, Mr. Buckley asks ingenuously: what Popes anathematized his position? (The answer is, of course, the Popes I quoted.) He then goes on to explain that he doesn't agree with such extreme exponents of his [sic] school of thought as Bentham, Spencer and Miss Rand. This is irrelevant. For one thing, I didn't single out Bentham, etc., so why does he?" Distinctions are irrelevant when one has a handy phrase for branding an opponent in debate. Presumably Mr. Corrigan would learn to distinguish if Mr. Buckley were unscrupulous enough to say that since Pius IX had condemned a free press, and Leo XIII had condemned freedom of religion, Mr. Corrigan "is at grave variance with the social teaching of the Church." To complete his performance, Mr. Corrigan expressed regret that Mr. Buckley had apparently never *heard* of that very natural law philosophy to which Mr. Buckley expressly subscribed in his response.

22. Newman put this thought in another form—that all doctrinal propositions *are* propositions, not decisions on contingent particulars (except those that have to do with the very nature of doctrine—e.g., scriptural events). *Cf.* "Letter," p. 193, *Grammar of Assent*, p. 108.

23. *Cf.* Newman, "Letter," p. 189, and Josef Rupert Geiselmann, in Callahan *et al.*, *Christianity Divided*, pp. 43-4.

CHAPTER THREE

KNOWLEDGE

THERE ARE, in the conventional division used by theologians, three degrees of faith—divine faith, accorded the truths that have been revealed; ecclesiastical faith, given to truths necessarily derived from, or correlative with, the revelation (the necessity of this connection guaranteed by the Church's infallible *assistentia*); and religious faith, given to other teachings of the Church, not part of the deposit of revealed truths, but called forth by her divinely imposed duty of protecting and expounding and applying the truths that are contained in that deposit. This latter form of belief is a true and internal assent, but it is not irrevocable —that is, the Church's teaching in this area can change without disturbing the security of the deposit. An instance of this is the change in the teaching concerning the interpretive norms for dealing with Scripture's purely historical and literary aspects.[1] Because religious faith can have many degrees of stringency, according to the objects proposed and the mode of proposal, this is the assent most frequently discussed when encyclicals are at issue. This degree of faith extends, in fact, to all the doctrinal teaching done by the Church that is not exigent of irrevocable assent. Even when the Pope proposes an opinion for the belief of Catholics, this should receive the assent of religious faith—though, as Father Benard shows, the directive itself demands an acceptance of the opinion *as an opinion,* open to the legitimate forces of change that work on opinion.[2] Things morally certain, or "safe," or merely recommended for respectful consideration, are to be accepted—when

proposed for the acceptance of the faithful—with an internal deference calibrated to correspond to the exact terms of the proposed teaching.

Such is the traditional theology of the handbooks. But the "degrees of faith" are often raised, in a discussion of the encyclicals, to
make one or the other of these two points:

1) The correct interpretation of encyclicals depends, primarily,
on deciding which of these three responses is appropriate for each
sentence contained in them; or

2) encyclicals as a whole demand an assent of religious faith.[3]

This latter application of "the degrees" is another version of the
false view already rejected—that encyclicals maintain a steady pitch
of authoritative exigence. There are obviously many matters of
divine faith proposed as the basis of discussion in an encyclical.

But, more important, there many things in encyclicals not proposed for belief at all—though the discussion takes place in the
context of the faith, and with an understanding that a uniquely
important teacher is speaking. When the Pope says that a certain
view must be adopted or rejected, he is obviously proposing a doctrine, whether infallible or not; and that doctrine must be accepted
with the degree of certitude indicated by the Pope's own presentation of it. But in discussing and expounding that doctrine, suggesting possible relations with contingent circumstances, exhorting
men to make its implication fruitful, and removing possible misunderstandings, the Pope makes observations not proposed as formulae of belief in any sense at all. A case of this is the illustrative
use Leo XIII made of the mediaeval guilds. Other instances could
be collected in great quantities. The Pope presents some examples
as hypothetical—one is not to believe the events actually take place.
Or the Pope may say he takes pleasure in the activities of those trying to fulfill aspects of the papal teaching—a form of felicitation
used of every group that seeks out an audience or receives an allocution. What is the proposition offered for belief here—that the
group is *in fact* trying to achieve the goals of Catholic doctrine, or
in fact succeeding? To make such propositions the object of an act
of faith would violate the norms concerning historical fact discussed
in the last section; and, besides, that is not the immediate assertion

made by the Popes, who merely state that they *do* congratulate, felicitate, take pleasure in, etc. It would verge on the ridiculous to take, as object of a Credo, the proposition: "The Pope congratulates this organization."

If response to every statement in a papal document were reduced to such a "belief in the proposition that . . ." the Pope's hands would be tied. He could talk only in doctrinal formulations, a privilege as inconvenient as King Midas' magic touch, which turned even food and drink to gold.[4]

Nor is the problem of belief solved, normally, when it is established that certain social proposals are expressly condemned, or expressly enjoined, by the Popes. Individualism (i.e., economic liberalism) and socialism are both condemned, it is true, by the social encyclicals. The primacy of the individual and the importance of the common good are both asserted. The sacredness of private property and of legitimate political authority are declared as enduringly valid aspects of the human condition on earth. Thus a Catholic cannot hold even moderate liberalism or socialism (as these are defined in the condemning documents),[5] cannot maintain that the state has no authority in economic affairs, or, on the other hand, that private property is not a fundamental human right. So far, it is true, the duty to believe is clear. But this is just the beginning of most discussion based on the encyclicals.

As befits solemn teaching, all the propositions so far referred to are given careful formulation. Liberalism and socialism are both condemned as *philosophies*—the economic concomitants of a rationalist-naturalist materialism.[6] The social right to property, the sacred nature of political authority, are defined in terms that apply to every historical situation. But the Pope's teaching role does not stop at this level. After establishing the framework of proper political discussion—establishing this principally (as in most doctrinal discussion) by ruling out errors at either end of the scale—he offers certain illustrative applications of his doctrine. Some of these are of universal applicability, but of relative priority in each circumstance. Such is the so-called "principle of subsidiarity":

Still, that *most weighty principle, which cannot be set aside or changed, remains fixed and unshaken* in social philosophy: Just as it is *gravely wrong* to take from individuals what they *can* accomplish by their own initiative and industry and give it to the community, so also it is *an injustice* and at the same time *a grave evil and disturbance of right order* to assign to a greater and higher association what lesser and subordinate organizations can do.[7]

I have added emphasis, to illustrate what has already been said about the clear marking of relative import that takes place in papal documents. There is no principle of political organization that has been more weightily proposed than this. It has been repeated, never diluted, never altered.[8] Nonetheless, it is, in its very terms, of varying applicability; a necessary scale, but a sliding one, whose fulfillment depends on a prudential estimate of the capability of lesser bodies to perform any specific activity under consideration.

When to the principle of subsidiarity are added other normative principles—in politics, the principle of the common good; in economics, that of the just wage; in education, the rights of the family and of society—a difficult set of adjustments is made necessary between standards doctrinally complementary but with practically competing demands. The effort at this adjustment will be defeated at the outset if stress on one principle in one situation is read as a denial of the other principles. For instance, to say that a Catholic proponent of welfare measures does not, as such, accept as a principle the teaching on subsidiarity is not a valid inference. To say that he *does* accept the condemned philosophy of socialism is an injustice of the harshest sort. In the same way, to say that a Catholic opponent of certain welfare measures is indifferent to the principle of the common good is invidious; but to say that he denies the very authority of the state is to take on oneself the severest of judging functions.

Admittedly, it is possible for a Catholic to be holding, secretly or in astonishing ignorance, one of the condemned philosophies we have considered. In such a case, the man's Catholicism is either feigned or terribly fragile, since economic liberalism and socialism both deny the foundations of faith, founded as these defined philosophies are on a secular rationalism.

It is also possible that a Catholic thinks the Church has no teaching function at all in areas where it regularly asserts that office. But this, too, is only possible in the case of hypocritical or astonishingly uninformed faith.

Far more likely is the final possibility—that men accept the doctrinal context of discussion, but differ on the relative applicability of a large set of the accepted principles. Most serious debate among Catholics takes place, or should take place, at this level. And when one remembers that even Cardinal Newman was barred from this legitimate arena by intolerant opponents (who thought *his* faith feigned or uninformed) , prudence as well as charity dictate a presumption that one's fellows intend to operate within these limits. In such cases, there is no question of defection from Catholic principle or doctrine, no doubt that others can accept the teaching role of the Church and make different applications of its teaching. Discussion should proceed on the prudential level, through analysis of the possible relevance of each principle that has been assembled in the Catholic social teaching. To keep insisting on belief, acceptance, "degrees of faith," at this level of discussion, is insulting, and betrays a misunderstanding of the dynamics of Catholic thought.

Faith does not homogenize human response, making it single in action, more intense here, less there, but qualitatively uniform. Faith informs the total human person; it does not supplant it. And all the activities of that humanity can and should be pursued with the added vigor lent by faith. Critical faculties are to be sharpened, not dulled; debate is made meaningful, not superfluous. The Church does not stand off to one side of this full human activity, speaking only to one level of man. It enters the human endeavor, guiding it, learning from it, leavening it.

When a man totally animated by the faith seeks knowledge, within the context of the faith, he is not seeking some *substitute* for the truths available to reason. His is a *fides quaerens intellectum,* faith ranging throughout the knowable world. Faith is a *guide* to him, leading him to the perfection of his person—using, therefore, a true *intellectus,* understanding exercised according to its internal structure.[9] Faith, it is true, is the acceptance of a truth on grounds extrinsic to its own internal cogency.[10] Catholics believe because God has told them. Without this warrant they would not even be aware that God is triune, that the proper worship of him is in the

Sacraments, or any of the other mysteries in the strict sense. If, on the other hand, compelling evidence of an intrinsic sort is given to the mind, they have *knowledge* not *faith*.[11] Thus, when the Pope marshals arguments to prove that the state is a natural society meant to perfect man in the order of society, he is not deriving a truth from revelation. Guided by revelation's affirmation of the goodness of created order, he is reasoning, and inviting men to reason. For those who see the cogency of his reflections, knowledge is attained. Although the Pope has talked within the protecting guide lines of, and with the aid of, the divine warranty, they arrive at a truth naturally available to the mind as God created it. The Pope has deliberately appealed to knowledge, led men to it, so that faith will no longer be necessary on this point; for even on earth, in matters not strictly mysterious, there can be a foreshadowing of that final moment when faith will disappear as man is perfected in knowledge. "Now I know in part, but then I shall know even as I am known" (I Cor. 13.12). The logical character of many encyclicals shows that the Pope does not want to keep men bound to him by intellectual swaddling clothes, unable to know, in a state of unreasoning faith.

Without making a sterile division between faith and reason— for the two interact at every level of Catholic life—it is possible, for the sake of analysis, to separate two emphases proper to two "situations," or a-temporal "moments."[12] Doctrine, taken strictly, is that set of beliefs that must be held if one is to be saved—*quam nisi fideliter firmiterque receperit, justificari non poterit*, as the Athanasian Symbol puts it. Here, the primary emphasis is on acceptance. As a Catholic, one does not understand the Trinity, though he can trace the reasons for accepting this doctrine *on God's word*. And the primary urgency, prior to all other considerations, is toward this *acceptance*. Any consideration of the mystery's beauty, implications, analogues, etc., is secondary in importance to that. Definition at this level takes the form of exact enunciation of obligatory content, accompanied by a formal command to accept, and severe warnings about the consequences of disbelief.

Once acceptance is assured, Catholics can exercise their understanding on the implications of doctrine, the relation of one point to another, the possible repercussions of the doctrine in every area of life and thought. This process, too, is guided by the Church. But her voice has a different accent here.[13] She assembles the material that facilitates belief, initiates the reasoning process for some of the faithful, expedites it for others, only obstructs it when a false set of considerations has led to barren debate or scandal for the rest of the body. The distinction between these two accents in the voice of the teaching Church is well put by Dom Paul Nau:

Doctrinal decision is presented complete as a categorical affirmation, in precise form, where the ruler of the faith is expressly using his authority (and, in formal definitions, using it to its fullest extent and without possible appeal), to impose a doctrine as part of the believer's faith, or to exclude false doctrine from that faith. The Church's wider teaching role, on the other hand, does not irrevocably fix doctrine, but gradually explains it; does not condemn false doctrine so much as inform and remind men of truth.[14]

For Newman, the distinction between these two "moments" was symbolized in the Blessed Virgin's instant response to any of her Son's words, followed by a prolonged consideration of them. Her invariable *Fiat mihi* was followed by a long course of meditation, during which she pondered in her heart the words acted on with instant trust:

She does not think it enough to accept [divine Truth], she dwells upon it; not enough to possess, she uses it; not enough to assent, she develops it; not enough to submit the Reason, she reasons upon it; not indeed reasoning first, and believing afterwards, yet first believing without reasoning, next from love and reverence reasoning after believing.[15]

It is especially to this task—"from love and reverence reasoning"— that the Pope calls modern man in his encyclicals. We are invited to reason, to ponder, to apply.

The papal documents themselves furnish us with frequent illustrations of the two attitudes. One such instance occurs in the encyclical *Mystici Corporis*, one of Pius XII's richest statements. When he is discussing the mode of union that exists between God and the faithful, he establishes the area of legitimate speculation on this mystery by forcibly condemning an error to be avoided:

Let all agree uncompromisingly on this, if they would not err from truth and from the orthodox teaching of the Church: to reject every kind of mystic union by which the faithful of Christ should in any way pass beyond the sphere of creatures and wrongly enter the divine, were it only to the extent of appropriating to themselves as their own but one single attribute of the eternal Godhead (par. 78).

In this statement the accent is clear; all the stress is on what *must* be repudiated. A *duty* is declared. The error is given very specific statement, with a legal thoroughness that allows no loopholes.

But it will be noticed that, as is customary in such statements of obligation, the procedure is by way of negation. The mystery itself is not reduced to a single formula; error is excluded. But then, within the safe boundaries traced by this analysis, the Pope encourages investigation of the doctrine's rich content:

We know, too, that from well-directed and earnest study of this doctrine, and from the clash of diverse opinions and the discussion thereof, provided that these are regulated by the love of truth and by due submission to the Church, much light will be gained, which, in its turn, will help to progress in kindred sacred sciences. Hence we do not censure those who in various ways, and with diverse reasonings make every effort to understand and to clarify the mystery of this our wonderful union with Christ . . . [and] let us not neglect the method strongly recommended by the Vatican Council in similar cases, by which these mysteries are compared one with another and with the end to which they are directed, so that in the light which this comparison throws upon them we are able to discern, at least partially, the hidden things of God (pars. 78-9).

If this "clash of diverse opinions" is encouraged by the Pope even in matters strictly theological and mysterious, then an even more thorough work of reasoning, applying, comparing, refining, is necessary in the area of politics. A nagging attempt to return all discussion to the first "moment" of passive acceptance goes against the manifest intent of these discursive and analytic documents. In an article devoted to the study of the Popes' terminological *mode,* whereby papal documents establish their own authority. Alfred de Soras, S.J., says:

The Papacy itself, repeatedly, by its manner of presentation, has made it clear that, in the documents issued by the pastoral magisterium, it has in mind a purpose more rich, more fertile, more supple, than a mere repetition of eternal principles or unvarying enunciation of doctrines general and immutable.[16]

When the Pope argues and reasons with his flock, he is not merely "going through the motions." In the freedom of the faith, he is inviting men to argue and reason. Anything less than this would constitute a lack of contact between teacher and pupil. When Catholics propose objections, examine problems, link inferences while moving toward conclusions in the practical order, they are not pretending to do this while *simulating* the motions of another's illative processes—making an act of faith, as it were, in the logical dexterity of any particular Pope. To contend otherwise would amount to one of two things—either a) it would make it impossible for the Pope to use reasoning in his teaching role, since use of reasoning necessitates submission to the rules of reason, established in nature by God;[17] or b) it would make it impossible for Catholics to reason honestly when discussing papal arguments.

Once commentators leave the acrimonious atmosphere in which Catholics propose excerpts of encyclicals, unqualified, separate from their context, as occasions for a profession of blind faith, then we can usefully ask, What is the character of an encyclical? We are not asking, at this point, What degree of faith does it, invariably, elicit? but, What is its tone, its tactical use and intent?

The first and most obvious observation to be made about the form of an encyclical is one that is rarely made. As Dom Paul Nau remarked, the primary characteristic of an encyclical is that it is a *letter*.[18] It is not, by its stylistic bearing or *genre,* an instrument of legislation, like a Bull or Constitution. It is not disciplinary, like the normal Motu Proprio. Its form is more diffuse, its phrasing more discursive, its tone more that of discussion than enactment.[19] At times the Popes have emphasized this character of encyclicals by issuing formal proscriptions as a *supplement* to their letters—as Pius IX did when he made two documents of *Quanta Cura* and the *Syllabus,* or as St. Pius X did when he discussed modernism in the encyclical *Pascendi,* and formally condemned its tenets in the Brief *Lamentabili.*[20]

The papal intention in renewing the epistolary form is clearly marked in the history of modern encyclicals. Nau considers the evidence in his chapter called "Letters of Unity." Benedict XIV renewed the term "encyclical letter" just as historians were re-emphasizing the importance of that term in the early Church. In 1728 Dominic Bencini published his two-volume study, *De Litteris Encyclicis,* and twelve years later Benedict, the eminent canonist, issued the first modern encyclical.

The "circulating letters" of the early Church were missives, sent from bishop to bishop, meant to maintain the unity and authenticity of Christian teaching. At a time when the Church was without means of easy communication, bishops kept informed and united through such a document, to which each added his name before passing it on. The letters became the instrument and sign of orthodox teaching. A bishop in one part of the world could initiate a letter telling of developments in his quarter, warning against heretical teaching he had encountered, affirming belief in the traditional doctrines, applying these tenets to new events. The result was a kind of gradual, epistolary "council," maintaining union in the episcopacy when all physical factors made for division.[21]

Benedict and his successors have demonstrated again and again that much of the early motive has gone into the revival of modern encyclicals, addressed to the Pope's brothers in the episcopacy. These "letters of unity" assess trends, encourage the entire Church, reaffirm ancient truth in new contexts. Their tone is that of formal correspondence rather than formal command.[22] Thus Nau could conclude—after making the most extensive study currently available of the modern encyclicals' formulae, history, and uses—that the *de facto* function of these letters has not been so much to create a juridical obligation with regard to doctrine, but to perfect the union of the faithful in understanding and application of doctrines already received.[23]

At this stage of the discussion it is necessary to reassert the fundamental oneness of the Catholic's response to the divine authority that is so dear to him. In a schematic figure, I have separated a "moment" of reflective activity from a "moment" of passive acceptance, but the reality is both simpler and more complex than this kind of analysis can indicate. A more exact approach would have to take into account the many shades of meaning in a Catholic's use of the word "faith." Catholic theology has traditionally provided for the instruction of men in the essentials of belief; it had to insist with particular emphasis, in an apologetic period dealing with certain theologies denying the validity of human reason, on the *intellectual* nature of the act of faith. And so most theologians use "faith" in what Gabriel Marcel calls a "belief *that . . .*" context. For this kind of *Credo,* concrete objects or events do not form a meaningful object.

But another use of the verb "to believe" has the most extensive scriptural warrant, and corresponds to a psychological dimension of Catholic life that is not often brought forward in the discussion of faith.[24] This is the "belief *in . . .*" of Marcel's treatise on faith and reality. We do not only believe *that* there is a God, that Christ is God, etc. We believe *in* the one God, as the abrupt Latin of our creed puts it: *Credo in unum Deum.* This is not the *in* that fixes something locally; it transfers all the motion of the verb into the accusative object.[25] There is a transfer of self, a surrender of one person to another.[26] This is the use of "belief" that St. John found so striking in Christ's words, remembering and recording it in the Gospel that bears the marks of unique personal relationship with our Lord, the testimony of the "beloved disciple."[27] Though Christ demands belief in specific predications of himself, the living relationship that leads to such articulation is a belief *in* him—in his total reality and everything that results from it.[28] It is *within* this relationship that all Christian thought and action is to take place.

To believe in someone . . . is to say: "I am sure that you will not betray (que *tu* ne trahiras pas) my hope, that you will respond to it, that you will fulfill it." I have purposely used the second person singular—one cannot have confidence except in a *toi*, in a reality which is capable of functioning as *toi*, of being invoked, of being something to which one can have recourse.[29]

This is the context in which pastoral letters of such warmth as the encyclicals—so often echoing their Pauline models—should be read. The letter is not to be transformed into a list of definitions or demands. It is the living voice of a teacher, representing by his office the Supreme Teacher *in whom* Christians believe. Faith is not to be reduced to the reception of propositions. It is directed to the total reality of the Church. An atmosphere of suspicion, a fear of discussion, is out of place here. Catholics are not afraid of knowing the Church's exact nature, her human elements, her less than fallible efforts. As the disciples grew to know each other, their failings and personalities and human features, they did not lose faith in the sacred office they administered. Karl Adam points out that the Church does not follow the false ideal of heretics like the Cathari, pretending that nothing but purity exists in its human organization. Knowledge in and of the Church is *knowledge,* knowledge totally animated by love, but for that very reason not afraid to look on the Church's leadership in all its complexity.

The Catholic affirms the Church just as it is. For in its actual form the Church is to him the revelation of the divine Holiness, Justice and Goodness. The Catholic does not desire some ideal Church, a Church of the philosopher or the poet. Though his mother be travel-stained with long journeying, though her countenance be furrowed with care and trouble—yet, she is his mother. In her heart burns the ancient love. Out of her eyes shines the ancient faith. From her hands flow the ancient blessings.[30]

We hear much today of Catholics with dormant consciences and rebellious dispositions, of "unprofitable servants" who do not heed the Popes' words. Yet, when these charges are examined, it often turns out that the offenders are simply not following a partisan political program for which the Popes' "support" has been constructed out of disparate texts; and texts thus used tend more to intimidate the faithful than to elucidate the faith. Perhaps the reaction of Catholics to such factional treatment of the papal letters comes from the deep instinct of the faithful, telling them that this is not the accent of their Shepherd:

The sheep follow him because they know his voice. But a stranger they will not follow, but will flee from him, because they do not know the voice of strangers.[31]

Perhaps the cold reception given to *America*'s treatment of *Mater et Magistra,* a reception that made Fathers Davis and Graham fear a great spirit of laicism and anticlericalism was upon us, arose not as some nascent American apostasy, but out of deep Catholic instinct—part of the *sensus fidelium* which, as Newman pointed out, is a sign of, as well as an assent to, the truths of the faith. The reaction of many to the dispute recorded in this book's early pages was simple bewilderment, a feeling that pronouncements of the Church were being used divisively. And the Catholic who encounters a partisan edge in the presentation of encyclicals may instinctively close his mind to the investigation of truths proposed by the Popes. This is not necessarily a denial of the papal teaching function; it may stem from a sense of personal inadequacy to reconcile what some teachers propose with what other, deeper guides to the faith indicate as central. Such Catholics may withdraw into a defensive ignorance, saying that interpretation of the documents is too difficult for them, that the acrimony surrounding this discussion does not impress them as an exercise in characteristically Catholic life, that their faith is itself more important than instruction in current political trends. It was just this reaction that Newman lamented, and Msgr. Talbot welcomed, among the laymen of the last century.

Only when sharply partisan use of the encyclicals is foresworn can such dangers be removed from modern life. Then Catholics can learn more of their faith, and of the world illumined by it, seeking deeper knowledge together, weighing every word of the Pope with exact scales, recognizing each other's weakness, their own limits, the limits of the world, and the declared limits of ecclesiastical leadership in political matters. Then there will be no distraction from, no adventitious obstacles to, the teaching of the Church. Catholics will receive, unintercepted, the clear voice of Catholic authority, encouraging freedom, uniting men in charity, recognizing the place and usefulness of argued disagreement. Catholics, once repelled by the hostile use made of the Pope's words, will encounter them in the context of the dialogue modern Popes have opened with the faithful, will see how the words are softened or made more pointed by the whole trend of Catholic teaching, will be persuaded from error, freed from exaggerations and unconsidered assertions. Then modern man will have co-operated fully in the effort initiated by the great modern "letters of unity."

NOTES TO CHAPTER THREE: KNOWLEDGE

1. Msgr. Charles Journet shows that the decision in the Galileo case must be considered in this context—not merely as a disciplinary measure, but as a *teaching* that could be and was altered (*Church of the Word Incarnate* I, pp. 354-8).

2. *Loc. cit.*, p. 98. For further treatment of the freedom of conscience within the proper assent, *cf.* Canon J. M. Herve, *Manuale Theologiae Dogmaticae*, p. 523.

3. Msgr. Fenton, of course, edges encyclicals up from one "degree" to the next, whenever this can be attempted. In fact, many modern theologians object to the three-fold division (which was invented in the wake of Molina's teaching on the severe limits within which divine faith is confined) for its tendency to blur various obligations into each other. These men, especially Marín-Sola, but also Schiffini, Gardeil, Beraza, Gits, Msgr. Journet, and others, argue that the basis of divine faith and so-called ecclesiastical faith is the same—belief in the revelation as made to the Church; so they would do away entirely with the misleading concept of ecclesiastical faith. *Cf.* Most Rev. Fidel G. Martinez, "Ecclesiastical Faith: a Modern Misconception," *Theology Digest* 1 (1953), pp. 59-63, Msgr. Journet, *op. cit.*, pp. 343-5, and Father Benard, *loc. cit.*, p. 92.

4. The Midas comparison was used by Father Henry Ryder in describing W. G. Ward's theory of infallibility (Ward, *Life of Newman* II, p. 225).

5. *Cf.* Pius XI, *Quadragesimo Anno*, pars. 117-20; John XXIII, *Mater et Magistra*, par. 34.

6. See, for example, Leo XIII's *Libertas Praestantissimum*, par. 15 (Gilson, p. 66): "What naturalists and rationalists aim at in philosophy, that the supporters of liberalism, carrying out the principles laid down in naturalism, are attempting in the domain of morality and politics."

7. *Quadragesimo Anno*, par. 79 (McLaughlin, p. 247).

8. The principle has become increasingly pertinent as the need for a state with extensive powers has grown. Pius XII frequently maintained this, as in his address to the Christian Union of Executives and Businessmen, March 7, 1957 (*The Pope Speaks* 4.1, pp. 88-9): "When we declare that the proper regulation of the future economy is the duty (or rather part of the duty) of the whole populace, We are far from agreeing that this duty should be committed to the State as such. If you follow the proceedings of certain Congresses—even Catholic ones—on social and economic matters, you become aware of an ever-increasing tendency to call for the intervention of the State, to such an extent that sometimes you get the impression that this is the only expedient imaginable. Now undoubtedly, the social doctrine of the Church clearly states that the State has a role of its own in bringing right order into social affairs. And if it is to carry out this role, it must be strong and have authority. But those who continually invoke it and who throw all responsibility onto it are leading it in the direction of ruin and serving the cause of powerful groups with interests of their own. The end-result is that there is no longer any personal responsibility in public affairs, and when someone speaks of the duties or negligence of the State, he means duties or faults of anonymous groups (among which he naturally would not dream of including himself). . . . As a matter of fact, problems such as that of the economy and social reform have only a superficial relationship to the proper functioning of any particular institution or organization, as long as the latter are not in opposition to natural law; but they are necessarily and intimately bound up with the personal value of men, their moral strength, and their sincere determination to meet responsibilities and to understand and then deal ably and intelligently with matters that they undertake or to which they are bound. No recourse to the State can create men like this. They must arise in the midst of the people."

Five years before this address, the Pope had seen the same forces at work, as one discovers from his talk to the Congress of Administrative Sciences, August 5, 1950: "In every era it has been necessary to deplore, here and there, excesses in the power of the State. In this era, however, the instances of abnormal growth succeed one another almost without interruption; with what consequences, one can see only too well. Naturally, we have in mind here real excesses. For, in the tangled confusion of existing conditions, especially social conditions, no one doubts the necessity for the State to widen its field of activity and also to increase its power. This expansion could be without danger, if clear knowledge and exact appreciation of the real importance of the role and of the purpose of the State had progressed in the same ratio. Had this pari-passu development taken place, the State would have found therein a regulating, controlling principle which would have prevented it from extending its power—in virtue of considerations quite different from economic and social needs—to realms which it would have been better to leave to the free initiative of citizens. This applies with special force to the cultural areas. However, what has actually happened? Too frequently, this knowledge and this understanding (of the role and purpose of the State) have been present in an inverse ratio to the growth of the powers of the State. This is not only true among those who see in the State merely the source of their profits or those who suffer in its name, but also among those whose calling it is to give the State its constitution and its form. Men in this category, however, should really live and breathe with a sound concept of the State as their constant inspiration. This is their primary duty and, so to speak, the justification for their existence. What, therefore, is the true concept of the State if not that of a moral organism based on the moral order of the world? The State is not an omnipotence crushing all legitimate autonomy. Instead, its function, its magnificent function, consists in favoring, helping and promoting an intimate coalition, an active cooperation aimed at a higher unity of members who, while respecting their subordination to the purpose of the State, contribute in the most effective manner to the welfare of the whole community, precisely in so far as they preserve and develop their individual and natural character. . . . The present era witnesses a luxuriant blossoming of 'plans' and 'unifications.' We recognize willingly that, within legitimate limits, these can be desirable and even required by circumstances, and, once more, what We condemn is but the excessive seizure of power by the State" (Yzermans I, pp. 140-1).

9. The dynamics of St. Anselm's phrase *fides quaerens intellectum*, "faith out on quest of knowledge," retrace the lines of force in Augustine's definition of prudence as "love led by wisdom in its choices" (*amor sagaciter eligens*). One might also compare Saint Paul's characteristically compressed phrase at *Eph.* 4.15, αληθεύοντες ἐναγάπῃ "finding the truth in love." St. Thomas analyzed Augustine's definition of prudence as offering a possible objection to his own treatment of prudence as an intellectual virtue; how can it be this if it is an *amor*? He answers that prudence is at the service of a directing *amor*, choosing the proper means for it to achieve its desire. The activity of prudence is in itself an intellectual act, but *amor movet ad actum (S.T.* q. 47, a. 1 ad 1). An analogous explanation must be made of Anselm's statement about the relation of faith to reason: *fides movet ad intellectum.*

10. *Cf.* Father Benard, *Proc. Cath. Theol. Soc. of Am.* 6 (1951), pp. 92 ff., Walter J. Ong, S.J., *The Barbarian Within*, pp. 103-20.

11. *Cf.* St. Thomas, *In Sent.* d. 1, q. 1, a. 2 *sol.: ad ea quae fidei sunt, ratio demonstrativa haberi non potest,* "in matters of faith, the grounds for strict demonstration are inaccessible."

12. Henri de Lubac, S.J., uses two such extra-temporal "moments" to deal with a different problem concerning the nature of faith (see his "Credo Ecclesiam" in *Sentire Ecclesiam,* edited by Danielou and Vorgrimler, Herder, 1961, p. 15).

13. Pope John XXIII characterized Leo XIII's social encyclical as made up of "solidly grounded principles, practical directives and fatherly appeals" (*Mater et Magistra,* par. 9); and Pius XII had described the same encyclical as presenting "principles, concepts, and norms" (Yzermans I, p. 34).

14. *Une source,* p. 72.

15. "The Theory of Development in Religious Doctrine," *University Sermons,* no. 15.

16. Rev. Alfred de Soras, S.J., "La facture," p. 261.

17. As Newman says, in the "Letter" (p. 133), "The Pope, who comes of Revelation, has no jurisdiction over Nature" (to repeal its laws).

18. *Une source*, p. 33.

19. *Ibid.*, pp. 29-31.

20. *Ibid.*, pp. 27-8.

21. *Ibid.*, pp. 47-8.

22. *Ibid.*, p. 34.

23. *Ibid.*, p. 73.

24. But St. Augustine and St. Thomas were very conscious of the distinction. *Cf. S.T.* II-II, q. 2, a. 2, commenting on Augustine's *Sermo 144* and *Super Joann.* 29.

25. *Cf. ad 4* of the *Summa* passage cited in the last note: *credere in Deum . . . importat motum in finem.* This is the Greek *eis* of the passages listed in note 27.

26. The difference between these two aspects of faith corresponds (partially, not perfectly) with Newman's distinction between notional and real assent, between theology and religion, between "believing the propositions that there is a God, that there is a Saviour, that our Lord is God, that there is a Trinity" and "believing in God, in a Saviour, in a Sanctifier" (*Grammar*, p. 108).

27. *Cf.*, for instance, John 2.11, 3.18, 3.36, 6.35, 6.40, 7.38, 9.35, 11.25, 12.44, 12.46, 14.1, 14.12.

28. The two activities are clearly marked, and demanded, at John 11.25-6; "Jesus said to her, 'I am the resurrection and the life; he who *believes in* me (*pisteuōn eis eme*), even if he dies, shall live; and whoever lives and believes in me, shall never die. Dost thou *believe this (pisteueis touto)*?' "

29. Marcel, *The Mystery of Being, II: Faith and Reality* (Gateway, 1960), p. 89. For some reflections on faith as an encounter of persons, *cf.* John Courtney Murray, S.J., "The Root of Faith," *Theol. Stud.* 9 (1948), pp. 31-2, Newman's treatment of conscience as a constant awareness of a *Person's* attention (*Grammar of Assent*, pp. 97-107), and Father de Lubac, *loc. cit.*, commenting on St. Thomas *S.T.* II-II, q. 11, a. 1, resp. (faith *that* something is true flows from faith *in* the one who reports it: *principale videtur esse, et quasi finis, in unaquaque credulitate ille cujus dicto assentitur*).

30. Adam, *The Spirit of Catholicism*, p. 242. Father de Soras contrasts the Church, a human body traversing history, with the structure of Platonic ideas that some critics seem to have in mind in their discussion of response to the encyclicals ("Portée des documents," p. 142). Pius XII, too, criticized "the pernicious error of those who dream of an imaginary Church," indulging in "a false mysticism" (*Mystici Corporis*, pars. 65 and 9).

31. John 10.4-5.

CHAPTER FOUR

PROVIDENCE

I N the Catholic's attitude toward the Church, belief and obedience are intimately related: he *obeys* the Church because he believes in her divine nature and warrant; and, conversely, he *believes* what she teaches as part of his general obedience to her divinely established authority. But the very language used in stating the connection indicates that these interconnected duties *are* two duties, not one and the same. An illustration used in the preceding section may clarify this. When the Pope offers argument and evidence for things that can be discovered by the human intellect in the natural order—e.g., that obedience is due to temporal authorities—understanding of the evidence makes faith no longer necessary on that central point, though general respect for the Church's teaching role, and regard for the educating or confirming aspect of her timely reminders, keep faith present in the Catholic's response to papal exposition of this natural truth. But someone unable to follow the argument or assess the evidence would have faith also on the central point. In both cases, faith is present, but in a different way, though *obedience* to the Church's command that man heed her teaching is equally observed in either case.[1]

Although belief and obedience are not the same thing, they are even more closely connected than many Catholics realize. Pope Pius XII made a point of this in an address delivered to laymen engaged in Catholic action. He reminded them that they partake of *one* of the Church's two principal powers, *sanctifying*, by their part in the sacramental life and priesthood of the whole Church, which

offers the redeeming Victim to God. But the other power—ruling
—is not theirs, nor even their priests', to dispose of; it belongs to the
Bishops, the successors of the apostles, in union with the possessor
of Peter's primacy. And this governing power includes the teaching
primacy.[2]

The distinction between these two aspects of the Church's activity can best be brought home to modern Catholics by an illustration admittedly fanciful. The priest does not as such participate in
the governing body of the Church; so true is this that, in theory, a
layman could be elected Pope.[3] This distinction between the
Church's two powers is very important; when the sacrificing, sacramental side of her activity is considered, men speak of the Church
as a totality, though with a hierarchy of functions in the living of
the divine mystery. On the other hand, where the *governing* task
of the Church is at issue, prelates rule the Church and are the supreme authorities of the Church; but they *are not* the Church. The
Church is made up, under this aspect, of the governing *and the
governed.*[4]

Now where, in this distinction of functions, does the teaching
role of the Church belong? Some might put it in the sacramental
life of the Church, since knowledge of the mysteries of the faith
grows by one's living of the supernatural life. But Pope Pius warned
the Catholic action groups against this error. The teaching authority obviously belongs to the governing body of the Church, under
its Supreme Pontiff, since only that body has the right to formulate
doctrine in terms of a formal obligation to believe. The magisterium, or teaching primacy, is simply one aspect of the general primacy bestowed on Peter and the apostles.[5] As the Church is composed of both the governing and the governed, so is it made up of
the *ecclesia discens* and the *ecclesia docens.*

The fact that the magisterium is part of the Church's *ruling*
power reminds us that the magisterium is directed to the preservation of a truth *given* to the Church; it is a treasury to be preserved,
ut . . . sancte custodiret, in the language of the First Vatican Council, forming Canon 1322 of the Canon Law. This does not mean
the Church guards *formulations,* merely, or exacts only formulaic
assent. She is not given guardianship over magic phrases, effecting

their work outside the knowing apparatus of the faithful. In order to guard the given truths, she must *teach* them, draw out their meaning, connect them, cast them in manageable language: *ut . . . sancte custodiret et fideliter exponeret,* to finish the phrase quoted above. All of this is clear; yet this task exists only because of the earthly career of the Church—because of the need for an external authority, with an infallible warrant, to help fallen man in his passage through a world of change and confusion.[6] In heaven, the Spirit holds sway in the triumphant Body of the Church, dispensing with that juridical structure which governs the faithful in history. The task of the Pope, like that of Moses, ends at the Promised Land.

Thus it is necessary to understand with precision the jurisdiction that exacts *both* belief in and obedience to the Church, but with differing modes in its different acts. Peter's scriptural commission is to be a rock of foundation, to keep the keys, to bind and loose, to strengthen his brethren, to feed Christ's flock.[7] By virtue of this commission, the rulers of the Church can exercise any of the prerogatives necessary to its fulfillment. Given the authoritative institution of a society—the State, by natural law; the Church, by direct revelation—the right to achieve the degree of *organization* necessary to that society is also sanctioned by the instituting power. Where the Church is concerned, the historical situation of man demands a clear preservation of revealed truth, as well as the maintenance of an ordered society (since Christianity is not just a teaching, but a *body* united to Christ, offering a redemptive sacrifice in *community*). Newman, discussing the scriptural passages in which authority was bestowed on the apostles, remarked that these passages

involve, in consequence, though they do not mention, a complex organization, and a combination of movements, and a variety and opposition of interests, and other similar results of extended sway. Of course, too, they involve vicissitudes of fortune, and all those other characteristics of the history of a temporal power which ever will attend it, while men are men—whether, as in the case of the Jews, they are under a supernatural Providence or no.[8]

Thus, though the papal authority was given directly from Christ, the means necessary for fulfillment of this task derive from the di-

Church have the power to issue commands to temporal society, as well as teachings to the faithful? At one time, such a power was defended, as a direct right of the Church. Then a theory of indirect power became popular. Finally, in modern times there has been a learned defense of the view that this power is not a proper part of the Church's mission, even though it may have been a necessary condition for the fulfillment of that mission at various points in history. Temporary suspension of functions normally belonging to the State does not in any way constitute a denial that these faculties *do* belong to the State. Though the Church has the right to take every moral means to fulfill her spiritual end, and though circumstances sometimes make the exercise of some temporal prerogatives necessary for fulfilling that end, nonetheless the spiritual end is the basis of her actions, even in these cases. There *is* no "temporal power" as separable from the spiritual power of the Church. It would be more precise to say the Church's actions have an indirect *effect* on the temporal order, by way of her role as guardian of doctrine and teacher of the faithful, than to say she possesses an indirect *power,* or principle of rule, in this sphere.[12] To take a parallel from Newman (speaking of the Church's infallibility) : "It could not act in its own province, unless it had a right to act out of it" (for any necessary defense of the proper province) .[13] Any power affecting men intimately is bound to have repercussions throughout their life. The superiority of the spiritual to the temporal order means that, when waves from such influence cross or clash, the spiritual has prior right. But this is not a right (which would not be a right, but a degradation) of the spiritual to *become* the temporal. If, for instance, the State and the Church both undertake the education of children, for their own aims, to form citizens and to inform the faithful, these efforts must be harmonized; and, should there be direct clash, the temporal power must give way to the spiritual as having prior right. The supremacy of the spiritual has been asserted, but no temporal act has been usurped by the Church.

At certain periods, no education would have been possible—including the teaching of the faith—unless the Church, which alone was stable enough, or could call on civilization in other parts of the world, initiated the entire educational process. This happened in the homeland of Europe, during the periods of tribal anarchy following on the Roman Empire's dissolution. It has happened in mission fields, as in the Jesuit "Reductions" of Paraguay. But the Church was not displacing a temporal authority in these situations, or even assuming it as such; she was supplying whatever effects of temporal rule were necessary for her to accomplish her spiritual aims.

To say that the Church, with her divine assistance, was merely exercising her spiritual right in these situations is not the same as saying that all the churchmen involved understood these distinctions, or, even if they understood them, that their formulations of the problem were exempt from the prejudices of the time. Nor is it to say that all acts of churchmen are exercises of the Church's power. At various times it has been tolerable or desirable—or simply the sole conceivable arrangement—that men have held both ecclesiastical and temporal power; as, today, it is a normal thing for priests to be teachers. The priest teaching physics or art in a high school is not asserting some necessary connection between his two roles, some direct or indirect power of the Church over science or art. He is not, by virtue of his priesthood, a better or worse teacher of those subjects than a layman or non-Catholic would be (though he may be given more respect in personal dealings, here as in everything he does). In such cases as this, it is clear that two separate tasks are undertaken by the same man. And in other societies, at other stages of development, the powers of priest and king, without being merged in their principles and separate bases, could be combined in one man. This was not an ideal arrangement; it showed an immaturity in the temporal order. For that matter, it is not an ideal arrangement to have priests spending their time teaching physics; it is a concession to the shortage of lay teachers and to the normal economics of the academy (which dictate that a student of a subject do some teaching in it). It is good for priests to know physics, and for Catholic schools to teach physics; and priest-teachers are the accidental byproduct, in an imperfect world, of these two goods.

Naturally, circumstances in which the Church must supply some temporal discipline if she is to fulfill her divine mission are also the ones in which the accidental combination of roles is likely to take place; that is, the *Church's* proper power is at work at a time when the accidental exercise of power by some of her *ministers* is also necessary or convenient. This has led to confusion in retrospective analysis, but only because some men tried to read the complexus of mediaeval events, in which the Church was intimately involved, as normative of the Church's role in *all* periods. Needless to say, it is logically and theologically absurd to go at the problem in this fashion. The mediaeval Church is not an ideal to which men should strive to return. It is the mark on history of a Church that is still living, and making a quite different mark in our quite different times. Her life is present to men, they still have her teaching voice with them. We do not have to go back to earlier centuries to find her in her "real self." She is always her real self.

By way of reaction to the error of those who would make the mediaeval arrangement of spiritual and temporal power an extrahistorical ideal, some Catholics fall into the opposite exaggeration, denying or belittling the juridical structure of the Church, and her disciplinary responsibilities to the faithful. Pope Pius XII described this error in *Mystici Corporis* (par. 65), when he wrote:

We deplore and condemn the pernicious error of those who dream of an imaginary Church, a kind of society that finds its origin and growth in charity, to which, somewhat contemptuously, they oppose another, which they call juridical. But this distinction which they introduce is false: for they fail to understand that the reason which led our Divine Redeemer to give to the community of man He founded the constitution of a Society, perfect of its kind and containing all the juridical and social elements—namely, that He might perpetuate on earth the saving work of Redemption—was also the reason why He willed it to be enriched with the heavenly gifts of the Paraclete.

"The saving work of Redemption," the *spiritual* aim and power, is at the base of all the Church's decisions, disciplinary as well as doctrinal. Those who belittle the juridical structure of the Church invite a misunderstanding that acts against their own intentions. By proclaiming an ideal Church, the "dream Church" of Pius' condemnation, they are, sooner or later, forced to justify *all* of the

Church's proper actions as *doctrinal*. By trying to "purify" the Church of its earthly power, they invite the simplifications of the "angelistic" faithful, who avoid the complexities of the incarnation of God's power in earthly society by theocratic claims for the Church.

Even Msgr. Journet's great book on the Church shows some traces of this mentality. The Church's powers are based on a direct mandate from God, in the supernatural order, but elaborated according to the natural laws of society given to us in nature (as faith is a direct gift of the Spirit, but reflection on the truths of faith, and formulation of them in human language, goes forward by the rules of the mind). Yet, in order to emphasize the pre-eminently spiritual character of the Church, Msgr. Journet maintains that "society" is a term that can be applied only analogously to the Church and to civil societies.[14] Such a position is a dilution of the mystery of the Incarnation as that is reflected in the structure of Christ's Mystical Body, where there is a union of the divine priesthood and kingship with *a real human society*. The result is unique, but the Church is no more "analogously" a human society than Christ's is analogously a human nature. The mystery of Christ, true God and true man, is reflected in the Church, which is a truly divine society and a truly human one.[15] This is clearly taught in the encyclical *Mystici Corporis*. I have already quoted the passage from paragraph 65, where it is said that the Redeemer intended "to give to the community of man He founded *the constitution of a Society*, perfect in its kind and *containing all the juridical and social elements. . . .*" The same paragraph goes on to describe the Church as "a real kingdom," and to describe "the juridical commission as Ruler" that is given to the Church. In paragraph 63 there is another treatment of the Church as a natural society; I give this below, in note 37 to this chapter. But the clearest statement of the Pope's teaching on this matter occurs in paragraphs 60 and 61, which are central to his exposition. There he distinguishes physical bodies from moral bodies (civil societies, voluntary organizations, etc.). On the basis of this distinction he teaches that the Mystical Body is clearly not the physical body of Christ, which suffered and is glorified; but it *is* a moral body. He adds that it is something more than a moral body, since it is "supplemented by another internal principle," i.e., the indwelling of the Spirit; but it *is* a moral body, a real society.

Msgr. Journet's unwillingness to grant that the Church is a human society has unfortunate consequences throughout his work. One effect is his preference for terms like "organism" and "biological" to explain the legislative discipline which is a necessary condition of coherence in the Church's body.[16] He dislikes political terms. Yet Christ regularly referred to the Church as His kingdom, and Newman, in his sermon on the Church as an empire, shows how extensive the political terminology is throughout Scripture. In fact, it was the example of the Old Testament writers that led Saint Augustine to take *civitas* as the key term for his great work on the Church. The importance of this usage was reaffirmed by Pius XI in *Quas Primas,* the encyclical on the sacred kingship of Christ.

The denial of the true humanity of the Church is motivated by the kind of timorous piety that led early heretics to deny the full humanity of Christ—a refusal to admit the original nobility of creation, and the thoroughgoing nature of the rescue achieved in the Incarnation. Where the Church is concerned, men want to lift its administration and history above the variables of human legislative process and imperfection.[17] Msgr. Journet is far too learned and wise to do this in the normal way, by refusing to admit that there is any imperfection in the Church's human activities. But he recasts the definitions of the Church's powers in order to separate them, as far as he can, from the human reality of the Church.

He writes, for instance, that "it is precisely inasmuch as she possesses the supernatural powers of order and magisterium that the Church is social and visible."[18] But the historical role of the Church does not arise solely from the eternal life given her; it arises from the fact that this mandate was given *to* men, *in* time. Thus, insofar as the earthly administration of the Church's order is concerned, the divine mandate is fulfilled in a community of men blinded and weakened by the effects of their fallen condition. "This power, viewed in its fulness, is as tremendous as the giant evil which has called for it. . . . It is a supply for a need, and it does not go beyond that need."[19] As Msgr. A. Pailler, Auxiliary Bishop of Rouen, puts it:

The justification *here and now* of authority in the Church under the present dispensation must therefore be found in the nature of this present dispensation, which is that of original sin with all its consequences for man in his concrete historical situation. The hierarchy of the Church is then seen to be mediatory and so subordinate to the mediation of the Incarnation. This is also true of her authority, which is therefore intrinsically justified by the historical fact and state of sin, remedied as it is on the plane of the Incarnation. It is only from this standpoint that authority can be actively integrated by the individual believer into an authentic view inspired by faith.[20]

In carrying out the divine mandate, rulers and teachers of the Church are not *inspired* as to the positive forms which definition and discipline should take, only *assisted,* negatively, from doctrinal error or such prudential disaster as would make the gates of Hell prevail against the Church.

The even more direct consequences of Msgr. Journet's attitude can be seen in his treatment of the Church's powers—"direct" or "indirect"—in the temporal order. Like Father Murray, Msgr. Journet denies that the Church has any direct commission to the ruling of civil society as such. But Msgr. Journet goes much farther than Father Murray. The latter says that circumstances, acting as a kind of "historical middle term," can make certain temporal powers the necessary condition of the spiritual power's activity; when this happens, *that spiritual power itself* will act through political means in a *particular* moral situation (without asserting any *general right* to the disposition of these means).[21] Msgr. Journet, on the other hand, puts the temporal activities of the Church entirely outside its canonical or legislative power. He finds these exercises of power sometimes valid, as a condition "juxtaposed" to the Church's canonical power, but not as an exercise of that power itself.[22]

It is easy to see the problems that make men try to distinguish a "soul" of the Church from the less ethereal aspects of its corporate rule.[23] If the power of the Church is divine, how can men attribute any imperfection to its exercise? One way is to face down fact, and find nothing but perfection in the historical career of the Church; another way, more reasonable but as little tenable in the long run, is to say that all imperfection occurs outside the Church's proper sphere.

This ecclesiastical argument parallels, in much of its process, the specious reasoning that led man into various theories of "divine right" for kings. Because the Church is founded on a divine mandate, runs the argument, all its *proper* actions are exempted from the laws of nature. In the same way, men argued: because all authority is from God, we cannot attribute to any king actions unworthy of heaven's king. Again there is an attempt to simplify, to "homogenize" the character of authority.

The truth, of course, is that the Church's rulers *can err even in the exercise of her divinely granted authority,* so far as the administration of the earthly society is concerned. In the entire course of the education Christ gave his disciples—an education not concluded with his departure from earth, or even with the descent of the Holy Ghost, as the vision to Peter in Acts 10.9-16 proves—we are taught that the Lord meant to create his kingdom of truly human materials, only exempted from the vicissitudes of human rulers to the degree necessary for preserving the truth of revelation and the unity of his mystical body.

In this union of the divine and human there is exemplified an economy or ordinance that is a leitmotif of Scripture. Christ continually acts through material agencies. In feeding the multitude, he uses the bread and fish offered by a boy, and has the disciples take care of its distribution. Even in the miracle itself, real bread is used, as real water was used at Cana—and as material conditions are necessary in the Church's administration of the Sacraments. When blind eyes are opened, it is by his word, but also through the instrumentality of clay. In a thousand ways, the redemptive act is achieved or signified through a symbolic re-enactment of the mystery that made salvation possible—the Incarnation of the Word in flesh. The Church is subject to the same law of divine action; it is a *magnum sacramentum*—the clay, the stuff of earth, that is quickened by the Holy Ghost:

Almighty God, in what He has graciously done for man from the beginning, has not acted against the appointments of this world, but through them. . . . When God would raise up a people to be a witness of His name, He did not send on earth a race of Angels, He did not frame a polity such as man had never seen, but He took a polity of earth, and breathed His Spirit into it, that it became a living soul. Of course the Jewish government and nation were in many respects peculiar and unlike the nations around them; but they were peculiar much more in the object aimed at, viz., the worship of the true God, than in the means of promoting it . . . though the outward form of Judaism was earthly, God had secretly inspired it and used it for His purposes.

The case is the same with Christianity also. Unbelievers have been busy in assigning human causes for its rise—such as the discipline of the Church, or the doctrine of a future life; and some of its defenders have been as eager to show that these cannot be assigned. . . . Now we need not deny that in one sense it is human; that is, as far as it is viewed externally. It is a divine treasure, but in earthly vessels. . . .

The peculiarity of God's Providence which has now been noticed, is almost seen in the creation of man himself. Man was made rational, after he was made corporeal. "The Lord God formed man of the dust of the ground, and breathed into his nostrils the breath of life, and man became a living soul." Here are two acts on the part of the Creator—the forming the dust, and the breathing the life; and they are to the point here as illustrating the principle I have been insisting on. Man is confessedly formed on the same mould as other animals; his skeleton is like theirs; he is very like some of them. And unbelievers, in consequence, have been forward to assert that he does not really differ from them; and because he is outwardly like them, and has an organized body, and can be treated by medical art, as if he were but a framework of matter, and is obliged to employ his brain as an instrument of thought, that in consequence, he has not a soul; just as in regard to Judaism they have denied it to have a heavenly spirit in it, because it had an earthly body.

And the case is the same as regards the Sacraments of the Gospel. God does not make for us new and miraculous instruments wherewith to convey His benefits, but He takes, He adapts, means already existing. He takes water, which already is the means of natural health and purity, and consecrates it to convey spiritual life. He changes the use of it. Again He selects bread and wine, the chief means and symbols of bodily nourishment—He takes them, He blesses them; He does not dispense with them, but He uses them. He leaves them in appearance what they were; but He lifts them with a Divine Presence, which before they had not. As He filled the Jewish Temple of wood and stone with glory, on its consecration, as He breathed the breath of life into the dust of earth, and made it man; so He comes down in power on His chosen symbols, weak though they be in themselves, and makes them what they were not.[24]

Though few Catholics will deny that the Church is a human society, with human imperfections, some soften the mystery of the Church by a line of thought more or less resembling that of Msgr. Journet. They say, for instance, that the Church's rulers remain men, and their purely administrative acts are not part of the infallible deposit, but that the divine exception of the Church from that eventual decay which overcomes other societies gives a special guarantee to the wisdom of any act originating from the Church. There is a broad sense in which this is true: Catholics must believe there is a special Providence guiding the Church's actions. Theologians even apply the term "infallible" to the prudential actions of the Church, insofar as these are unable to destroy the Church. Since the gates of Hell cannot prevail against her, one can say that, in terms of a society's life and death, the Church is protected from the misstep that might be fatal. But can one proceed from this *infallibilis securitas* (as Cardinal Franzelin called it) to a judgment about the wisdom of any particular act? It is often asserted—and particularly in the treatment of encyclicals—that one *can* make this step, directly and without qualification. The Rev. Norman Galloway, O.S.A., for instance, reasons from the providential protection of the Church to the following assessment of encyclicals:

The possibility of error in these documents is so utterly remote that it is practically non-existent, even as a possibility.[25]

But we have already seen that the encyclicals are not a special variety of teaching. In them, the whole range of papal teaching can be voiced; and who, looking at the facts of history, can claim a preternatural protection from error in the papal conduct of all ecclesiastical affairs? As Newman put it,

Was St. Peter infallible on that occasion at Antioch when St. Paul withstood him? was St. Victor infallible when he separated from

his communion the Asiatic Churches? or Liberius when in like
manner he excommunicated Athanasius? And, to come to later
times, was Gregory XIII, when he had a medal struck in honor of
the Bartholomew massacre? or Paul IV in his conduct towards
Elizabeth? or Sextus V when he blessed [and helped finance
(G.W.)] the Armada? or Urban VIII when he persecuted Galileo?[26]

An analogue, from the individual's life in grace, may help explain
the "prudential infallibility" of the Church. St. Thomas teaches
that the virtue of prudence is not innate, but acquired, the result
of discernment exercised on experience. When it is objected that
there is an *infused* virtue of prudence in the baptized Christian,
he says that this grace makes man *sufficiently prudent, with regard
to the things necessary for salvation, to reach heaven*; but extension
of this prudence to the wise regulation of the affairs of life, and to
the directions of others' lives, has to be won by experience.[27] In
much the same way, the Church's prudential infallibility guarantees the achievement of her essential aims; but, within this containing *assistentia*, divine Providence commits the earthly government of the Church to its earthly rulers, men of varying capacities
and experience.

The deep error encouraged by passages like that quoted from
Father Galloway is a misunderstanding of Providence. The Christian believes in a mysterious, not a manifest, Providence.[28] God's
actions are not bound by necessity, or by the expectations of human
reason, as St. Thomas said in refuting the demonstrative force of
St. Anselm's "proofs" that God *had* to become man.[29] The simplistic view that Providence is manifest, that God's ways are ours,
is not confined to things like the Anselmian treatise on the Incarnation. Men deny the existence of God, arguing that Providence
could not allow the presence of evil in the world, by much the
same reasoning that leads men to think God could not allow a taint
of human imperfection in His Church.[30] In reflections on the political order, Edmund Burke could argue that what *is*, in the social
arrangements of mankind, is as it *should* be, since events took this
shape under a superintending Providence. Using the same arguments, de Tocqueville argued that the forces making for *change*
were evidently divine, so powerful were their converging pressures.

Such errors, recurring in a thousand shapes, reduce Providence to the status of an evident pattern sanctioning some institution or action.

The error as it applies to the Church might be supported by urging that God's will is more manifest in things connected with his direct revelation than in the darker hieroglyph of nature. But one might as logically argue that Providence would not allow misunderstanding to take place over the written record of revelation. This is, after all, an activity not only *assisted,* as the Church is, but directly *inspired.* And so, by an a priori approach such as Anselm took with the mystery of the Incarnation, one might construct a set of rules that Providence *must* fulfill in revealing the essential truths of salvation. It would be easy to argue, for instance, that words in an inspired account must be perfectly clear on the nature of God and his Church. With this pattern in mind, we could search the written records of mankind for the kind of syllogistic revelation that would satisfy us. Whatever the results of this search, it would not lead us to accept the Christian Scripture as a vehicle of revelation. For there is, in the Bible, no careful sorting of doctrines, no technical language, no unambiguous testimony. As Newman remarked,

the structure and style of Scripture [remain] a structure so unsystematic and various and a style so figurative and indirect that no one would presume at first sight to say what is in it and what is not. It cannot, as it were, be mapped, or its contents catalogued; but after all our diligence, to the end of our lives and to the end of the [earthly career of the] Church, it must be an unexplored and unsubdued land, with heights and valleys, forests and streams, on the right and on the left of our path and close about us, full of concealed wonders and choice treasures.[31]

Nor is the *relative* clarity or explicitness of a text the gauge of its importance—as defenders of a manifest Providence would be forced to maintain.[32] On this subject Newman wrote:

First, the word Trinity is not in Scripture. Next, I ask, How many of the verses of the Athanasian Creed are distinctly set down in Scripture? and further, take particular portions of the doctrine, viz., that Christ is co-eternal with the Father, that the Holy Ghost is God, or that the Holy Ghost proceedeth from the Father and the

Son, and consider the kind of texts and the modes of using them, by which the proof is built up. Yet is there a more sacred, a more vital doctrine in the circle of the articles of faith than that of the Holy Trinity?[33]

The Catholic may say that he is given the authoritative exposition of doctrines covertly present in Scripture by the correlative side of revealed truth—tradition, embodied in the teaching of the Church. But that, too, is an historical teaching, tangled up in lesser matters, enunciated through controversy, often defending doctrine in response to a particular challenge, exhibiting "the growth of an idea under successive emergencies."[34] In short, the teachings of the Church make themselves known through a set of human circumstances and accidents (and even misunderstandings) consonant with the apparently casual structure of Scripture, the personal peculiarities in the style of each inspired author, the current concepts and language (and even the errors, on non-doctrinal matters) that make interpreters of that source proceed as men who "have to wind their way through obstacles, in and out, avoiding some things and catching at others, like men making their way in a wood, or over broken ground."[35] Is it likely that God would exempt the large body of the Church, as it takes its course through time, from conditions under which he let the inspired writers of the apostolic age compose the record of his Son's life and work? Is it likely that Popes and Bishops have been blessed with a more evident degree of holiness and wisdom and foresight than were granted to the Apostles? Rather, is there not an economy here, which reveals truth not in such a way that it overwhelms man, or compels assent, but according to the partial knowledge, the trials exacting great effort and confirming good faith, that condition all our human striving after God? Newman writes of the sacred books,

Though the Bible be inspired, it has all such characteristics as might attach to a book uninspired—the characteristics of dialect and style, the distinct effects of times and places, youth and age, of moral and intellectual character.[36]

And in another essay he traces the parallel mystery by which Israel's history—and, we may add, the Church's—has all the characteristics of any other national history. Yet the literary structure of the one, the political structure of the other, though perfectly human, are something more than human also; as man, though an animal, is more than animal:

> Till the comparative anatomist can be said by his science to disprove the rationality and responsibility of man, the politician or geographer of this world does nothing, by dissertations in his own particular line of thought, towards quenching the secret light of Israel, or dispossessing its angelic guardians of the height of Sion or of the sepulchers of the prophets. Its history is twofold, worldly to the world, and heavenly to the heirs of heaven.[37]

Those who would have the Church shine with unquestionable wisdom on every subject are indulging in the kind of escape that is manifested, by the simpler-minded, as a wish that every Good Friday be a rainy day. In each case, there is a desire to overwhelm with signs of authority, when God has conspicuously observed a different dispensation, challenging men to seek, exacting faith where unaided reason cannot go, granting even to those who accept his word only disturbed vision, as in a clouded mirror (*per speculum in aenigmate*).[38]

How often Christ could have dispelled misgivings, during his life, by a miraculous revelation of his power, yet forebore. When He worked miracles, He frequently asked whether the recipient believed in his power *before* it was exercised—so that faith led to the manifestation, instead of arising from it. "Thy faith hath saved thee." Man is not lifted, by the new dispensation of the Gospel, above the conditions of *trial* that characterize earthly life.

And if Christ did not present his own actions in an unquestionable light, did not discourse wisely on philosophy and politics, did not avoid temporal connections that obscured his eternal glory (coming from the improbable village of Nazareth, gathering an unlearned following, speaking among those who claimed to know of his father, a carpenter), what right have we to expect such marks of glory and unfailing wisdom in his Church? Even Christ "grew in wisdom and knowledge and grace *in the sight of men*."[39] Is the Church to avoid, or hide, the historical task of learning from experience, correcting itself, maturing in consideration of this problem or that? When men asked for an unambiguous sign, that Christ might certify himself by the credentials *they* established, he did not come down from the Cross. When the devil tried to put his powers to the proof in a "test case," he did not leap from the temple or turn stones to bread.

With even more direct reference to his vicars, Christ did not choose men extraordinary for their learning. He did not grant them an instant *gnosis* that made his mission evident to them. He did not protect them from the pettiness of ambition. Nor, in the Spirit's inspiration of Scripture, did God hide the long record of the disciples' failure to understand his work. After that very mission in which they first wielded supernatural powers, Christ rebuked them for their impure elation and self-confidence (Luke 10.17-24). He appointed as chief of the disciples a man who seemed to have a positive talent for getting into trouble. In the timidity, followed instantly by presumption, that made Peter fear the waves, then venture out beyond his own faith—or, reversing the order, strike with a sword, then run away—many will see an image of the timidity or overextension with which the Church has met different challenges in different ages.[40] Even after the revelation that no man is common or unclean (Acts 10.28), Saint Peter seems to have held, as a matter of prudential discipline, that the Old Law observances should be retained—which led to the confrontation at Antioch (Gal. 2.12). By his quick action (the baptism of Cornelius) and timorous withdrawal from it, Peter's volatility and fluctuant temper are made evident even after Pentecost. Christ's words to the disciples have a special significance for Peter, who has so often "known not the times": "It is not for you to know the times or season which the Father hath appointed by his own authority; but ye shall receive power. . . ." (Acts 1.7.)

All this is true even of a great saint like Peter, and true of the saintly men who have inherited his office and been as confused as he was by historical tides and storms. Think of Pio Nono, tossed from the most optimistic liberalism to the most oppressive reaction by the trials of his office. Yet a darker mystery is contained in the leaders of the Church who were actually evil men. The luxurious princes of the Church, with their nepotism and absenteeism, their mistresses and children and boy lovers—all of this corruption reaching, at times, up to the throne of Peter himself—show how fully God has committed the earthly side of his Church's fortunes to human care. In this society, as in others, evil men exist and hold office and affect issues. As Saint Paul felt rebellion in his own body, flesh warring with spirit; as all men feel tempted in this place of trial; so the earthly body of the Church contains a struggle between good men and evil:

> Thus, at the flood, there were eight men in the Ark, and one of them was reprobate; out of twelve Apostles, one was a devil; out of seven Deacons, one (as it is said) fell away into heresy; out of twelve tribes, one is dropped at the final sealing.[41]

The attempt to deny or simplify this interaction of human and divine, of the eternal and the temporal, of good and evil affecting the Church's earthly history, has the most serious, yet the most unpredictable, consequences. It acts, with equal regularity, in almost opposite directions. When men try to efface the boundary between God and man, this world and the next, they can treat earth as *nothing* compared with heaven or, with equal logic, treat earth as heaven. In the early history of the Church, the immanentizing of the kingdom of God led, in some cases, to a justification for the powers-that-be as a City of God, or, on the other hand, to a denial of the validity of earthly life and rule, of marriage, civil allegiance, temporal responsibility. Absolutism, precisely because it does not correspond to nature's order, is lawless, touching reality at unrelated points. Antinomy is its law. The psychology of this has been studied, at the individual level, in Msgr. Knox's *Enthusiasm,* which records how the belief that sex is irrelevant or unworthy can lead either to hysterical abnegation or to the Adamite brand of promiscuity, can do this even in the same movement or individual. A refusal to come to grips with the complexity of reality introduces men into ever further reaches of the unreal. In the same way, the simplistic domestication of Providence can support, equally, Burke's belief that God willed the establishment of the English Church as an unchangeable dispensation, or de Tocqueville's belief that the strong forces working toward equality were a sign of divine intent.

These views, developed further than these philosophers themselves ever carried them, lead logically to a radical theocracy on one hand, or a radical anarchy on the other, and both aberrations *have* arisen from the work of such men.

Here, I think, is the explanation of something that will at first bewilder the observer of ecclesiastical controversy today—the fact that homogenization of response to papal guidance is encouraged both by the upholders of mediaeval ideas about the Church's power over states (that group which Father Weigel called the "static" school), and by some of those who defend "modernization" and a fashionable "liberalization." There is a connection between these positions: it is the antinomian connection that existed between the milleniarists of empire and of anarchy. Each errs on the nature of Providence.

One way of expressing the coalescence of the Church's temporal rule and the City of God is to make the blunt assertion that all kings should be subject to the Pope in everything. But a slight change in viewpoint will put the same absolutism at the service of the world—of the Holy Empire, of the future, of the spirit of this age. In both cases, the gap between heaven and earth is closed, not by the divine mediation of the Church, but by a human forcing of reality. The ultimate homogenization of reality is probably that which sees no break between the kingdoms of this earth and the City of God. This latter temptation is especially strong by reason of the neglect, in a great deal of modern thought, of Christianity's eschatological teaching. Father Yves Congar and Father Karl Rahner have pointed out the dangers in this for Catholics,[42] and C. S. Lewis notes the same forces at work in Anglican thought.[43] Yet it is precisely the apocalyptic doctrines so prominent in the New Testament, so significant for early Christians, that confirm the view of Providence we have been taking. The Church's relation to the world is essentially transitory, dark, a trial and conflict not to be eased until the ending of the world. No other aspect of Christianity is so fundamentally at odds with the accommodating temper of the modern world; and, correspondingly, no aspect has been so softened by those who try to merge Providence with their chosen pattern of recent happenings.

The history of modern culture . . . is dominated by various forms of immanentism, rationalism, the spirit of Faust; and eventually there is Marxism, the most consistent endeavour that has ever been made to give the world a purely immanent meaning, excluding all transcendence; an endeavour to overcome all contradictions and to attain integrity without any reference to God. Even things that are in themselves good and true, authentic earthly values, are susceptible of becoming idols and a "home-ground" for the Prince of this world. Think what can happen to country, production, progress, class, race . . . we must be on our guard against setting up as judge and arbiter before the time that God decrees. As we have seen, it is not till the end of the time that He has put between his ascension and his coming again that the Son of man will take his winnowing-fan and sweep clean his threshing-floor. *Nolite ante tempus judicare*, says St. Paul, "Pass no judgment, therefore, before the time, until the Lord come, who shall both bring to light what is hidden in darkness and manifest the counsels of hearts; and then' shall every man have due praise from God" (I *Cor.* 4.5). The Portuguese proverb that Father F. Portal loved to quote, and that Claudel inscribed at the beginning of *The Satin Slipper,* "God writes straight with crooked lines," is a remarkable version of one of the deepest truths of Christian wisdom. We believe that Christ alone holds the secret of the ambivalent world in which the history of salvation is worked out; there was reason perhaps in St. John's tears before the sealed book (*Apoc.* 5.1 ff.), but it is precisely in the fact that only he breaks the seals that the sovereign power of the immolated and conquering Lamb is made manifest. We are not able to know which of the forces in history may not in the end work for the Kingdom. God, who is lord of the world of nature as well as of grace, has everywhere sown seed which by his power contributes to his work, and it is beyond question that we shall one day be very surprised to see in which ways it has been done.

The rightful order between nature and grace is certainly a harmony, the order which the Creator has willed and the Saviour will re-establish. But this rightful order is obstructed by a factual order, the order of sin and redemption by the Cross. Hence, the tension inherent in Christianity and the kind of dialectical character of the pattern it imposes: "use the world as not using it to the full"; "he that hath lost his life for my sake shall find it."

At the beginning of modern times Christian thought was rather losing sight of the eschatological sense that gives movement and balance to the economy of salvation, *in Christo et ecclesia*; while at the same time men were beginning to discover history, not simply events and their chronological order, but history as a movement towards something—the eighteenth century said towards enlightenment and reason, towards progress. By so doing men were really providing an eschatology for themselves, an equivalent of a religion. But it was a religion of man and a kingdom of the world and of history.[44]

Father Congar gives, as an example of a Catholic teacher who neglects eschatology, Pierre Teilhard de Chardin, S.J. Teilhard, ignoring the assurance that man will not know the day or hour of Christ's coming to establish the Kingdom in its eternal form, believed that knowledge of the day and hour would itself *effect* the day and hour, that the "noosphere" would purge away, by stages, the noxious aspects of a fallen world and *earn*, as it *became*, heaven.[45] With no regard for the scriptural language of crisis, of things become worse, of trial unintermitted, of error grown more plausible than ever at the last stage when anti-Christ appears, Father de Chardin dismissed the entire eschatological segment of Scripture, hoping that the world would pass through stage after stage that modified those limitations God has hitherto put upon the nature of his revelation and the working of his Providence. Here is Gnosticism and Illuminism, here is Anselm's anticipation of necessities that *dictate* God's ways, done on the grand scale. For such a mentality, the immanentizing tendencies of modern thought are clear signs of Providence. Paradise is to be regained by making one's surroundings Paradise, in the best Adamite tradition:

All over the world, men are toiling—in laboratories, in studies, in deserts, in factories, in the vast social crucible. The ferment is taking place by their instrumentality in art and science and thought, is happening for your sake. . . . Accept it, this sap—for, without its baptism, you will wither, without desire, like a flower out of water. . . . The temptations of too large a world, the seductions of too beautiful a world—where are these now? They do not exist.[46]

But the scriptural assurance that the world will hate the Church until the end of time is not so easily dismissed as this. Darwin has no more ended the duality of spirit and flesh, of time and eternity, than did Calvin or John of Leyden or the Eastern emperors. It is no wonder that, carried away by his vision of heaven informing all earthly powers, Teilhard took the International Geophysical Year (1957) as "Year One of the Noosphere."[47]

For those so easily brought to a boil, the Popes' cautious endorsement of modern trends is read, not in relation to the Holy Spirit's ageless superintendence of the Church, but as evidence of a *new* spirit remaking history.[48] The believer in modernity is not counseled to moderation by a memory of the uses his own "immanentist" arguments have been put to, against the innovators of other ages, since he thinks history has forever put off such unenlightened ways. The absolutist never fears that absolutism can serve another part of reality; for him, there *is* no other part. The direction of this hope is indicated in a sentence from de Chardin's 1934 work, *Comment je crois*:

If by some interior collapse I came to lose my faith in Christ, my faith in a personal God, my faith in the Spirit, I think I should continue to believe in the World. The World, its values, its infallibility and its goodness—that, in the last analysis, is the first and last thing in which I believe. It is by this faith that I live and it is to this faith that I feel I should, beyond all doubts, abandon myself at the moment of death.[49]

It is easy to see why such a teaching would appeal to a world affected by what Father Congar calls "immanentism." And a similar "immanentism" prompts men to cite encyclicals in piecemeal excerpts and "homogenizing" vagueness. De Chardin, certain that *all* things were now divinized, felt no uneasiness about his departures from the careful language of theology; one need not preserve, cautiously, the truth of the old formulae, of the infallibility of the Church, where *all* things are "speaking" truth, when the earth itself has become infallible, when everything suffers the influence of the noosphere.[50] Similarly, some proponents of modernity, with their hasty exegesis of encyclicals, their certitude about "papal teaching," seem convinced that the Spirit of the Age and the Holy Spirit have somehow intermingled flames, and that difficulties in the letter of the Church's teaching are to be read in the light of this heavenly-earthly spirit: as Mr. Clancy told us earlier,

The clear, over-all direction of papal teaching on political-social problems has been in the general direction of what we in this country, rather loosely, for lack of a better term, call "Liberal."

If it is asked how this judgment could be formed, how difficulties arising from the very text of the Pope can be brushed aside so easily, is not part of the answer to be found in a conviction that the spirit of this age and the Spirit that guides the Church must be the same?

The thing that bothers me most about "Conservative" Catholicism is its essential pessimism toward history and I think if I could briefly describe the attitude of "Liberal" Catholicism I would say it is an essential openness, and perhaps an essential hope, about the providence of God in history.[51]

It is interesting to recall that the liberalism of Acton led him, in his later days, to condemn Newman's "pessimism" as a sin against the Holy Ghost, who is also the *Zeitgeist*: "Providence means progress. . . . God is active in history. . . . Not to believe in Providence is to question the divine government." And therefore, since his old ally did not submit to the Third Person in the spirit of progress, "Newman denies the divine government of the world."[52] History *vindicates* God, for without manifest progress divine wisdom is senseless, its action is wasted: "My theory is that divine government is not justified without progress. There is no *raison d'être* for the world. . . . It is the only point of view from which one discovers a constant progress, the only one therefore which justifies the ways of God to man."[53] For Acton, Newman became an "evil man," head of a "school of Infidelity," because he withheld the assent to history's beneficent and single course toward Acton's nineteenth-century version of "the Omega point." To retain the apocalyptic teaching of Scripture was a denial of that Christ who is history. And Newman *did* retain the scriptural teaching all his life, the teaching he phrased so eloquently in this passage:

When the Christ had come, as the Son over His own house, and with His perfect Gospel, nothing remained but to gather in His Saints. No higher Priest could come—no truer doctrine. The Light and Life of men had appeared, and had suffered, and had risen again; and nothing more was left to do. Earth had had its most solemn event, and seen its most august sight; and therefore it was the last time. And hence, though time intervene between Christ's first and second coming, it is not *recognized* (as I may say) in the Gospel scheme, but is, as it were, an accident. For so it was, that up to Christ's coming in the flesh, the course of things ran straight towards that end, nearing it by every step; but now, under the Gospel, that course has (if I may so speak) altered its direction, as regards His second coming, and runs, not towards the end, but along it and on the brink of it; and is at all times equally near that great event, which, did it turn towards it, it would at once run into. Christ, then, is ever at our door; as near eighteen hundred years ago as now, and not nearer now than then; and not nearer when He comes than now. When He says that He will come soon, "soon" is not a word of time, but of the natural order. This present state of things, "the present distress" as St. Paul calls it, is ever *close upon* the next world, and resolves itself into it. As when a man is given over, he may die any moment, yet lingers; as an implement of war may any moment explode, and must at some time; as we listen for a clock to strike, and at length it surprises us; as a crumbling arch hangs, we know not how, and is not safe to pass under; so creeps on this feeble weary world, and one day, before we know where we are, it will end.[54]

Providence is the mystery on which the old "fundamentalist" reading of encyclicals and the "modern" fundamentalisms share common ground. The "static" theologians of Father Weigel's analysis think that Providence acts in a manifest and final way through every pronouncement of authority: to question, to see crossing tides or historical currents, to hang back from a blind obedience elicited without interpretive subtleties, is to defy the clear will of God; so that Msgr. Fenton can say that encyclicals are to be explained, not interpreted.[55] The *modern* fundamentalist thinks that Providence acts in a manifest and final way in the very order of history, so that hesitation about those enlightened political enthusiasms which lay claim to papal warrant is a repudiation of God's divine government in time; and Father Davis writes "Encyclicals should be interpreted, not controverted."[56] Those out of tune with authority or modernity do not need to be questioned closely about their reading of the papal text; their lack of consonance with the Spirit is clear. To differ on a particular *application* of a teaching is as grievous as to question the most general statement of that teaching. Prudential judgments are as subject to the *Zeitgeist* as doctrinal formulations are to the papal *assistentia*. Even those who pronounce judgment from the encyclicals do not need to read or cite the Popes with care, since the mind of the Pope at once pervades and is vindicated by the modernity which the Holy Spirit has made his own. Msgr. Fenton and Father Davis can with equal equanimity ban speakers from campuses,[57] call men's faith in doubt, anathematize, find anticlericalism in any disagreement with them.

Not that the false views on Providence would be given the assent of either man. Luckily, the error is inchoative, cloudy. unformulated. Yet this error, however vaguely held, alone seems adequate to explain the otherwise incomprehensible nonchalance with which men extract convenient meanings from a literature for which they profess such reverence; they must have a certainty that their meaning is the right one, *no matter what the text says.* That is, they interpret the documents by a certitude about God's will that comes from some source other than the magisterial doctrines themselves. They interpret the texts by their times, and not *vice versa,* fully confident that the divine plan is manifested through either channel. Such men can be unperturbed by any words of Father Teilhard which seem to conflict with the Pope's, since the same Spirit that wrote through the one works through the other, and apparent discrepancies can safely be left to the Spirit of history, who will reconcile the phrasing of *both* of *his* revelations. On the other hand, any tag or phrase that *suggests* a departure from papal thought on the part of men who are not attuned to the times must be branded as coming from bad faith, selfish desire for gain, dormant conscience, or sheer determination to overthrow God's authority. What other explanation can one find for conduct such as this?

There is nothing surprising about this: man always tries to escape the doubts that a mysterious Providence raises, the clouded mirror in which men read revealed words. This longing is intensified, today, by all the anxieties that come from the demonic achievements of science, reason, and that history which men feel *must* be either beneficent or, if opposed to human longing, invincible. Out of this longing is born the immense emotional appeal of Father Teilhard, linking non-Christian evolutionists and Liberal Catholics in an alliance that Teilhard himself felt more intimate and important than his ties with fellow Catholics.[58]

But the world has not escaped its status as the domain of the Prince of this World (whose presence Father Teilhard refused to face);[59] and even the Church on earth has not transcended this dispensation—since, as Monsignor Pailler points out (page 113, above), the Church's ruling apparatus is called up precisely by this dispensation, to save men existing in a fallen world.

It is with this understanding of Providence that we must interpret the Church's relation to the world. And the papal encyclicals, firmly based on the Church's true nature, not only exist in this dispensation, but explicitly recognize and formulate its economy:

Pains and hardships of life will have no end or cessation on earth; for the consequences of sin are bitter and hard to bear, and they must accompany man so long as life lasts. To suffer and to endure, therefore, is the lot of humanity; let them strive as they may, no strength and no artifice will ever succeed in banishing from human life the ills and troubles which beset it. If any there are who pretend differently—who hold out to a hard-pressed people the boon of freedom from pain and trouble, an undisturbed repose, and constant enjoyment—they delude the people and impose upon them, and their lying promises will only one day bring forth evils worse than the present. Nothing is more useful than to look upon the world as it really is, and at the same time to seek elsewhere, as we have said, for the solace of its troubles.[60]

So, Leo XIII. Pius XII also spoke out against utopianism of any kind, technological or economic,[61] evolutionary or revolutionary:

The Christian statesman does not serve the cause of national or international peace when he abandons the solid basis of objective experience and clear-cut principles and transforms himself, as it were, into a divinely inspired herald of a new social world, helping to confuse even more minds already uncertain.[62]

He warned men against relying on the delusion that history is self-purifying, on the clock as an instrument of redemption:

A one-sided supernaturalism might refuse entirely to take such an attitude into consideration, [i.e., that the bridge between East and West cannot be built on any recognition of Russia's *system*, only of her people's rights], alleging the reason that we live in a redeemed world and are therefore withdrawn from the natural order; or some might say that the collectivist character of that system ought to be recognized as a "historical truth," in the sense that it too corresponds to the will of God—but these are errors to which a Catholic can by no means submit.[63]

NOTES TO CHAPTER FOUR: PROVIDENCE

1. For other aspects of the relation between belief and obedience, see John Courtney Murray's critique of Scheeben's theology (the subject of Father Murray's disser-
tation): "The Root of Faith," *Theological Studies* 9 (1948), pp. 34-46.

2. See, especially, the address to the Second World Congress for the Lay Apostolate
(Oct. 5, 1957, *The Pope Speaks* 3, pp. 119 ff), and the treatment of the layman's mission
in the Pope's two addresses to the hierarchy on Nov. 2 and Nov. 4, 1954 (Yzermans
I, pp. 284-301). The latter addresses make a distinction, for convenience of treatment,
between the tasks of ruling and teaching; but the 1957 address makes it clear that
there are only *two* principal powers: "Christ granted His Apostles a twofold power:
first, the priestly power to consecrate which was given in its fullness to all the Apostles;
second, the power to teach and govern . . . the power to teach and govern belongs
to the Pope and bishops." Cf. *Mystici Corporis*, where the triple division is used in
par. 38, and the double one in par. 65 (which contrasts the Spirit's sanctifying work
with the Church's *"juridical* commission of Ruler and Teacher").

3. Rev. Yves Congar, O.P., *Lay People in the Church*, p. 249.

4. Cf. Congar, "The Historical Development of Authority in the Church," in Todd,
Problems of Authority, pp. 140, 155: "It is a fact that 'Church' is sometimes understood
by the theorists of ecclesiastical power or papal authority as indicating clerics, priests
and the Pope. This use of the word was completely unknown to the Fathers and the
liturgy. It is a fact that in a large number of modern documents the word 'Church'
indicates the priestly government or even quite simply this government's Roman
courts. It is distinct from the faithful, from men in general and outside and above
them. Here is one example from hundreds which could be given: 'The Church is
given the task of feeding the flock of Jesus Christ.' But the Church is herself this
flock. . . . It is most essential and important that we should restore, not only in erudite
theology, but in catechetical instruction, in preaching, and in pastoral documents, the
true sense of words. We should not use 'Church' when we really mean the leaders of the
Church, the Church's government, in short, the *Praepositi Ecclesiae*. The Church is the
Christian community. She has her leaders, but she is not just an authority with a
juridical organization." The same care to keep the term Church for the whole body
of the faithful, rather than its ruling part, informs much of Msgr. Journet's great
book, *The Church of the Word Incarnate*; see especially pp. 45-9. Cf. Pius XII's remarks on the sickly members of the Church's sound body (*Mystici Corporis*, pars. 23
and 24), and Newman, *Plain and Parochial Sermons*, vol. 3, pp. 223-5.

5. Some theologians, notably Cardinals Franzelin and Billot, used to consider the
teaching power a third *and distinct* part of the Church's mission. But *cf.*, besides the
teaching of Pius XII (note 2 above), Vermeersch-Creusen, *Epitome Juris Canonici*, II,
p. 457, and Msgr. Journet, *Church of the Word Incarnate*, pp. 163-6.

6. Cf. Newman's famous exposition of this matter in the *Apologia*, pp. 319-29.

7. Matt. 16, 18-9, Luke 22.32, John 22.15-7. Msgr. Journet's *The Primacy of Peter* is
devoted to an examination of these passages.

8. "The Christian Church an Imperial Power," *Sermons Bearing on Subjects of the
Day*, no. 16. And see *Mystici Corporis*, par. 21 (NCWC translation) for God's willing
the means when he willed the end of the Church; along with par. 69 on the Church's
visible character as establishing the need for social articulation and discipline.

9. For the Thomistic presentation of this cf. Thomas Pègues, "L'autorité des encycliques pontificales d'après St. Thomas," *Rev. thomiste* 12 (1904), pp. 513-9.

10. It may be well to guard against a confusion in terminology that is liable to arise
in discussions of this sort. Men often refer to disciplinary actions of the Church's
rulers as "pastoral," contrasting these actions with the more strictly "doctrinal" actions.
(Placing a book on the Index, when there is no specific condemnation of its teaching,
may be a prudent measure meant to prevent scandal or misunderstanding, even when
the book's doctrine, rightly understood, is sound.) This distinction is a key one, for instance, in Father de Soras' discussion of the different kinds of teaching in the encyclicals (*Rev. de l'act. pop.* 1961, pp. 141 ff.). It must be remembered that these are two

aspects of a single jurisdictional power, that even the prudential acts are taken with a view to preserving doctrinal purity. But another use of "pastoral" refers to the *other* power of the Church, the sacrificial-sacerdotal role. Thus men talk of giving the papal teaching a "pastoral" character when they refer to the apt presentation of doctrine in the sacramental life of Christians (*cf.* Todd, *Problems of Authority*, pp. 13, 25, for examples of this usage). It is this latter use that makes us speak of the local priest, the confessor, the immediate guide in spiritual matters, as "the pastor." These two uses should be kept distinct; and, to avoid misunderstanding, I shall call the former the "disciplinary" power; the latter, with which this essay is not immediately concerned, is the "pastoral" solicitude that characterized Pope John XXIII, and which was perfectly defined by Pope Paul VI who, writing while still Msgr. Montini in 1957, said: "By pastoral is meant that the teaching is prompted less by the intrinsic requirements of doctrine—although that is also involved—than by the extrinsic needs of specific groups" (*Osservatore Romano*, May, 1957).

11. *Cf.* Pius XII's words at Yzermans I, pp. 297-8.

12. Although Father Murray, S.J., argues, if I understand him, that the Church has this indirect *effect* in the temporal order, he holds that some statements of the indirect *power* theory—notably, the first great one, by John of Paris—can be upheld, even in the light of historical development and modern findings. The same is not true of, e.g., Bellarmine's theory of the indirect power. *Cf.* especially "Governmental Repression of Heresy," *Proc. Cath. Theol. Soc. of Am.* 3 (1948), pp. 26-98, "Bellarmine on the Indirect Power," *Theological Studies* 9 (1948), pp. 491-535.

13. *Apologia*, p. 332.

14. *Church of the Word Incarnate*, pp. 180-1, 194 ff. Msgr. Journet argues that "society" is used, of Church and State, in an "analogy of proportion"—that is, the word is predicated of both by reason of their relation to a *third* use, which is the first most proper one. But he does not give this third usage. Saint Augustine called the Church the *Civitas Dei*, using the scriptural term for Jerusalem, and frankly proceeded from political analysis of the meaning of *civitas*; this *would* afford a third use for both Jerusalem and the Church—with the disturbing implication, a kind of "reverse Platonism," that heaven is patterned on earth. But Saint Augustine makes his procedure clear at Book XIX of the *City of God* (section 24), where he gives a univocal definition of society equally applicable to civil societies, to the Church, and to other ordered communities. Msgr. Journet, by the vagueness of his reference to a third usage, actually seems to be referring to some such generic word, without admitting that the application of that term is made by univocal predication. It is hard to imagine a more proper use of society than can be exemplified in the Church and the State, which are Saint Thomas' "perfect" (i.e. self-sufficient) societies.

15. *Cf. Mystici Corporis*, par. 64: "As Christ, Head and Exemplar of the Church 'is not complete, if only His visible human nature is considered . . . or if only His divine, invisible nature . . . but He is one through the union of both and in both . . . so it is with his Mystical Body' since the Word of God took unto Himself a human nature liable to sufferings, so that He might consecrate in His blood the visible Society founded by Him and 'lead men back to things invisible under a visible rule.' " (Pius XII's own quotations in this passage are from Leo XIII and St. Thomas.)

16. *Church of the Word Incarnate*, pp. 181-2, 184, 371 ff. It is ironic that the endeavor to lift the Church's activities above the murky level of human activity leads Msgr. Journet to talk as if biological process, unmuddied by rational interplay of persons, were a *higher* form of activity than the union of men in love. Yet the highest union men can conceive is not a biological one; it is the Trinity, a union of three *persons*. Another irony: in order to avoid the "juridical," Msgr. Journet criticizes the use of "society" as inadequate because analogous. In point of fact, the term is *not* analogous, yet the scriptural term *Body*, which he prefers, *is*. St. Paul traces the analogy at length (I Cor. 12-31), and Pius XII considers another aspect of it at par. 21 of *Mystici Corporis*.

17. That this consideration is present even in Msgr. Journet's brilliant work can be seen by his use of Samarine's attack on the use of "institution" with regard to

the Church: "It brings the idea down to too mundane a level, makes it too crudely familiar" (Journet, *op. cit.*, p. 181).

18. *Ibid.*, p. 180.

19. Newman, *Apologia*, pp. 326, 329.

20. *Cf.* Todd, *Problems of Authority*, p. 22. This is a particular application of the general rule that "the order established in things by the divine wisdom . . . is not an adequate representation of that wisdom, since the divine wisdom is adapted to the order that receives it" (St. Thomas Aquinas, *S.T.* I, q. 25, a. 5 *resp.*; *cf. C.G.* III, 97.2). The principle is exemplified at Matt. 19.8, Mark 10.5, John 3.12-3, 4.17.

21. The mediating historical "term" does not intercept the spiritual power, blocking it off from its particular exercise—any more than the middle term in the act of conscience makes the moral duty specified by it less binding. See the discussion of conscience below, in Chapter Eight.

22. *Church of the Word Incarnate*, pp. 255-62. Msgr. Journet defines the Church's canonical power as its "legislative power, taking this last word in its broadest sense" (p. 157).

23. *E.g.*, "She [the Church] must be considered as an essentially supernatural society through and through, having a simple likeness of analogy and proportion to political society, not a univocal likeness, even a generic one" (*ibid.*, p. 180). The trouble with this sentence can be identified by substituting "Christ" for the Church and "God" for supernatural society—but further we cannot go, for Christ does not have a mere *likeness* to man, analogous or otherwise. Neither is the Church only *like* society.

24. Newman, *Sermons on Subjects of the Day*, pp. 97-103. These thoughts are developed in the essay on "Milman's View of Christianity," (the Harrold edition of *Essays and Sketches* II, esp. pp. 223-5). See also the sermons "Submission to Church Authority," "Contest Between Truth and Falsehood in the Church," "The Church Visible and Invisible," and "The Visible Church an Encouragement to Faith," vol. 3 of *Parochial and Plain Sermons*.

25. "How Binding Are the Encyclicals?" *Catholic Mind*, Nov., 1956, p. 625.

26. "Letter," p. 135. The list, of course, could be indefinitely extended—was Pope Hormisdas infallible when he rejected formulations John II had used; or Virgilius when he first conspired with Justinian and then refused to join him in condemning Nestorians; or Honorius when he recommended the teaching of Sergius, Patriarch of Constantinople (for which he was later censured by the Third Council of Constantinople); or Pius IX when he conceived the Papal States as necessary to his spiritual role?

27. *S.T.* II-II, q. 47, a. 14.

28. "This is the law of Providence here below; it works beneath a veil, and what is visible in its course does but shadow out at most, and sometimes obscures and disguises what is invisible" (Newman, "Milman's View," p. 221).

29. *In Sent.*, d. 1, q. 1, a. 3, *S.T.* III, q. 1, a. 2. A crudely Anselmian view that Providence *had* to use the means it did is the basis of an article in the *Am. Eccles. Rev.* for 1946 called "The Necessity for the Definition of Papal Infallibility" (pp. 439-57). *Cf. S.T.* I, q. 25, a. 5, *resp.*, "nullo modo iste cursus rerum sic ex necessitate a Deo provenit, quod alia provenire non possent"—"this (Providential) course of events does not proceed from the determination of God in any way that would allow us to say alternative dispensations were impossible." (*Cf. S.T.* I, q. 19, a. 3.)

30. Thus the more general observations of St. Thomas on Providence and the presence of evil in the world can be applied, in proper measure, to the imperfection of the human elements in the Church: *cf. S.T.* I, q. 22, a. 2, *C.G.* III, 71; and, for the action of Providence through the inferior ordering capacities of men, *S.T.* I, q. 103, a. 5, ad 3, *C.G.* III, 77, 78, 79, 111, 112, 113.

31. *Essay on the Development of Christian Doctrine*, pp. 90-1, bracketed phrase added (G.W.).

32. *Ibid.*, p. 118.

33. "Holy Scripture in its Relation to the Catholic Creed," Harrold's edition of *Essays and Sketches* I, p. 232.

34. *Essay on Development,* p. 89. There is good reason why the teachings of Scripture and of the Church's tradition should present similar obstacles to the student. Theologians are currently reminding us that Scripture and tradition are interpenetrating aspects of a single revelation—that tradition established the canon of Scripture, and that the authoritative interpretation of Scripture is the task of tradition. These theologians feel that only apologetic pressures and a mistaken concept of the Church's power to declare the meaning of Scripture have led men in the past to treat these as two sources of revelation. Revelation has only one source—God; and only one authoritative interpreter—the magisterium of the Church. *Cf.* Newman, *Essay on Development,* pp. 323-5, where he describes Christian teaching, in all its manysidedness, as having "a reference to Scripture throughout," and writes: "Scripture may be said to be the medium in which the mind of the Church has energized and developed. . . . Nor am I aware that later, Posttridentine writers deny that the whole Catholic faith may be proved from Scripture, though they would certainly maintain that it is not to be found on the surface of it, nor in such sense that it may be gained from Scripture without the aid of tradition." See also *Grammar,* pp. 107-8: "The long history of the Church, with its fresh and fresh exhibitions of Divine Agency, the Lives of the Saints, and the reasonings, internal collisions, and decisions of the Theological School, form an extended comment on the words and works of our Lord."

35. "Scripture in Relation to Creed," p. 230.

36. *Ibid.,* p. 234.

37. "Milman's View," p. 225. Pius XII used the same illustration in *Mystici Corporis,* par. 63: "The Church in its entirety is not found within this natural order, any more than the whole of man is encompassed within the organism of our mortal body." The comparison itself shows that the Church *is* in the natural order, as man is in the animal order, but that both of these orders are *transcended* as well.

38. I Cor. 13.12. And see St. John Chrysostom's description of Christ's way of teaching through enigma (*In Joann. hom.* 34, PG 59, col. 194).

39. Luke 2.52. That this refers to a real growth in Christ's human, experiential knowledge, St. Thomas teaches at *S.T.* III, q. 12, a. 2.

40. Newman saw the Church's historical fortunes figured in the incident of the storm at sea: the Church is "always going, and never gone; ever failing, yet ever managing to explore new seas and foreign coasts. . . . He who could walk the waters, could also ride triumphantly upon what is still more fickle, unstable, tumultuous, treacherous—the billows of human wills, human purposes, human hearts. The bark of Peter was struggling with the waves, and made no progress; Christ came to him walking upon them; He entered the boat, and by entering it He sustained it" ("Christ Upon the Waters, I" in Harrold's edition of *Sermons and Discourses,* pp. 313-4).

41. *Plain and Parochial Sermons,* vol. 7, p. 207.

42. Congar, *Lay People in the Church,* pp. 93 ff. Rahner, *Free Speech in the Church,* pp. 90-4.

43. *Cf.* title essay in *The World's Last Night,* Harcourt, Brace, 1959.

44. Congar, *Lay People,* pp. 93-5.

45. In *The Divine Milieu* (Harper and Brothers, 1960), selective treatment of fact (e.g., this is a spiritual treatise that dismisses sin as irrelevant to its purpose) leads Teilhard to discern a "general 'drift' of matter toward spirit" (p. 86), leading to this "totally human hope": "To desire the Parousia, all we have to do is to let the very heart of the earth, as we Christianize it, beat within us" (p. 137).

46. *Ibid.,* p. 138. It is to be noticed that the redemptive work takes place, in de Chardin's system, in the laboratories, in factories, and on expeditions. Where sacraments are (infrequently) referred to in this connection, it is usually as a metaphor for this scientific redemption (the "baptism" of the quoted passage). *Cf. Letters From a Traveler* (Harper and Brothers, 1962), p. 86: "I keep developing and slightly improving, with the help of prayer, my 'Mass upon things.' It seems to me that in a sense *the true substance* to be consecrated each day is the world's development during that day—the bread symbolising appropriately what creation succeeds in producing, the wine (blood) what creation causes to be lost in exhaustion and suffering in the

course of its effort." Though it is not easy to see why wafers and Mass wine could not be packed in the supplies of an expedition, we find Teilhard praying thus: "Since, once more, my Lord, not now in the forest of the Aisne but in the steppes of Asia, I have neither bread, nor wine, nor altar, *I shall rise beyond symbols to the pure majesty of the real,* and I shall offer you, I your priest, on the altar of the whole earth, the toil and sorrow of the world. . . ." (From unpublished *La Messe sur le monde,* quoted in *Letters,* p. 141, emphasis added.)

47. *Letters,* pp. 354-5.

48. *Cf.* de Chardin, *Letters:* "I have been deeply interested to see even Chinese thought, in its own way, taking the same direction as my own and that of my friends. Moreover, it's a most encouraging confirmation of the idea—very close to my heart, as you know—that in future the faith of Christ will never hold its own or be extended except through the intermediary of faith in the world" (p. 177). "It seems to me that on a higher level than the confused currents of moribund democracy and nascent Communism and Fascism—*and of an ageing Christianity, too, that no longer informs the material world* [it is to be recalled that informing the material world is the prime redemptive act of de Chardin's 'ever-greater Christ']—there should be some way of grouping the 'elect' who have made up their minds to build the earth on the three 'columns' of Universalism, Futurism and Personalism" (p. 228). Emphasis added.

49. Cited in *monitum* of the Holy Office censuring Teilhard's work. *Cf. Letters,* p. 205: "I am studying the successive development of an adherence which, proceeding from faith to faith, rejoins the Christian current (or *phylum*) by convergence: faith in the world, faith in the spirit in the world, *faith in the immortality of the spirit in the world, faith in the ever-growing personality of the world."* Emphasis added.

50. *Cf.* Teilhard's description of "my effort to re-think Christology and Christianity in terms of a humanity in process of biological convergence" (*Letters,* p. 321). The *human* is the *norm,* not Christianity, since Teilhard is interested in "the neo-humanism on which, I am convinced, our future salvation depends" (*ibid.,* p. 359). Even God must rely on this salvific process, "God as He thrusts His roots downward in the direction of Earth, and nourishes Himself from below" (*ibid.,* 273). "Christ saves, but should not one add that He is also saved by evolution?" (*Le Christique,* 1955). The real faith, for Teilhard, is faith in the world—"the faith of Christ will never hold its own or be extended except through the intermediary of faith in the world (*Letters,* p. 177)—so interpretation and action must be oriented primarily toward this earthly spirit of success, and to God only *through* its mediation, its terrestial pontificate.

51. Mr. William Clancy, Debate of May 25, 1960, p. 35. (I do not mean to suggest that Mr. Clancy is trammeled in all of the theological idiosyncrasies of Teilhard; only that a certain line of Liberal thought, reaching an extreme statement in de Chardin's work, has left the Catholic Liberal defenseless for distinguishing adequately between the aberrations of de Chardin, the welfare programs of various twentieth-century governments, and the social teaching of the Church. Such a Liberal has, in effect, two sources of revelation, the Church *and the will of God made manifest in modern Liberalism:* "Modern Liberalism has fought and won battles for which we Catholics should have fought but which, in our blindness, we too often opposed. Thus does God's providence work in men's affairs. Those Catholics who are described as 'Liberal'—*who are 'open' toward modern civilization—are at their best, I think, when they are in search for such evidences of God's providence in history, even in movements where they may least expect to find God's hand"* (Clancy, Debate of October 23, 1960). Again we are urged to look for (or demand) a *manifest* Providence.

52. Quotations from Acton's later thoughts on Providence are gathered by Hugh A. MacDougall, O.M.I., in *The Acton-Newman Relations* (Fordham, 1962), pp. 168-75.

53. *Ibid.,* p. 140.

54. *Parochial and Plain Sermons,* vol. 6, pp. 240-1.

55. See page 85 above.

56. *America,* Oct. 28, 1961.

57. For *America's* ban on uncongenial speakers, see page 13 above. The Catholic University made a similar judgment against some of the most distinguished American

and European theologians, early in 1963, because they held "controversial" opinions on the Second Vatican Council—a decision *America* criticized as a failure in good press relations (*America*, March 9, March 30, 1963, pp. 329, 430).

58. *Commonweal*, for instance, reporting the *monitum* issued by the Holy Office on the subject of Teilhard, agreed that specific objections had force, but regretted the fact that the warning "does not give full credit to Teilhard's general aim" (editorial, July 27, 1962). This readiness to gloss over doctrinal error where the other source of divine guidance—the spirit of the age—is vouchsafed, is not a phenomenon confined to the Liberal devotion to de Chardin: *cf.* Clancy, Debate of October 23, 1960: "Dorothy Day's vocation has been a historic one. It has been to witness in the world to the corporal works of mercy. Here she has been a light before men. She has been a light to all of us. There have been intellectual aberrations in the Worker movement. I don't subscribe to its political anarchism. I think that, philosophically, the movement is sometimes childish. . . . But this isn't the point when you talk about Dorothy Day." The far different standard by which presumed deviation from doctrine is handled in Mr. Buckley must arise from the fact that he has not been certified by the historical spirit who issues Liberal vocations.

59. Since divinization of the world is a growth of personality in Teilhard's scheme, it is more than an embarrassment to have a formed, higher than human, personality standing at the beginning of history as the enemy of man. It is just as embarrassing to have a formed personality as the *source* of a self-personalizing universe. Thus Satan and God the Father are absent from de Chardin's thought. He can call his scheme "Christocentric," since "Christ" is seen as the saving, immanent, growing "ever-greater Christ" of the world. But this Christ does not take men back to the Father; rather, forward to Omega, a goal which itself grows.

60. Leo XIII, *Rerum Novarum*, par. 18 (Gilson, p. 214).

61. See his attack, in the Christmas Message of 1954, on the "blind faith which confers on economics an imaginary mystic force," and holds that "since man has given proof of such great power as to create the marvelous technico-economic composite of which he boasts today, he will also be able to organize the liberation of human life from all the privations and evils from which it suffers, and in this way effect a kind of self-redemption." Compare with this Teilhard's letter to a prosperous businessman: "You are still having some difficulty in justifying to yourself the euphoria of a soul immersed in business. I must point out to you that the most important thing is that you *do* have that feeling of well-being. Bread was good before we knew about the chemical laws of assimilation. . . . 'How,' you ask, 'can the success of a commercial enterprise bring with it moral progress?'; and I answer, 'In this way, that since everything holds together in a world which is on the way to unification, the spiritual success of the universe is bound up with the correct functioning of every zone of that universe and particularly with the release of every possible energy in it. Because your undertaking—which I take to be perfectly legitimate—is going well, a little more health is being spread in the human mass, and in consequence a little more liberty to act, to think and to love" (*Letters*, p. 164).

62. Christmas Message, 1953 (Yzermans II, p. 181).

63. Christmas Message, 1954 (Yzermans II, p. 194).

CHAPTER FIVE

THE TERMS OF AUTHORITY

In the preceding chapters of this section I raised four of the difficult matters involved in interpreting encyclicals—authoritative terminology, historical particulars, degrees of belief, and Providence. Since my aim was to show that these *are* relevant subjects, and to suggest their interconnection, I could do little more than point to the places where attention must be directed if we are to discuss encyclicals more usefully than has been the practice. Now, in a kind of second go-round, I propose to make some beginning of the kind of discussion that seems called for under each of these headings. There is not time or space to do more than start an argument or two; but in the areas where argument can be conducted fruitfully.

In the chapter on "Authority," it was argued that the range of injunctive force in encyclicals is potentially as wide as the Pope's powers, running all the way from the ability to fix belief down to recommendation. Father Philip Land, S.J., writes that there should be

a manifest distinction made between statements of what is truth, generally and everywhere applicable, and what is rather exhortation to a line of action which, according to circumstances, is mandatory or advisable or less advisable in one part of the world or another.[1]

The impression that may be given by this is that the Pope gives directives that are more or less important, but always directives.

Yet this impression will not stand if we look to the Popes' own words, which are the gauge of his intent. He may say, for instance, that a certain movement or organization is not necessarily forbidden. He *allows* men to participate in it. There are many observations that fall within this category, where there is no positive exhortation—of even the mildest sort—to co-operate in the activity mentioned.

A clear example of this is St. Pius X's modification of Leo XIII's judgment that Catholics should avoid the labor organizations that were not formally Catholic. St. Pius said that, at the discretion of the Bishop in each diocese, Catholics *could* belong to these. There is no judgment that they *should*. (That was to follow in Pius XI's great encyclical of 1931.)

Another example is the treatment of the corporatist, or syndicalist, state in *Quadragesimo Anno*. The Pope's attitude toward this phenomenon is clearly marked by his introduction of the subject:

Recently, as all know, there has been inaugurated a *special* system of syndicates and corporations of the various callings which in view of the theme of this encyclical *it would seem necessary to* describe here briefly and comment upon appropriately.[2]

In the following paragraphs, the Pope outlines the scheme in its essentials, commends the "obvious advantages" it offers, draws attention to grave dangers in it,[3] and remarks that the scheme, if it is to be undertaken at all, will profit by the leaven of Catholic principle. Nowhere in the discussion is there a recommendation that men *should* adopt this system—merely the remark that, under the proper conditions, Catholics *may* participate in it. Thus it would be a violation of the interpretive norms of encyclicals to state flatly that the Popes "supported" a system that forbids strikes, a system that contributed to Mussolini's and Salazar's organization of their regimes.

The famous comments of Pope John XXIII on "socialization" are to be read in this same way. The Pope does not "recommend," far less "impose," upon Catholics a process that clearly threatens freedom but which is an inescapable fact of modern life. He merely says that, if the dangers are foreseen and allowed for, it is not *neces-*

sary to oppose the process of complexification as such. The terms are very important here. After describing the forces that work against freedom in the modern world, and insisting on the contrary principles that must be asserted against this tendency, he comes to this conclusion:

> *So long as* social relationships do *in fact* adhere to these principles *within the framework of the moral order,* their extension does not *necessarily* mean that individual citizens will be *gravely* discriminated against or *excessively* burdened. On the contrary, we *can hope* that they will help him to develop and perfect his own personal talents, and lead to that organic reconstruction of society which our Predecessor Pius XI advocated in his encyclical *Quadragesimo Anno.* . . .[4]

To claim, on the evidence of this encyclical, that the Pope is "for" the process called "socialization"—in the sense that he urges Catholics to further it, with any degree of *injunctive* force—is to follow standards that automatically disqualify one for serious discussion of papal language. Yet many newspapers took the encyclical's description of "socialization" as a *recommendation* of various national "Welfare States," American, British, and even Russian; and others predictably used it as an endorsement for their favorite theories or projects.[5]

The Pope often speaks to assert or aid or encourage Catholic freedom of action—saying this or that organization is not contrary to Catholic principle in its professed aims and methods, that Catholics *may* (not *must*) join or co-operate with it. He allays doubts, while reminding Catholics that they must follow the basic principles of morality in *any* social situation. But it is surprising to see these counsels of Catholic freedom turned to *limits* placed around Catholic debate for or against the political organizations concerned.

An example of this arose in connection with two passages from the encyclical *Mater et Magistra.* It was argued that the Pope had given a binding directive to support the UN *because he had praised the work of its Food and Agricultural Organization* (a thing Pius XII had done five years earlier). The same kind of inference was based on a mention of the International Labor Organization. But what, exactly, was said? Here are the two passages:

Here we would like to express Our sincere appreciation of the work which the F.A.O. has undertaken to establish effective collaboration among nations, to promote the modernization of agriculture especially in less developed countries, and to alleviate the suffering of hunger-stricken peoples.[6]

We must also express here Our heartfelt appreciation of the work that is being done by the International Labor Organization—popularly known in various countries as the O.I.L. or I.L.O. or O.I.T. For many years now it has been making an effective and valued contribution to the establishment in the world of an economic and social order marked by justice and humanity, an order which recognizes and safeguards the lawful rights of the workingman.[7]

There is here no command, exhortation, or recommendation to Catholics—either to join, support, or speak well of these organizations. There is simply an expression of gratitude for good things done. Unless the Pope is a ruler whose winks and nods and merest sighs dispatch men to do his implied bidding—as the murderers sped after Thomas à Becket from Henry II—such expressions of gratitude should not be translated into doctrinal or programmatic urgings.

It will be urged, in answer, that the Pope would not have taken a public occasion to thank the ILO, in an important teaching document, unless it were his intent to single out a key example of the kind of work he is proposing to Catholics. In short, his words are implicitly in the imperative mood throughout an encyclical. We have returned, through the back door, to the place where these documents are homogenized.

Such argument is invalid, based as it is on the assumption that no other motive can be found for the mention of a specific organization except the desire to give all Catholics directives about it. The Pope is a ruler whose subjects live under a variety of other legitimate authorities.[8] Toward these rulers, so easily represented as his rivals, he must maintain the most scrupulous impartiality and neutrality, where there is no absolute repudiation of his own basic rights. This involves the Papacy in a necessary diplomacy of conciliation, if the father of all the faithful is to maintain maximum access to his flock—and to those who are not yet of it, but groping toward its fellowship. Thus, even in encyclicals, he "expresses congratulation, benevolence, *etc.*"—to use Cardinal Cicognani's description of one aspect of these letters[9]—wherever it is possible to do this. His aim is not to take a partisan position toward any of the regimes in which his flock conducts its political affairs, but to express his willingness to co-operate with all of them, so long as there is no express use of their powers to undermine the moral order.

The severest test of this neutrality occurs when wars are waged between nations. Catholics on both sides often express impatience that the Church does not commit itself to one side or the other— thus, in effect, closing the avenues of Grace for those on the other side, and making it impossible for the Pope to minister to one part of the world, or urge moral considerations within it. Faced with such arguments, Benedict XV remarked, during the First World War,

It is, for every thinking man, abundantly clear that in this frightful conflict the Holy See, whilst unceasingly watching it with the closest attention, must preserve the most absolute neutrality. The Roman Pontiff, as, on the one hand, the Vicar of Jesus Christ who died for all and each, and, on the other, as the Common Father of all Catholics must embrace all the combatants in the same sentiment of charity. He has on both the belligerent sides a great number of sons for whose salvation he must have an equal solicitude. He must accordingly not consider the special interests which divide them, but the common bond of faith that makes them brothers. Any other attitude on his part not only would not assist the cause of peace, but would, what is worse, create a lack of sympathy with, and hatred against, religion and expose the tranquillity and internal concord of the Church to grave disturbances.[10]

The same attempt to recruit the Papacy in political conflict led some to denounce the Papacy for allowing Catholics to fight on the Nationalist side in Spain, or for maintaining diplomatic relations with the Japanese during the Second World War. Msgr. Knox addressed several published letters to Catholics who were disturbed in conscience over these events.

The silly modern point of view seems to be that if the Pope had denounced (say) Franco's bombardment of Barcelona (the big one) he would have done his duty and could have sat back and twiddled his thumbs, like Pilate washing his hands. Because in fact he preferred to deal diplomatically, and succeeded to such an extent that there has been no real big-scale bombardment since, he gets no credit at all.[11]

If I had to make a decision of this kind (God forbid that I ever should, in the humblest way), I should argue with myself thus. To refuse to have diplomatic representation in a country which has so flagrantly violated the principles of international morality might win me credit as a gesture, both now and when history comes to be written. But charity is more important than making gestures, and charity demands that I should be represented in Tokyo, because it is my only chance of finding out what is happening to the prisoners and internees in Japanese hands, or sending them relief if and when they need it. The Archbishop there has tried to find out what was going on, and has been snubbed because he had no status. If the Red Cross is doing all it can to establish relations with Japan, it is my business to do the same. That is how I would argue, and how I believe the Pope did argue; over and above the fact that it is more important than ever to keep in touch with the Missions, when a country goes to war.[12]

Another, more recent example of the misconception Msgr. Knox was dealing with can be found in the controversy over Rolf Hochhuth's play *Der Stellvertreter,* the drama that accused Pius XII of callous disregard for the plight of the Jews under Hitler's persecution. Hochhuth realizes that Pius did a great deal for Jews, but he condemns him for not making a public and specific condemnation of the persecution. Yet the history of the Dutch Bishops' formal statements indicates that the Jews would be harmed by such public stir and flourish. And even if the persecution were not made fiercer by such a statement, many channels open to the Pope and other Catholics, lay and clerical, would undoubtedly have been closed—channels for aiding Jews, influencing their persecutors, alleviating their sufferings. This was not an ambiguous moral question to be settled by sound teaching, but a diabolical force consuming lives at every moment, a force to be countered by every practical means; so Pius chose to use his power, openings, influence, prestige and money to intercede for and aid and protect Jews all over the world. The Pontiff now reigning, and others best equipped to know, agree that this course best served the Jews themselves, even if it leaves the Pope vulnerable to those more interested in a propaganda "image" than in concrete good done. It would, indeed, have ingratiated Pius with many to make a gesture for the benefit of historians; but this act of "political exhibitionism"[13] would have tied his hands as an intercessor and condemned hundreds of thousands to death.

The Pope's formal neutrality is not only maintained in time of war. It is his position at all times; and Pius XII explicitly affirmed this with regard to the Cold War and the various political solutions proposed for it:

Now those who wrongly consider the Church as an earthly power or a kind of world empire are easily led to ask from her also, as from others, that she renounce her neutrality and make a clear choice in favour of one side or the other. However, there can be no question of the Church's renouncing her political neutrality, for the simple reason that she cannot serve purely political aims. . . . Statesmen and, at times, even churchmen, who would make the Spouse of Christ their ally or the tool of their political alliances, whether national or *international,* do injury to the very essence of the Church and would inflict damage upon the life proper to her. In a word, they would drag her down to that level where conflicting temporal interests are locked in struggle. *And this is and remains true even when there is question of ends and interests in themselves lawful.*[14]

Why, then, has the Pope so frequently commended the work of various UN organizations, if he is officially neutral on political organizations? Because he does not take a position of surly independence, saying a plague on both your houses.[15] Rather, he is ready to co-operate with any moral effort put forth by men of good will.[16] This does not constitute a declaration on his part that this is the best effort possible, that others are not to be advanced, that men of good will cannot oppose the program as less effective than an alternative plan, or as entailing serious disadvantages. He is not an arbiter or partisan of these purely political questions. And, by reason of his co-operative attitude toward any and all efforts not formally immoral, he is in a peculiarly good position for offering sound advice to *all* groups on the moral aspects of political life. Msgr. Knox noted this advantage with regard to Spain. The same thing can be seen in the Pope's kindly reception of various groups in audience. Welcoming the various professions and organizations, he is able to bestow fatherly admonitions on them all, equally, precisely because he has put his good will toward them all beyond question. Receiving the representatives of the ILO, Pius XII reminded them that care for the "human factor," in direct contact with employers and good relations with them, must now be one of the foremost concerns of a moral labor movement.[17] Then, speaking to business men, he said they must consider the good of the whole community when undertaking profitable projects in one sector of it.[18] In a similar way, when Pius addressed representatives of the Movement for World Federation, he warned them against the delusions of "artificial uniformity" unrelated to the processes of true social formation.[19] Because he speaks as a father, he can engage in paternal correction, without suspicion that his words are to be treated as partisan sniping.

To ignore this active and benevolent neutrality, which was so signally reaffirmed by Pope John XXIII,[20] is to invite endless misunderstandings. Pius XII indicated one such confusion when he said that concordats are not to be interpreted as endorsements of the political regime with which they are concluded, but of "toleration"—that is, of co-operative neutrality as we have been considering it, with fuller *agreement* only on specified matters in the concordat.[21] Yet, despite the Church's long record and policy in these matters, Pope John XXIII's reported negotiations to achieve some freedom of religious practice for Catholics behind the Iron Curtain were read as an endorsement of Communism. This misunderstanding filled the newspapers, despite the fact that the principles of the Church's neutrality were spelled out again in Pope John's last encyclical. In a passage that did not expressly mention Communism,[22] the Pope pointed out that any human effort that is good in itself will be recognized as such, and encouraged by the Church. This is not a political statement, as Father Thurston Davis made perfectly clear;[23] nor is it a new principle, thrown up by the wash of history; it is the reaffirmation of the principle on which the Church's practice has been based throughout modern times. Yet many rejoiced or grieved over what they supposed was an "endorsement" of Communism in *Pacem in Terris*. In *National Review*, Mr. Frank Meyer called Father John Courtney Murray's careful explanation of the document "patently absurd" (a judgment that is itself absurd), and treated the encyclical as "collaborationist."[24] The motive for the Pope's solicitude was more reasonably analyzed by Mr. Erik Kuehnelt-Leddihn:

For even a small opportunity to spread the word, through sermons, instruction or periodicals, the Church is prepared to pay the price of confusion among naïve voters (and intellectuals) in the West. This can be understood in the light of the Church's two main tasks; to administer the Sacraments and to teach. To carry them out, she has time and again co-operated with powers she rightly regards as evil. . . .

If I were a Hungarian Catholic, my main interest would be to get a minimum of religious freedom for myself and my family, regardless of election results in Rome or Quebec. I would want to go to church without thereby losing my job, and I would be desperate about the impossibility of getting religious education for my children.

An armistice between the Church and Communism does not imply an armistice between the Catholic faith and Communist doctrine. That is impossible.[25] . . . It only means that an agreement has been reached as to the rules, by-laws and regulations of an intellectual and spiritual warfare, with a certain disengagement in the political sphere. It is true that the Communists will be able to abrogate the agreement whenever it suits them, while the Church is always, in St. Augustine's words, *inops ecclesia,* the "helpless Church." Still, she is bound to enter the struggle and to accept the best deal she can make, and it will then be up to the Catholic (lay) leadership to pursue the fight against materialism with more zeal than ever.[26]

The encyclical *Pacem in Terris* was criticized for not making a thorough analysis of the political realities that obstruct progress toward the ideals explicated in it. At this level there is some warrant, Father Murray said, for disappointment.[27] But the encyclical was clearly not meant to be read at this level, and this for two reasons; first, the Pope does not "take sides," but preaches to all sides, so far as he is allowed to; and second, he lets the specific application of the ideals he proposes be worked out by competent men engaged in the practical areas affected—a principle restated in the document itself.[28] The Church, as Pope John insisted in his most famous phrase, is both mother and teacher—mother to persecuted Jews, to the Hungarians deprived of the Sacraments, to men seeking her light but easily baffled of this light by an external bearing that does not welcome them. To turn expressions of good will voiced by the Church as *mother* into doctrinal positions bearing her whole weight as *teacher* is not only an error, but an error that would paralyze the effort to understand papal statements. The Church must imitate her head, who ate with publicans and sinners, let Pharisees come to him secretly, asked the notorious outcast of Sichar to give him a drink of water. Those who want crusades on every moral issue, who, with Rolf Hochhuth, want a condemnation of Nazi treatment of the Jews even at the cost of worse treatment for the Jews, who, with Frank Meyer, want Catholics to avoid all contact with Communists, even when it is the contact of a priest with the Communist jailors who might admit him to the deathbed of a Catholic prisoner—men using such norms will never make sense of the papal mode of address, a mode that is benevolent to any men who show signs of good will. This benevolence will, necessarily, be given to some who only feign good will; it will be exploited, as it has been in the past. But the cost of abandoning it—the cost in terms of men's access to the Pope, and the Pope's access to the faithful in all lands—would be terrifying.

One of the many related mistakes in this matter arises from the good wishes the Pope extends to any Catholic participating in legitimate political enterprises. This is sometimes interpreted as having doctrinal force—as if the Pope urges that Catholics should hold all the positions of power in this world, or that *they* should be supported rather than other legitimate contenders for positions of responsibility. But when Pope John XXIII felicitated John F. Kennedy on his election to the Presidency, he was not asserting, or implying, or in any way semaphoring an opinion, that Catholics who voted for Richard Nixon were less truly his sons than President Kennedy himself. In the same way, the good will expressed toward Catholic rulers in Spain or Portugal or Italy does not in any way add up to a recommendation of these "Catholic" governmental forms for other countries. The Pope can have a concordat with Mussolini, can make any reasonable arrangement for the freedom of Catholics in Gomulka's Poland, without expressing support of the party or program in force there except as it regards the one point praised or negotiated—i.e., recognition of the Church's freedom.

In this connection, it is amusing to imagine the plight of a Catholic journalist like Mr. Donald McDonald (who professes to know the Pope's mind on most matters, and was sure that papal winks were indicating a "Catholic line" on Senator Joseph McCarthy not long ago), had the same Senator McCarthy chosen to visit Rome before his death. As a validly elected official of the United States Congress, and a Catholic in good standing, he might well have been received in the normal course, and offered papal good wishes. Men who read party platforms into felicitations addressed to the World Federalist delegation in Rome, or to the F.A.O., would have been highly discomfited by this exercise in common politeness toward the political representative of a free state, this fatherly expression of good will toward a Catholic participating freely in the political activities of his time. Such an audience, such good wishes, would not have bound Catholics to support McCarthy, any more than similar expressions have bound them to support Mussolini, Franco, the corporatist state, the UN, or the ILO. What such felicitations *do* signify is the Papacy's enlightened effort to further Catholics' freedom and initiative, their full participation in proper debate and experiment.

If the extent of power exercised is marked, in each case, by the Pope's own terminology, then it is clear that he sometimes tells us that he is not commanding at all. His *diplomatic* role, his neutrality on matters of partisan debate, give a formal character to much that he says. As always, his precise terms are to be considered. When addressing the ILO, Pius XII said:

The International Labor Organization was never intended to represent only one social class or to become the means of expression of one tendency exclusively. It welcomes everything that is constructive, everything that meets the real needs of a harmoniously constructed society. . . .[29]

This is not the language in which a Pope commends doctrine to the faithful. Of what human organization, in a world weighted with the legacy of original sin, could that statement be made in a critico-historical sense? Not even of the Church itself, which, on its human side, has certainly resisted constructive elements of change, or been for a while unaware of the means that might lead to a harmoniously constructed society. The Pope is clearly speaking the language of diplomacy. By courtesy, and a recognized convention of diplomatic language, he implies what the organization *should* do by saying that it *is* doing it.

It is distressing to see the Pope's very counsels of liberty, his invitations to political freedom, turned into weapons of intimidation which can be brandished over the heads of the faithful. The kind of felicitation we have been considering, the expression of a co-operative neutrality, is often presented as *more* binding than a doctrinal discussion. The misuse of such congratulations and commendations is particularly marked in the case of the United Nations Organization. The Pope cannot refer favorably to any of its operations or agencies without having the compliment turned by zealots into a political imperative for Catholics around the world.

I am not dealing with the merits of the United Nations Organization (which are outside the scope of this book), or the papal teaching on the relevant topics of international order (though norms for judging this will be taken up in the last chapter). The subject here is papal terminology, and its binding force. If there is a papal mandate to "support the UN," it must be formulated in one of the many expositions of the duties of states, not in one succinct directive to take a specific political act. At any rate, I can find no such unequivocal sentence of command. But large expositions of the natural law are not a handy instrument for the polemicist; so even the vaguest commendatory references to the UN are tailored to meet the requirements of speaker and moment. The result is haphazard interpretation, a blurring of papal terms, and the dimming of respect for encyclicals in the mists of political passion. The papal teaching on international organizations, balanced as it is with provisos and warnings, and leaving room for the exercise of prudence in the particular act, is not easily compressed into an unambiguous plank for a political platform; but men circumvent this difficulty by turning papal amenities into campaign directives. The strategy is clearly marked in this excerpt:

There is also a clear teaching of the Church on the international order, particularly in pronouncement after pronouncement of Pius XII; and this teaching is *not merely an abstract, disembodied generality*. The late Pope, time after time, gave *positive encouragement* to the United Nations. He sent a delegate to UNESCO. . . .[30]

The exposition of international duties is, you see, not as useful as the speaker would desire; it is "abstract, disembodied generality." But wait! We do not need to submit to its dialectic, weigh its arguments, apply it to reluctant particulars in order to get our "clear teaching of the Church." That teaching is *not merely* "abstract, etc." It is conveyed to us also in any *positive encouragement* the Pope gives to the UN; and, to clinch things, to make the magisterium's action perfect, we need not wait for a definition or directive. *Habemus doctrinam*: the Pope "sent a delegate to UNESCO"![31]

But if the Pope's ambassador at UNESCO is a hieroglyphic form of doctrinal pronouncement, was the ambassador in Tokyo during the last war a command to support the Axis; is a telegram of good wishes sent to President Kennedy a command to vote for him; is a papal diplomat sent to Poland a recommendation of Communist atheism? Is every "positive encouragement" the Pope gives to an organization a positive *command* that Catholics join or support that organization, refrain from criticizing it, exempt it from political investigation or assessment? That seems to be the basis—if a logical one is to be supplied—for statement after statement purporting to tell Catholics their duties. The crudity to which these statements can descend will be illustrated by this example:

There is an old political maxim, "No man votes against his own bankbook." If the Holy Father agrees with Father Harnett that the U.N. is a "fatuous institution," why does he make such frequent contributions to U.N. agencies?[32]

Cynical maxims about the politicians' pocketbook are hardly adequate norms for dealing with the Pope's contributions to charitable agencies. As one author puts it,

No intelligent European in the sixteenth century would have thought that if the Emperor and the Sultan had concluded an armistice, polygamy would become licit or drinking wine a crime. After the treaty of Westphalia in 1648, no sane Spaniard thought the time had come to show the Inquisition his treasured secret copy of Calvin's *Institutiones*.[33]

The laughable and yet not funny lengths to which the "escalating" of papal praise can go are best measured from the popular syndicated column, Msgr. Conway's "Question Box." In a column that the editors of *America* saw fit to reprint in *The Catholic Mind* (March, 1963), Msgr. Conway would have us run through all the organizations the Pope has praised (even *inferentially* praised, even the Peace Corps) in the style of those confessional booklets that help the Catholic examine his conscience:

Have you been opposed to the ILO? Then you should definitely re-examine your prejudices.
    Have you been opposed to the FAO? Better review your thinking.
    Have you been opposed to foreign-student exchange? To the rights of immigration? To the principles and ideals of the Peace Corps? To foreign aid? To idealistic concepts of a world community? Then you need to read *Mater et Magistra* carefully, as a humble Catholic, with deep faith in the Church as Mother and Teacher.

It is difficult to determine which is the more remarkable—that this talismanic procedure should be recommended, in the first place, as an intelligent response to an encyclical, or that the editors of *America* should consider it a valuable contribution to the process of ingesting papal precept. The actual wording is as lamentable as the conception: for one thing, Pope John made it very clear that *he* was opposed to "idealistic concepts of a world community." *Pacem in Terris* demands the utmost realism in forming the universal agencies of peace.

Even those who do not rely on merely *congratulatory* formulae tend to create obligation out of phrases as little binding, as little injunctive. Father Robert A. Graham, S.J., for instance, a recognized authority on the subject of papal diplomacy, once said it is as offensive to criticize the UN (even to criticize those who are "bewitched" with the UN as a "superstition") as to criticize religion itself (*America*, October 10 and December 7, 1957). When a

Catholic journalist wrote in to protest that debate on these matters
is still possible among Catholics, Father Graham, relying on a text
of Pius XII, declared that the UN is *not* a debatable subject:

Quite recently the Holy Father gave earnest exhortation to our
Catholic élite to work actively with international institutions. To
the Congress of the Lay Apostolate he said on Oct. 5: "We give you
two directives: First, collaborate with the neutral and non-Catholic
organizations and movements to the extent that and on condition
that you serve the common good and the cause of God. Secondly,
take a greater part in international organizations." . . . I am charged
with "upsetting the conscience of Catholics" in debatable matters.
If by quoting the Pope's words I succeed in awakening dormant
consciences, I suppose I can be said to have an "upsetting" influence. But is this quite so debatable? No doubt there is nothing
shockingly new in the regrettable fact that perfectly orthodox
Catholics (priests and laymen) can live a compartmentalized life
in which their social views bear no relation to their private conscience. It is not necessary to challenge their orthodoxy; but it is
difficult to see how they can explain, among other things, their
habitually "contemptuous" attitude toward international problems. At least it can be said that they are out of touch with the
current thinking of the Church and that, as far as the Pope is concerned, they are unprofitable servants. . . . This is not an issue of
conservatism vs. liberalism, as Mr. Morriss assumes throughout.
Fundamental modern issues on which the Church has so much to
say should not be reduced to such a fragile basis.

There are many interesting things in this passage. Father Graham
avoids the temptation of calling his opponents heterodox. He contents himself with the even less palatable and provable assertion
that they are acting from "dormant consciences"—in the scriptural
language, "unprofitable servants." He assumes that for one to criticize excessive expectations about the UN is, in itself, to be habitually contemptuous about international problems. Contempt for
any human problem is, of course, sinful in itself, an attack on the
"fundamentals" every Pope has emphasized for decades. But the
point at issue is whether debating the merits of the UN *is* synonymous with such contempt, whether this one thing has been lifted
above the "fragile basis" of a political issue. The UN involves, it
is true, issues "on which the Church has so much to say." The
Church has much to say about the State; can we no longer vote,

argue, have opinions on politics itself? We are back at Msgr. Fenton's numerical test for recognizing "closed issues."

But this matter of reading an inference, even a valid one, from the text *as part of the text's explicit enjoinders* will be discussed later. What is at issue here is the particular text offered as proof that the UN is no longer debatable on the fragile basis of political argument. Look again at Pius XII's words. The first thing one notices is that the UN is not mentioned here; nor is it mentioned anywhere else in the address (which will be found in *The Pope Speaks* 4.2, pp. 119-34), though *other* international organizations *are* mentioned (*e.g.*, catechetical groups). A second point is that the UN, since it is not a formally Catholic organization, comes under the general norms given in the very sentence Father Graham quotes— that action must go forward *on condition* and *to the extent* that the common good is being effectively served. That is, the Pope imposes the duty of making just those prudential decisions on which Father Graham, using this text, closes debate. But the third and most important point is the context. Father Graham quotes the sentence as if it were a command issued to all Catholic men, who must now "*play an important part in*" international organizations. The form of the injunction is strange, as if the Holy Father were saying "*Be very successful* in labor unions." The reason for this choice of phrase reveals itself if we consider where the sentence occurs—at the end of a list of such suggestions: teach the fundamentals of their faith to Catholic workers in the European Coal and Steel Community, teach catechism in Africa, enter political life, work in the field of communications. These are suggestions of the range of activities open to his particular audience in their particular work. He was speaking to the World Congress of the Lay Apostolate, telling them what useful tasks they could perform in the world. If Catholics are *all* commanded to play important roles in international organizations, are all of them equally commanded to teach catechism in Africa? Can Father Graham accuse the editors of *National Review* of being unfaithful to the Church's teaching if they fail to do this? Yet if Catholics did all the things the Pope suggests to his audience, they would be severely fatigued. The emphasis throughout this talk has been on services Catholics *may* per-

form, especially charitable ones. Political organizations are nowhere at issue, a thing that Father Graham's audience might have
suspected had he continued his citation for one more sentence.
The work in international organizations is recommended; then
the Pope adds, "This recommendation applies to all, *but particularly to agricultural specialists.*" The Pope is not thinking of a
Catholic editor writing about the UN, but of Catholics in a lay
apostolate movement working with the Red Cross, with agricultural aid missions, with catechetical guilds in underdeveloped
areas. To make of these recommendations for Catholic action a
direct statement on the particulars of the political order is to ignore
the clear teaching of Pius XI, who repeatedly said that Catholic
action is not to be a *political* program, or replace the competent
political parties.[34]

I think it reasonable to say that something is seriously wrong
when a respected journal prints a recognized scholar performing
these operations on a papal text, *in the name of loyalty to papal
teaching,* and with the purpose of branding other Catholics as disloyal to that teaching.

Mr. Donald McDonald, a Catholic journalist who often accuses
his fellows of working counter to the Pope's directives, gave this
text as proof that they can no longer indulge in criticism of the UN:

The Church desires peace, and therefore applies herself to the promotion of everything which, within the framework of the divine
order, both natural and supernatural, contributes to the assurance
of peace. Your movement dedicates itself to realizing an effective
political organization of the world. Nothing is more in conformity
with the traditional doctrine of the Church, nor better adapted to
her teaching concerning legitimate or illegitimate war, especially
in the present circumstances.[35]

This passage, too, has a context. It was delivered to the Congress
of World Federalists, received in audience. The Pope says, in this
introductory passage of felicitations, that he supports *every* effort
that dedicates itself to the realizing of an effective political organization of the world. This is a statement of fact, not a command. It
makes no decision on the matter of fact whether the World Federalist Movement, or the UN, or any of the other efforts at effective

order, are succeeding in their aims. Even in the passage cited, he takes occasion to remind his audience that the Church has a teaching on legitimate war (a reminder not likely to coincide with certain pacifist tendencies within the World Federalists). He then goes on to warn his audience against the ideal of "artificial uniformity." Even in the passage cited, we are told that the Catholic's commitment should be to an *effective* political organization, which must therefore exist within the framework of the divine order, both natural *and* supernatural. The Pope says of these bases for the authority he is describing:

Unless the universal political organization rests upon these indispensable foundations, there is risk of its being infected with the deadly germs of artificial uniformity. We would like to invite those to reflect on this point, precisely from a federalist viewpoint, who dream of setting up a world parliament. Otherwise, they would subject themselves to the play of those disintegrating forces from which our political and social order has already suffered too much. They would only finish by adding one more legal automaton to the many others which threaten to stifle and to reduce men to the condition of inert instruments.

Instead of contenting himself with the obvious truth that the Pope has here put forth a teaching of great subtlety and realism, calling for the highest exercise of prudence ("work, study, and action" Pius asks for in his final words), this journalist takes another of the Pope's expressions of good will toward all sincere effort, and turns it into an indictment of his fellow Catholics. This use of isolated fragments from the papal speeches is not the way to arrive at the Church's teaching on international order.

Nor is distortion restricted to the "escalating" of actual phrases from one context or mode of speech into another. Sheer inference, not related to the papal text in any discernible way, is presented as the Pope's own mandate. Mr. Donald McDonald, for instance, who has long made the claim that he reads papal messages "straight," and has had to suffer for his strict standards in this matter,[36] offered this exposition of *Mater et Magistra* in his syndicated column:

The Holy Father has reminded Catholics and the world that peace must be preceded by social justice, that Communism is as much a symptom as it is a cause of world disorder, that ownership of property and accumulation of wealth are neither sacred nor absolute rights, and that there is nothing inherently pernicious in "socialization."

Although the Pope said nothing about Communism in the encyclical, either as cause or symptom, and though his treatment of "socialization" does not present it as inherently good either (but as a natural human tendency, morally indifferent in itself, at present dangerous, but capable of being put to man's use by strenuous efforts directed at obviating the dangers), these *inferences from* the text are in varying degrees defensible. "The Holy Father has reminded" is perhaps not the happiest way of introducing Mr. McDonald's own inferences, but even a man of his strict standards can be allowed this liberty, so generally taken. But where in the text did he find even the most flimsy basis for the inference that ownership of property is not a sacred right? Not an "absolute principle," perhaps, since the very concept may be contradictory in the realm of politico-economic programs. But if the phrase means anything, then the right to property can be considered absolute, since it serves as a fundamental norm and permanent standard. That is what the right of private property is and has been in all the papal documents. To take but one passage from them, Leo XIII wrote:

> *The first and most fundamental principle,* therefore, if one would undertake to alleviate the condition of the masses, *must* be the *inviolability* of private property.[37]

How did Pope John *remind* Catholics of the *opposite* of this principle? Here is the passage of *Mater et Magistra* that deals with this right:

> The right of private ownership of goods, including productive goods, has permanent validity. It is part of the natural order, which teaches that the individual is prior to society and society must be ordered to the good of the individual. Moreover, it would be quite

useless to insist on free and personal initiative in the economic field, while at the same time withdrawing man's right to dispose freely of the means *indispensable* to the achievement of such initiative. Further, history and experience testify that in those political regimes which do not recognize the rights of private ownership of goods, productive included, the exercise of freedom in almost every other direction is suppressed or stifled. This suggests, surely, that *the exercise of freedom finds its guarantee and incentive in the right of ownership.*[38]

That is, the Pope not only reaffirms the basic right to property itself (how *could* he change the natural law?), but introduces subsidiary advantages connected with that right (i.e., the indispensable protection given to *other* liberties by recognition of this one) , and does this in terms scarcely rivalled by any other papal statement.

I will not claim to have—since I do not, in fact, have—any suspicion about Mr. McDonald's loyalty, good conscience, or filial respect for the Apostolic See. When, in the heat of political journalism, he slips into a rhetorical denial of the first and most fundamental principle of Catholic social teaching, it would be petty to exploit this slip. Faced with the pertinent documents, and given time to cool his customarily high partisan temperature, there is no doubt that he would admit the principle of private ownership is sacred and absolute (according to the mode of all such principles). Yet Mr. McDonald himself has subjected many Catholics to the kind of suspicion mentioned here, and on far less substantive ground. A hint of disagreement on the inferential consequences of congratulatory words to UNESCO, a breath of criticism directed at governmental accretions of power, are enough to make Mr. McDonald accuse any critic of departure from the grounds of his faith.

Mr. McDonald is not himself defiant of authority; but he is strangely careless about the terms in which he adduces it. He does not encourage others to be defiant of authority, but he promulgates, in his measure, standards that make it difficult for them to react to it intelligently. His motives are manifestly pious; but he does the magisterium no favor when he suggests that its pronouncements are indistinguishable from his current preoccupations. Nonetheless, when his fulminations are met with disbelief or doubt of any sort, he presents himself as a type of "the mystification and frustration of the apostolic Catholic." He publishes the record of his "hollow victories" against the lost soul of one who refused to recognize Pius XII's command to support the UN: "I mailed him half a dozen full texts of pertinent Papal addresses."[39] This bombing with mail sacks, like the incantatory summoning of papal names in the informal excommunications we are increasingly favored with, reduces the Catholic's participation in politics to the level of caricature. As Father Yves Congar says,

It can hardly be denied that, in taking a side or expressing an opinion, Catholics often try to shelter behind some authority, some law or decision or extract from an encyclical letter or Papal address; in other words, they try to find a shell. Is it because they have no skeleton, no backbone, no nerves, and no muscles?[40]

The encyclicals are not meant to encourage this parody of obedience to just authority, but to aid in the formation of responsible, adult, and free men.

Improvisation from, and often very far from, the papal texts goes on in quarters where one least expects it. One of the editors of a full-scale scholarly book on *Mater et Magistra,* Mr. Justus George Lawler, writes in his brief introduction to the book:

The Catholic Council on Civil Liberties is carrying out the mandate of the encyclical by such important initiatives as supporting the film "Autopsy on Operation Abolition," by filing *amicus curiae* briefs, and by speaking out against infringements of personal liberty by the state or by private groups and individuals. This I suggest is the kind of "translation" of doctrine into action which the Pope advocates.[41]

He suggests, in short, a translation of the Pope's terms into *his* terms, and the publication of the latter as the former—as "the mandate of the encyclical," as the "action which the Pope advocates." But is the author perhaps saying that this is merely one application of papal teaching, not an *authoritative* adaptation to local circumstances by a Bishop, but the effort of one layman to apply the teaching to his own circumstances, an effort that does not rule out disagreement on the application other men might make? This is what one would expect, or hope for. But the author is ready to say that

those who disagree with *him* are defying the Pope, that his *is* the
one valid interpretation of the encyclical. He argues that, since

the "free world" is in fact now utterly enslaved in its inner spiritual
depths . . . it is apparent that every mute Catholic tax-payer, every
Catholic defender of our national adventures in *Realpolitik,* tacitly
views the admonitions of *Mater et Magistra* as "trivial."[42]

It is apparent that *every one* of these reprobates is dismissing as
trivial *not* Mr. Lawler's own judgment that "the 'free world' is enslaved in its spiritual depths,"[43] *not* the other judgments he deems
relevant in his ten pages on how to approach *Mater et Magistra,*[44]
not the application of papal principle to these historical judgments,
not Mr. Lawler's first reading of those principles themselves. Not
any of these things, you see, but *Mater et Magistra* is being scorned,
since its whole mandatory weight is coming at us from behind each
word of Mr. Lawler. And those who deny this are not making an
honest mistake, and certainly not differing from his views because
he has made a mistake anywhere along the line; they are register-
ing contempt for the papal document itself as a trivial thing.

Mr. Lawler is not applying the Pope's teaching by an individual
act of conscience, he is interpreting that teaching authoritatively
for others. He is not afraid to do this, since he conceives the normal
instruments of authoritative local interpretation—the Bishops—
as watchdogs of logical consistency, who must let *laymen* declare
the Pope's intentions on what movies to see or support.

The bishops are primarily witnesses to Christian truth; that is,
their dedication is first of all to the absolute norm of things. It is
the role of the layman, though certainly not his exclusively, to apply this ideal norm to the circumstances and realities of the here
and now situation.[45]

As a statement that there is a duty of the individual to follow conscience in the particulars of his individual acts, there is some truth
to Mr. Lawler's statement. But as a claim that laymen can formulate interpretations of binding force, can in fact make statements
with the *same* binding force that the original document had—and
this is the claim Mr. Lawler's own proclamations must be based on

—this is simply another example of polemical impatience. Like so many others, Mr. Lawler is certain that the Pope would do whatever he wants him to do, if only the overworked Pontiff had time; and the solicitous servant, relying on his own instincts about the implicit papal teaching, kindly promulgates this teaching without having to bother the Pope himself.

I shall take, at a little more length, one last example of interpretive liberty with the papal texts—again from *The Challenge of Mater et Magistra*. That book is meant as a survey of the major topics treated in Pope John's first social encyclical. Each topic is assigned to an appropriate expert, and some of the essays do proceed by sound scholarly methods. This gives special significance to the chapter on labor, which was assigned to a man with what should be a qualifying background. Mr. John C. Cort was for many years labor editor of *The Commonweal*. He was a founder of the Association of Catholic Trade Unionists, and he is currently a field director for the Peace Corps. His contribution is worth close examination, not because it is more irresponsible than many of the things that are said about papal documents, but because he offers us so detailed an account of his *mode* of forming judgments and attitudes toward Catholic social teaching. He approaches his subject by way of the following clearly delineated steps:

1) In 1937 he construed a passage in "the original Vatican translation" of *Quadragesimo Anno* as advocating "profit-sharing," because the passage did indeed use the words "profits" and "share." Then he found support for his interpretation of this sentence in another part of the encyclical, which used the word "profits," even though it did *not* contain the word "share." He gives us the two passages, in the translation he was using at that stage of the game. The first is from paragraph 57 of Pius' letter:

By these principles of social justice one class is forbidden to exclude the other from a share of the profits.

The other is from paragraph 54:

It is flagrantly unjust that either capital or labor should deny the efficacy of the other and seize all the profits.

2) "Using these texts as our justification," Mr. Cort and his fellows wrote a profit-sharing plank into the program of the Association of Catholic Trade Unionists. This, too, happened in 1937.

3) Later on, Mr. Cort read a different translation of the encyclical, which used "benefits" instead of "profits" in the first passage, and "what has been produced" for "profits" in the second passage. On the basis of "this presumably more accurate translation," he concluded that "this translator was apparently thinking of profits in the broad, general sense of 'fruits of production.' . . . As a result, the whole question of profit-sharing as understood by Pius XI has become completely confused." There is some mumbling, here, about the "murky beam" of "inaccurate or vague translation." One does not know, yet, which translation he thinks is guilty of this; not until

4) the appearance of *Mater et Magistra* removes all Mr. Cort's doubts, since "in the first official Vatican translation of *Mater et Magistra* the original translation of *Quadragesimo Anno* appears again. If one is concerned with preserving the continuity of papal thought as well as with setting this thought in its proper context, it may now be seen in the light of *Mater et Magistra* that the original passage from Pius XI should be read as an encouragement of profit-sharing." He finds that a number of morals might be drawn from the discrepancy in translations, but contents himself with a single one, "the need for authoritative translations of the papal pronouncements"—which in this case means the "original translation" released from the Vatican.

5) But Mr. Cort does not depend only on his searching textual analysis, this drama of certitude-doubt-certitude that extends over twenty-four years. He adds three other arguments to establish that the texts referred to supported profit-sharing. One is from authority: he quotes "Benjamin Masse, S.J., a distinguished expert in Catholic social theory," who says that Pius XI made several practical suggestions in *Quadragesimo Anno,* "and one of them was profit-sharing." Father Masse happens to differ with Mr. Cort on the binding nature of these remarks, but at least there is an understanding on both sides that Pius *was* talking about profit-sharing.

6) His second and third arguments are from personal preference

the relation of a particular statement to a general one. The preceding passage deals with the correct norms for the distribution of goods in society; it reads: "Wealth, therefore, which is constantly being augmented by social and economic progress, must be so distributed among the various individuals and classes of society that the common good of all, of which Leo XIII spoke, be thereby promoted. In other words, the good of the whole community must be safeguarded. By these principles. . . ." It is clear then that the "sharing of profits" intended here is that participation of the whole community in the common good which is the basis of Catholic social teaching. The Pope states the general principle, then gives it the particular statement which forms the basis of *economic* justice. He even further specifies the matter in the sentence immediately *following* the one Mr. Cort cites, a sentence which gives our *second* indication of context: "This sacred law is violated by a wealthy class who, as it were carefree in their possessions, deem it a just state of things that they should receive *everything* and the laborer *nothing*." Again, it is made perfectly clear that *some* participation in the good effects of his work is due the worker, that he cannot be *excluded* from these benefits. This is not a world-shaking statement, to anyone familiar with Catholic thought, or with the most rudimentary concepts of justice. Mr. Cort might well be disappointed with it, if it stood alone; but that is no reason for rewriting it to his own standards or veiling the Pope's express meaning. With a little patience, and willingness to read further, Mr. Cort would find that these first and most general statements of principle do *not* stand alone, but lead to sections of greater specificity. Our *third* indication of context comes precisely from the fact that this passage *does* occur in a section of the letter which is laying down the broadest basis for practical action. Specific recommendations we would expect to follow these passages. And this expectation is confirmed: we are given our *fourth* contextual determinant when in a later passage (paragraph 65), the Pope finally does raise the question of profit-sharing in the most explicit terms. Mr. Cort, our expert on encyclicals, thinks this passage is by way of *brief supplement* to his primary text, since he turns for enlightenment on that primary statement's meaning to an even earlier and even shorter excerpt, from paragraph 54, which in fact gives us our *fifth* and conclusive guide to the meaning of Cort's primary text.

The supporting text ran, as you remember, "It is flagrantly unjust that either capital or labor should deny the efficacy of the other and seize all the profits." And again I ask, entirely apart from the later translation that caused Mr. Cort temporary doubt ("what is produced" standing for "all the profits"), how the sentence, even in its first form, can bear the meaning he gives it? Note the terms: "*deny* the efficacy" and "*all* the profits." What does that first phrase mean? Look at the words that immediately precede this quotation: "Capital cannot do without labor, nor labor without capital. It is therefore entirely false to ascribe the results of their combined efforts to either party alone; and it is flagrantly unjust. . . ."If that is not plain enough, turn to the marginal summaries that are a part of the official text of *Quadragesimo Anno*. Next to the sentence from which Mr. Cort has excerpted his argument is the marginal statement that is rendered, in the translation he used, as this paragraph heading: "Each needs the other." Thus "to deny the efficacy" is to say that one partner in this combination *contributed nothing* and therefore is to *receive nothing*. This *reductio ad absurdum* is part of the general argument advanced here—that as all goods produced by an economy of capital and labor arise from the co-operation of these two elements, their real interests are not contradictory but complementary. And this argument, in turn, is part of the papal attack on class-war theories, which present social progress as the outcome only of opposition, of treating one's real allies as one's *enemies*. Leo XIII had made this argument, and Pius is here repeating it even more emphatically, since Communism had become a far greater menace in the forty intervening years. It is his point in this encyclical that the basic fallacy of Communism is its belief in the inevitability of class warfare (par. 112), and that the beginning of a Catholic social philosophy to counter this must be the recognition that labor and capital contribute to the common product and the common good, and are therefore complementary forces. That this principle is stated in its most general terms can be seen from the fact that the Pope says *neither* party is to deny the *other's* efficacy; he condemns a capitalist class that "claimed all the products and profits" *and* the workers' " 'intellectuals,' as they are called," who claim "that all products and profits, excepting those required to repair and replace invested capital, belong by every right to the workingman." He spells out both sides of the matter again, in the words immediately following the passage that Mr. Cort began with: "This sacred law is violated by a wealthy class who, as it were carefree in their possessions, deem it a just state of things that they should receive everything and the laborer nothing. *It is violated also* by a propertyless wage-earning class who demand for themselves all the fruits of production, as being the work of their hands." Yet this statement of barest principle, which says *neither* side should repudiate the *other,* is presented by Mr. Cort as if its only and first meaning were that the *employer* should not deny his workers a profit-sharing contract.

Let me repeat: I am using the very translation Mr. Cort read, and from which he finally vindicates his first impressions of the text. How *can* he insinuate into this careful statement of first principles a sudden command, which must be a very strict one ("it is forbidden," "this sacred law," etc.) , that men adopt one organizational or contractual device, a device which is later called one of many possibilities for a just arrangement? It takes an heroic resistance to meaning, a total dedication to one's preconceived notions, an absolute reliance on wishful thinking as the sole interpretive guide, to wrest Mr. Cort's meaning from Mr. Cort's favorite translation of the two passages from *Quadragesimo Anno* that Mr. Cort thinks are clearest and most relevant. In the light of his performance, it seems fair to suppose that anywhere the words "profit" or "sharing" might occur, in any context, in any papal pronouncement, he would be sure to clutch at them and assign his programmatic meaning to the whole text. And unfortunately, this approach to isolated tags used as shibboleths has proved effective in Mr. Cort's case. He candidly tells us the story in his first paragraph, which gives us such a vivid picture of the "magic-formula" approach to papal texts that I must quote it in its entirety:

Some time in 1937 I attended a week-end retreat for men near New York City. Along with the specifically religious conferences there were informal sessions on the social encyclicals of the popes. At one point in the discussion I maintained that Pius XI, in *Quadragesimo Anno,* upheld the right of the workers to a share in the profits. The priest who was moderating the discussion said that this was not true, while I reasserted my belief that it was. A copy of the encyclical was sent for and I read the following passage from the original Vatican translation: "By these principles of social justice one class is forbidden to exclude the other from a share in the profits." The moderator agreed I was right, and my fellow retreatants looked at me with a new respect. As a matter of fact, another passage of the same encyclical, which at the time I had not noticed, also affirmed that, "it is flagrantly unjust that either capital or labor should deny the efficacy of the other and seize all the profits." Using these texts as our justification, in 1937 we wrote into the original program of the Association of Catholic Trade Unionists the following declaration: "The worker has a right to a share in the profits after a just wage and a fair return to capital have been paid."

This shamanistic approach to encyclicals, as instruments of power (so that one's fellows look at one "with a new respect," in what Mr. Cort later calls his retreat-house "victory"), is familiar to many Catholics; but rarely has it been recorded in all its naked superstition. Nor is it surprising, any longer, that even the priest who presumed to "direct" discussion of the encyclical was unaware of the later section on profit-sharing, and willing to surrender his point at the incantation of a phrase. In case anyone thought I was exaggerating in my earlier description of what goes on in encyclical discussion groups (to two of which I have belonged), let him consider this scene, evidently recalled with pride many years later, and published for all to rejoice in.

2) After his retreat-house success, Mr. Cort's exegetical powers were relied on by the founders of the Association of Catholic Trade Unionists, who, confident that they had the voice of the Pope with them, declared that the worker has the *right* to demand a profit-sharing scheme—a point that is expressly denied by Pius XI in a part of the encyclical Mr. Cort never deals with. We shall consider that passage in its place, but here the haphazard way of founding practical political movements on papal texts deserves a word. Were a political opponent of Mr. Cort to say that Pope John XXIII favors right-to-work laws because he wrote in paragraph 18 of the original Vatican translation of *Pacem in Terris,* "Human beings have the

natural right to free initiative in the economic field, and the right to work," presumably even Mr. Cort would acquire the minimal interpretive sophistication required to point out that coincidence of phrases is not sufficient to translate a fundamental statement of human right into a practical plan for achieving or impairing that right. Mr. Cort would be perfectly justified in objecting to such simplistic use of papal texts; *Pacem in Terris* as it stands does not command men to support right-to-work laws. Yet over the last two and one-half decades no one has suggested to Mr. Cort that a coincidence of phrase far less misleading, far less justifiable from context, far more far-fetched, does not justify his assertion that *Quadragesimo Anno* as it stands *orders* men to adopt profit-sharing schemes.

3) It is true that Mr. Cort had some doubts during this period, but they arose from the appearance of a different translation, the National Catholic Welfare Conference version, which has been used in almost all subsequent English printings of the encyclical. The interesting point here is that when doubts arose it never occurred to Mr. Cort to go back beyond the "original translation" [sic] to the *original*. Because of this he is able to say, later on, that Pope Pius *could* not have written "what is produced" in the second of his chosen passages. Yet a glance at the Latin text—*quidquid effectum est*—would have settled the issue instantly. Pope Pius not only *could* but *did* write this. Furthermore, the context, clear even in the Vatican translation, is further sharpened if one turns to the document itself. The language throughout is about the mutual *product*, in the widest sense, as affecting society. The marginal summary translated in his version as "Each needs the other" is, more precisely, "Neither is able *to produce anything* without the other" (*Neutra sine altera quidquam efficere valet*). It is the mutual productivity that is not to be denied (*alterius efficacitate negata*) by the total arrogation of the product (*quidquid effectum est sibi arrogare*).

So much for the second passage, which Mr. Cort concludes *had* to have "profits" in it. What of the first? The word used there is *emolumenta*, of which "benefits" is not only the more normal and accurate translation, but which is later given a definition within

Pius' own document. When he *does* speak of modifying the wage-contract wherever sufficient advantages justify this, the word for advantages is *emolumenta,* and the range of such advantages is suggested by the Pope when he names three possibilities—that the laborers might share somehow (*aliqua ratione*) in ownership (*dominium*) or management (*curatio*) or profits (*lucra percepta*). It is manifest then, that *emolumenta* is a general term, with profit (*lucrum*) as one possible kind of advantage, but not as a synonym for it. We saw how, even in Mr. Cort's preferred translation, other phrases, about "common advantage" and "common good," indicated the meaning of "share in the profits" (or "benefits"). In the Latin this interconnection of meanings is even more manifest. We are told that *participatio emolumentorum* is the result of the *communis utilitas* served by any enterprise as part of its duty to the *commune bonum* of society.

Perhaps Mr. Cort knows no Latin. But does he know no priest, no layman who can read the very simple text of the Pope? Do the editors of his book, who let him speculate thus freely, in total isolation from the text, know no Latin, or consider that a point of translation can be settled by doing everything *but* look at the text being translated? After all, one of Mr. Cort's main points is that "inaccurate or vague translation" casts a "murky beam," that we have a "need for authoritative translations of the papal pronouncements." A prior need would seem to be that those who talk about "authoritative translations" have some rudimentary notion that *translation* is from an *original,* and that the original possesses whatever *authority* can be attributed to an accurate version.

The cast of Mr. Cort's phrases in this section helps explain what otherwise would be inexplicable carelessness on his part. You will recall that a "presumably more accurate translation" did not make Mr. Cort feel that the *original* was perhaps not dealing with profit-sharing at this point, but only that "*this translator* was apparently thinking of profits in the broad, general sense of 'fruits of production,'" with the result that "the whole question of profit-sharing *as understood by Pius XI* has become completely confused." But at this stage, of first encounter with the presumably more accurate translation, Mr. Cort had no basis for assuming that Pius XI ever had any understanding of profit-sharing, that he dealt with the matter at all in the only two texts Mr. Cort considers important. Yet this possibility is so intolerable to him that he speaks about the *mind* of Pius XI as if it *must* have busied itself with this issue, whether this was made clear to others by external pronouncement or not, so that only poor translators or other accidents can act as obstacles between *our* confusion and *his* understanding of profit-sharing. There could be no better illustration of the process I described in the last chapter—the interpretation of papal teaching in terms of one's own sense of history or of political urgencies. Mr. Cort begins from the need for profit-sharing as the one certain thing in his life, and arrives, by way of hasty snatchings from *Quadragesimo Anno*, at the papal intentions; and even when those texts begin to crumble in his hands, he is left with the original certitude about profit-sharing, and a presumed certitude about the Pope's concern. He cannot entertain the supremely insulting suspicion that the Pope did *not* favor profit-sharing. Since the Pope is infallible, he must have held to this absolutely certain doctrine. The text does not judge the times; our times, or one view of them, make their demand upon the text, and a translator who will meet Mr. Cort's standards of the authoritative must live up to that demand. The authoritative text is that which will authorize what *he wants* authorized. It is as simple as that; and this approach, which seems the only explanation of many similar claims about the Pope's mind, is given by the ingenuous Mr. Cort as his *declared* procedure.

4) But even the small degree of doubt Mr. Cort allowed himself —not about the concern Pius XI had with profit-sharing, but about the success of various translators in conveying this concern—was resolved when "the first official Vatican translation of *Mater et Magistra*" reproduced "the original Vatican translation of *Quadragesimo Anno*." *This* makes it possible to preserve the continuity of papal teaching. To our good fortune "it may now be seen in the light of *Mater et Magistra* that the *original passage* from Pius XI should be read as an encouragement of profit-sharing." Mr. Cort asserts this without ever having seen the original passage, without considering it necessary to look it up or ask a competent friend to translate. Furthermore, what translation did he expect the Vatican

to use except the *Vatican translation*? The translations put out by
the Vatican Press Office for the convenience of those who know no
Latin are not "authoritative." If they were, men would not be permitted to make *other* translations, at greater leisure and after long
study of the original. The Vatican offers a convenience to newspapers and other channels of information by giving out renditions
into the different vernaculars. This would hardly be a convenience
if the Polyglot Press were not to cite its own press releases when the
time came to issue more such releases, so that there is at least consistency within this set of translations given to the public. Does Mr.
Cort expect the Vatican to pick and choose a different translation
each time, thus giving preference to one or other of the versions
Catholic scholars are encouraged to make in the name of accuracy
and idiomatic ease? As a matter of fact, by the end of his tortuous
soritical acrobatics, Mr. Cort, with his demand for an "authoritative" translation and his complaints about the confusion that was
caused him when a different version came along—with his confidence that one Vatican rendition, quoting another, establishes the
continuity of papal thought—is really arguing that no other translations should be allowed to confuse us after the Vatican has released its newspaper version. Luckily, few scholars would agree
that the Vatican is wrong in allowing other translations to be made.
In fact, the majority of English-speaking scholars have made their
choice in favor of the very NCWC translation that Mr. Cort accuses of casting a "murky beam." And few would claim that the
Vatican's vernacular texts are models of idiomatic precision, to be
preferred, say, to Msgr. Knox's rendering of *Humani Generis* or
Father H. E. Winstone's Englishing of *Mater et Magistra*. Once
again, Mr. Cort is certain that the continuity of papal thought is
to be established by congruence with the continuity of *his* thought
on profit-sharing. By clairvoyance he has arrived at the Pope's mind,
and that is murky which does not fit his own mystic vision of the
future, in which profit-sharing has a very prominent (and perhaps
central) place.

5) Now we must leave the text of the letter for a moment, while
Mr. Cort quotes Father Masse rather than Pope Pius: here is the
entire citation as given in *The Challenge of Mater et Magistra*.

Has it [the UAW] a right to demand profit-sharing for workers? If there is a question of moral right, a right founded on the natural law, the answer is "no." Workers have a right to a just wage, which imposes a correlative duty on employers. But once employers have discharged this duty, they have no further obligation in justice to their employees. It is true that in the encyclical *Quadragesimo Anno* Pius XI mentioned several ways in which the wage contract might be liberalized, and one of them was profit-sharing. It is evident, however, that the Pope was not talking in terms of an obligation. In the present condition of human society, he wrote, "We consider it more advisable . . ." that the wage contract be modified in various ways. Employers are not morally bound to follow that advice.

To which Mr. Cort's immediate answer is: "That seems clear and positive enough. One cannot help wondering if it is as clear and positive today as it was in 1958." Then he adduces *Mater et Magistra,* quoting *Quadragesimo Anno,* to establish that, in the "continuity of papal thought," he and his fellows were perfectly justified when they made their program read in 1937, that "The worker has a *right* to share in the profits *after* a just wage. . . ." (It does not, apparently, strike him that the very concept of a *just wage* would be impossible if justice of itself demanded a system based *not* on wages but on sharing the profits.)

But the most important thing in this interchange between Mr. Cort and Father Masse is that the latter refers to, *and actually quotes,* the section of the encyclical where Pope Pius *does* consider profit-sharing (pars. 64 ff.) . Yet Mr. Cort continues the discussion as if the real basis for it were the two scraps of evidence he first fastened on and later "vindicated" from *Mater et Magistra.* That is, he not only ignores the key passage in the encyclical, but treats it as unimportant when it is quoted by the authority he adduces and reprints. Nor does he discuss, now or later (when he finally admits there was "another" mention of profit-sharing in the encyclical) , the basis of Father Masse's assertion that Pius does not present profit-sharing as *demanded* under strict moral *obligation.* He acts as if Father Masse had spun all of this out of the two passages which alone express Pius' "understanding" of the scheme, spun it as freely as Mr. Cort spins his own certitudes.

At last, then, let us turn to the place where Pius XI does raise the question of profit-sharing (or, in Mr. Cort's tardy gesture to it, the "one short observation" that was not important enough to consider while establishing Pius' understanding or the continuity of papal thought). The passage occurs at the beginning of the discussion of the just wage; I shall emphasize the terms relevant to Mr. Cort's confusion:

First of all, those who declare that a contract of hiring and being hired is *unjust* of its own nature, and hence a partnership-contract *must* take its place, are certainly *in error and gravely misrepresent* Our predecessor, whose encyclical not only accepts working for wages or salaries but deals at some length with its regulation in accordance with the rules of justice.

We consider it more *advisable,* however, *in the present condition of human society* that, *so far as is possible, the work-contract be somewhat modified* [aliquantum temperetur] by a partnership-contract, as is already being done [more properly, *is beginning* to be done, *fieri jam coepit*] in *various ways* and with no small advantage [emolumenta] to workers and owners. Workers and other employees thus become sharers in ownership *or* management *or* participate *in some fashion* [aliqua ratione] in the profits received.[47]

It will be seen from the first two paragraphs how precise Father Masse was in representing all sides of the Pope's argument at this point. (He must have been working from the Latin, since "in some degree *liberalized*" is a better translation of *aliquantum temperetur* than the phrase used in either of the major Englishings.) Furthermore, Pius' aim in making "workers and other employees" become "sharers" is not primarily economic but social, as we find when, in the next section of the encyclical, he goes beyond the recommendations of Leo XIII and presents his concept of the *ordines,* or groupings according to profession and product, meant to restore social harmony through "a graduated order" (par. 80). The evil he is trying to rectify is made clear in paragraph 78: "Following upon the overthrow and near extinction of that rich social life which was once highly developed through associations of various kinds [consociationes] there remain virtually only individuals and the State." The Pope is talking in this last place about "the reform of institutions," and his terminology makes it clear that the role he wants *consociationes* to play was in his mind when he said that

it is advisable *in the present condition of human society* that workers and other employees become in some degree "sharers" (*con-
sortes*) in the work they do—not *necessarily* in financial returns,
since one of the possibilities he suggests is a share in the cares and
plans of the management (*curatio*). At the end of the quoted passage on profit-sharing, the Pope continues with his immediate topic
—the several factors that enter into the just wage (he lists three
main ones), and then he arrives at his other principle, with which
the wage system might be "tempered"—the voluntary organizations
by profession (*ordines*), meant to restore order and harmony to an
atomized society.

Now we must deal with a very difficult question: Why, faced
with that passage, has Mr. Cort continued to wring out of his unlikely clauses "the whole question of profit-sharing as understood
by Pius XI"? Why, if he was not faced with the whole passage, but
only that segment of it he later quotes, does he accept offers to ex-
pound the papal teaching on labor? Why, if he does such things, do
presumably competent men call on him, print him, refrain from
correcting him or gently edging some of the relevant literature into
his admittedly restricted field of vision? That is, there are two
questions—How can he be so casual in his tossing of papal texts
around? and, How can he be allowed to be so casual? The question
is directed not only to him, but to his sponsors, and to his audience.

But before we face this problem there is more work to do on his
confident assumptions. His argument is not only based on a very
selective reading of the 1931 encyclical, but on the assumption that
there was no other source of light in 1958, when Father Masse
wrote; none, in fact, till *Mater et Magistra* appeared in 1961. On
these two points alone—the wrong passage in Pope Pius and the
right passage in Pope John (he *did* choose the right section of *Mater
et Magistra*, which suggests that the twenty-four years were not entirely wasted)—on these two points he strings "the continuity
of papal thought." It does not strike him as odd that a right *demanded by justice* should have been so thoroughly neglected by the
Papacy in the intervening decades. Pope Pius XII spoke many
times on the subject of the just wage, which is a contradictory concept in Mr. Cort's system, yet rarely mentioned profit-sharing—in

fact, so far as Mr. Cort gives evidence of knowing, he never spoke of it. He addressed many labor organizations at the Vatican, including the ILO; he delivered a major message to the world on the fiftieth anniversary of *Rerum Novarum*; yet this "right" of the worker is, by Mr. Cort's assumption, completely ignored.

Actually, of course, Pius delivered some famous cautions on all the aspects of labor's and management's "codetermination" of the conduct of a business. To take a very relevant text: one month before his famous address on *Rerum Novarum*, Pope Pius XII gave an address primarily concerned with *Quadragesimo Anno*.[48] Here he develops the same thoughts that first misled Mr. Cort, but anticipates misunderstanding, and answers it. First of all, he deals with the share in the common product exactly as his predecessor had— as an answer to the theory of class warfare. He says, of labor and capital:

Erroneous and baneful in its consequences is the prejudice, unfortunately too widespread, which sees in them an irreducible opposition of conflicting interests. The opposition is only apparent. There are, in the economic field, *activities and common interests* which concern both management and labor. To want to disregard this *mutual link* and to attempt to break it is the result of the whim of blind and irrational despotism. Management and labor are not irreconcilable adversaries. They are co-operators in a mutual work. They eat, as it were, at the same table since, after all is said and done, they live by the *net total profit* of the national economy. Both have their *own profit,* and in this respect their reciprocal relations by no means make one side subject to the other.

Here no room is left for the kind of ambiguity Mr. Cort imports into the parallel discussion in *Quadragesimo Anno*. In terms of that earlier document, the *emolumenta* men share are the net total profits of the national economy, which serves the common advantage (*communis utilitas*). But, like his predecessor, Pius goes on to suggest ways in which this mutual contribution of the two to social profit might be expressed:

If, therefore, the interest is mutual, why should it not be expressed in a common formula? Why should it not be right to assign the workers a fair share of responsibility in the formation and the development of the national economy?

It will be noticed that his emphasis, like that of Pius XI, is primarily on the joint *responsibility* (*dominium* or *curatio*), rather than the *lucrum*. Both men are dealing first of all with ways of increasing harmony in the social order, not with the minimal demands of a just economic return. But Pius then goes on to say that the *ordines* his predecessor hoped would secure this organic unity of society seem no longer feasible.[49] Since this plan failed, many have suggested that the *State* step in and organize society; but Pius opposes this desperate remedy as self-defeating: "To want to make of State ownership the general rule in the public organization of economies would mean subverting the right order of things." Others would like to make a share in ownership or *in profits* a matter of obligation; and to them Pius answers:

It would be *equally a mistake* to affirm that any individual enterprise is by its nature a partnership where the relations between the partners are determined by the canons of distributive justice and where all, indiscriminately—whether owners or not of the means of production—have a *right* to their share of the property, *or at least of the profits*. A conception of this kind presupposes that every enterprise, by its nature, is in the sphere of public rights; but this supposition is incorrect: whether it be constituted in the form of a trust or association of all the workers as joint owners, or whether it be the private property of an individual who stipulates a working contract with all those employed by him, *in either case, the enterprise falls within the private juridical order of economic life.* What we have said applies to the juridical character of the enterprise as such, but for its members it may also entail a complex of individual relations and mutual responsibility, which must be taken into account. *Whoever owns the means of production*—either as an individual or as an association of workers or as a trust—*must be the master of his own economic decisions,* though always within the limits of the public economic law. It follows that his profit must be greater than that of his collaborators, but at the same time, the individual material well-being of all, which constitutes the object of social economy, must still further impose on him the duty of contributing through his savings to the increase of the national capital. Nor must it be forgotten that just as it is extremely useful to a sound social economy that this increase of capital should come from the greatest possible number of sources, so is it most desirable that the workers also should contribute with the fruits of their savings to the formation of the national capital.

The Pope, then, like his predecessor, calls it mistaken to urge that profit-sharing is the *duty* of any employer. To serve the common good is his duty, as it is all men's. But this can often be done by contributing to the *national* wealth by the increase of output and of savings and of capital.[50] Even the workers must serve the common good by considering their contribution to this. The Pope urges that the mutual nature of their undertaking be expressed, if possible, by some joint formula, by some sharing of responsibility; but he expressly excludes three ways of doing this—by the *ordines* of Pope Pius XI, by state confiscation, *and by compulsory contracts of shared ownership and/or profit.*

Mr. Cort is "concerned with preserving the continuity of papal thought." Here he has two very clear texts which say that profit-sharing is not a *right to be demanded*; that those who maintain this "are *certainly* in error and *gravely* misrepresent Our predecessor"; that to separate property from *responsibility* for that property, to maintain that specific contributions to the production process cause a necessary antagonism of interests, to treat the just wage as *un*just, is to show ignorance of the very basis of Catholic teaching in this area. Yet remember that it was on the authority of words from *Quadragesimo Anno* that the Association of Catholic Trade Unionists declared "The worker has a right to share in the profits *after* a just wage and a fair return to capital have been paid."

What, then, of that original plank Mr. Cort is trying to vindicate? It is interesting to recall that students of the social order in Germany made a claim that resembled this proclamation of the American trade unionists. Despite Pius XII's words in the 1941 Allocution quoted above, the *Katholikentag* at Bochum issued a statement, in 1949, that the worker has the *right* to a share in the management of an enterprise. We have already seen that this plan is more often recommended by the Popes than a share in the profits; and to this extent, the Germans were on firmer ground than the Americans. But Pius XII returned to the subject, with even greater emphasis, in 1950. Speaking to a meeting of students of the social sciences in Rome, on June 3, 1950, he recalled Pius XI's teaching that labor and property need each other, and must recognize each other's contributions to the productive enterprise; both members of the contract enter into it equally as persons, not as mere objects to be disposed of. But Pius goes on:

There is nothing in the nature of the just relations between individuals, such as are normative for the simple wage contract, which denies this basic equality. Pius XI, our wise predecessor, made this clear in the encyclical *Quadragesimo Anno*; and therefore he denied any intrinsic necessity for adjusting the work contract to a partnership contract. We do not deny that good has been done by arrangements of this sort, variously carried out to the mutual advantage of workers and owners; but both in principle and in practice, the *right* of economic co-management that has been claimed is beyond the limits of possible endeavor. [51]

Here, then, we have an authoritative exposition of the very passage Mr. Cort has been studying in his eccentric manner, one that comes to conclusions far removed from his, and one which should have at least some weight with a man trying to establish the continuity of papal thought.

Pius XII re-emphasized his teaching in 1952. On January 31 of that year, in an Allocution, he commented on a process that was still going on eleven years later when Mr. Cort published his exegesis of *Quadragesimo Anno*:

We can no longer ignore the false interpretations which are given to the words of great wisdom of our glorious predecessor, Pius XI. The weight and importance of a social program of the Church are being given to an *obiter dictum* on the subject of eventual juridical modification in the relations of workers, as subjects of the work-contract, with the other party to the contract. [52]

In a radio message to the Austrian *Katholikentag* in that same year, he said:

The Popes who wrote social encyclicals, and We ourselves, have refused to derive from the nature of the wage-contract a right of the worker to share, either directly or indirectly, in the ownership of capital and, by way of this, to share in management. This claim must be denied, for out of it there arises an even greater problem: the right of the individual and of the family to ownership flows directly from the nature of the human person, a right that is part of his individual dignity, though it involves social obligations as well. But this right is not merely a function of society. [53]

And in the 1952 papal greeting to the Semaine Social, issued over the signature of the then Msgr. Montini, he said

In principle, therefore, a true right of co-management does not belong to the worker. [54]

6) After his arguments from the text and from authority we come (and by now we come without unbounded confidence) to Mr. Cort's argument from *logic*. The Pope *cannot* have meant, by *quidquid effectum est,* "what is produced," since that would be an *obvious* statement: "Even the most unjust employer does not 'arrogate to (himself) what is produced.' He pays some kind of wages. What he arrogates [sic] is the profits after paying wages." The logical progression is this: Minor: The sentence in its NCWC form is obvious. Conclusion: The Pope cannot have said that. Try to find any major for this except the principle that the Pope cannot say anything that is obvious in his encyclicals. It is a formula few will accept. Mr. Cort's own prose suggests that his reading runs toward pamphlets and manifestos,[55] but the papal literature is not afraid of basic truths, or even of platitudes, so long as they be sound and true and timely. And on these rather tame-sounding principles, it constructs infinitely more flexible recommendations, in the practical order, than Mr. Cort seems capable of grasping. But let us put the syllogism to the test. What cannot the Pope say? "This sacred law is violated by a wealthy class who, as it were carefree in their possessions, deem it a just state of things that they should receive *everything* and the laborer *nothing*"? But he *did* say that. In fact, these are the *very next words* after one of those passages that Mr. Cort is using to prove that the Pope could *not* say this. And when Mr. Cort uses sentence A to prove that its author *cannot* write what he *did in fact write in sentence B,* then we must put his logical dexterity on the same level as his textual and translating skills.

7) Here we reach the point where the earlier encyclical and the "continuity" strung from it to Pope John can be dismissed; on the strength of *Mater et Magistra* alone, we are told, it can be estab-

lished that the 1937 founders were right, even though they had no
proper warrant for thinking so at the time. Clairvoyance wins out
after all: what was a grave mistake and misrepresentation in 1931
and in 1941 has become, in 1961, the representation of a demand
in justice. 'Twere strange, if it were so. But is it so? "Now turn we"
(in Msgr. Knox's favorite rendering of the scriptural refrain) to
Pope John. Here is the passage Mr. Cort cites, in the translation he
cites *(which, it will be noticed, does not use the translation to
which he is so partial, but one of those confusing ones whose murky
beam obscures the key word "profits" in the citation from Pius
XI)*:

We must here call attention to the fact that in many countries today, the economic system is such that large and medium size productive enterprises achieve rapid growth precisely because they
finance replacement and plant expansion from their own revenues.
Where this is the case, *we believe* that such companies *should grant*
to workers *some share* in the enterprise, *especially* where they are
paid no more than the minimum wage.
    In this matter, the principle laid down by our predecessor of
happy memory, Pius XI, in the encyclical letter, *Quadragesmio Anno,* should be borne in mind: "It is totally false to ascribe to a single
factor of production what is in fact produced by joint activity; and
it is completely unjust for one factor to arrogate to itself *what is
produced,* ignoring what has been contributed by other factors."
    The demands of justice referred to can be met in various ways,
as experience shows. *Not to mention other ways,* it is *very desirable*
that workers *gradually* acquire *some share* in the enterprise *by such
methods as seem more appropriate.* For today, more than in the
times of our Precedessor [Pius XI], "every effort should be made
that at least in the future, only an equitable share of the fruits of
production accumulate in the hands of the wealthy, and a sufficient
and ample portion go to the workman."[56]

I repeat, this is the translation, the very words, Mr. Cort uses to
conclude that "sharing in ownership . . . is said to be demanded by
justice" (the words are Msgr. Higgins', who should know better).
Surely this is an odd way to publish an obligation binding upon
all as a basic right, especially since Pius XI and Pius XII had expressly said that the partnership contract was *not* a basic right. It is
like saying one should not commit murder, at least not after 10:00
P.M., since "experience shows" that screams disturb men's sleep

after that time. Seriously, who can derive from this passage a command of duty corresponding to that which was put in the 1937 platform by Mr. Cort's zealous friends? We are told that the owner of a business who is returning the firm's profits into rapid expansion should, especially when he is paying no more than minimum wages, "grant" (and who can grant, but one who possesses by right?) "some share in the enterprise" (*dominium* or *curatio* or *lucrum?*). When talking of the strict demands of justice the Pope does not say, for instance, "In certain circumstances, we believe an employer should grant a just wage, especially when working his employees to the maximum legal limit." The just wage is not the owner's to *grant*. It *is* the worker's. Nor does he go on to say, "Remuneration of the worker could take many forms, satisfying these demands; but not to mention others, one of the ways that would be very *desirable* is the just wage." The difference in language should be obvious to anyone, even in this translation.

But lest Mr. Cort find some more "authoritative" (i.e., congenial) translation than the one he himself uses, let us look at some of the key terms in the original. Of the three paragraphs quoted, the first gives a specific instance where an obligation *can* make itself manifest. The second paragraph gives the principle on which such obligation would be based. The third gives various ways of achieving a more desirable distribution of goods.

In the first paragraph, that in which some form of sharing is indicated as a possible obligation, the words given as "Where this is the case, we believe that such companies should grant to workers some share in the enterprise" run this way in the Latin: *Quod ubi contingat, hoc statui posse putamus, ut hac de causa societates eaedem nomen aliquod a se solvedum opificibus agnoscant. . . .* Here is a very literal translation: "Wherever this should be the case, we think it is possible for it to be demanded that such companies on these grounds allow to their workers some claim to be met by them." It will be noticed that *posse* ("we think it is *possible* for . . .") is left out of the translation Mr. Cort uses. So is *hac de causa*, "on these grounds." And what are the grounds?—that a company be achieving rapid growth by financing replacement and expansion with its revenues, and (where the prescription is most binding, *si maxime . . .*) at the same time paying minimum wages. With great care Pope John spells out the situation. He does not, for instance, say that *more than* the minimum wage *must* be given by such a successful business of the first or second class (*vel magni vel medii ordinis*). But he does say that if the company is putting off the worker's increased return from the success of the business, since all the funds are going back into production, then it should admit some claim upon itself (*nomen aliquod . . . agnoscant*) to a *future* return from these growing resources (*a se solvendum*) , a claim which is not further specified. This is the case of which it is said, with many provisos (*ubi contingat, hac de causa, si maxime . . .*), that an obligation is *possible* (*hoc statui posse putamus*). This is hardly the general command Mr. Cort makes of it. It is a model instance of the kind of demand justice makes in the economic order if there is to be a fair distribution of the goods produced for society. As such, it is easily deduced from the general principles that Pius XI promulgated *even while denying that the partnership-contract is in its nature a right of the worker.* And, lest there be any doubt of the matter, notice that Pope John *does* appeal, in his second paragraph, to Pius' general principle in this matter—that labor and capital must recognize that they need each other, and that they share in the benefits created by their co-operation.

Mr. Cort takes Pope John's citation of one of his favorite passages from *Quadragesimo Anno*, following as it does the paragraph on the "granting of some share" in an enterprise, as the final proof that the original passage *was* after all a command to adopt profit-sharing arrangements. But notice that, after citing this maxim, the Pope continues with a relative adjective referring to it, and says *"This* title of justice is not satisfied by any one arrangement (*non uno modo*) , as practical experience (*usus rerum*) teaches." In other words, the passage Mr. Cort offers as final proof that his maxim *did* enjoin one economic system is a passage that itself says just the *opposite.*

The third paragraph does not deal with the kind of obligation imposed by special circumstances, as the first had. It recommends some form of joint ownership as one among many other possible schemes (just as Pius XI had in his paragraph 65) . The passage goes: "Aside from other ways (*ceteris missis*), it is today greatly to be hoped (*hodie magnopere optadum*) that, by the means which seem suitable (*magis consentaneae*), workers should arrive by stages (*sensim*) at some part in the ownership (*in partem possessionis*) of the company for which they work." The only words that Mr. Cort is true to in that sentence are "apart from other ways." Such *cetera* are indeed *missa*. For him there is only *one* way, not presented as desirable or to be hoped for, just *imposed*. Furthermore, Mr. Cort concludes that *profit-sharing*, the original plank of his association, is now imposed, whereas the Pope has recommended some form of joint *ownership*; and in another section he expressly recommends some share in management. That is, he raises the question of *dominium* or *possessio*, of *curatio* or *partes in negotiis* (par. 91); the one thing he does *not* raise is the question of sharing the *lucra percepta* of the business. Now it is true that there may be some profit-sharing in joint ownership, but that is not what is normally considered under the various schemes of profit-sharing (such as that proposed in the 1937 program of Mr. Cort's association), since that also involves loss-sharing. It can also be urged that from the principles that lead Pope John to recommend two of the three forms of sharing Pius XI mentioned a reader can construct a sound case for the third mode too. All this is true. What is *not* true is that the Pope has now made profit-sharing the *only* just arrangement for all businesses above the "Mrs. Murphy" level. Not only does he propose alternatives, and recognize the existence of others which he does not himself propose for consideration; even when recommending a share in management, he says, of that recommendation:

It is not, of course, possible to lay down hard and fast rules regarding the manner of such participation, for this must depend upon prevailing conditions, which vary from firm to firm and are frequently subject to rapid and substantial alteration.[57]

8) And now we come to Mr. Cort's belated recognition that there was another passage in *Quadragesimo Anno* which had something to do with the problem he agonized over, fighting his way through murky beams—the problem he finally resolved in isolation from

this passage. Again, his whole treatment must be given, or I may be suspected of concocting this astonishing passage:

Other than the passage quoted above, Pius XI had only one short observation on the subject in *Quadragesimo Anno*: "In the present state of human society, however, we deem it advisable that the wage contract should, when possible, be modified somewhat by a contract of partnership, as is already being tried in various ways to the no small gain both of the wage-earners and of the employers. In this way wage-earners are made sharers in some sort in the ownership, or the management, or the profits."

And that, so help me, is all he has to say of the passage that *does* concern profit-sharing in *Quadragesimo Anno*. As a matter of fact, we saw above that this is not "only one short observation on the subject." Immediately before this sentence comes the paragraph that denies partnership contracts are demanded by justice. Mr. Cort had to edge by that paragraph with averted eyes in order to excerpt the subsequent "short observation" he admits thus late into his discussion. But even this "observation" should be enough to make his long manipulation of Pius' words manifestly irrelevant. The careful spelling out of the Pope's recommendation in paragraph 65 is a "short observation" for Mr. Cort, while the far shorter and totally misread passages given earlier are *commands*. Mr. Cort does not even offer an explanation why, if a command had been given earlier, the Pope should suddenly soften his imperative to an "observation" on what is "advisable . . . when possible . . . in the present state of human society," or why, if profit-sharing has been expressly enjoined in the two places that used the word "profits" (in one translation) , a whole *list* of things is suggested here, with profit-sharing merely *one* of the alternatives. We could not have been given a better example of what was mentioned earlier, in connection with the UN—the tendency of propagandists to avoid the passage where obligation *is* discussed, with all its refinements and complexities, and to seize on any phrase or comment that can be presented as a simple order.

And, with all his zeal, what service has Mr. Cort done for his cause? Pope John *did* recommend plans for joint ownership and management (and, one may safely extend the matter, profits) ; he kept alive a very old recommendation, one that has not dropped out of the papal literature, as Pius' syndicates and other aspects of *Quadragesimo Anno* have; he did it in an important new discussion of the worker's dignity and initiative. All of these points could have been made without the hanky-panky Mr. Cort resorts to. Yet it is so much simpler to produce a magic phrase and make a sweeping claim; and then to look around and see opposition crumble before this papal imperative. Mr. Cort does not realize that the game is self-defeating in the long run, that men who make the encyclicals sound so one-dimensional, who wield them so absolutely, who make anything they wish of their text, are undermining the respect of thoughtful men for Catholic leaders who can live with such oversimplifications. For Mr. Cort is not alone; not even in this particular appearance is he alone. He was called on to write this essay in the first place; the editors—one of them Mr. Lawler, who edits the quarterly *Continuum,* the other (Joseph N. Moody) an associate editor of the new *Catholic Encyclopedia*—accepted the travesty he submitted; he appeared in some very good company; so far as I can find, reviewers have not pointed to a single one of his distortions; he quoted men making statements quite as silly as his, men like Msgr. Higgins. I did not have to seek this sadly silly discussion out of some obscure place. It came before the public in the first and only American book on *Mater et Magistra.* Nor have I ferreted out the enormities quoted elsewhere in this book. They are the words of past or present editors of *America,* of *The Commonweal,* of *The Catholic World,* of what has at times been considered the leading diocesan paper in this country. They are the words of respected spokesmen for the National Catholic Welfare Conference, of columnists who appear throughout the Catholic press. These men apparently have no qualms about writing themselves, and quoting from others, and refraining from criticism of, the wildest assertions about what the papal literature contains.[58] They simply must not advert to what is going on, so much has it become a habit, so lacking in critical standards is this whole process.

It is time someone called these things to their attention. It is time these things stopped. The encyclicals and other formal statements of the Roman Pontiff are very carefully written. They should be carefully read and carefully quoted. They are the words of a man who wields an awesome power, and has the duty of using it with the greatest circumspection. At least equal caution should be displayed by those who appeal to this power. And those who would usurp it should be greeted, not with "looks of new respect" for such a "victory," but with the critical standards that will call discussion back to order and give it viable norms of procedure. To say this is not to treat the Pope's teaching office as trivial. It is to protect it from trivialization and worse at the hands of men who are making opportunism the sole criterion of exegesis in these matters. It was the great defender of the Pope's teaching role, the man who did so much to make the encyclical an important instrument of the modern magisterium, it was Leo XIII, who wrote:

There is no doubt that in the sphere of politics ample matter may exist for legitimate difference of opinion, and that, the single reserve being made of the rights of justice and truth, all may strive to bring into actual working the ideas believed likely to be more conducive than others to the general welfare. But to attempt to involve the Church in party strife, and seek to bring her support to bear against those who take opposite views is only worthy of partisans. Religion should, on the contrary, be accounted by every one as holy and inviolate. [59]

NOTES TO CHAPTER FIVE:
THE TERMS OF AUTHORITY

1. *America*, Nov. 4, 1961, p. 150.

2. *Quadragesimo Anno*, par. 91 (McLaughlin, p. 251).

3. *Ibid.*, par. 95 (p. 252): "We are compelled to say that to our certain knowledge there are not wanting some who fear that the State, instead of confining itself as it ought to the furnishing of necessary and adequate assistance, is substituting itself for free activity; that the new syndical and corporative order savors too much of an involved and political system of administration; and that (in spite of those more general advantages mentioned above, which are of course fully admitted) it rather serves particular political ends than leads to the reconstruction and promotion of a better social order."

4. *Mater et Magistra*, par. 67 (*The Pope Speaks* 7.4, p. 308).

5. Perhaps the most common aberration was to treat the complexification of relations as a Teilhardian "convergence," as "that socialization to which mankind seems summoned." Rev. Donald Campion, S.J., lists three such treatments in *The Challenge of Mater et Magistra*, p. 163, and Mr. J. G. Lawler refers to a fourth before adding a fifth (*ibid.*, p. 5).

6. *Mater et Magistra*, par. 156 (p. 325).

7. *Ibid.*, par. 103 (p. 314).

8. For a description of this diplomatic aspect of the Church's activity, *cf.* Robert A. Graham, S.J., *Vatican Diplomacy* (Princeton, 1959), pp. 7 ff.

9. *Canon Law* I2, Newman, 1934, p. 84.

10. Allocution, Jan. 22, 1915.

11. *Off the Record* (Sheed and Ward, 1954), p. 90.

12. *Ibid.*, p. 80.

13. This is how Paul VI, then Cardinal Montini, described the gesture Hochhuth desired in the London *Tablet* for June 29, 1963.

14. Christmas message, 1951 (Yzermans II, p. 150), emphasis added. *Cf.*, further in the same message (p. 151): "The Church cannot consent to judge according to exclusively political norms. She cannot tie the interests of religion to particular policies of a purely earthly scope. She cannot run the risk of giving any reason for doubting about her religious character."

15. *Ibid.*, p. 151: "She cannot come down from the lofty supernatural sphere where political neutrality has no meaning, in the sense in which this concept is applied to earthly powers [i.e., an official indifference]. This does not exclude, but rather increases her share in the toils and sufferings of her divided members in either camp. . . ."

16. *Cf.* Pius XII, Allocution, April 27, 1957 (Yzermans I, p. 406): "Without by any means forgetting that his goal is to contribute to his neighbor's salvation, the Christian must be ever mindful that the establishment of God's Kingdom in men's hearts and in social institutions very often requires a minimum of human development, a simple demand of reason to which a man normally assents even if he does not have the grace of faith. For this reason, the Christian will always be ready to work for the relief of every material distress and for the development of some common basis of knowledge. It is desirable, therefore, that Catholics co-operate in any undertaking which bases its activity on a theoretical and practical respect for the data of the Natural Law. . . . In any group which aspires to a humanitarian goal, they will find men of generosity and superior character, who can rise above material considerations and understand that any truly collective destiny for mankind presupposes the absolute value of the persons who compose it and the existence, outside of time, of that true society of which a world community can only be a reflection." Although the Pope is speaking, in particular, of the Catholic intellectual's participation in projects not formally Catholic, the two principles he enunciates can be taken as directive of the Church's own attitude: a) The posture of the Church as such should be one of encouragement extended toward any effort corresponding with man's nature, and so reaching toward completion of that nature in the supernatural; and b), while encouraging the natural movement, the Church should seek out and encourage the supernatural considerations that complement the humanitarian motives. This religious attitude of the Church, and religious duty of the individual, does not conflict with a *political* duty, of the *citizen*, to criticize any movement from the viewpoint of practical effectiveness and strategy. This passage from Pius XII may be said to characterize the whole reign of his successor, who developed these points at length in Part Five of *Pacem in Terris*. The passages cited in the last few notes should be considered by those who have tried to construct a deep disagreement between Pope Pius and Pope John on papal "openness" toward modern movements.

17. Pius XII, Allocution, Nov. 19, 1954 (Yzermans I, pp. 302 ff.).

18. Pius XII, Allocution, June, 1955 (Yzermans I, pp. 337 ff.).

19. Pius XII, Allocution, April 6, 1951 (Yzermans I, pp. 142 ff.).

20. *Cf.* Pope John's speech in receiving the Balzan Peace Prize, March 7, 1963.

21. Pius XII, Allocution, December 6, 1953 (Yzermans I, p. 277): "When the Church has set her signature to a Concordat, it holds for everything contained therein. However, with the mutual acknowledgement of both high contracting parties, it may not hold in the same way for everything. It may signify an express approval, but it may also mean a simple tolerance, according to those two principles which regulate the coexistence of the Church and the faithful with the civil powers and with men of another belief."

22. About the famous passage (pars. 158-9) distinguishing abstract doctrine and

concrete historical movements, Rev. John Courtney Murray, S.J., wrote (*America*, April 27, 1963): "I am not sure just what 'historical movement' the Pope chiefly had in mind. I suspect that it was Continental Socialism, whose primitive inspiration was largely atheist. Perhaps the Pope's distinction has some relevance to the whole Marxist movement, but here its application would have carefully to be made."

23. See his article "Pope John's Letter," in *America*, May 18, 1963: "*Pacem in Terris* is a religious, not a political, document . . . the Pope has decided to try to break through the rigidities and ice jams of the Cold War with a purely religious, doctrinal, non-political appeal to the rulers of the world. . . . The Pope wants to relieve tensions, break through the Iron Curtain and perhaps bring some relief to his people in the captive nations. This is no act of *Realpolitik*. It is the spontaneous gesture of a warm, priestly heart, and its motivation is totally spiritual."

24. *National Review*, May 21, 1963. Mr. Meyer calls his column "*Divini Redemptoris* to *Pacem in Terris*," a phrase obviously meant to suggest a long distance, and steep descent, from the one document to the other. A close reading of both will not support this simplification.

25. This was a point made also in *America*'s editorials for April 20, 1963 (pp. 518-9).
26. *National Review*, April 23, 1963.
27. *America*, April 27, 1963. It is interesting that respected spokesmen of the two other faiths represented in largest numbers in America came to a similar conclusion about this aspect of the encyclical. Reinhold Niebuhr wrote, in *The New Leader* for July 22, 1963, "*Pacem in Terris* has the disadvantage of proclaiming the rather easy optimism which has characterized classical liberalism, with its disregard for the power realities of the political order. . . . It disregards the power realities of the cold war." And Will Herberg wrote in *National Review* (May 7, 1963): "The vision of peace and unity possesses him; and a generous vision it is. But it is a vision of *ultimates*; it looks beyond, perhaps overlooks, the nearer world of immediates. But we, on our part, must live in both." (Mr. Herberg was subjected to a characteristically tasteless attack by the Catholic press for this last remark. The diocesan paper of Baltimore wrote, on May 3, 1963: "Herberg has taken his stand squarely, not on the issue of whether it is possible to divorce principle and practice, but on that of whether it is possible to practice principles. . . . Herberg, mighty Herberg, has struck out. Lamely he concludes . . ." —and Herberg's sentence, quoted above, is given). The pleas of these theologians for realism should not mislead us on the significance of the encyclical. The Pope *did* prescind somewhat from the particulars of world politics. But he did not relax any of the norms by which realistic policy must be guided. It is certainly not possible to infer from the text that papal teaching endorses any current regime based on Communist atheism. It was at the very time when Red Chinese refugees were streaming into Hong Kong, when there were daily skirmishes and murders along the Berlin Wall, as men tried to escape the confines of East Germany, that Pope John issued these words of *Pacem*: "Every human being has the right to freedom of movement and of residence within the confines of his own country; and, when there are just reasons for it, the right to emigrate to other countries and take up residence there (par. 25) . . . The sentiment of universal fatherhood which the Lord has placed in Our heart makes Us feel profound sadness in considering the phenomenon of political refugees: a phenomenon which has assumed large proportions and which always hides numberless and acute sufferings. Such expatriations show that there are some political regimes which do not guarantee for individual citizens a sufficient sphere of freedom within which they can lead a life worthy of man" (pars. 103-4). And it was to a world, one of whose current fixtures is the satellite system behind the Iron Curtain, that Pope John said "Relations between States should be based on freedom, that is to say, that no country may unjustly oppress others or unduly meddle in their affairs" (par. 120). He struck even deeper at this system in the paragraphs that assert that a police state ("where authority uses as its only or its chief means either threats and fear of punishment or promises of rewards") lacks juridical force (pars. 48-9, 61). These observations can be compared to the general admonitions and laments that Pius XII issued during the persecution of the Jews, admonitions on human rights which, though not expressly

applied to the Nazi terrorists by name, lest these criminals be prodded into even more hideous crimes, obviously had a direct application to their crimes, for anyone willing to listen. It should also be remembered that *Pacem in Terris* insisted on the rights of free speech, on the freedom of the press, and on free access to information; and that the very Communist papers which cynically praised the Pope's letter printed it only in partial and distorted forms!

28. *Pacem in Terris,* par. 160, especially the words "this decision rests primarily with those who live and work in the specific sectors of human society in which those problems arise."

29. Pius XII, Allocution, November 19, 1954 (Yzermans I, p. 301).

30. Mr. William Clancy, transcript of May 25, 1960, debate, *Public Forum,* p. 18, emphasis added.

31. The same standards are implicit in Msgr. Higgins' assertion that praise of the FAO and ILO in *Mater et Magistra* was *"extraordinarily significant in view of the fact that so many Americans, Catholics included, have been sniping at the United Nations and all its agencies lo these many years"* (*Ave Maria,* Aug. 26, 1961, p. 7, emphasis added).

32. Editor's answer to a correspondent in *The Catholic World,* May, 1961, p. 68.

33. Erik Kuehnelt-Liddihn, in *National Review,* April 23, 1963.

34. Pius XI, *Quadragesimo Anno,* par. 96 (and see his letter to Msgr. Perdoma, Feb. 14, 1934, and Apostolic Letter, *Con Singular,* Jan. 18, 1939).

35. Yzermans I, p. 143. This passage has been worked very hard by men who want to extract a simple command from Pius' praise of various groups. For a typically hazy use of the text, see Mr. William Clancy, *Public Forum* transcript, May 25, 1960, p. 20. Mr. McDonald's use of it is in *The Commonweal,* March 16, 1956, p. 619.

36. See his statement to this effect in *The Commonweal,* Feb. 10, 1956, pp. 480-2.

37. Leo XIII, *Rerum Novarum,* par. 15 (Gilson, p. 215), emphasis added. There is no mention of this "first and most fundamental principle" in the UN's Covenant on Economic, Social and Cultural Rights.

38. Par. 108, *The Pope Speaks* 7.4, p. 315, emphasis added.

39. *The Commonweal,* Feb. 10, 1956.

40. Congar, *Laity, Church and World,* p. 26. Mr. Buckley tried to make a similar point in his debate with Mr. Clancy (May 25, 1960): "I myself do not intend to live out my life as an exegete of every editorial that appears in *Osservatore Romano.* I do not believe that Catholic arguments, that arguments between decent and self-respecting Catholics, are settled on the basis of an internecine saturation with Catholic papal encyclicals" (p. 8). Mr. Clancy chose to interpret this remark as an attack on the encyclicals themselves (much as *America* was to interpret the *"Mater sí"* remark) when he referred to "Mr. Buckley's sallies against *L'Osservatore Romano* and papal encyclicals" (*ibid.,* p. 15), and said "It is very nice to make fun as you did before of papal encyclicals, of the [sic] *L'Osservatore Romano:* but is there any discernible papal teaching. . . ."

41. *The Challenge of Mater et Magistra* (Herder and Herder, 1963), pp. 8-9.

42. *Ibid.,* pp. 10-11.

43. Although Mr. Lawler finds, on page 10, that freedom has been swallowed up in slavery throughout the free world, he was just as certain, on page 5, that the world is undergoing "what Teilhard called 'the divinization of human action.'" And in this optimistic vein he remarks that *"Mater et Magistra* echoes in its central themes the voice of Teilhard."

44. Since our freedom is so vestigial for Mr. Lawler, at least in one of his moods, his sense of urgency is easily triggered. He finds it necessary, even in a brief essay on the Pope's message, to attack "campaigns for Sunday closing laws, for the introduction of Christian symbols *qua* Christian symbols in public buildings, and for the censorship of the public arts on exclusively confessional grounds." An example of his style: "Because the Church is the best temporal expression of the spirit-matter construct, more nearly perfect even than the sacrament—which is defined as the inward spiritual grace and the outward material reality—this supremely oxymoronic nature must itself

be expressed by a chiasmic redoubling if it is to be grasped in all its richness. . . . Matter only becomes *mater* when it is informed, so that motherhood is itself a state of the merging of polarities." What is "the sacrament" he refers to, than which the Church is a greater example of the union of matter and spirit (which is what he *must* be driving at in his word "construct," which nonetheless implies that there *is* no union)? In the general sense he gives of "sacrament," the Church is a *magnum sacramentum*, as many Christian writers have taught us; and how can the Church be greater than herself? There is hardly a paragraph in his ten pages without similar contradictions. Consider, for instance, the sentence "As *mater* she is committed to matter, as *magistra* she is committed to spirit," a sentence that has no meaning and seems to have only one purpose—the linking of matter and *mater* so as to set up the later pun on these words. I quote these excerpts, from many others, to show what can be perpetrated in scholarly books on the encyclicals.

45. *Ibid.,* p. 9. It is not surprising, after this passage, to find that the paragraph attacking those who treat the encyclical as trivial goes on to find this attitude not only in "Catholic groups" but coming "from some Catholic prelates in this country. One can only hope that the voice of the supreme pontiff will help them bridge the gap between their 'spiritual' ideals and their practical conduct." That is, Mr. Lawler not only takes over the episcopal function of local explicator of the Church's teaching, he exercises it against the bishops themselves. And it is a little unfair to say their practical conduct is inconsistent with their spiritual ideals when he has earlier said that they are to be concerned *only* with those ideals, and *not* with their application.

46. The citations could, of course, be indefinitely extended without leading to any useful conclusions on the specific legislation called "right-to-work." (See, for instance, Yzermans I, p. 33, asserting that the "right to work is imposed on and conceded to the individual in the first instance by nature, and not by society.") For texts that *might* have a bearing on intelligent discussion of that legislation, see the next chapter.

47. *Quadragesimo Anno,* pars. 64-5 (McLaughlin, p. 242).

48. Allocution, April 27, 1941 (Chinigo, pp. 307-9).

49. See note 17 to the next chapter.

50. This teaching is in accord with *Quadragesimo Anno,* par. 51 of which reads: "Expending large incomes so that opportunity for gainful work may be abundant, provided, however, that this work is applied to producing really useful goods, ought to be considered, as we deduce from the principles of the Angelic Doctor, an outstanding exemplification of the virtue of munificence, and one particularly suited to the needs of the times" (*cf. S.T.* II-II, q. 134, a. 3, ad 3).

51. AAS 42, p. 487. Just above this passage, on the same page, the Pope said with equal clarity, "But neither the nature of the work-contract, nor that of the productive enterprise, necessarily entails a right of this sort."

52. DC 1952, 200. The Pope is referring, here, to misinterpretations of par. 64, the place where Pius XI did discuss profit-sharing, a passage Pius XII calls an *obiter dictum*. Mr. Cort, with his two sentences from the encyclical, is not even able to find the right passage to misinterpret. He has not the talent to make *quite* the mistake that Pius criticized.

53. AAS 44, p. 792.

54. DC 1952, 1359.

55. See, for instance, p. 261: "It is obvious that if we are going to wait until either the law of supply and demand, or the National Association of Manufacturers, or the United States government, or the United Nations, enforce some kind of ideal arrangement whereby the economic worth of an individual's contribution equals a living wage, then we are going to wait a long, long time. Fortunately, the AFL-CIO is not yet persuaded that a reliance on abstract theories, or management's generosity, or on legislation, is the only instrument for achieving economic justice." But if theory, charity, and law cannot achieve a just order, what is left? Brute violence? Mr. Cort treats profit-sharing as the means of acquiring a minimal just wage (which he implies is not given in America, even to Detroit's auto workers, see p. 254), while the Popes treat the various partnership contracts as ways of expressing a higher degree of amity

and social harmony after the minimal requirements of justice are satisfied through their proper instrument (the just wage).

56. *Mater et Magistra,* pars. 75-7.

57. *Ibid.,* par. 91.

58. Only one example comes to mind of the public refusal to let political sympathies or opportunism obscure the dangers and injustice that can result from the misuse of papal texts. This occurred in the August 28, 1962 issue of *National Review*:

> A Mr. Gordon Fitzgerald has published a little book called *A Catholic Rebels.* This is a right-wing version of the conventional left-wing ploy—page after page of excerpts from the Popes' encyclical letters marshaled to "prove" that one's political opponents are living in a state of criminal defiance of their own faith. The victim of the procedure is, in this instance, John F. Kennedy. Catholic Conservatives will be tempted to take secret satisfaction on seeing the Liberals' own weapon turned against them. Mr. Fitzgerald's performance, after all, is at least as skillful and well-documented as the standard Liberal pronouncement *ex cathedra sinistra.* But Catholics of all political positions, it would seem, must resolutely deny themselves this particular kind of satisfaction. The rummaging of the papal documents—or, for that matter, Bible-picking—for partisan tags is undignified, divisive, and unjust, whether engaged in by the left or the right. The encyclical literature establishes a meaningful context for political discussion, but not if parts of that literature are torn from the whole and used talismanically to hex one's foes. Mr. Fitzgerald thinks that the papal teaching makes it a Catholic's clear duty to oppose Mr. Kennedy—just as Liberals were saying, not so long ago, that the Pope had anticipated the Senate in censuring Senator McCarthy. Although practical political positions cannot, and should not, be wholly divorced from theological social doctrine, Catholics can oppose the New Frontier without constructing a Vatican imperative for this. It is as insulting to Catholics of all parties to say the Vatican has "purged" the present Administration, as it is to claim that the New Frontier is the rim of the Roman Empire.

59. Leo XIII, *Sapientiae Christianae,* par. 29 (Gilson, pp. 262-3).

CHAPTER SIX

CONTINGENCY

In the chapter on historical judgments it was argued that the Pope can err on matters of fact *propter falsos testes,* and that his broad historical generalizations are characterized, by the very terms in which they are advanced, as hypothetical rather than definitive. To the extent that available testimony is imperfect, in itself and because of man's fallen intellect, nothing even remotely resembling the doctrinal certitude of revealed truth can be derived from this kind of knowledge, however useful, even necessary, it is as part of the teaching Church's general repertory.

The practical effects of this argument are extensive. If the Pope is not guaranteed against error in the description of past events, he can scarcely be granted unfailing insight into the men, institutions, and movements of his own time. The lapse of time allows men to organize and assess evidence in a perspective denied the actual participants in events. To be immersed in an historical moment is to see actions without knowing their outcome, to make decisions under the press of immediate necessity; to go, steering one's way by prudence, into the future, not to judge the sifted records of history.

Can we say that the Pope is spared the trial of this partial vision and difficult steerage? Can he, like Macbeth's tormentors, "look into the seeds of time/And say which grain will grow, and which will not"? Were one to claim this, he would reduce the papal prerogatives to the level of astrology. Revelation does not satisfy any of those itches which turn to magic for their easing, which bargain for knowledge of the future. God reveals himself in a providential order that demands faith and hope, where Christians know not the day or the hour, but, as Chesterton put it in his ballad, "go gaily in the dark."

There is, then, no difficulty posed to the Catholic's faith by the fact that papal teaching fluctuates on points of particular fact, that decisions concerning these particulars are reversed or discredited, without unseating the firm, defined doctrines that may have entered into any decision. Refined testimony on medical affairs brought about, for instance, a change in the Church's teaching on ectopic pregnancy. The principles of the sacredness of human life were not revoked, but the medical estimate of the mode of preserving human life changed. The Church must use all of this testimony, apply relevant principles of morality to the data supplied, and, when added facts or an altered estimate of fact call for it, make new applications, correcting or even canceling the old ones. For a Catholic to make these observations does not constitute a denial of his Church's right to judge the moral implications of human action and knowledge; they merely describe the way it *exercises* that right.

What is true of medicine is true of economics. Pope and Council have infallibly condemned usury, the use of *money* as a weapon against *men*.[1] But new knowledge of new conditions—a grasp of the structure of productive trade—has led to a reassessment of the moral effect of certain devices. Throughout mediaeval times, and as recently as 1745 (in Benedict XIV's encyclical *Vix Pervenit*), the taking of any interest was condemned under the ban on usury. Leo XIII made an obscure reference to *modern* forms of usury in *Rerum Novarum,* a reference never expanded or explained by the Pope.[2] But it is clear that extortion of *disproportionate* interest is the kind of usury now envisaged by the doctrinal condemnation. This is the teaching of Canon 1543 of Canon Law, and Pius XII explicitly taught that taking interest is not sinful in itself, but conducive to productive service of the common good.[3] In these new conditions, he has even *urged* men to use modern devices (such as interest on savings) for mobilizing capital, so that better economic conditions may be established for the poor.[4]

If testimony on medical and economic fact can be obscure or misleading, then surely matters of political fact can be imperfectly discerned, in themselves and in their formulation by observers. These are matters of great complexity in themselves, influenced by sudden developments, reported through the mists of principled zeal, political rhetoric, unconscious bias, or sheer cupidity. The Roman Pontiff has, it is true, a uniquely serene position from which to observe this clouded scene, and a body of normative doctrines divinely guaranteed and carefully formulated over the centuries. But during much of her history, the Church was herself a temporal power, at the center of conflict and confusion; and, though the divine assistance never failed her, the marks of a turbulent history are printed on her. Even in more recent times, during which the Vatican has enjoyed a comparatively lofty vantage point above purely national strife, Pope Leo XIII entertained fears concerning neutral labor unions (i.e., those not formally Catholic) which time assuaged, and Pope Pius XI could muster some hope of good from a system (the "corporatist state") that has had a poor history. The Pope is not blessed with an infallible *political* judgment.

The effect of variable constituents in a papal teaching can be illustrated by a famous pronouncement, Boniface VIII's Bull *Unam Sanctam*, which contained an *ex cathedra* definition of the Pope's ruling prerogative. This definition was imbedded in a document severely conditioned by its historical context. The Bull solemnly affirms Peter's position as a universal ruler; but the practical effect of his rule on other ruling powers is formulated in terms of one era, of mediaeval Christendom. Nor is this surprising; it would have been truly surprising if anything else had occurred. After all, the scriptural authors were not freed from prevailing opinion concerning the structure of politics, or even of the universe. Pope Boniface could teach with a practical assumption that all politics would be formally Christian, much as the Bible could describe the universe on an assumption that the sun circles the earth. Man's conception of the historical role of the Church

is often influenced, even as regards its essentials, by the kind of ideal society which is predominant in any given historical context and then spreads, by a sort of unconscious osmosis, if we may be allowed the expression, to the life of the Church. It is in such a context that different temperaments, social phenomena, political ideas, vocational activities (with their professional bias), fear and recklessness, play their part.[5]

The application of these principles to the Bull *Unam Sanctam* has long been accepted by theologians:

A careful distinction is to be made between the fundamental principles concerning the Roman primacy and the declaration as to the application of these to the secular power and its representatives. . . . The statements concerning the relation between the spiritual and the secular power are of a purely historical character, so far as they do not refer to the nature of the spiritual power, and are based on the actual conditions of a mediaeval Western Europe.[6]

Father Murray says that "the doctrinal tendency of the *Unam Sanctam*, just so far as it reflects this transitional concept, is not moving in the main stream of Catholic tradition. This is not to diminish the truth but to define it."[7]

Not only was Boniface's political application of doctrine hemmed in by historical limitations; even in this context, Catholic scholars have considered his act imprudent in terms of the best analysis of the period itself. Infallibility does not make Popes unfailingly prudent. The eminent political philosopher Heinrich Rommen wrote that the mediaeval powers of the Papacy found "last and proudest expression in Boniface VIII's bull *Unam Sanctam at a time when the realization of this claim was already an impossibility.*"[8]

Here, then, we have *a doctrinal pronouncement of the extraordinary magisterium motivated by, imbedded in, and meant to be useful for, a misconception of the relation of that doctrine to the political order.* There could be no more striking example of the Pope's ability to misunderstand the drift of events in his own time, *even when exercising his infallible power.*

Almost any papal teaching based on an estimate of contingent events must undergo change at certain intervals if it is to stay relevant. And, since each adjustment will depend on testimony of varying clarity and judgments of varying prudence, principle will be oriented toward practice with more or less success from moment to moment.

A good example of this is the ever-changing yet continuous teaching on modern labor unions. The principle here is the right of men to organize freely for their own good and that of the community, without interference from other groups or individuals. Not only may the state not prevent these organizations from their effort at self-improvement, but, so far as these groups contribute to the good order for which the state is responsible, the state should encourage them. That is the principle from which all Popes have proceeded in their discussion of labor organizations. But the application of principle has depended on the assessment of real needs and of the means at hand for satisfying them.

Leo XIII first treated the labor organizations at length in *Rerum Novarum*. Taking the mediaeval guilds as his models, he proposed that Catholics should form organizations formally religious, with joint worship and education as part of their regime. Catholics were expressly warned against joining the organizations already in existence:

Associations of every kind, and especially those of working men, are now far more common than heretofore. As regards many of these there is no need at present to inquire whence they spring, what are their objects, or what the means they employ. Now, there is a good deal of evidence in favor of the opinion that many of these societies are in the hands of secret leaders, and are managed on principles ill-according with Christianity and the public well-being; and that they do their utmost to get within their grasp the whole field of labor, and force working men either to join them or starve. Under these circumstances Christian working men must do one of two things: either join associations in which their religion will be exposed to peril, or form associations among themselves and unite their forces so as to shake off courageously the yoke of so unrighteous and untolerable an oppression. No one who does not wish to expose man's chief good to extreme risk will for a moment hesitate to say that the second alternative should by all means be adopted.[9]

In terms of our analysis of papal injunctive formulae, the last sentence is a strong recommendation. But, as we shall see, it is an exhortation tempered by the historical analysis and the institutional realities to which Catholic attention is called. The Pope obviously had in mind the Masonic lodges in the paragraph just quoted; and Father Murray has demonstrated, by an analysis of the entire Leonine *corpus*, that Freemasonry held the central place in Leo's picture of the social evils of his time.[10] Once this is understood, the Catholic organizations recommended by Leo are seen in their true light. They are not only inspired by the mediaeval guilds —(as secular forms of the Catholic "orders," resembling the military orders in their devotion to a temporal task)[11]—but they are antitypes of the Masonic lodges, counter-lodges. Pope Leo's references to the guilds' mediaeval heraldry, communal worship, welfare and educational provisions, are aimed at the paraphernalia of the lodge. We must at least advert to Leo's historical analysis if we are to understand the conclusion from that analysis, the famous conclusion that "the most important of all [organizations promoting social justice] are workingmen's unions, for these virtually include all the rest."[12] His ideal organizations "include the rest" by being *guilds*—religious, educational, social units of the broadest scope.

Whatever judgment historians may make of Pope Leo's attitude toward the Masonic threat, Father Murray is obviously on safe ground in asserting "No such diagram would correspond to the realities of the new phase of the perennial struggle between the Church and the world through which we are now living."[13] As a matter of fact, Pope Leo's analysis, based as it was on the European experience, did not hinder Catholics, with the open or implied permission of the hierarchy, from joining *American* unions of the "neutral" sort, a development which occasioned these words of St. Pius X:

The Bishops, therefore, should consider it their sacred duty to observe carefully the conduct of all these associations and to watch diligently that the Catholic members do not suffer any harm as a result of their participation. The Catholic members themselves, however, should never permit the unions, whether for the sake of material interests of their members of the union or for the union cause as such, to proclaim or support teachings or to engage in activities which would conflict in any way with the directives proclaimed by the supreme teaching authority of the Church, especially those mentioned above. Therefore, as often as problems arise concerning matters of justice or charity, the Bishops should take the greatest care to see that the faithful do not overlook Catholic moral teaching and do not depart from it even a finger's breadth.[14]

Pius XI went further, and counseled that:

It is clearly the office of bishops, when they know that these [neutral labor] organizations are on account of circumstances necessary and are not dangerous to religion, to approve of Catholic workers joining them, keeping before their eyes however the principles and precautions laid down by Our predecessor Pius X of holy memory. Among these precautions the first and chief is this: Side by side with these unions there should always be associations zealously engaged in imbuing and forming their members in the teaching of religion and morality so that they in turn may be able to permeate the unions with that good spirit which should direct them in all their activity.[15]

Pius XI gave the discussion of unions a new context, with reference to certain organic theories of society (especially Heinrich Pesch's "solidarism") espoused in Catholic circles (e.g., the study group at Königswinter) . Pius recommended that employers' organizations be formed to balance the workers' organizations, or, better yet, that organizations, formed by trade or profession, include both employers and employees.[16]

This "solidarist" ideal, and the restriction against membership in unions not formally Catholic, both disappeared from Catholic teaching during Pius XII's reign.[17] He recognized a new danger. The *right* to organize was no longer disputed; rather, the extent and intensity of organization had become a matter demanding close moral scrutiny. In his famous address on "the demon of organization," he wrote:

How, therefore, can it be considered normal that the protection of the personal rights of the worker be placed more and more in the hands of an anonymous group, working through an agency of immense organizations which are of their very nature monopolies? The worker, thus wronged in the exercise of his personal rights, will surely find especially painful the oppression of his liberty and of his conscience, caught as he is in the wheels of a gigantic social machine.[18]

More and more, toward the end of his life, Pope Pius saw how freedom of association might be restricted by the very extent and rigidity of the modern organizations that had developed. Working men's organizations were supposed to encourage direct relations with employers; yet modern unions, organized on a national or international scale, could draw workers farther than ever away from their immediate employers. The Pope reminded representatives of the ILO that good relations between employers and employees should be personal relations.[19] Increasingly he feared the impersonality and anonymity of large-scale organizations:

In democratic systems one can fall easily into such an error, when individual interest is placed under the protection of these collective organizations, or of a party, where one seeks protection for the sum total of individual interests, rather than the promotion of the good of all; under such a guise the economy becomes easily subject to the power of anonymous forces which dominate it politically.[20]

May it please God that the day be not far off when those organizations of self-defence which the defects of the economic system, and especially the lack of Christian outlook, have made necessary may cease to function. [21]

His concern shows itself in many warnings. In 1945 he said:

If, as a result of political and economic betterment, the trade union comes one day to assume a patron's role, or the right to dispose of the worker at will, of his strength or his possessions, as has happened in some places, the very concept of a trade union as an association for self-help and self-defence will be altered and destroyed.[22]

And in a 1948 allocution to the Christian workers of Italy, he said:

If the unions seek after exclusive domination in the state and in society, if they want to exercise absolute power over the worker, if they spurn a strict sense of justice and lack a sincere readiness to cooperate with other social classes, they will disappoint the expectations and the hope which every honest and conscientious worker puts in them. What must be thought when a worker is denied the opportunity of working because he is not in the union's good graces, when a stoppage of work is enforced for political ends, when unions take not a few false turnings, which lead them far from the real good and unity which is asked of the working class?[23]

At this stage, then, a new emphasis was put on a continuing aspect of the encyclicals' teaching—on the principle that membership in the unions should be a matter of free choice. Pope Leo's basic argument for such organizations had been based on the *right of free association*. He was presumably criticizing more than the irreligious bent of those organizations that

do their utmost to get within their grasp the whole field of labor, and force working men either to join them or starve.[24]

And when he called for counter-societies of Catholic workers, he based this call to unionism on a freedom *not* to join the existing groups.

Pius XI described in *Quadragesimo Anno* the professional organizations he wanted to flourish:

Just as inhabitants of a town are wont to found associations with the widest diversity of purposes, *which each is quite free to join or not,* so those engaged in the same industry or profession will combine with one another into associations *equally free* for purposes connected in some manner with the purposes of the calling itself. Since these associations are clearly and lucidly explained by Our predecessor of illustrious memory, We consider it enough to emphasize this one point: People are *quite free* not only to found such associations *which are a matter of private order and private right,* but also in respect to them *"freely* to adopt the organization and the rules which they judge most appropriate to achieve their purpose."[25]

Those final words are quoted from Leo XIII's description of working men's organizations. And in the section of Pius' encyclical devoted exclusively to the governmental supervision of trades and professions in the corporatist state, it is said that men must be free to join or not to join the syndicates (membership in which is the channel of parliamentary representation) ; in fact, only this right makes it possible to call the system free, even though membership dues are exacted of *everyone* within a certain profession. Furthermore, the right not to join can be protected by organizations *other than* the politically recognized ones. The Pope was laying down, in this paragraph, the specific form of syndicalist *state* to which he gave a minimal, conditioned approval, so his terms are carefully chosen; and it will be seen how great an emphasis is placed on the right to join or not to join:

Anyone is free to join a syndicate *or not,* and *only within these limits* can this kind of syndicate be called free; for syndical dues and special assessments are exacted of absolutely all members of every specified calling or profession, whether they are workers or employers; likewise all are bound by the labor agreements made by the officially recognized syndicate. Nevertheless, it has been officially stated that this legally recognized syndicate does not prevent the existence, without legal status however [i.e., the right to direct participation in government], of other associations made up of persons following the same calling.[26]

Emphasis on the freedom-to-join principle, even within the confines of a system where unions have been replaced by syndicates, indicates that the principle is relevant in many contexts, even unlikely ones. And emphasis on this principle has become sharper in more recent times. Pius XII wrote,

Again, access to employment or places of labor is made to depend on registration in certain parties, or in organizations which deal with the distribution of employment. Such discrimination is indicative of an inexact concept of the proper function of labor unions and their proper purpose, which is the protection of the interests of the salaried worker within modern society, which is becoming more and more anonymous and collectivist.[27]

Pope John XXIII, in his 1959 Christmas message, repeated Pius XIII's fear that men were becoming cogs in the great social machinery[28]—a warning that was repeated in the letter issued by Pope John's first secretary of state to the Semaine Sociale July 12, 1960. This famous letter was devoted to the subject "Socialization and the Human Person," and it presents the thoughts repeated in *Mater et Magistra,* expressly connecting this problem with the term Pius XII used so often—the "dehumanization" of modern man. Cardinal Tardini's letter refers to the dangers outlined in the subsequent encyclical, and takes the same attitude toward the possibility of circumventing these dangers. One passage has to do with the "right-to-work" principle:

One sees the role that can be played in this perspective, for the purpose of safeguarding the rightful autonomy of the person and the family, by the "intermediate bodies," as they are often called, that is, those forms of free and voluntary associations, well ordered and well oriented, so often advised by the sovereign pontiffs and so constantly invoked by the Social Weeks. By taking charge of tasks too weighty or too complex for the individual and the family to handle alone, these groups liberate new individual or collective capabilities. But this is to be done on the condition that each of these institutions remains within its own sphere of competence, *that it be offered to, not imposed upon, the free choice* of mankind. They must under no circumstances look upon themselves as an end and make their members an instrument of their activity.[29]

In the encyclical itself, Pope John made another pointed reference to freedom of association as the law of these organizing efforts:

Pope Leo XIII also defended the worker's natural right to enter into association with his fellows. Such associations may consist either of workers alone or of workers and employers, and should be structured in a way best calculated to safeguard the workers' legitimate professional interests. And it is the *natural right* of the workers to work without hindrance, *freely, and on their own initiative* within these associations for the achievement of these ends.[30]

In the treatment of labor organizations, then, we have a clear instance of moral teaching variously applied to historical circumstance, which is never frozen. Papal teaching in this area, though it has worked from the same fundamental principle, and maintained a continuity of reference, has undergone frequent changes, based on successive Popes' estimates of the situation they confronted. Much of the teaching has been cumulative, forming a core of permanent principle. Pope Leo emphasized the right to form organizations, Popes Pius X and Pius XI stressed the adaptability in organization allowed to Catholics, Pius XII warned against the loss of a human perspective when organization reaches a complex stage, and Pope John XXIII laid particular emphasis on the benefits to be derived, in an era of "socialization," from multiple and flexible "intermediate organizations" (intermediate, that is, between the lone individual's or family's efforts, and the universal action of the state).[31] At a level of more particular observation, less permanent elements have also appeared in this teaching; and, in time, disappeared. Pope Leo, for instance, basing his judgment on an estimate of the Masonic lodges' force, insisted that unions be guild-like in their religious organization. Pius X spoke within this context, though allowing Bishops to dispense Catholics from the effort to form their own guilds. Pius XI spoke in a context tempered by "organistic" theory, and recommended that unions play a role in the general grouping of society by the professions. Pius XII and John XXIII also made particular recommendations whose practical consequences have still to be tested. Pius XII especially recommended decentralizing the larger organizations, and Pope John put new emphasis on the desirability of profit-sharing, as we saw in the last chapter. It is too early to see whether these specific suggestions will prove fruitful, like the extension of Catholic membership to non-Catholic unions, or prove ineffectual against the practical difficulties, like Pius XI's ideal of social organization by the professions.

Clearly there are elements of more and of less adequate historical judgment at work in the shifting course of this moral instruction. These cause problems even at the general level, and the problems multiply as we consider particular situations in terms of this general yet contingent teaching. For instance, important as the papal teaching has been as a model for the proper application of principle, the applications made by the Popes have been unrelated to the realities faced in some dioceses. A clear indication of this is the American experience of "neutral" unions. Leo XIII's warning against them was obviously more applicable to the European situation, where specifically Catholic national traditions were under attack by specifically anticlerical societies, than to the United States. Americans therefore belonged to neutral unions long before *Quadragesimo Anno* incorporated this principle into the encyclical literature.

Other accommodations to reality were necessary too. The Popes have consistently opposed use of the concept of "class struggle" as a moral basis for social reform; yet, with varying degrees of seriousness, American and other unions have used this rhetoric of antipathy to gain their goals. Because of fluctuations in particular circumstance, Bishops have been able to assess the real force of this rhetoric in each case, and allow Catholics to work with some movements whose stated principles were in opposition to the Popes' teaching. The prudential decision to be made was indicated by Archbishop Alter of Cincinnati, who said in 1952:

Doubt and confusion arise concerning the nature and purpose of labor unions as they now exist. Can they be classified as functional and vocational groups, as conceived in the mind of the Popes; or are they primarily class conflict and class interest groups?[32]

Another problem was caused by the Popes' decision that Catholics are not to co-operate in Communist-dominated organizations, even when these work for immediate goals that are good, since such efforts are placed at the disposal of the Communist cause. It had to be decided, in certain instances, when union leadership had become effectively Communist. Thus some European Bishops forbade Catholics to belong to unions taken over by Communist organizers (an exercise of the Church's freedom that would be made impossible if compulsory unionism were enacted everywhere).

This brings us to another accommodation made by Catholics in their treatment of the encyclicals. It is argued that special circumstances in America make it necessary to by-pass the papal admonition that workers should be free to join, or not to join, unions. Considering the other adjustments made to specific reality, there is no reason why this adjustment might not be made in certain circumstances. But there should be a clear identification of the circumstances' force, which involves a clear understanding of the rule against which exceptions are being made. For the principle of free membership is not as fluctuating as other aspects of papal thought on these matters. Every Pope who has treated this subject has upheld this principle, since it is a part of that right—free association to promote legitimate interests—on which the very existence of the unions is based. And the papal assertion of this rule has undergone an intensification in recent years.

The arguments used for compulsory unionism are often not conclusive. It is said, for instance, that a man may have a *duty* to join a union because in this way he can contribute to social justice and the betterment of his fellows. But even if this argument is factually established in the particular case, the individual's duty to contribute to just social activity is not necessarily an assertion that the law must *compel* him to fulfill this duty. To take an instance Pius XII treated, voters sometimes have a duty to contribute to just government by going to the polls. This is the contribution, small but important, of the socially responsible citizen. But this argument would not normally be a sufficient warrant for laws *compelling* men to vote. There are several kinds of obligation intermixed, here, which must be sifted and dealt with separately. First, a man might be able to contribute to the social good in some way without being *obliged* to do so. Second, even if he were morally obliged, this would not necessarily mean that legislation should enforce the obligation. Third, even if he were obliged, and some legislation were called for, it would be difficult to formulate the legislation in a way that would correspond to the moral imperative (e.g., abstention from voting can sometimes be the most effective *use* of one's vote).

Another argument sometimes used is that the closed shop is "equitable on the grounds that workers who receive the benefits of union protection should pay for its costs."[33] This argument, too, is not sufficient in itself to cause the suspension of an important principle. Every social aim legitimately undertaken should, by helping some, promote the general good. An attempt to restrict the social good effects to those who hold membership in one organization is expressly warned against by Pius XII when he criticizes those organizations "where one seeks protection for the sum total of individual interests, rather than the promotion of the good of all."[34] It is easy to see the inadequacy of the argument if we transpose it: suppose that a refrigerator factory were built in an area whose economy is languishing, and that this caused a general upsurge of employment, services, peripheral benefits. The manufacturer could not impose a legal obligation that all local residents buy *his* brand of refrigerator, on the grounds that the area benefits by his business, and so should help pay for it.

The arguments so far considered fail of conclusiveness because they point out *advantages* or *goods* that can be attained by the closed shop, without creating an *obligation* of sufficient gravity to suspend the operation of the primary principle of *free* association. Another line of argument could establish such a necessity and obligation.

The actual circumstances may be such that the common good demands some legislative action, to overcome selfishly entrenched power. On the principle of subsidiarity, it could be maintained that the government can more fittingly act through the intermediary of a smaller organization, which, though no longer voluntary, *is* a subsidiary unit. In this situation, the union would no longer be performing one of those legitimate services that voluntary societies can undertake; it would be performing a service so necessary to the common good that the state has *commissioned* it to do this, and lent *its* power to the undertaking, without entirely supplanting the organizations themselves or their partial independence of government supervision.

This latter argument, I say, could be validly made, if the conditions were such as I have described. But it cannot be offered as a realization of the plan for those "laboring men's organizations" that have been the subject of most papal discussion. The argument I present is based on the contention that such organizations are *insufficient*, that power more like that ascribed, in the papal literature, to state *syndicates* is needed. Such an argument must work from papal teaching on the state, the common good, and subsidiarity, not from the organizations described as "intermediary" and free of state control. These latter organizations were not only recommended on the principle of voluntary association;[35] their voluntary character was presented as one of their principal advantages. Pope Leo said of them: *"In order to supersede undue interference on the part of the State,* especially as circumstances, times, and localities differ so widely, it is advisable that recourse be had to societies or boards such as We shall mention presently."[36] And Pius XI gave as his motive for introducing a "graduated order" based on "observance of the principle of subsidiary function" the fact that society had been atomized, so that "there remain virtually only individuals and the State."[37] John XXIII emphasized this aspect of Pius XI's teaching, when, in a summary of its essential points, he singled out the proposals for "establishment of economic and vocational bodies *which would be autonomous and independent of the State."*[38] Thus, whether it be a question of Leo's *collegia,* of Pius XI's *consociationes* (labor unions) or *ordines* (organizations by profession), of Pope John's *so-*

cietates, the basis in papal literature for a discussion of labor unions is solidly established on two points—that they be free of state direction, and that they be voluntary.

If it be maintained that the voluntary organizations *can* do the job, but that particular difficulties in a particular sector demand emergency measures achieving the effect of the closed shop, then again one should be clear about the principles involved. In such a case, it should be explicitly maintained that the principle of free association is still valid, but that a suspension of its action has been undertaken for a particular good, a good weighty and urgent enough to justify this suspension; and the action should be taken precisely to *remove* those circumstances that impede the functioning of right principle (in this case, the principle of free association).

It should be clear that I am not saying the Pope supports or condemns any particular form of legislation over union membership. I am only exploring the *kinds* of relationship one must consider in order to bring papal principle to bear on particular fact. It is *not* sufficient to advance the pseudo-syllogistic argument that "the Popes are for unions, and unions are against right-to-work laws, therefore the Popes are against right-to-work laws."

In fact, one should say the Popes are "for" unions only with the understanding that they are for certain principles of social action and organization. To say that these ideals are concretely realized in a specific union is an inference from the principle, not a mere rephrasing of it. Something has been added—the concrete order of fact. The union movement has not taken, in all respects, the course of development anticipated by Popes Leo XIII or Pius XI or Pius XII. Unions have not become as guild-like, as corporatist, as despotic as those Popes respectively anticipated. Accommodations have often been made, as when Catholics were allowed to join non-Catholic unions or groups using violent rhetoric. In other matters, no accommodation has been made—e.g. Catholics still cannot join Masonic lodges or the Communist Party. Whether suspension of the principle of free association is to be treated as subject to accommodation, and to what kinds of accommodation, must be decided by competent men weighing each concrete situation—a kind of study I am not engaged in here.

The important thing to notice about the history of the Catholic labor movement is that principle had to be combined with historical circumstance, often in a way that was not foreseen by the encyclicals, or even in a way that *canceled* recommendations made on the assumption that other conditions did or would prevail. *And this did not involve disloyalty to the papal teaching.* Pius XI specifically commended the adaptability which had led the labor movement to develop in ways not foreseen by Leo in *Rerum Novarum*; he refers to the departure from Leo's teaching that unions must themselves be religious and educational in scope when he says:

These counsels and instructions of Leo XIII were put into effect differently in different places according to varied local conditions. In some places one and the same association undertook to attain all the ends laid down by the Pontiff; in others, because circumstances suggested or required it, a division of tasks developed and separate associations were formed. Of these some devoted themselves to the defense of the rights and legitimate interests of their members in the labor market; others took over the work of providing mutual economic aid; finally, still others gave all their attention to the fulfillment of religious and moral duties and other obligations of like nature.[39]

Pipe Pius does not merely say that *now* men can act on different orders, that the "line" has been changed. He praises the adapting efforts made by conscientious Catholics, even when these efforts involve an analysis of existential fact different from that made by Leo XIII in his encyclical.

This latitude must be permitted if the Church is to have any flexibility at all, any response to the constant flux of political reality. If all teaching comes ready-formed from on high, when is one to change one's estimate of the guild organization, the corporatist order, or the neutral union? Are all Catholics to be for or against these until the moment when another papal statement is made; then, overnight, are they all to change their views? And, if a teaching merely drops out of sight, when are they to judge that it is no longer central to the social ideals of the Popes—after five years of silence, after ten?

Merely to pose these questions is to show the misunderstanding from which they take their origin. This nervous regard for "official" views is not part of the Catholic's approach to prudential political choices. But the kind of questions prompted by it *are* familiar today. They are the agony of the Communist, whose actions depend on the precise ascertaining, at each moment, of the Party line. The *procedural* aspects of the Marxist revolution, the sheer *technical* demands placed on one who tampers with history's mechanism in order to accelerate it, the importance of each instant in a world-view limited to time and concerned only with the material, the relative insignificance of the individual where masses are to be saved by an immediate and messianic politics—all these considerations lead, for the Communist, to an exaggerated emphasis on "orthodox" politics. But this "social conscience" is not in any way like the Catholic regard for justice.[40] The Communist is a determinist; for him history's laws are clear and irreversible. A dark Providence has no meaning for him. Nor the rights of conscience. Nor the division between sacred and secular authorities. But all of these *are* elements in the Catholic system, elements leading to a freedom of action, a personal responsibility, that render monolithic social action undesirable and, indeed, impossible.

Insofar as historical analysis is fallible, and insofar as it enters into a proposed application of principle, to just that extent the specific directive is contingent. It cannot be immutable, since it has as one of its constitutive elements a judgment merely temporal or hypothetical. This is the principle that Father John Courtney Murray formulated concisely in his general law that "an immediate illation from the order of ethical and theological truth to the order of constitutional law is, in principle, dialectically inadmissible. If such an illation is to be made, it depends for the validity of its conclusion on the mediation of an historico-social middle term."[41] Using the syllogistic motion toward an intellectual conclusion, one must apply principle by uniting it with a "minor" assertion of fact—fact complex, changing, different in each case. Something resembling this process is also true of *moral* "conclusions." Given papal teaching on the free association of workers for the common good, and given model applications of this to particular circumstances, we are not to go away with a fixed conclusion, exempted from the task of performing the illative operation ourselves. We must test the Popes' factual "minor"—which cannot be applicable everywhere, which is therefore an instance or hypothesis, meant as a model— against the pressure of fact at work on us at the moment. It is this "historical middle term" that has changed, in politics, since Boniface VIII's day, and leads us to different conclusions from the doctrine of papal supremacy. In small ways and large, the "historical middle term" of labor organization has changed from year to year, from country to country. And even in the same area and instant, men with different information and mental equipment and insight into history's forces can come to a different estimate of that "minor."

Alfred de Soras, S.J., makes an analysis very similar to Father Murray's, in everything except terminology. The "major" in Father Murray's analysis is called a "doctrinal" statement by de Soras. And the conclusion to which a mediating historical "minor" has contributed some of its contingency is called, by de Soras, an "historico-prudential" directive. Of such directives he remarks:

Statements of the historico-prudential sort, viewed in their logical structure, have a hybrid character. They admit of a double reference, by reason of their components and the mode of union between them—on the one hand, a reference to absolute and unchanging principle; on the other, to the contingent and changing facts of history. Viewed under one aspect, they are presented as absolute assertions, categorical and unchanging by virtue of the principles they manifest. From another point of vantage, they are presented as statements with all the contingent character, the historical limitations, of the situation to which they have reference.[42]

Obviously, statements into which both "major" and "minor," both principle and history, have entered, must be assessed with very delicate instruments where the binding of conscience is concerned. One must, in many cases, resort to the six diagnostic guides that are suggested by de Soras; namely,[43]

1) Precise understanding of the meaning, *in the text,* of the terms used. For instance: "freedom of the press," as this was condemned by Pius IX, was given a deep and defined meaning; ignorance of this meaning would vitiate analysis of the text.

2) Investigation, so far as is possible, of the history of the con-

troversy and discussion that preceded the official teaching on any subject. Father Fransen has shown how a consideration of the preliminary formulations, of the debates, the schemata of a Council helps fix the exact meaning of a Council's pronouncements. A similar regard for the subject matter of encyclicals is in order (e.g., the relation of Cardinal Tardini's letter on social complexity to the section in *Mater et Magistra* that treats the same subject). Newman quotes one version of this counsel from the Jesuit journal in England, *The Month*: "To understand the real meaning of a decision, no matter how clearly set forth, we should know the nature of the difficulty or *dubium,* as it was understood by the tribunal that had to decide upon it."[44]

3) Consideration of the document's relation to its historical context, with especial regard for the particular facts, institutions, and ideologies under discussion. An example would be the work Father Murray has done in showing what sort of society Pope Leo XIII had in mind when he opposed Catholic membership in the existing labor organizations.

4) Awareness of the relation of a specific pronouncement to the general tradition of Catholic teaching. When a Pope criticizes certain vices endemic to political life, one should not turn this into a denial of the rights of the polity itself, of the State's legitimate authority; it is precisely within the context of a teaching that recognizes these rights that the Pope finds his norms for criticizing political *abuses.*

5) An estimate of the weight acquired by repetition of a certain teaching. Mere return to a subject may show that it is of itself a matter closely involved with the contingent, and needing constant surveillance. But repetition of one principle in many different contexts —e.g., the principle of subsidiarity—gains a certain force by this repetition, even within discussions greatly tempered by historical contingency.

6) Knowledge of the technical terminology for condemning and commanding, discouraging and recommending. As de Soras points out, the papal literature is official; all of it is on a plane above the familiar language of everyday life. Observations that rank low on the scale of papal injunctive emphasis may seem severe to those not

acquainted with that scale. This is part of the beneficence of anathema we have already considered.

Only by careful attention to factors like these can we be sure that we are understanding the terms in which authority declares itself. In the very language of historical application and illustration—more general, at once, and more particular, than the doctrinal precision of revealed dogma—one can find the intent of the author. As de Soras says:

Although doctrinal pronouncements, in the encyclicals, demand an unconditioned assent, the historico-prudential statements exact an assent conditioned by the facts of place, time, emphasis and detail that modify their formulation; and conditional assent can take many forms, according to circumstances. This makes clear the care that must be taken, in a correct exegesis of papal documents, to distinguish assertions of the first sort, *doctrinal* in a strict sense, from assertions of the second sort, which are *historico-prudential,* if we are to avoid creating a kind of assent in the reader that works against the gifts of prudence and wisdom kept alive by that Spirit who abides in the heart of the baptized, to Whom they must be responsive even in defiance of ecclesiastical superiors.[45]

It is on such principles that the historical course of Catholic work within labor unions can be assessed and explained. The apparent contradictions between formal statement and actual application are *not* contradictions, but examples of a living response to a guiding voice; and this is not a voice imposing patterns on some inert stuff, but a voice *teaching men,* forming them for intelligent action.

The Popes do not mean to short-circuit the prudential application of truth, to prevent study of the "middle term." In fact, much of Catholic experience, discussion, trial and error, goes into the formulations each Pontiff makes for our guidance. The Pope does not shut himself up and commune only with the moral theologians of the past when he writes encyclicals. He draws on the accumulated efforts of Catholic historians, scholars, leaders, who supply him with the data of that Catholic life to which he ministers. And normally the Pope thanks these people for making new applications of his teaching—as Pius XI did when commenting on the departures from the contingent recommendations in *Rerum Novarum.*

The Pope speaks, then, after making an analysis of contemporary fact, and he *concludes from this* that certain things are desirable. The analysis, general or hedged or purely historical in approach, helps to temper the stringency of the recommendation based on it. This is made even more explicit by frequent limiting phrases— phrases like "so far as conditions allow," or "so far as possible," or "in accord with actual institutions and circumstances."[46] Pius XI said, for instance, that changes were made in Leo's teaching "according to local conditions" and "because circumstances suggested or required it." Pope John XXIII, in turn, said of Pius XI's own social encyclical, that it not only "reiterated the principles of the Leonine encyclical and stressed those directions which were applicable to modern conditions," but "took the opportunity . . . to reformulate Christian social thought in the light of changed conditions."[47] Here again, then, authority sets its own terms, allows, always, for adjustment to particular circumstance. This could not be done with matters that are doctrinal in the strict sense; truth cannot be offered as subject to accident.

But we are not merely to infer the Pope's mind in this matter from his rhetoric, or from *obiter dicta*. It has been repeatedly stated in a direct way:

When one comes down from abstractions onto the solid earth of facts, one must indeed be careful not to deny the principles just established; they remain firm. However, in becoming incarnate in factual situations the principles are invested with a stamp of contingency determined by the environment in which they find application.[48]

We do not judge it possible to enter into minute particulars touching the subject of organization; this must depend on national character, on practice and experience, on the nature and aim of the work to be done, on the scope of the various trades and employments, and on other circumstances of fact and of time—all of which should be carefully considered.[49]

Indeed the Church holds that it is unlawful to mix without cause in these temporal concerns; however she can in no wise renounce the duty God entrusted to her to interpose her authority, not of course in matters of technique, for which she is neither suitably equipped nor endowed by office.[50]

Leo XIII [in *Rerum Novarum*] had no intention of laying down guiding principles on the purely practical, we may say technical, side of the social structure; for he was well aware of the fact—as our immediate predecessor of saintly memory, Pius XI, pointed out ten years ago in his commemorative encyclical *Quadragesimo Anno*—that the Church does not claim such a mission.[51]

Within the divine laws given not only to the individual, but also the nations, there is a wide sphere in which the most varied forms of political life have ample freedom of expression. The effects of one or other political system, however, depend on circumstances and reasons, which, considered in themselves, are beyond the scope of the Church's activity.[52]

Apart, even, from these specific statements, the Pope often clarifies his relation to civil rulers in his form of address, or in asides of this sort, given to a Congress of Administrative Sciences:

In your convention, you have discussed mainly practical problems of administration. We, on Our part, have wished to add thereto a consideration of matters of principle. You will endeavor, We are certain, to fuse these principles into the life and functioning of public administration.[53]

This passage returns us to one of the primary principles of papal teaching—the fact that the Papacy is not wedded to any particular form of government. Leo XIII was particularly insistent on this principle, probably to reassure those who, mistaking the "middle term" as a permanent thing, feared that Pius IX's condemnations of the "modern freedoms" had condemned not only the false philosophy and its direct expression but all modern kinds of free activity. To guard against this misunderstanding, Leo stressed the Papacy's openness to different governmental forms—including, explicitly, those of democracy—in almost every one of his important encyclicals on the State.

This, then, is the teaching of the Catholic Church concerning the constitution and government of the State. By the words and decrees just cited, if judged dispassionately [the Syllabus of Errors has just been cited], no one of the several forms of government is in itself condemned, inasmuch as none of them contains anything contrary to Catholic doctrine, and all of them are capable, if wisely and justly managed, to insure the welfare of the State. Neither is it blameworthy in itself, in any manner, for the people to have a share greater or less, in the government; for at certain times, and under certain laws, such participation may not only be of benefit to the citizens, but may even be of obligation.[54]

If the Church does not prefer one form of government—the most drastic instrument for ordering society, an instrument whose uses have been analyzed by centuries of discourse—it is hardly likely that she will condemn procedural modes in other areas, of less drastic importance and less defined status. That is, if Pius IX's strictures against the democracy based on false philosophic principles were not a condemnation of democratic forms in themselves, then it is not likely that Leo XIII's condemnation of materialistic capitalism represents any judgment on economic *techniques* as these are separable from the philosophic denial of moral law. And if no one form of *government* is dictated to the nations from Rome, it seems safe to suppose that no single economic arrangement—whether profit-sharing, corporatism, highly complexified capitalism-"socialization" —is imposed on mankind as the "true solution" to its problems. Express warrant for extending this openness toward governmental forms into other areas is supplied by Pius XI, who wrote:

The teaching of Leo XIII on the forms of political government, namely, that men are free to choose whatever form they please, provided that proper regard is had for the requirements of justice and of the common good, is equally applicable, in due proportion, it is hardly necessary to say, to the guilds of the various industries and professions.[55]

But the clearest statement of these various considerations is given by John XXIII in the course of his last encyclical, *Pacem in Terris*. On the Church's neutrality toward any governmental form as such, he has these three paragraphs (52, 67, 71):

It must not be concluded, however, because authority comes from God, that therefore men have no right to choose those who are to rule the State, to decide the form of government, and to determine both the way in which authority is to be exercised and its limits.

It is impossible to determine, once and for all, what is the most suitable form of government, or how civil authorities can most effectively fulfill their respective functions, i.e., the legislative, judicial and executive functions of the State.

And yet, social life in the modern world is so varied, complex and dynamic that even a juridical structure which has been prudently and thoughtfully established is always inadequate for the needs of society.

In these and other ways, Pope John spelled out with greatest clarity the difference between the authoritative principle of the common good and the political means elaborated to achieve that good, between the claims of society as such and the limits of power given to the political representatives of society.[56] This led Father John Courtney Murray to say:

In dealing with the problem of political order, Pope John XXIII represents a development of the tradition. He leaves behind the predominantly ethical concept of the society-state which was characteristic of Leo XIII. He adopts the more juridical conception of the state that was characteristic of Pius XII, and he carries this conception to new lengths. For instance, he clearly accepts the distinction that seems to be missing from Leo XIII, namely, the distinction between society and the state. His general conception of the political ideal is fundamentally that of St. Thomas, "the free man under a limited government."[57]

Furthermore, in urging men to come to grips with what has been discussed here as "the middle term" of historical reality, Pope John gave a very full statement of the Church's teaching on the indispensable role of *prudence* in political life:

To lay down the ways and degrees in which work in common might be possible for the achievement of economic, social, cultural and political ends which are honorable and useful—these are the problems which can only be solved with the virtue of prudence, which is the guiding light of the virtues that regulate the moral life, both individual and social. Therefore, so far as Catholics are concerned, this decision rests primarily with those who live and work in the specific sectors of human society in which those problems arise, always, however, in accordance with the principles of the natural law, with the social teaching of the Church, and with the directives of ecclesiastical authority.[58]

The Church helps shape history because it enters history, honestly, on the necessary terms of action in this dark world of trial. She learns, on the human level, even as—by the divine truth granted her, and the human lessons she has already learned—her teaching effort goes forward. She is the more effective teacher for her willingness to learn from the human intellect and experience, from created fact, in all areas where such witnesses are competent. No human skill will be denied that can contribute to her social teaching and historical experience. Even by human norms, she is an institution with a career of experienced trial that commands respect. In her life, new truths connect with old; the scholar and the practical man, the theologian and the layman enrich each other's work.

A sign of this is the very fact that encyclicals *maintain* a dialogue with the world. If Leo XIII had given the kind of final pronouncement on social affairs that some men imagine, there would have been no reason for Pius XI to write *Quadragesimo Anno*. But the Pope is engaged in a continuing task of education and exhortation.[59] Later Popes did not merely parrot Leo. They added, deleted, adjusted. Ideas had to be recast whenever the friction of events sharpened or wore away their applicable edges. The Church has ever stimulated change, even as it responded to it. As Pius XII put it, "Social action not only firmly guides, but is itself guided by practice."[60]

NOTES TO CHAPTER SIX: CONTINGENCY

1. Usury is a good "test case" for the relation of defined truth to historical context. As such, it is prominent in several of the better discussions of this problem, including Newman's "Letter" (pp. 195-6) and Alfred de Soras, S.J.'s "La portée des document pontificaux" (pp. 138-9). For the successive analyses of economic fact which were the vehicle of change in this regard, *cf.* John T. Noonan, Jr., *The Scholastic Analysis of Usury*, Harvard, 1957.

2. *Cf.* Noonan, *Scholastic Analysis,* p. 389.

3. Allocution, June 19, 1950.

4. *Cf.* Allocution, April 27, 1941 (Chinigo, p. 309): speaking of "whoever owns the means of production," Pius said "his profit must be greater than that of his collaborators, but at the same time, the individual well-being of all, which constitutes the object of social economy, must still further impose on him the duty of contributing through his savings to the national capital. Nor must it be forgotten that, just as it is extremely useful to a sound social economy that this increase of capital should come from the greatest possible number of sources, so it is most desirable that the workers also should contribute with the fruits of their savings to the formation of the

national capital." See also the Christmas Message of 1952 (Yzermans II, p. 1965): "Let those who are able to invest capital consider in the light of the common good— and with due regard to their economic condition, to risks involved and opportunity offered—whether they can reconcile with their conscience their neglect and failure to make investments because of unreasonable caution."

5. Msgr. Pailler, Auxiliary Bishop of Rouen, "Considerations on the Authority of the Church," in Todd, *Problems of Authority*, p. 15.

6. J. P. Kirsch, s.v. "Unam Sanctam," *Cath. Encyclop.*

7. Murray, "Governmental Repression of Heresy," p. 37.

8. Rommen, *The State in Catholic Thought*, p. 535 (emphasis added).

9. *Rerum Novarum*, par. 54 (Gilson, p. 234).

10. In reconstructing the diagram of social forces described by Pope Leo, Father Murray finds that "sects" were the militant agents most to be feared in this outline, and that the Masonic Society was considered the most dangerous sect ("Leo XIII on Church and State," *Theol. Stud.* 14, pp. 3-7).

11. The rights of religious orders are discussed as an aspect of the freedom of organization Pope Leo has in mind for laborers (*Rerum Novarum*, par. 53).

12. *Rerum Novarum*, par. 49 (Gilson, p. 231). Pope Leo first advocated restoration of the guilds in his encyclical on Freemasonry, *Humanum Genus*, par. 35 (Gilson, p. 135), which appeared seven years before *Rerum Novarum*. He wrote there, "If our ancestors, by long use and experience, felt the benefit of these guilds, our age perhaps will feel it the more by reason of the opportunity which they will give of crushing the power of the sects." It is, alas, typical of the historical scholarship available to laymen that, in the standard expositions of *Rerum Novarum* (e.g., Cronin, Husslein), working men's organizations are discussed without any reference to Freemasonry.

13. "Leo XIII on Church and State," p. 8.

14. *Singulari Quadam*, par. 7 (Yzermans, *All Things in Christ*, p. 193). But Saint Pius said that Catholic unions were still "to be most approved and considered as most useful" where they were still feasible. And he recommended *co-operation* with non-Catholic unions rather than actual *membership* in them: "We would rather see Catholic and non-Catholic associations unite their forces through that new and timely institution known as the *cartel*." (*Singulari Quadam* is, by the way, the only encyclical devoted exclusively to the subject of labor organizations.)

15. *Quadragesimo Anno*, par. 35 (McLaughlin, p. 230).

16. *Ibid.*, pars. 37-8 (pp. 230-1), pars. 81-7 (pp. 247-9). The formation of these extra-governmental groups should not be confused with the use of them as political units in a corporatist *state*. The two are often confused in references to Pius' encyclical. But he makes the distinction between them clear when he raises the subject of the corporatist state as a new topic after he has discussed the *ordines* or *corpora*, and states its distinctive feature: "The *civil authority itself* constitutes the syndicate as a *juridical* personality . . ." (par. 92). The corporatist *state* does not offer what Leo XIII took to be a prime advantage of his *opificum collegia*—the resolution of conflicts without the intervention of the state (see note 35 below).

17. In an Allocution in 1941 (April 27, Chinigo, p. 308), Pius referred to his predecessor's treatment of "professional organizations" and stated that "this part of the Encyclical seems, unfortunately, to offer us an example of those propitious opportunities that are lost because they were not taken advantage of in time"—a sentence that offers *us* an example of the changes that can take place in the papal teaching under the force of changed circumstances.

18. Christmas Message, 1952 (Yzermans II, p. 168). And see the Allocution of March 11, 1945 (Chinigo, p. 317): "As for the democratization of the economy, it is threatened no less by monopoly, that is by the economic despotism of an anonymous conglomeration of private capital, than by the preponderance of organized masses, ready to use their power to the detriment of justice and the rights of others."

19. Yzermans I, p. 304.

20. Yzermans II, p. 197. This problem was one of Pius XII's deepest concerns, and it called forth a sustained and penetrating analysis of modern society. He criticized

five interconnected aspects of the social pressure exerted on the human person in our time:

1) First, the scientistic approach to organization treats society as an entity that is *mathematical* (Yzermans II, pp. 53, 167, 179) or *mechanical* (*ibid.* I, pp. 141, 144, 216; II, 58, 81, 105, 163, 166, 168), an entity adjustable on the considerations of efficiency that are proper to a *mechanism,* but which make living *men* "run up against the provisions of organized society as against an inexorable law, against pure mathematics." In the words of his 1952 Christmas message:

> Indeed, modern society, which wishes to plan and organize all things, comes into conflict, since it is conceived as a machine, with that which is living, and which therefore cannot be subjected to quantitative calculations.

2) Organization based on such principles fittingly tends toward *anonymous leadership* (II, pp. 156, 168, 197, 218), to "the anonymity of power, the swallowing up of the individual in the mass." Men act not as persons, but as parts of large blocs, and freedom is endangered

> when individual interest is placed under the protection of these collective organizations, or of a party, where one seeks protection for the sum total of individual interests, rather than the promotion of the good of all; under such a guise the economy becomes easily subject to the power of anonymous forces which dominate it politically (1954).

3) *Technology,* a set of devices neither moral nor immoral in themselves (II, 174, 176), is naturally a favored instrument for the work of men whose very principles are mechanistic, and it can be used to lure others to these principles (I, 141; II, 174-80, 189-91). The vision of power it opens to men

> is a deceitful panorama, that finishes by shutting up as in a prison those who are too credulous with regard to the omnipotence and immensity of technology (1953).

4) All these tendencies converge to maximize the *powers of the State* (I, 140; II, 84, 97, 163, 166), so that "instances of abnormal growth succeed one another almost without interruption":

> This sad reality is already with us: wherever the demon of organization invades and tyrannizes man's spirit, there are at once revealed the signs of a false and abnormal orientation of society. In some countries, the modern state is becoming a gigantic administrative machine. It extends its influence over almost every phase of life. It would bring under its administration the entire gamut of political, economic, social and intellectual life from birth to death (1952).

This resembles the warning Pius had issued ten years earlier:

> Whether this slavery arises from the exploitation of private capital or from the power of the State, the result is the same. Indeed, under the pressure of a State which dominates all and controls the whole field of public and private life, even going into the realm of ideas and beliefs and of conscience, this lack of liberty can have the more serious consequences, as experience shows and proves.

5) The result is a *depersonalization* of modern life (I, 32-3, 141, 304; II, 163, 166, 167, 197), causing men to forget "the indispensable primacy of personal impulse and responsibility in social life":

> Here may be recognized the origin and source of that phenomenon which is submerging modern man under its tide of anguish: his "depersonalization." In large measure his identity and name have been taken from him; in many of the more important activities of life he has been reduced to a mere material object of society, while society itself has been transformed into an impersonal system and into a cold organization of force (1952).

21. Radio message to *Katholikentag* of Bochum, Sept. 4, 1941 (Yzermans I, p. 128). Pius said, in a 1946 allocution to Italian electricians, that "professional and trade unions are provisional aids and transitional forms" (DC 1946, 382).

22. AAS 37, p. 70.

23. AAS 40, pp. 336-7.

24. *Rerum Novarum,* par. 54 (Gilson, p. 234).

25. *Quadragesimo Anno,* par. 87 (McLaughlin, p. 249).

26. *Ibid.,* par. 92 (p. 251).

27. *Christmas Message,* 1952 (Yzermans II, p. 168).

28. Thus recalling not only a major theme of his predecessor, but his very language (*e.g.,* Yzermans II, pp. 156, 168). Pope John's words are: "The disturbances which unsettle the internal peace of nations trace their origins chiefly to this source; that man has been treated almost exclusively as a machine, a piece of merchandise, a worthless cog in some great machine or a mere productive unit" (*The Pope Speaks* 6.2., pp. 201).

29. *The Pope Speaks* 6.4, pp. 422-3.

30. *Mater et Magistra,* par. 22 (*The Pope Speaks* 7.4, p. 300).

31. Pope John stressed the role such organizations must play as society becomes more complex, both in *Mater et Magistra* and even more insistently in *Pacem in Terris* (pars. 24, 53, 64, 69, 100).

32. *Cf. Singulari Quadam,* par. 7 (Yzermans, *All Things,* p. 193): "Furthermore, if Catholics are to be permitted to join the trade unions, these associations must avoid everything that is not in accord, either in principle or in practice, with the teachings and commandments of the Church or the proper ecclesiastical authorities. Similarly, everything is to be avoided in their literature and public utterances which in the above view would incur censure."

33. Cronin, *Catholic Social Principles,* p. 427.

34. *Christmas Message,* 1954 (Yzermans II, p. 197).

35. *Rerum Novarum* treated the proper activities of the State and of working men's organizations as supplementary, rather than directly linked. Only after a long treatment (pars. 32-47) of the *State's* duty to prevent violence, oppression of the poor and violation of property, does it go on: "In the last place, employers and workmen may *of themselves* effect much, in the matter We are treating, by means of such associations and organizations as afford opportune aid to those who are in distress, and which draw the two classes more closely together. Among these may be enumerated societies for mutual help; various benevolent foundations established by private persons to provide for the workman, and for his widow or his orphans, in case of sudden calamity, in sickness, and in the event of death; and institutions for the welfare of boys and girls, young people, and those more advanced in years. The most important of all are workingmen's unions, for these virtually include all the rest. History attests what excellent results were brought about by the artificers' guilds of olden times . . ." (pars. 48-9). Thus the discussion of unions is launched. Paragraph 53 puts these organizations in the same situation as religious orders, so far as their relation to the State is concerned: "The rulers of the State accordingly have no rights over them, nor can they claim any share in their control; on the contrary, it is the duty of the State to respect and cherish them, and, if need be, to defend them from attack." Then, after recommending Catholic organizations to oppose the godless ones already formed, Pope Leo writes (par. 55) "The State should watch over these societies of citizens banded together in accordance with their rights, but it should not thrust itself into their peculiar concerns and their organization, for things move and live by the spirit inspiring them, and may be killed by the rough grasp of a hand from without." *Quadragesimo Anno* is as clear on this matter as *Rerum Novarum* (*cf.* references in note 16 above). In fact, by treating the "syndicates" apart from the strictly free "self-governing" organizations (par. 83), whether of workers, or employers, or entire professions, the Pope made the same kind of distinction that I make in the model argument advanced. The practical effect of such distinctions is made clear by Pope Pius himself when he says that syndicates, as having a directly political function, cannot be considered a project of Catholic action associations (whereas *private* associations, with good aims, can).

36. *Rerum Novarum,* par. 45 (Gilson, p. 230).

37. *Quadragesimo Anno,* pars. 78, 80 (McLaughlin, pp. 246, 247).

38. *Mater et Magistra,* par. 37 (*The Pope Speaks,* 7.4, p. 302).

39. *Quadragesimo Anno,* par. 34 (McLaughlin, p. 229).

40. Yet the extraordinarily inept comparison is sometimes made: "If we had the same devotion to the social encyclicals as Lenin had to Communism, we could lead a Christian revolution to Christianize the social and economic life of the world" (Rev. Norman Galloway, O.S.A., in *The Catholic Mind*, November, 1956, p. 628). Fr. Galloway apparently refers only to the *quantity* of devotion, not the quality of it. But such comparisons can be misleading in an article concerned precisely with the *kind* of response to authority that Catholics should have. And even the *quantity* of a Communist's zeal is intimately connected with the fact that he can conceive *no other kind* of justice than social, earthly, economic good order.

41. "The Problem of 'the Religion of the State,'" *Am. Eccles. Rev.* 124, p. 343.

42. "La facture des documents pontificaux," p. 266.

43. *Ibid.,* pp. 271-3. I give de Soras' list, but the examples appended to each point are my own, with reference where possible to things treated somewhere in this book.

44. "Letter," p. 165.

45. "La facture," pp. 268-9.

46. *Cf.*, for instance, in *Mater et Magistra*: (of the principles involved in the right to a just wage) "Their degree of applicability to concrete cases cannot be determined without reference to the quantity and quality of available resources; and these can—and in fact do—vary from country to country, and even, from time to time, within the same country"; (of gradual inclusion of workers in ownership of companies) "by ways and in the manner that seem most suitable"; (of worker participation in management) "It is not, of course, possible to lay down hard and fast rules regarding the manner of such participation, for this must depend upon prevailing conditions, which vary from firm to firm and are frequently subject to rapid and substantial alteration"; (of Catholic social teaching generally) "It is essential that this doctrine be known, assimilated, and put into effect in the form and manner that the different situations allow and demand," a process in which "Differences of opinion in the application of principle can sometimes arise even among sincere Catholics" (*The Pope Speaks* 7.4, pp. 309, 310, 312, 336, 338).

47. *Mater et Magistra*, par. 28 (p. 300).

48. Leo XIII, encyclical *Au milieu.*

49. Leo XIII, *Rerum Novarum*, par. 56 (Gilson, pp. 235-6).

50. Pius XI, *Quadragesimo Anno*, par. 41 (McLaughlin, p. 232).

51. Pius XII, radio message on anniversary of *Rerum Novarum*, June 1, 1941 (Yzermans I, pp. 27-8).

52. Pius XII, Christmas Message, 1940 (Yzermans II, pp. 35-6).

53. Yzermans I, p. 141.

54. *Immortale Dei,* par. 36 (Gilson, p. 177). For other passages, see Gilson, pp. 65, 81, 222, 262.

55. *Quadragesimo Anno*, par. 86 (McLaughlin, p. 249). And for the interconnection of the political and economic forms, see Pius XII's statements at Yzermans II, p. 62 and *The Pope Speaks* 3, pp. 443-6.

56. *Cf.* the praise given to the principles of a limitation of political authority by constitutionality (pars. 75-8), a division of powers (pars. 67-8), and a limited term of office (par. 74). *Cf.* Newman, *Parochial and Plain Sermons*, vol. 3, pp. 221-2: "When we speak of the Nation we take into account its variety of local rights, interests, attachments, customs, opinions; the character of its people, and the history of that character's formation. On the other hand, when we speak of the State, we imply the notion of orders, ranks and powers, of the legislative and executive departments, and the like." Pius XII made the same distinction when he talked of virtuous men as the source of good order in *any form* of government (Chinigo, pp. 295-9, *The Pope Speaks* 4.1, p. 98).

57. "Things New and Old in *Pacem in Terris,*" *America*, April 27, 1963, p. 612.

58. *Pacem in Terris*, par. 160 (Gibbons, pp. 54-5). And see par. 69 (p. 27): "Public officials must strive to meet the problems that arise in a way that conforms both to the complexities of the situation and the proper exercise of their function. This requires that, in constantly changing conditions, legislators never forget the norms of morality, or constitutional provisions, or the objective requirements of the common

220 POLITICS AND CATHOLIC FREEDOM

good. Moreover, executive authorities must co-ordinate the activities of society with discretion, with a full knowledge of the law and after a careful consideration of circumstances. . . ."

59. This makes mere repetition of certain points an insufficient norm for measuring the mandatory weight of the Pope's words. Msgr. Fenton actually uses a numerical gauge for edging propositions into the realm of infallible statement: "It would appear . . . that especially when a number of these documents deal with a certain individual subject, and when the more recent letters repeat and emphasize teachings which have been stressed in previous encyclicals, that *some, at least,* of the doctrine thus presented to the Church universal should be considered as taught infallibly by the Church's ordinary and universal magisterium. . . . In such a case, as for example in *the series of pontifical pronouncements on Church and State,* the teachings of the earlier documents are *repeated and re-stated* in more recent letters. Thus there is *an indication* that the Sovereign Pontiffs wished to *close discussion* on the points at issue and have the *teachings thus repeated* accepted *always* by the members of the Church" (*Am. Eccles. Rev.* 121, 1949, pp. 213, 215, emphasis added). We are told that where there is a return to certain subjects we have "an indication" that the Pope wants to close discussion (of the relation of Church to State!) and that on such vague grounds we must suppose that "some, at least" of the pronouncements are infallible! (That "some, at least" is very touching, as if the Msgr. were pleading for a little more *ex cathedra* activity; he seems to think the Pope is being mistreated, or wasting his time, if he does not get some doctrine pronounced to supply the breakfast tables of latter-day William Wards.) Certainly one might conclude that the Pope has taken an odd way of indicating that a question is closed when he keeps *raising it over and over;* but according to Msgr. Fenton we are to consider a discussion *more* closed the *more* it is raised again. It seems more economical to infer that the Pope returns to the discussion of a problem like the Church's relations with the State precisely because this matter is so deeply imbedded in the obscure texture of history, and needs constant reassessment. The Pope means to guide and take part in a continuing discussion, not abruptly break it off.

60. Letter to International Federation of Christian Workers' Movements, May 8, 1955.

CHAPTER SEVEN

FAITH

F AITH, it was observed in Chapter three, above, should not be conceived exclusively as *faith that* God exists, etc. Animating the acceptance of these propositions is an attitude toward a Person—*faith in* God. In one sense we can apply this two-fold language to the Church. Catholics believe *that* the Church is the body of Christ, that it teaches infallibly, that it cannot succumb to its Enemy, etc. They also believe *in* the Church, insofar as they recognize Christ in his mystical body, in his members. It was this faith *in* the Church that was considered in Chapter three. But modern theologians remind us that it is more proper, more traditional, to speak of believing *in Ecclesia* than *in Ecclesiam*.[1] Catholics are not faced with the Church as with an object or person placed over against them. Its life is the one they live. They believe *in* it as *acting in* it, as part of it; its act of belief is theirs. They *are* the believing Church. As Saint Augustine says, "We, who are Christ's even by our name, do not believe *in* Peter, but *with* him, strengthened by him as he tells us of the object of his faith, Who is Christ."[2] In this sense the Christian is pious toward the Church, loyal to it as part of it, animated by its supernatural life; his is an *anima ecclesiastica*.

Such faith can inform men's lives without displacing the intellect's proper activity. Where mystery in the strict sense is at issue, revealed truth necessary to salvation, Peter makes it clear that adherence is, for his subjects as for him, the primary duty and the origin of all further light in an area that is mysterious of its nature. But in matters reached by historical analysis or natural reasoning, men can reason with Peter, even when "strengthened" by him. He leads, and lights the way, but they must journey with him. They are not to wait supinely for the process to reach some conclusions they can carry away unexamined.

But there is a tendency to reduce the mystery of man's participation in the Church's life by treating it as a great and imposing structure they confront with submission, yielding to it rather than living in it. This attitude, of submission in all things, is sometimes presented as an ideal of piety toward the Church. One does not enter, ask, question, reason. One simply listens, with the highest degree of passivity that can be maintained. Peter's historico-prudential teaching is received with the same attitude as definitions of revealed dogma. The Church is an oracle, a cave out of which rigid formulae are dispensed. The faithful approach it, receive such packages of truth, and take them away unopened, untampered with. The hierarchy and the priesthood are not diaconates of service to the Church's life, but resonators, at the door of the cave, of these magic phrases.[3]

Men who take this posture toward the Church use a language that *sounds* pious. Their attitude is accepted, often, as a sign of great faith. And departures from it are, in varying degrees, represented as failures in belief, or at least as dangerous tendencies.[4] It is said that "questioning" the Church's meaning in any area may undermine faith in things revealed, may lead to rationalism. Even if the particular question raised be a justifiable one, it should be repressed lest it lead to questioning in other areas. And by raising doubts such as these, it is possible to discredit the views of those who take a less passive stance toward the Church's historical mission, toward theologians who show originality, toward those who examine the meaning of the official phrases used as counters in political or intellectual life. This was the power of that great weapon invented by W. G. Ward and still wielded by Msgr. Fenton and others—the word "minimist." Those who try to describe the exact structure of the diaconate's activity are treated as niggling and ungenerous in their response to the inestimable goods offered them by the Church.

This resembles the argument sometimes used against the precise case-work of moral theologians. Mistakenly fervent Catholics make light of this science on the ground that a person should not ask what he must, at the *minimum,* do to avoid sin. It is not enough to answer such arguments with the command Christ gave to the Phar-

It is in this context that the either-or mentality already referred to finds its home. *Either,* we are told, there is a Catholic moral doctrine on a social question, *or* there is not. If there is *not,* the Church would not have spoken at all on these matters. Since the Church has spoken, there *is* a doctrine; and our duty is to find it and accept it, not to delimit it, or discuss variant lines of conduct possible among Catholics. One must not make this doctrine the subject of debate. It was for such debating, for precise dissection of difficult pronouncements, that Newman was branded a minimist by the papal "maximizers" of his day. The importance of interpretive subtlety to his whole moral theology is registered in the angry pages of the *Apologia.* Kingsley maintained that his finesse in discussing the problem of truthfulness amounted to a Jesuitical defense of lying. The massed artillery of Newman's response is explained by the fact that his entire intellectual effort was at stake. He spent most of his life arguing, in various ways on various subjects, that religious ardor is the ally, not the foe, of refined reasoning on moral matters. The honesty with which Newman discussed problems posed by the faith made Huxley suspect him of being a rationalist in his heart of hearts; and Swinburne called his work the greatest defense of agnosticism. Both were making the same mistake that Kingsley made in morals, William Ward made in dogma, and Acton made in politics. Newman was convinced, from the actual history of the Church, that discussion of problems was the only way to anticipate those errors that will inevitably come, in endless waves until time ends, against truth and against truth's citadel, the Church. A platitude about "telling the truth" may hide errors that will spell spiritual ruin for confused consciences. Hasty submission to a simplistic view of the Church's power may lead to the gravest consequences.

To the attitude represented by Newman, it is sometimes objected that we must follow St. Paul's advice about feeding the spiritually weak on intellectual milk. Preoccupation with all the difficulties of interpreting moral obligation will dampen the certitude on which resolute action is based. The same argument has been used to justify suppression of the facts of history, when these did not seem edifying, or even to praise ignorance and "peasant faith" to the denigration of intellect. This explains how encyclical "study groups" can be used to stir up "social conscience" (read here: emotions), with the implication that the *intellect,* reasoning on the structure and limits of papal authority, has no real bearing on the act of conscience. A distinction is made between "devotional study" and intellectual "scholarship."

Perhaps in some societies, or at certain points in history, the suppression of information can be justified. It is an obvious truth that all things should not be presented indiscriminately to all men.[6] For a Catholic to elaborate on all the plausible arguments against the faith before a young man not equipped to handle them would be, it seems, like giving a baby his "free" choice of matches, knives, or poison as playthings. But there are degrees of educational guidance. Preventing the young man from doing anything that might expose him to such arguments is not the same as omitting the persuasive presentation of them oneself. And saying or implying that such arguments *do not exist,* so that the man need not *equip* himself to deal with them, would be a use of immoral means to achieve a moral end. Pope John XXIII wrote, in *Pacem in Terris,* that man has "the right to freedom in searching for truth and in expressing and communicating his opinions . . . and he has the right to be informed truthfully about public events."[7] Newman wrote:

Facts are omitted in great histories, or glosses are put upon memorable acts, because they are thought not edifying, whereas of all scandals such omissions, such glosses, are the greatest.[8]

In the past, social conditions made it impossible for large parts of the faithful to become learned, or even literate. Education was a prerogative of the clergy. But with the growth of education and leisure and books, restrictions suitable for an earlier day become increasingly meaningless—a fact recognized by the Popes in their statements on the freedom of Catholic scholarship, biblical study, and the exercise of political responsibility. Censorship should always be a means of education, a strategic pruning of knowledge to be followed by growth. It should have a "planned obsolescence" with regard to the progress of human maturity. And certainly there can be no suspicion of obscurantism in the papal teaching that has been presented through the encyclicals. These are commended to the study of all the laity. Though they discuss difficult problems at a depth and with a subtlety that is demanding, they are not circulated privately among an elite, for later elucidation to the unread. They are all of them implicitly addressed—as *Pacem* was formally addressed—"to all men of good will."

It is therefore necessary to scrutinize with some care the all-too-familiar claim that people who do not agree with some particular teacher are flouting the papal authority; that "the tendency toward an unhealthy minimism [is] current in this country and elsewhere in the world today";[9] that Catholics are deliberately refusing to take papal teaching "straight";[10] that political disagreement among Catholics is caused simply by dormant consciences;[11] that even *silence* on the subject of a particular encyclical implies, among priests, that they "reject the Pope's right to teach in these [social] fields";[12] that this silence is eagerly caught at by laymen who "find encouragement for their own rejection of papal authority on social questions";[13] that matters of continuing political dispute have, unknown to many Catholics, been removed from the sphere of the debatable;[14] that those who continue to discuss these things must be ignorant of the papal teaching;[15] that this ignorance makes one's words "almost as obnoxious to a well-instructed Catholic as [do] assaults on religion";[16] further, that it is the "stuff from which seedling schisms sprout,"[17] is actively related to laicism[18] and anticlericalism;[19] that reservations on the timeliness of certain emphases in a certain document constitute a denial of the *right* of the Pope to teach;[20] that, to avoid questioning this right, one must not only avoid such observations, but generally observe a tactic of "interpretation" rather than controversy,[21] or of explanation rather than interpretation[22]—in short, a mode of exegesis guaranteed to reach the conclusions upon which this whole line of accusations proceeds, namely that (again, from the top) "the tendency toward an unhealthy minimism. . . ." Enough!

More than enough. The words of Newman return, with the persistence of the phenomenon they describe—"that day of tyrannous *ipse-dixits*."[23]

It is too familiar, from too many areas of the Church's life, to continue its way unchallenged. This refusal to see honesty in disagreement; this suspicion of defection hidden in silence; this anticipation of heresy in tiny "seeds"; this concentration on motive, on bad conscience, on everything but the *possibility* of disagreeing rationally, of distinguishing, of discerning alternatives—the history of the Church is already too full of these sad, zealous endeavors to promote a position by moral blackmail rather than intellectual exposition.

This whole misunderstanding is furthered by the confusion between *faith-that* and *faith-in* situations. Faith *in* God can deepen immeasurably, with the generous outpouring of grace; but men tend, subconsciously, to talk of an increase in faith as if there were always to be an increase in the propositions believed—that more perfect faith *accepts more,* that the Church's teaching "spreads," that her guidance is accepted as infallible in more and more areas, her recommendations escalated, her teaching homogenized in an ecstacy of acceptance.

But the true significance of a careful and legitimate "minimism" is this: precision in the statement of the propositions *that* we believe is the safeguard for faith *in* God's manifold guidance and mysterious nature and directing love. A minimum in the one aspect of faith, the (mainly negative) definitions protecting endangered propositions, allows a free and doctrinally sound maximum in the other aspect, in personal knowledge, individual yet guided by grace. Newman was the champion of this increase in love to be attained by the careful contraction, into defined statement, of obligatory doctrine. He fought the drift of Catholic sentiment into a view that faith grows by accretion of the things one can accept. As he says, intellectual honesty, belief in the ordinances of natural law, and trust in Providence, demand that we approach all truth with the critical standards of mature examination. To know perfectly what one must believe, one is obliged, also, to ascertain the points where he need *not* believe, or, even, *must not* believe. Newman describes the growth of his realization that

we were bound to be more or less sure, on a sort of (as it were) graduated scale of assent, viz., according as the probabilities attaching to a professed fact were brought home to us, and, as the case might be, to entertain about it a pious belief or a pious opinion, or a religious

conjecture, or at least a tolerance of such belief, or opinion, or conjecture in others; that on the other hand, as it was a duty to have a
belief, of more or less strong texture, in given cases, so in other
cases, it was a duty not to believe, not to opine, not to conjecture,
not even to tolerate the notion that a professed fact was true, inasmuch as it would be credulity or superstition, or some other moral
fault, to do so.[24]

And so one can say that there is a *duty*, for an intelligent man looking at the mosaic of truth and argument and conjecture that make
up the papal teaching documents through history, to deny the apparently pious or "faithful" idea that "the possibility of error in
these documents is so utterly remote that it is practically non-
existent even as a possibility."[25]

Minimist, that passage of Newman's? Perhaps—minimizing er-
ror, scandal, expenditure of effort in defense of the indefensible.
And maximizing understanding, co-operation, exploration of the
Church's mystery.

NOTES TO CHAPTER SEVEN: FAITH

1. *Cf.* Karl Rahner, S.J., "Dogmatische Randbemerkungen zur 'Kirchenfrommig-
keit,'" pp. 769-93, Henri de Lubac, S.J., "Credo Ecclesiam," pp. 13-16, in *Sentire Ecclesiam*, edited by Jean Danielou and Herbert Vorgrimler (Herder, 1961).

2. *The City of God*, 18.54.

3. Rev. Peter Fransen, S.J., describes this mentality as opposed to the very concept
of ministry (*diaconia*), making the Church serve its ministers rather than *vice versa*:
"I must apologize for insisting so much on this basic principle, but history shows that
unfortunately few truths are so easily forgotten as this one. How many times did not
our Lord have to return to it as he taught the Apostles! The neglect of it in practice
leads to clericalism in all its forms and this is a great cause of scandal to our separated
brethren. It is tragic even that it is this particular abuse of authority which so easily
arises in fervent Christian communities. It is true to say that the respect shown by
the faithful towards their pastors becomes a dangerous temptation for the latter to
fail to recognize the profound religious and christocentric nature of every form of the
exercise of authority in the Church" (Todd, *Problems of Authority*, p. 49). The concept of *diaconia* was perfectly expressed by Pius XII, when he said that ecclesiastical
authority "spreads its maternal arms towards this world not to dominate but to serve"
(*Summi Pontificatus*, par. 92, NCWC, p. 41).

4. Msgr. Fenton is convinced Newman could not have been a great teacher because
he was critical of Cardinal Manning and Msgr. Talbot, and even flippant about their
policies (*cf. Am. Eccles. Rev.* 113, pp. 300-20).

5. *Cf.* Msgr. Ronald Knox, *Enthusiasm*, pp. 584 ff.

6. I do not mean, here, to make any observations on the proper mode, extent, and
agencies of censorship, but simply to recognize the principle on which all legitimate
censorship is based—a principle sensitively expounded in Chapter seven of Father
Murray's *We Hold These Truths*.

7. *Pacem in Terris*, par. 12 (Gibbons, p. 9).

8. *Historical Sketches* II, p. 231.
9. *Am. Eccles. Rev.* 13 (1956), p. 100.
10. *The Commonweal,* Feb. 10, 1956, p. 480.
11. See page 151.
12. *America,* November 4, 1961, p. 149.
13. *Ibid.*
14. See page 151.
15. *Ibid.*
16. *America,* Nov. 17, 1951, pp. 173-4, Oct. 10, 1957.
17. See page 5.
18. See page 11.
19. See pages 17-20.
20. See pages 11-12, 48.
21. See page 128.
22. See page 85.
23. "Letter," p. 184.
24. *Apologia,* p. 141.
25. See page 116.

CHAPTER EIGHT

PRUDENCE

In the fourth chapter above, it was argued that Providence conducts man through trial, rather than lifting him above it—and that the Church is with man in this experience of history, riding above the waves of purely human activity, but *on* them, tossed by them, a vessel of passage *in* history. The model here, as everywhere, is Christ himself, who educated his disciples gradually, constantly throwing them back on themselves, testing their resources, seeming to abandon them in the boat, letting them act from imperfect knowledge in many areas. He demanded faith, encouraged freedom, and led them to maturity.

The Church, too, forms conscience, instead of replacing it. And the only way to form conscience is in freedom. Man's destiny is in his own hand, as the Wisdom Literature says; and the ability to affect that destiny forever—by a free act to be lifted high as heaven, or to sink oneself low as hell—is at the center of the Christian drama, which turns on such momentous choices, on Adam's decision in the Garden of Eden, on Christ's in the Garden of Olives. This accounts for what Chesterton calls "that external vigilance which has always been the mark of Christianity (the command that we should *watch* and pray)":

All Christianity concentrates on the man at the crossroads. . . . The instant is really awful; and it is because our religion has intensely felt the instant, that it has in literature dealt much with battle and in theology dealt much with hell. It is full of *danger*, like a boy's book: it is at an immortal crisis.[1]

The Church, by its teaching, makes choice a terribly significant act, fraught with eternal consequences for the soul. And precisely because choice is made so significant, because each point in time opens toward eternity, the Church cannot replace the choosing process.

It may be objected that the Church allows men to choose (because who, after all, *can* take away that right?) but that her authoritative teaching narrows the range of choice—allows the Catholic, in effect, but one choice: to obey, or not to obey. Man, in this view, is free only to make the first and last act—submission. Once this is made, all is mapped for him, all other decisions are included in that one. There is a profound truth hidden and caricatured in this oversimple objection to the moral authority of the Church; but truth so masked is not much better than a falsehood. The hidden truth is that all free acts should eventually lead to or come from one ultimate act of homage—which can only be made directly to God, if we are to avoid idolatry. The surface falsehood is that this act of adoration introduces a consequent atrophy of man's faculties, makes intellect and will superfluous once this most profoundly human act has been elicited, disqualifies man for the honest appraisal of reality. In this view obedience must be perfected at the cost of intellect and initiative, making man a holy zombie who serves his Creator by, in effect, uncreating himself.

The confusion arises from a misunderstanding of the phrase "freedom of conscience." There have been theological differences over the meaning of these words in the past; but they have been adopted, now, by secularists who give them *no* theological meaning. This drift was evident even in Newman's day, so that, as he said, freedom of conscience had come to mean freedom *from* conscience.[2] Freedom of conscience is not the freedom to do what one wants, what one thinks best for oneself, what seems noble in itself, or consonant with one's dignity. It is not "a long-sighted selfishness, nor a desire to be consistent with oneself."[3] Conscience implies a recognition that one is *bound* to do things, *obliged*. And reflection on this universal notion that we *must* do this or avoid that leads, as Newman argued, to the very roots of our personality: personality looks out, always, at another Person, either at the idealized "person" who possesses the Reason of the rationalist or the Humanity of the humanist, or (for those who have read this mysterious dependence more accurately) at God. Man's very nobility, his isolation from lesser creatures, his independent intellect and will, lead to a higher form of dependence. His thought is always a *logos*, a word spoken, a communication, something addressed to another.[4] His deepest need is to love another and be loved. Because of his high faculties, his very being is a being-toward other things, a contemplative and appetitive openness toward reality from which lower creatures are sealed off. Man's highest knowing is always a knowing *with* (*con*-scientia, *syn*-eidesis), his highest form of having is a having *with*: *Nullius boni sine consortio potest esse fecunda possessio* ("There is no sure having of a good thing that is not also a sharing of its good, since to get is to beget").[5] Furthermore, his acts of reason are tested by reason itself—and reason is the act of a person. He judges his own moral acts against a higher rectitude of will—and only a person wills.

Thus, in a thousand ways, man's acts reveal themselves as related to another, as an accountability in that other's presence: "Conscience implies a relation between the soul and something exterior, and that, moreover, superior to itself; a relation to an excellence which it does not possess, and to a tribunal over which it has no power."[6] This is not merely a sense of the Good, or Beautiful, which can be rested in and controlled. Conscience is the recognition that one *must* choose the Good or Beautiful, not as compelled by a good or beautiful thing in itself (which would be idolatry, submission to something less than man, below his dignity as a person). Obligation is of one *person* to another:

Conscience does not repose on itself, but vaguely reaches forward to something beyond self for its decisions, as is evidenced in that keen sense of obligation and responsibility which informs them. And hence it is that we are accustomed to speak of conscience as a voice, a term which we should never think of applying to the sense of the beautiful; and moreover a voice, or the echo of a voice, imperative and constraining, like no other dictate in the whole of our experience. . . . Inanimate things cannot stir our affections; these are correlative with persons. If, as is the case, we feel responsibility, are ashamed, are frightened, at transgressing the voice of conscience, this implies that there is One to whom we are responsible, before whom we are ashamed, whose claims upon us we fear.[7]

This experience is partially repeated or prefigured in our dealings with other men. We recognize claims upon us, we owe others loyalty or obedience or gratitude. But all such claims are judged against a higher claim: those who recognize no God must, to turn Voltaire's dictum around, invent some ideal person, some "superego" or "unconscious of the race," some abstract bearer of such rationality or benevolence as can *exact* their likeness from us.[8] Conscience, if it does not answer to a Person, answers to the abstract (i.e., impersonal) "person" which alone gives conscience a residue of meaning in some modern moral systems. Freedom of conscience is based on the recognition of the higher authority of God (or some substitute for God). It means that no third person can intervene to break this bond between God and the individual, can annul the dictates of this voice—just as freedom to marry means that no third person can make or break the partners' own vows to each other. Should a man's relationship, not with this higher authority, but merely with *himself* become the only source of norms for his moral acts, he can no more claim to possess "freedom of conscience," he can no more make an act of conscience, than he can be a married bachelor or a religious atheist.[9] Conscience, like marriage, like *re-ligio,* is binding; it obliges; it prevents usurpation on the part of lesser authorities by asserting man's prior subjection to the *supreme* authority. In Newman's words,

It *commands,* it praises, it blames, it threatens, it implies a future, and it witnesses of the unseen. It is more than a man's own self . . . from the nature of the case, its very existence carries on our minds to a Being exterior to ourselves; for else, whence did it come? and to a being superior to ourselves; else whence its strange, troublesome peremptoriness? . . . Its very existence throws us out of ourselves and beyond ourselves, to go and seek for Him in the height and depth, whose voice it is. As the sunshine implies that the sun is in the heavens, though we may not see it, as a knocking at our doors at night implies the presence of one outside in the dark who asks for admittance, so this Word within us, not only instructs us up to a certain point, but necessarily raises our minds to the idea of a Teacher, an unseen Teacher.[10]

Conscience is therefore man's channel of direct communication with God, of commands coming from him. It keeps a way open, a bridge or *pons,* between divinity's solicitings and man's devout attentiveness, so that Newman calls it the *pontifex primus:*

Conscience is the aboriginal Vicar of Christ, a prophet in its informations, a monarch in its peremptoriness, a priest in its blessings and anathemas, and, even though the eternal priesthood throughout the Church could cease to be, in it the sacerdotal principle would remain and would have a sway.[11]

Freedom of conscience does not mean that one can ignore this authoritative voice, but that nothing external can take its place. No one can act as his conscience *for* a man; it is *his* act, his living link with, his receiver of, God's voice:

Conscience is a personal guide, and I use it because I must use myself; I am as little able to think by any mind but my own as to breathe with another's lungs. Conscience is nearer to me than any other means of knowledge.[12]

By placing man in the presence of that Person he must above all others please, conscience is "adapted for the communication to *each separately* of that knowledge which is most momentous to him individually."[13] Its task is "to tell us duty on every emergency, to instruct us in detail."[14]

Part of the confusion that has made freedom of conscience stand for freedom as such comes from the fact that conscience is not only a sanction for right action, having the imperatve authority of the divine voice; it is also the *critical* faculty which weighs the morality of each individual act. In its first aspect, conscience looks to the *why* of morality, and makes man obedient to authority; in the second aspect, it looks to the *how* of moral life, and makes man discover the means of obeying God when faced with practical alternatives.[15] These two sides of the matter are complementary, mutually necessary; and fortunately they have each been the object of a searching analysis—the former by Newman, the latter by Thomas Aquinas. Newman was especially interested in the passive side of man's duty—in conscience as *commanding* right action. St. Thomas concerned himself more with the active role of man in discerning what right conduct is. By his etymology, *con-scientia* is a knowing of particulars *along with,* or as measured *up against,* the norms of rational action.[16] And this involves judgment, prudence, choice. The need for making this measurement from act to act has led some men to talk of conscience as if it were simply a principle of idiosyncratic estimate, of choice as somehow separated from the imperative of pleasing a present God in all one's choices. Yet personal choice flows from this imperative, since man is not given a revelation on each event or idea that comes before him. The revelation we have been granted is from the God who created nature, and who sent a super-natural revelation as nature's "complement, re-assertion, issue, em-bodiment, and interpretation."[17] Conscience, if it is to carry God's command, must do so through the channels God ordains—through the structure of reality made available to the intellect. Natural law and supernatural law give us a set of commands, but the application of these to the material of actual choice is not made for us by God or by any of his vicars—only by Newman's "aboriginal vicar," con-science.

St. Thomas tells us that the practical reason acts, in reaching a judgment that binds in conscience, somewhat as the speculative reason works in reaching a conclusion in the demonstrative order. As the minor premise of a syllogism specifies the principle stated in the major, making the conclusion follow of necessity, so the facts of a moral situation specify the moral law, leading to a morally neces-sary decision:[18]

—I must not commit usury.

—Taking *this amount* of interest on a loan is usury.

—I must not take this amount of interest on a loan.

In the act of conscience, there is no *descent,* or *motion away* from the voice of God. The conclusion has the same "ought" force that the major does. But the middle term is of a different order—an "is" proposition. Newman, one supposes, would think of conscience as looking at God in and through the particular realities man con-fronts in the act of choice; and the "majors" of the moral law he would consider a *frame* focusing one's vision in the area where God is to be found, at each instant, and followed. Conscience is not pri-marily introspective, a searching of one's own motive, turned back on one's own act. It is, rather, the searchlight of action, turned outward to find God: "Let thy eyes look straight on, and let thy eyelids go before thy steps" (Prov. 4.25). All of the paradoxes of the Christian attitude toward the world are contained in this quest for the God who is acting with and in one, making authoritative the very light that *seeks* him: the Christian ascetic does not seal himself off from the world to find God, but goes in and through it. Like Augustine, we go out to search for what was most intimate to us all the time: *Ego foris eram, et tu intus*. God is our source *and goal*.

The whole of this complex process cannot be encompassed in St. Thomas' illustrative moral "syllogism." He himself points out that it is not a strict demonstration in the speculative order.[19] But it is a useful parallel, so long as one remembers its limitations. It *does* put in a vivid way the different elements that enter into the act of conscience. The "major" is an imperative of the moral law as grasped by Newman's "conscience" or St. Thomas' "synderesis." The conclusion is the same imperative made specific to one person at one point in his life. But the thing that gives it this greater specificity is a judgment of fact made in the "minor."

We considered the same kind of "syllogism" at a different level when we talked about Father de Soras' "historico-prudential" category of teaching, qualified as that is by Father Murray's "historical middle term." There the conclusion was not an individual's act of conscience, but a statement of duty in terms partly specific and partly general. In mediaeval times, for instance, the facts and conventions and categories available to men went into their judgments of specific acts: taking any interest on a loan was conceived as a necessarily non-productive exploitation of man's need. The conclusion reached from such a middle term was that taking interest is usurious in itself. At present the facts, and men's estimate of them, have become far more complex, and a middle term is far more difficult to formulate. And even when this statement of economic fact is formulated with the proper delicacy, the substantiating of it in particular circumstances takes balance and discernment. As Pius XII said of a comparably difficult moral situation—a healthy pluralistic society—"Before all else, the Catholic statesman must judge if this condition is verified in the concrete—and this is the 'question of fact.' "[20]

For no matter how the Church specifies her universal teachings of the historico-prudential sort, the "conclusion" must remain a *general* directive for all the faithful, while the act of conscience is particular in the strictest sense. It tells the individual what he must do in a set of concrete circumstances no one else shares with him.[21] The Pope, a Bishop, a confessor, can supply necessary elements for making the act of conscience, can explain the moral law, the Church's directives; but the obligation must be grasped by the individual if he is to be capable of making a moral act at all. And it will be grasped with a particularity that gives conscience its immediacy and absolute sanction. There is no escaping the command of conscience, precisely because its "middle term" is the individual's own act of existing in a unique relationship with other existents, with a specific range of alternatives, and a specific equipment for judging these realities. As Msgr. Nedoncelle writes,

Our experience of the short or long term results of our actions, the influence of our love or hatred of given leaders, information received (and, of course, the historical momentum of the groups in which we have been brought up), reflection on the changing nature of circumstances, etc., all combine to give their verdict and are involved in the authority of conscience itself. St. Thomas Aquinas clearly saw that synderesis is only one of the factors in total judgment.[22]

Other laws must allow for things not foreseen in their formulations, must leave room for equity, for extenuating circumstance, for immunity, for exceptions. But conscience binds with unique finality precisely because all of these things go into its command; it need not adjust its terms to allow for any act but the specific one it orders, since its decision is reached, its command issued, only for the single act. This is the reason that even an erroneous decision is binding.[23] Man must follow his conscience, even when the information that was the best he could get remains incorrect; otherwise, omniscience would be a necessary condition for a moral act. The act of conscience mobilizes all the knowledge available for making a responsible choice. And just as the strictly demonstrative syllogism can form a logical necessity without making the conclusion true in the existential order, so the "syllogism" moving from synderesis to conscience forms a moral necessity, even when the facts are different from the presentation of them in the middle term.

In some cases, the very principles out of which the Church's prudential teaching arises may call for an act of conscience that seems to go counter to it. For instance: a doctor who had reached and tested a new conclusion on, say, the treatment of ectopic pregnancy might be obliged, by his responsibility for the life put in his hands, to follow a different procedure than the one that had been formulated as the policy of his Bishop; it might oblige him to do this before the theologians have had time to become acquainted with these facts and reformulate moral teaching under the Bishop's guidance. Such a decision would involve, of course, an understanding on the doctor's part of the moral principles at work in the original policy. And it is precisely such understanding that the encyclicals, with their discursive mode of presentation and their teaching on prudence, are meant to further. The Church must teach man according to the principles that are at work in his own act of conscience, if the Catholic is to be able to relate moral law to the realities that call for its exercise, if this law is to enter into the binding legislation of conscience. Furthermore, in the Church's teaching, it is precisely the structure of the moral act that is being taught whenever a specific moral duty is enjoined. This is the reason Newman wrote "I shall drink—to the Pope, if you please— still, to Conscience first, and to the Pope afterwards."[24] As Father Congar remarked of this sentence, "It is the honoring of the first toast that would give meaning and value to the second."[25]

In the encyclicals that have to do with social and economic and political action, there is continued reference to the normative role of prudence. That is, the kind of decision suggested by the case of a doctor who must save a life with new information is very close to the *normal* situation for one at work on the shifting scene of political activity. No one formula can be taken by the Catholic as a simple answer to such problems. The *process* and *principles* of Catholic social thought must be understood, as we saw when we considered the adjustments that Catholics made, and were praised for making, when dealing with Leo XIII's doctrine on the guilds. But to raise the subject of prudence is to introduce a factor of first importance into the act of conscience, a factor I deliberately left out in the preceding paragraphs, to keep the "model" of that act simple in its first exposition.

So far we have considered only the judgment of present fact that goes into the "middle term" of an act of conscience. But since decisions of the practical intellect are concerned with alternative means to an end,[26] they look forward. *Prudentia*, says St. Thomas, is oriented to the future (*porro videns*).[27] Thus the "minor" of an act of conscience that involves a prudential choice will have a doubly contingent nature: as concerned with historical particulars of the present situation,[28] and as concerned with the future effects of an action, which, insofar as they are future, are unknowable in themselves.[29] And since political virtue is prudence exercised in the area of the common good,[30] all acts of conscience that are concerned with the political must have this two-fold contingency.

It is in the nature of prudence that we find the nexus between the subjective act of conscience and the objective order of Providence. St. Thomas says that the principal constituent of prudence is "foresight" (*providentia*).[31] Human foresight is concerned with things that are not necessary, since the future has not been determined in act. But necessity is the condition of true knowledge. How, then, is prudence to operate?

Future things are necessary as they are present to God's timeless vision, his Providence. Since these divine determinations are not open to man's knowledge in themselves, man can only know Divine Providence in its actual fulfillment—in the events of the past and present. On these necessary events man bases his "educated guesses" about the future.[32] Thus it is essential to know the mode in which God's Providence is discernible in history. It is not to be sought in the manifest signs some men demand of God, but in created nature with its regular patterns and in the specific revelation made to men "darkly as in a mirror." The man for instance who would base his estimate of the future on the certitude that the Church has an unfailing wisdom in its earthly government would be *imprudent*; he would not have contemplated and understood the *history* of the Church. The man who would base a decision on the belief that grace cancels nature, or on the expectation that miracle will foreseeably contravene the natural order of things, would be imprudent; he would have misread the impact of grace on events of the past, or ignored the scriptural mode of revealing divine truth. Prudence demands a submission to the ordinary operation of God's Providence.

And, paradoxically, by this very submission man overcomes determinism. Using his "foresight" about the probable effect of various actions, man *affects* the future; he helps to determine it as it is "foreseen" (i.e., *seen*) by God. The mystery of knowledge (which deals with things already *ordered*) and free will (which deals with things as open to ordination) interact, to make man actually participate in God's providential government of the universe.[33] This is the reason prudence is put at the head of the cardinal virtues. By its light, man incorporates reality's laws in his own action, lives intimately in the rhythm of created order, and helps enact that order. He *enacts the truth*, as Scripture puts it (ποιῶν τὴν ἀλήθειαν, John 3.21, ἀληθεύοντες, Eph. 4.15).

The Church's social teaching comes out of the very heart of this scriptural understanding of Providence, which St. Thomas helps us interpret by his teaching on prudence. Pius XII said of the section on prudence in the *Summa*:

His treatise shows his understanding of a sense of personal activity and of actuality, which contains whatever true and positive elements there may be in 'ethics according to the situation,' while avoiding its confusion and wandering from the truth.[34]

As an example of the interplay between papal teaching and the conscience of the faithful, we might look at recent Popes' treatment of the subject of international order. No other matter in current politics is in the same degree presented as "settled." We are told that there is no more room for debate. For a Catholic to disagree with those who assure him that this is the case, is to invite censure as a renegade. Yet, after all, papal teaching on the formation of an international organization under the difficult circumstances of modern politics is bound to call upon the resources of prudence, and to leave *some* room for discussion of the way to proceed. How much room? What precisely is enjoined, and how far does this close debate? Does it not, in some areas at least, *open* debate, focus it and make it fruitful?

It is impossible, of course, to give the specific "syllogism" that the individual Catholic conscience would form at a certain moment in this discussion. But a schematic presentation of the main points at issue might go something like this:

—Major: Because of the Church's teaching, based on the natural law as that is discovered by reason and confirmed by faith, I am obliged to support the most inclusive organization or organizations that, based on the moral law and a true understanding of society, can effectively promote peace, and particularly disarmament.

—Minor: The United Nations is presently the most inclusive organization that, based on the moral law and a true understanding of society, can effectively promote peace, and particularly disarmament.

—Conclusion: Because of the Church's teaching, based on the natural law as that is discovered by reason and confirmed by faith, I am obliged to support the United Nations.

Needless to say, this purely illustrative "syllogism" does not exhaust the matter of obligation in the international order. Even if it were not necessary to support some measure because of the Church's teaching, it might be incumbent on a Catholic to do so for other reasons; or if not incumbent, advisable. And even if the United Nations were to be rejected because of some judgment of fact in the minor, one would still be obliged to seek a way of realizing the aim of the major. The demands of morality in this area cannot be reduced to a single decision. Moreover, I am not presenting this particular "syllogism" as the most accurate treatment of the real problems, since I am concerned only with procedure. But I think this model cuts close enough to the real issues to stand as an example, which is all that is needed. If it be argued that I have overlooked something—though I did not mean to, and shall be sorry to hear of it—the omission will not affect the essential point: even with a more accurate presentation of the Church's teaching, and with a decision rendered on the questions of fact (no such decision will be given here), one would still have to proceed by way of such a prudential act of conscience as I outline here. These reservations made, turn to the model I propose, in each of its terms:

I. THE "MAJOR"

Other kinds of teaching would proceed from a different introductory formula. In matters of direct revelation, the Pope would not have the constant reference to natural law that is evident in the discussion of good political order. But in this area, Pius XII spoke of "the unchangeable order which God our Creator and Redeemer has shown us through the Natural Law and Revelation, that two-fold manifestation to which Leo XIII appeals in his Encyclical [*Rerum Novarum*]."[35] The "am obliged" of any major will be calibrated to correspond with the terminological rigor used by the Pope. Without deciding the exact degree of urgency that has been registered in this matter of international organizations, it is enough for our purposes to recognize that it is a weighty one.

It would take some discussion to get all the elements of papal teaching expressed, in their proper relationship to each other, within a single proposition. This difficulty in formulating the obligation, even in its most general terms, arises from the fact that the Pope has not made a single inclusive pronouncement on these matters—the kind of formulation one finds, for instance, in *Casti Connubii*'s treatment of artificial contraceptives. For even the major here involves a number of contingent facts and prudential judgments. The stress on disarmament would not have been the same in a different era. For that matter, this teaching would not have been advanced in times when international organization was a physical impossibility. To this extent, the major is part of a soritical series stretching back through several larger generalizations about our historical situation.[36] But I think it safe to say that a study of the Popes' words—primarily of Pius XII's Christmas messages and allocutions, and of John XXIII's *Pacem in Terris*—would lead any responsible Catholic to accept some such major as the starting point of his act of conscience in this area.

There are some who would demand more specificity in the major, who would not, for instance, allow any talk of "organization or organizations." They flatly say that the Pope commands us to support the UN, that this is our only possible "major," that no "minor" looking toward the complexities of the real situation can discernibly qualify an order so direct. As we saw in the chapter oh terminology, this claim is most easily, and so most frequently, made by citing the Popes' praise or congratulations or hopes expressed for the UN as if these were policy statements to be subscribed to by every Catholic voter. But such words of encouragement— whether addressed to the League of Nations, the UN, the World Federalist Movement, the European Coal and Steel Community, the ILO—are not prudential judgments on the success of the organizations in *achieving* their aims, nor a judgment on alternative mechanisms for attempting these tasks.

It would be very strange if the Pope, who does not command men to accept this or that form of political or economic organization at the national level, were to endorse one specific form of international framework. One may argue that the UN is the only possible or likely channel for an organization with the kind of authority the Pope has called for, but that precisely *is* an argument, and involves the sort of minor I have supplied in our model. We do not begin with a specific injunction that can be slipped, without reference to the difficulties of the prudential order, into the conscience of every Catholic. The Pope's own attitude in this was expressed by Pius XII in 1951:

Statesmen, and at times even churchmen, who want to make the Spouse of Christ their ally or the instruments of their political alliances, either national or international, would do injury to the very essence of the Church and would inflict damage on the life which is proper to her; in a word they would bring Her down to the same level on which conflicting temporal interests are locked in struggle. And this is and remains true even where there is question of ends and interests legitimate in themselves. Whoever then would wish to detach the Church from her supposed neutrality, or bring pressure to bear on her in the question of peace, or diminish her right to determine whether, when, or how she may wish to come to a decision in the various conflicts, such a one would not make the Church's co-operation in the work of peace easier. For any decision on the Church's part, even in political questions, can never be purely political, but must always be *sub specie aeternitatis,* in the light of

divine law, of its order, its values, its standards. . . . The Church
cannot consent to judge according to exclusively political norms.
She cannot tie the interests of religion to particular policies of a
purely earthly scope. She cannot run the risk of giving any reason
for doubting about her religious character.[37]

After each papal reference to the UN, those inclined to find a
direct command in these references have, predictably, found it.
Some examples were considered in Chapter five; from three different sources in Pius XII, Mr. Clancy, Father Graham, and Mr. Mc-
Donald told Catholics that it was now formal: the Pope had made
belief in the UN a necessary part of every Catholic's faith. More
recently, men have rediscovered this mandate in Pope John's social
encyclicals. (Since the earlier interpretations never seem to "take,"
these critics usually forget that they have already established the
obligation; as each new document comes out, they present *it* as the
one that makes the matter clear at last.) At first, in *Mater et Magistra,* the simple command had to be constructed out of kind words
addressed to the FAO and ILO; and even from such unpromising
materials the desired command was patched together.[38] Then came
Pacem in Terris, which *did* discuss the duty of forming an effective
international authority, and gave more direct praise to the UN.
With such promising material available, the publication of the
Pope's command was no longer left to individuals and groups. A
general impression got abroad that there was an irrevocable Catholic "line" on the UN. So strong was this impression, so bolstered
by apparent authority, that even a man who was naturally skeptical
about the matter, and unwilling to think that the Church makes
such simplistic pronouncements, had reluctantly to conclude that
it had done so in this case. Reinhold Niebuhr wrote:

Pacem in Terris had the disadvantage of proclaiming the rather
easy optimism which has characterized classical liberalism, with its
disregard for the power realities of the political order. Thus Pope
John declared "It is Our earnest wish that the United Nations Organization—in its structure and its means—may become ever more
equal to the magnitude and nobility of its tasks. May the day soon
come when every human being will find therein an effective safeguard for the rights which derive directly from his dignity as a
person." The concept of the UN as an embryo world government
is breathtaking. It is so breathtaking, it cannot be shared by even

the staunchest advocates of the UN. It disregards the power realities of the cold war, and seems to be of a piece with the sort of liberalism which animates all proponents of world government.[39]

That is, even Niebuhr, like so many *Catholics* before him, quotes one of those expressions of good will and hope that should not be read as a command. The Pope hopes that the UN may make itself more adequate to its stated task, that it may "be able to adjust its structure and appropriate instruments" to the task (*valeat formam atque idonea instrumenta sua . . . accommodare*). There is an implication that the UN is not presently adequate to its tasks—a judgment that is more than implied in an earlier section (par. 134-5, 140-1), where it is said that changes must be made in the present international structure. In the passage Niebuhr cites, Pope John, who had described the UN's Declaration of Human Rights as a kind of step in the right direction (*quidam quasi gradus atque aditus*), most urgently wishes (*vehementer expetimus*) that the organization might be able to protect human rights effectively (*humanae personae jura efficienter tueri possit*). It is true that the English translation did Niebuhr no service, with its extra little flourishes (like the insertion of "every human being will find," corresponding to nothing in the Latin, and the omission of the proper subject with *possit*). But even when men are dealing with the English version, they are not justified in taking this passage as the core of the Pope's teaching on international authority, and then, on the basis of this, rebuking him for a lack of realism.

Others gave the words that went before the passage cited by Niebuhr as *their* proof that Pope John was issuing an order to Catholics. This is the way that passage went in the English version released to the press:

Some objections and reservations were raised regarding certain points in the Declaration [of Human Rights]. There is no doubt, however, that the document represents an important step on the path towards the juridical-political organization of the world community.

Again, even in the English translation, this praise of a step in the right direction is hardly a command. And the passage is much less imposing in the original:

Nos sane non praeterit, quaedam Professionis hujus capita minus probanda nonnullis visa esse; neque id immerito. Nihilominus Professionem eandem habendam esse censemus quendam quasi gradum atque aditum ad juridicialem politicamque ordinationem constituendam omnium populorum qui in mundo sunt.

The English leaves out *neque id immerito*: "It does not escape us, indeed, that certain points in this Declaration seemed to some— *and not without cause*—less acceptable." It translates *quidam quasi gradus atque aditus* ("some sort of advance" in the direction of a juridical and political structure) as "an *important* step along the path," and turns "nonetheless We think" into "there is no doubt."[40]

But enough of the peripheral phrases dear to simplifiers. The Pope devoted a long section of this long encyclical to the subject of *publica universalis auctoritas*. Taking this in its entirety, can we justly say it is unrealistic, a form of naïve world-governmentism?

To make that judgment is to miss the entire point of the encyclical. Pope John's approach is first and foremost realistic. He begins from the fact that the present order is not adequate for giving security and ending the arms race (pars. 134-5, 140-1). And the first qualifying characteristic, the immediate test, of any change in this situation must be its ability to overcome this shortcoming. It must, above all, *work*:

There exists an intrinsic connection between the common good on the one hand and the structure and function of public authority on the other. The moral order which needs public authority in order to promote the common good in civil society, requires also that the authority be effective in attaining that end. This demands that the organs through which the authority is formed, becomes operative and pursues its ends, must be composed and act in such a manner as to be capable of furthering the common good by ways and means which correspond to the developing situation.[41]

And what precisely must be rectified in the present situation, to make it work? The Pope indicates the need in these words:

The public authorities of the individual nations—being placed as they are on a footing of equality one with the other—no matter how much they multiply their meetings or sharpen their wits in efforts to draw up new juridical instruments, they are no longer capable of facing the task of finding an adequate solution to the problems mentioned above. And this is not due to a lack of good will or of a spirit of enterprise, but because their authority lacks suitable force.[42]

The task is to give their authority (*ipsorum auctoritas*) suitable force (*idonea potestas*) in a structure that would look to the *universal* common good, and not merely to the good of each nation acting as an independent bargaining agent. That system of bargaining served the common good in the past (par. 134), but it is not doing so now. What form (*ordinatio, constitutio*) would this authority take? In accord with Vatican neutrality, the Pope does not prescribe a specific organizational mode; he only warns against the dangers to be avoided in any political form. His comments are all directed to what this public authority must *not* be:

1) It must not suffer the defects arising from the present system of action by equals dealing primarily for their own advantage (pars. 134-5).

2) Yet in forming a higher society, the nations must remain a) free to join of their own accord (par. 138), b) primarily responsible for their own destiny (pars. 92, 123), and c) possessed of all authority over their own actions, except that absolutely necessary to the higher authority's task of preserving peace (pars. 139-41).

3) The higher authority must be effectively prevented from a) letting component nations usurp the power belonging to the whole community of men (par. 138, compare pars. 87-8, 120), and b) from taking legitimate authority away from the lesser bodies, or diminishing their ability to handle their own problems (pars. 139-41).

Does this sound like the naïve love of world government that Niebuhr criticizes? Does the Pope make fun of those who are chary of surrendering sovereignty to a community so heterogeneous and hard to influence as a world executive must be? He writes

There would be reason to fear that a supranational or world-wide public authority, imposed by force by the more powerful political communities, might be or might become an instrument of one-sided interests; and even should this not happen, it would be difficult for it to avoid all suspicion of partiality in its actions, and this would take from the efficacy of its activity. Even though there may be pronounced differences between political communities as regards the degree of their economic development and their military power, they are all very sensitive as regards their juridical equality and their moral dignity. For that reason, they are right in not easily yielding in obedience to an authority imposed by force, or to an authority in whose creation they had no part, or to which they themselves did not decide to submit by conscious and free choice.[43]

Or are we to think of this *publica auctoritas* as replacing the authority of the nations themselves? Yet the Pope says the *universalis auctoritas* is justified precisely because it is necessary for restoring to each nation that *idonea potestas* that is lacking in the present arrangement (par. 141):

The public authority of the world community is not intended to limit the sphere of action of the public authority of the individual political community, much less take its place. On the contrary, its purpose is to create, on a world basis, an environment (*rerum status*) in which the public authorities of each political community, its citizens and intermediate associations, can carry out ther tasks, fulfill their duties and exercise [more properly, "protect," *sua jura vindicare*] their rights with greater security.

Or does the Pope say that the nations of the world are obsolete as political units? The English translation does suggest this in places, but only by blurring the exact terminology used by the Pope. Twice we are told in English that the present system *cannot* work any longer, where the Latin simply says that it *is* not working.[44] *Universalis auctoritas* is translated by various English phrases, such as "a supernational or world-wide public authority" (par. 138). *Public authority* itself is made to sound as if it were a *world government,* by the fact that the English refers to "public authorities" where the Latin describes the efforts of particular rulers and governments (*rerum publicarum rectores, moderatores, etc.*). This distinction between the *authority* that the common good has in any society and the *instruments* adopted for enforcing that authority cannot be dismissed as trivial in a document that puts heavy stress on the very difference. This can be illustrated by five points within the encyclical itself:

1) When discussing the juridical force of all public authority, in Part II of his letter, Pope John enunciates the distinction between authority and the agents that enforce it. In the case of a decided clash between the two, the Pope says that when rulers are not basing their actions on the natural law their orders have no juridical force (pars. 61, 49-54). Furthermore, even when an administrative system is founded on right principle, it will never be entirely adequate to its task: "And yet, social life in the modern world is so varied, complex and dynamic that even a juridical structure which has been prudently and thoughtfully established is always inadequate for the needs of society" (par. 71). This is said of the national governments. It must of necessity be more true for the international order. That is, when asking that the instruments for upholding universal authority be adequate to their task, the Pope is not expecting some magic solution to all the problems, as Niebuhr seems to think. It was, no doubt, the teaching of paragraph 71 that made Father John Courtney Murray list first, among the important new things in this encyclical, "the distinction between society and the state." Thus there is no warrant for translating the *universalis auctoritas* into a specific kind of world government or federation as *the* papal prescription. Such an organization may justify itself by the norms the Pope offers, but that will be through the kind of factual judgment treated here as the "minor."

2) The Pope said that at one time the *rerum publicarum rectores* did provide for the universal common good through normal diplomatic channels—which shows that the *publica auctoritas,* the international law based on a universal common good, could conceivably be administered without a world government—that the two are not synonymous. And if changes are to be made in the current situation, they are to restore, so far as possible, the conditions in which nations responsible for their own citizens will be working, as well, for the common good of *all* men (pars. 139-41).

3) The whole of Part II, devoted as it is to the traditional Catholic teaching on political authority, directly affects the question of international order—a connection that Pius XII often made in express terms. That is, such authority must be based on a consensus concerning the natural law and the derivation of authority from

God; it must oblige its citizens morally because of this consensus; it must consult this consensus in all its acts. In short, law arises from social unity, expresses and stabilizes it; it cannot *create* this unity by being imposed on elements that do not recognize a common authority.[45]

4) The Pope is very careful to state the need for a *publica universalis auctoritas* in terms which do not impose any one organization or procedural mode. The difficulties are immense, and must be met with the greatest prudential originality. Had the reigning Pope told the framers of the American constitution how to draw up their document, he would have been worse than imprudent. A new situation called, then, for new insights into the nature of federalism as a protection of freedom. We face such a situation today, and nothing the Pope has said acts as a barrier to a comparable originality; he merely tells us what must be avoided. The complexity of the task is suggested by the Pope when he describes the elements that must go into it and be protected:

Fickleness of opinion often produces this error: many think that the relationships between men and States can be governed by the same laws as the forces and irrational elements of the universe, whereas the laws governing them are of quite a different kind and are to be sought elsewhere, namely, in the nature of man, where the Father of all things wrote them. By these laws men are most admirably taught, first of all how they should conduct their mutual dealings; then how the relationships between the citizens and the public authorities (*magistratus*) of each State should be regulated; then how States (*res publicae*) should deal with one another; and finally how, on the one hand individual men and States (*civitates*), and on the other hand the community of all peoples (*universorum gentium societas*), should act towards each other, the establishment of such a world community (*societas*) being urgently demanded today by the requirements of the universal common good.[46]

There is here no simple pyramiding, citizens dealing with each other and their State, States dealing with each other and with some super-State. The demands of world community are far more subtle and complex than such a formula could capture in its net. That the Pope was consciously allowing for all these demands can be seen from a later paragraph, in which he again describes them:

There is an immense task incumbent on all men of good will, namely, the task of restoring the relations of the human family in truth, in justice, in love and in freedom: the relations between individual human beings; between citizens and their respective political communities (*civitates*); between political communities themselves; between individuals, families, intermediate associations and political communities on the one hand, and the world community (*universorum hominum communitas*) on the other.[47]

5) This encyclical, more than any other, has devoted attention to the necessary role of prudence in formulating any specific program for attaining social good:

We deem it opportune to point out how difficult it is to understand clearly the relation between the objective requirements of justice and concrete situations, namely, to perceive the degrees and forms in which doctrinal principles and directives ought to be applied to reality.[48]

The Pope can hardly be suggesting that this effort, necessary for the forming of any political policy, is *not* necessary for dealing with the problems of the international order.

Only a very simple reading of this encyclical can lead men to think it is a simple prescription for peace. The charge might rather be made that the Pope proposes so many realistic considerations as almost to paralyze the effort. He does not mean to pretend that it is a simple job, or that we are close to its achievement. He says, it is true, that one definitive statement of the *ideal* moves in the right direction. But he also says: "Admittedly those who are endeavoring to restore the relations of social life *according to the criterions mentioned above* are not many; to them We express Our paternal appreciation, and We earnestly invite them to persevere in their work with ever greater zeal. And We are comforted by the hope that their number will increase, especially among Christian believers."[49] It would seem, then, that the first task is to acquaint people with these criteria; and only then can operational directives be issued to a real community operating effectively to achieve the aims every sane man desires to bring about, one way or another.

The Pope is idealistic only in the sense that he proposes an ideal that is demanding. Faced with it, men may say that, in the present circumstances, they are willing to settle for the UN, even if it does not satisfy all the requirements. That is a prudential decision that might be justified, but only if one knows that one *is* "settling" for something by the application of an historical "minor." Men decided to support the labor unions, even though they were not the guilds Pope Leo had in mind *and expressly urged men to form.* In the same way, men can support *various* means of consulting the universal common good, especially since Pope John did *not* tell us to subscribe to one organizational mode.

There is no basis, then, for the joy of some, or the lamentation of others (like Reinhold Niebuhr), at a non-existent papal directive "To all Catholics: Support the UN"—not, at least, if this directive is presented as the "major" of a prudential choice binding in conscience. But what of the minor?

II. The Minor

In the middle term, we come to the analysis of political realities —which involves us in two questions: Is the UN the organization with the best hope of promoting peace and disarmament by the establishment of the world authority the Popes have told us to seek? And, second, will it be the best organization for achieving this in the future? That is, we must consider the question of fact in the world today, and the probable future effect of actions we take in such a world. The second question is the more important. Even the UN's most loyal advocates do not present it as fully responsive to the needs of the present situation. Pope John made it clear he thought the present international system—largely symbolized by the UN—is inadequate.

The prudential decision a Catholic must make is whether to treat the organization as the best transitional medium in which to work for fuller recognition of the natural law, or to seek some other means. Discussion of this matter must proceed with the greatest realism. Men using the same norms might come to different conclusions; but they must work from the norms. They must neither demand an imposible perfection of any earthly society, nor act as if anything meets the Popes' conditions for the establishment of just order (conditions which would thus go the way of provisos in Msgr. Fenton's hands—becoming no conditions at all). The problem is met in each of the complex decisions, affecting the UN's fate, that men are called on to make. For instance: would the organization best promote the recognition of human rights by *demanding* this recognition from its members? Concretely, do we deepen this basic recognition, or the bond of unity between those sincerely sharing it, by expelling South Africa, or Russia, or Cuba, or Spain, or Hungary from the UN; by admitting Red China; by letting protests against Hungary or Indonesia or Portugal lapse, or by prosecuting these objections; by prosecuting them with what degree of force, applied in what way? The dimensions of the problem were suggested by Pius XII when he said:

No one expects or demands the impossible, not even from the United Nations. But one should have a right to expect that their authority should have had its weight, at least through observers, in the places in which the essential values of man are in extreme danger. Although the United Nations' condemnation of the grave violations of the rights of man and entire nations is worthy of recognition, one can nevertheless wish that, in similar cases, the exercise of their rights, as members of this organization, be denied to states which refuse even the admission of observers—thus showing that their concept of state sovereignty threatens the very foundations of the United Nations.[50]

This is from the Christmas message following the Hungarian uprising, the message in which Pope Pius warned that "a false realism is succeeding in prevailing in not a few of its members," a "realism" that disposes men to sacrifice any principle in the name of an external show of coherence. Such a façade can shelter forces of disorder, which work more effectively in the dark.

Or, again, the primary aim of an international organization—in the words of Pope Pius and Pope John[51]—must be to effect disarmament. Yet all of the attempts and agreements in this line have gone on outside the elaborate and many-nationed corridors of the UN. The same is true of the negotiations over the most seriously troubled world areas—Berlin, Lebanon, Suez, Cuba. Father John Courtney Murray even thought it safe to predict that realistic negotiation is bound to go forward in this way: "If and when any agreement on disarmament is reached, it will be reached directly between the Kremlin and the White House, without the confusing assistance of additional nations, allied or neutral."[52] Should we say, then, that the UN is doing worthy work, but not precisely the work that the Popes consider the *first* task of a public authority? That such a public authority is taking shape through channels that do not include the UN? Should all efforts be made to inject the UN's apparatus into these negotiations? Or, rather, is it false to say the UN has not been an agent in these talks, by the atmosphere it established of constant interchange? Should it consciously take on this latter, more general role, satisfying John's requirement that a *rerum status* be established in which the nations themselves can consult their own interests and, at the same time, the common good of all men?

To return to Father Murray's mention of the "confusing assistance" of nations not directly concerned in delicate negotiations, should such assistance be encouraged, made less confusing? As areas of the world become independent, and nations are carved from them, should these be given equal power in the UN? Pius and John both recommended the formation of larger political units where political and geographical ties extend beyond national lines; yet, as an African proponent of federation in larger nations has remarked, the prospect of a vote in the UN, with all the bargaining power this gives a nation for playing bloc against bloc, is a powerful enticement luring tiny sectors toward independent sovereignty. Should these smaller nations be called into disputes, in the hope that power and friction will be diffused? Or should they be kept out, on the grounds that they add to the friction by leading the big powers to compete more vigorously, each "outbidding" the other?

And, since we are touching on the matter of local mergers and alliances, are these to be encouraged as elements of at least partial unity, constituents of a larger unity to be built from them; or should they be discouraged as rivals to the main organization? Should certain alliances be permitted, but not others? For instance, should defensive pacts be treated as implicitly divisive (as formed

for defense *against* possible enemies)? Or is this a kind of false
realism? Can military alliances contribute to other forms of unity,
as Western pacts and mutual economic recovery, connected with
NATO, have contributed to the Common Market? Pius XII
seemed at times to see the union of Europe as a necessary prelude
to any higher solidarity of men. In his 1956 Christmas message, he
said "a definite need of this period—a means of insuring the whole
world's peace and a fruitful share of its goods, a force which embraces, too, the peoples of Asia, Africa and the Near East, including Palestine with its Holy Places—is the restoring of European
solidarity."[53] He praised the European Coal and Steel Community,
which was to become the Common Market, especially for the realism of its approach:

A whole set of reasons urges the nations of Europe today to federate
in an effective way. . . . A moral lesson in energy and patience
emerges from the present situation of the ECSC, for it could achieve
the substantial results thus far attained only through a long juridical and technical preparation, without which it would never have
overcome difficulties of all kinds which confronted it during the
first months.

He also reminded them that "It is surely necessary to base the attempt at political union on sure economic factors" and "There is
no thought of abolishing allegiance to one's fatherland or of fusing
races arbitrarily. Love of the fatherland flows directly from the laws
of nature."[54]

Again, should local groupings seek to make themselves acceptable to all other groups by avoiding clear statement of principles
(tenets with which some might not agree)? Or is the open profession
of these standards the best way to approach others with realism
and honesty? In particular, when confronting Communism, should
the West make its opposition to the principles of this giant system
perfectly clear, even if this means, for a while, building a society
with whatever nations can subscribe to a Western code of justice?
Pius XII wrote, in 1954:

Now a bridge cannot be built in truth between these two separate
worlds, unless it be founded on the human beings living in one and

the other of these worlds, and not on her governmental or social systems. This is so because, while one of the two parties still strives in large measure, whether consciously or unconsciously, to preserve the natural law, the system prevailing in the other has completely abandoned this basis. A one-sided supernaturalism might refuse entirely to take such an attitude into consideration, alleging the reason that we live in a redeemed world and are therefore withdrawn from the natural order; or some might say that the collectivist character of that system ought to be recognized as a "historical truth," in the sense that it too corresponds to the will of God— but these are errors to which a Catholic can by no means submit.[55]

If we are to build world unity with the Russian people, not the Russian system, is the best way to do this by refusing to recognize the system, or by actively opposing it in every way?[56] Should complete tolerance, or a minimal courtesy, be given to the evil system, so that contact may be had with the men enslaved by it? When does contact increase that slavery, decrease men's hope of liberation from it, take away their very ability to conceive an alternative?

These are just a few of the problems that spring to mind when one must assess the record and present status and future prospects of the UN. They are not easy questions; I have no answers to them. But they must all be weighed:

If the UN were effective in no other way, is it worth support as a symbol? But when is the symbolic value of its existence diluted by the maintenance of low standards of admission and performance? Can it be a cover for disruptive forces? The Popes, after all, have made effectiveness the primary note of the authority they recommend.

Does the UN fail to affect the big powers, but provide a forum for the little nations? Or do the prestige and power of membership in the UN lead to fission among the small nations and friction between the large ones? Does "polycentrism" reduce nationalism and the polarity of the Cold War? Or does the fervent nationalism of the new countries and their bartering for aid, intensify nationalistic jockeying?

An assessment of these factors would go into any specific decision on the future of the UN; and which of these complicated matters has been frozen in a formulation by the Pope? And, for that matter, we are discussing throughout the consequences of different specific choices. What does it mean, for instance, to say that one should "support the UN"? The UN is a large and complex structure, of parts not necessarily related. It is a clearing house for information, an agent of education and charity through many channels. It has a judiciary body loosely connected with it, a spasmodically active executive department (weak in Hungary, strong in Katanga), and a shadowy legislative branch. The popular assembly is undergoing rapid expansion, diffusion of responsibility, and growth of power; the reviewing council is admittedly obstructive since counter-vetos can deadlock an issue affecting the interests of the major powers. Support of the UN can mean increasing or decreasing the executive power, altering the legislative structure, directing the whole body into a supplementary role (as "clearing house" of national viewpoints), or trying to diminish the independence of its components. In fact, one of the principal arguments made by those who support the organization is that it is "moving in the right direction," a step along the way. But it is moving in *many* directions. What particular one of these directions does the Pope support, in the view of those who consider him an "advocate of the UN"? Which particular one do they think Catholics are *bound* to endorse?

Some say that the trouble with the UN is its inability to enforce laws; that it needs a strong executive. Others say that it would be foolish to try to *enforce* laws before *making* them; that a strong executive, coupled with a powerless or confused or haphazard legislature, is the formula of tyranny.

All right, comes the answer, give legislative structure to the organization by making it a real government. Others object that to form a real government at this stage, even aside from scarcely masked animosities between the major camps, would be to defy the processes of growth, solidarity, articulation that alone animate a constitution. To form a government, today, of widely varying spiritual and physical regimens would, in their view, demand an over-all regime either irrelevant or oppressive, a form trying to affect its matter from outside, a stray ghost trying to get inside a crowd of bodies at one and the same time.

It is not enough, faced with these matters, to say that the Pope has praised the FAO, or hoped out loud that the UN will become more adequate to its task, or sent an observer to UNESCO. Even if one is to support the UN, should he do this as one of its leading servants and spokesmen now does, by withering criticism of wrong directions taken, disruptive forces growing—that is: if Charles Malik were a Catholic, would he be observing or defying the simple kind of order that is published, month by month, in the Catholic press?

III. THE CONCLUSION

The conclusion given in our model is obviously unrealistic. A specific decision binding in conscience would involve, presumably, a more limited act than the simple alternative of supporting anything and everything the UN votes to do, on the one hand, or, on the other, abolishing it overnight. Only the simpleton could find no good in the organization, or no bad. Men capable of understanding a moral teaching at all will be responding to a specific question of the sort exemplified in the discussion of the minor.

Once a Catholic has in good conscience come to a conclusion, working from the major we have given, the entire force of that major descends into the conclusion—which is therefore binding with the force of natural law and revelation. A man who has reached such a decision may wonder at a neighbor, who seems to have come to a different one. And since the urgency felt by the first man is of a *divine* law incumbent on him, he may imagine that his neighbor is denying the authority of God, treating papal authority frivolously. Such a man is forgetting that an "is" judgment went into his binding act of conscience—a judgment of present fact, and an estimate of future likelihood. Almost all informed discussion should, one would think, take place at this level. Yet apparently informed men are ready to say that a person who has not reached the same conclusion on the *organizational means* of promoting the universal common good does not want to promote the universal common good at all; that a man who finds more hope for a public world authority in Europe's renaissance than in Africa's painful time of birth is simply a disbeliever in the natural law; that one who finds hope primarily in negotiations that take place outside the UN is attacking the magisterium of the Church.

Even when there is some disagreement about the major, it does not usually concern the source of man's obligation in this area, but the precise formulation of a large and complex teaching. Some men, I imagine, would deny that freedom to join or not to join is part of the major that governs discussion of labor unions; others would admit that it is part of the basic principle we start from, but that its operation must be suspended in certain instances, instances analyzed in a "minor" concerned with factual conditions in a specific organization; some will deny that such conditions could exist, or that they do exist. Few would take the first position listed, however, so the debate would again center for most men on the question of fact.

Once this basic structure of moral choice is understood by Catholic polemicists, response to papal teaching will become informed and effective. Communication between men who differ will not instantly be reduced to the open doubting of the other's good faith. Disagreement can be focused, and dealt with. It will become impossible, for instance, to quote passages against exaggerated nationalism as if they imposed the duty of surrendering sovereignty to the first candidate for world power that came along. And, conversely, it would become impossible to use the praise of national cultures, of the virtue of patriotism, as an implicit criticism of all attempts at world-wide organization. The two stresses in Catholic thought must be united in a major that takes note of both, in balance—as both are recognized in Pope Pius' words on the organic nature of a genuine society. Once this formulation is reached, on a proper level of binding statement, then application of this principle to the intractable details of political life has some chance of succeeding.

It may be objected that in considering all of the procedural possibilities for a decision of conscience—suggesting for instance, the range of problems involved in the application of papal teaching to the UN—I am making the papal teaching ineffective.[57] This contention would betray a lack of understanding about what an "effective" teaching program by the Church means to *effect*: not submission to a set of formed conclusions, but the informed activity of conscience. And conscience is the voice of responsibility; it must deal with moral complexities. To say that the modern international problems are not complex, or to suggest that the Pope takes this position, would be an insult to intelligence. The papal teaching puts moral law clearly in command of the discussion; it marshals expert knowledge, indicates lines of application, commands (with the varying degrees of stringency studied earlier) certain lines of action. But the commands are rarely particular. Because the moral law is the monitor of men's discussion, that process must terminate on the scene of man's confrontation with moral imperatives—in conscience. The papal teaching gives structure to external discourse and useful argument, but its first and last aim is to supply judicial norms and quantities of evidence to the *internal* court, where man comes to grips with obligation in its direct form:

Conscience is like the most intimate and secret nucleus of man. There he takes refuge with his spiritual faculties in absolute solitude: alone with himself, or, better still, alone with God—Whose voice conscience echoes—and with himself. There he decides for good or for evil; there he chooses the road to victory and the road to defeat. Even if he wanted to, man could never succeed in getting rid of conscience. In the company of his conscience, whether it approves or condemns, he will travel the entire road of life and, again in its company, as with a truthful and incorruptible witness, he will present himself before the judgment-seat of God. Conscience, then, to describe it with an image which is as ancient as it is appropriate, is an asylum, a sanctuary, on the threshold of which all must halt—even, if there be question of a child, father and mother. Only the priest may enter there, as a guardian of souls and minister of the sacrament of Penance. But even here conscience does not cease to be a jealously guarded sanctuary, of which God wishes the secrecy to be safeguarded with the seal of the most sacred silence.[58]

The encyclicals are not to be used as means for Catholics to judge their fellow Catholics, or even for the Pope to judge Catholics. They are not even aimed, primarily, at making it possible for a Catholic to judge problems in the modern world, except as this is involved in the fulfillment of the letters' most sacred function: they equip man to judge himself, and to endure the scrutiny of the

Judge of all men. Here is the sacred and awful authority they have; yet, in the mystery of conscience, here is the pledge that they are a liberating literature; for freedom is guarded at its inmost citadel when it is recognized and demanded in the act of conscience.

NOTES TO CHAPTER EIGHT: PRUDENCE

1. G. K. Chesterton, *Orthodoxy*, Image edition, pp. 134, 136.
2. "Letter," p. 130.
3. *Ibid.*, p. 129. *Cf. Idea of a University*, pp. 203-4: "When the mind is simply angry with itself and nothing more, surely the true import of the voice of nature and the depth of its intimations have been forgotten, and a false philosophy has misinterpreted emotions which ought to lead to God. Fear implies the transgression of a law, and a law implies a lawgiver and a judge; but the tendency of intellectual culture is to swallow up the fear in the self-reproach, and self-reproach is directed and limited to our mere sense of what is fitting and becoming. Fear carries us out of ourselves, whereas shame may act upon us only within the round of our own thoughts."
4. *Idea of a University*, p. 270: "What does Logos mean? it stands both for *reason* and for *speech,* and it is difficult to say which it means more properly. It means both at once: why? because really they cannot be divided—because they are in a true sense one. When we can separate light and illumination, life and motion, the convex and the concave of a curve, then will it be possible for thought to tread speech under foot, and to hope to do without it—then will it be conceivable that the vigorous and fertile intellect should renounce its own double, its instrument of expression, and the channel of its speculations and emotions."
5. This compressed text from Richard of St. Victor is given brilliant exposition in the first chapter of Frederick Wilhelmsen's *The Metaphysics of Love* (Sheed and Ward, 1962).
6. From manuscript of Newman printed in Boekraad and Tristram, *The Argument From Conscience to the Existence of God According to J. H. Newman* (Louvain, 1961), p. 113.
7. *Grammar of Assent*, pp. 99, 101. Freedom arises from a consciousness that one can execute one's own acts, that one is responsible *for* them; freedom of conscience is the awareness that one is responsible *to* certain laws and to their Author. In St. Paul's analysis, one goes from the awareness of oneself as being in a legislative situation to the possibility that the law by which one prefers and rejects can be cited against oneself as well as others, and from this to an awareness of the supreme scrutiny man undergoes at the hands of the supreme Judge: "There are times when they [the Gentiles] carry out the precepts of the law unbidden, finding in their own natures a rule to guide them, in default of any other rule; and this shows that the obligations of the law are written in their hearts; their conscience utters its own testimony, and when they dispute with one another, they find themselves condemning this, approving that. And there will be a day when God (according to the gospel I preach) will pass judgment, through Jesus Christ, on the hidden thoughts of men" (Rom. 2.14-6, Knox translation).
8. Newman ms., *The Argument From Conscience* (see note 6 above), p. 118: "I have a feeling in my mind, which, as soon as I have occasion to recognize my feeling towards a parent or kind superior, I find *interpreted* by it."
9. Newman spoke of conscience as "a constituent element of the mind," such that "it cannot be resolved into any combination of principles of our nature more elementary than itself" ("Letter," p. 129). Yet this basic faculty can be impeded, its actions suspended; it can fail to reach its object. In the ms. printed in *The Argument From Conscience*, Newman wrote (p. 119) that "conscience, or the sense of an impera-

tive coercive law . . . when analyzed, i.e. reflected on, involves an inchoative recognition of a Divine Being." Yet this does not mean that this inchoative sense is the same as a fully formed one; these first motions can be extinguished or dimmed, partially or for long periods or for a lifetime. Thus Newman compares conscience to another basic action of the mind, man's memory: "After years, how easily may my memory be tampered with! You have a first and true impression—look hard at it and you lose it. Tamper with it, and it goes never to return. Distort it, and, after repeating your perversion a number of times, you will begin to believe in it, and will think you remember what you don't. Yet who will say still, that the faint representations of memory may not impress certainty? And when you get yourself back into old days, how much rises up clearly before you which you had quite forgotten! So Conscience may be improved."

10. *Occasional Sermons* V, p. 73. *Cf. Parochial and Plain Sermons,* vol. 8, pp. 24-5: "Whether He commands by a visible presence, or by a voice, or by our consciences, it matters not, so that we feel it to be a command."

11. "Letter," p. 129.

12. *Grammar,* p. 304.

13. *Ibid.*

14. *Discourses to Mixed Congregations,* p. 84.

15. These distinctions are made by Newman, *Grammar,* pp. 98-9.

16. Newman's conscience as sanction corresponds in some ways to St. Thomas' "synderesis," or grasp upon the basic principles of the natural law precisely as coming from a Legislator (*S.T.* I-II, q. 94, a. 1, ad 2). Conscience as a rule of right conduct in the individual action is the decision rendered on particulars in the light of the principles held by synderesis; and this Thomas calls conscience in the strictest sense, though he recognizes the wider and more popular usage, by which men talk of conscience not merely as evaluating an act but as passing sentence on it (*S.T.* I, q. 79, a. 13, ad 1 *et resp.*).

17. "Letter," p. 133.

18. For the analogy, *cf. In II Sent.* d. 24, q. 3, a. 4, *De Ver.* q. 17, a. 2, *S.T.* I, q. 79, arts. 12, 13, *C.G.* III, 97 (12). St. Thomas' etymological illustration, *cum (alio) scientia,* parallels the *syn (logōi) logos* of the verb *(syllogizomai)* on which "syllogism" is based.

19. *C.G.* III, 97 (12).

20. Yzermans I, p. 274.

21. Newman, "Letter," p. 134.

22. "Reflections on the Authority of Conscience," in Todd, *Problems of Authority,* p. 191.

23. St. Thomas, *In II Sent.* d. 24, q. 3, a. 4, *De Ver.* q. 17, a. 2, *S.T.* I-II, q. 19, a. 5. And see John Courtney Murray, *Theological Studies* 6, pp. 256-62, Msgr. Nedoncelle, *Problems of Authority,* pp. 197-8

24. "Letter," p. 138

25. *Laity, Church and World,* p. 26.

26. *C.G.* III, 97 (12).

27. *S.T.* II-II, q. 47, a. 1, *resp.,* q. 49, a. 6, ad 1.

28. *S.T.* II-II, q. 47, a. 3.

29. *S.T.* II-II, q. 47, a. 1, q. 49, a. 6.

30. *S.T.* II-II, q. 47, a. 10, ad 1.

31. *S.T.* II-II, q. 49, a. 6, ad 1.

32. *S.T.* II-II, q. 47, a. 1, ad 2 and a. 3, ad 2, q. 49, a. 5, ad 2.

33. *S.T.* II-II, q. 47, a. 6, I-II, q. 91, a. 2, *resp.*

34. Yzermans I, p. 212.

35. Yzermans I, p. 28.

36. The same is true of any historico-prudential teaching of the Church. At one time, a binding major for the act of conscience would have been the statement that taking interest is immoral. Majors of this sort can change, but are still authoritative under the conditions for which they are framed.

37. Christmas Message, 1951 (Yzermans II, pp. 150-1).

38. See pages 139-40, 150, 187n. 31.

39. *The New Leader*, July 22, 1963, p. 11.

40. The vernacular translations of *Pacem in Terris,* like those of *Mater et Magistra,* range remarkably far from the official text. (For some comments on the *Mater et Magistra* versions, see J. R. Kirwan, *Dublin Review,* Autumn, 1961, pp. 196-230.) When doubts were raised about the accuracy of the English *Pacem in Terris,* Father Thurston Davis tried to allay them with three arguments (*America,* May 25, 1963, p. 732):

1) Cardinal Suenens read a passage from the Vatican translation when addressing the UN in English.

2) And, anyway, "careful comparison of the authentic Latin text with this version reveals that the apparent discrepancies are little more than what one must expect when expressing complex ideas on technical subjects in two languages of such different character."

3) Appeal to the Italian version for "clarification of obscurities in the inevitably more abstract Latin phraseology" is justified by the fact that "as in the case of the great social encyclical *Mater et Magistra,*" encyclicals "are commonly drafted in a modern language."

The *New York Times* took these arguments of Father Davis as settling all doubts about the English translation. In fact, it presented the whole discussion in morality-play terms. Villains had tried to obscure the great peace encyclical, but the Pope really *did* say he wanted peace. The *Times* presumed, apparently, that some scoundrel like Buckley was the target of Father Davis' remarks, when in fact the doubts about the translation were raised by a Jesuit of the Creighton University Center for Peace Research, who thought the English *softened* the Pope's support for the UN. But Father Davis' arguments are more interesting for their mode of procedure than for the occasion that led him to make these efforts:

1) As for Cardinal Suenens' English excerpts, the question earlier addressed to Mr. Cort is relevant here: What translation did Father Davis expect a Vatican envoy to use, when giving a speech in English before the press of the world, but that which was released to the press of the world by the Vatican? Points of interpretation or translation are not settled by this, any more than Mr. Cort's idiosyncratic explication of the original text of *Quadragesimo Anno* was validated by the Vatican press's use of its own translation.

2) In the course of his "careful comparison" of the texts, what subtlety did Father Davis think was caught by the English translator who, in his agony of accuracy, had to leave out *neque id immerito*? Was the Latin so complicated that *no* English sentence could be constructed that might retain this element? After all, the exact English wording of this passage was used to arrive at very serious conclusions, and to impose very heavy burdens on the conscience. For ascertaining what was actually said, here and elsewhere, more "careful comparison" is necessary than that which Father Davis gave to the texts.

3) After telling us that the Latin's complexities are difficult to capture in themselves, Father Davis adds that the Latin is so abstract that one must turn to the vernacular in which it was presumably written to find what the Pope had in mind; that is, the complex text is further specified, and given new complexity, by the language in which the Pope is presumed to be thinking. One appeals from the Pope's words to the Pope's mind. But this surely is to write a commentary, not a translation. And even if the Italian version were the preliminary draft, it has no more force than any other sketch that might be dug out of the waste baskets of men writing formal documents. In fact, if one suspects that the Italian reflects some stage of the composition *prior* to the official text, one should *avoid* it when trying to give a reproduction of that text. For instance, if *neque id immerito* was not in the preliminary draft which the Italian and the English reproduce, but was *inserted* in the official text, it is even more important to reflect this change, since presumably the change was thought necessary before the binding document was issued.

To cap it all, Father Davis ends by saying that the English text is "substantially reliable" in its first form *and* "in the carefully edited versions now available in pamphlet form from sources such as the *America* Press, the Paulist Press and the NCWC Social Action Department." Faced with this assertion, one might reasonably ask, first, what standard of "substantial reliability" Father Davis thinks is high enough for formal documents of careful terminological calibration, and second, why we are allowed to have carefully edited and corrected versions if the first one was adequate? In the Paulist Press edition, many minor changes were made to bring the English into conformity with the Latin. This job was done by Rev. William J. Gibbons, S.J., by Urban P. Intondi, managing editor of the Paulist Press, and by Rev. James B. O'Hara. Yet not one of these men thought it worthwhile to include *neque id immerito* in their corrected version, or to wonder why scholars should be permitted what no first year Latin student could get away with—the translation of *quidam quasi* as "important." It seems that, although the emendators allowed themselves to change the sentence-breaks, etc., their attitude is that of Mr. Cort and Father Davis—that once the Vatican has issued a vernacular translation (and once this has been quoted by a Cardinal, or by another Vatican press release), men should refrain from any further attempts at supplying the most accurate reflection of the official text. As I said earlier, this is not the Vatican's view of the matter.

41. *Pacem in Terris,* par. 136 (Gibbons, p. 46). And see par. 138, on the things that might "take away from the *efficaciousness of its actions" (actionis vis et efficacia).*

42. *Ibid.,* par. 134 (p. 45). The Latin says only that the world rulers *are not achieving* a better order: *non assequuntur.* From these words we get the English "they are no longer capable of facing the task of finding a solution to the problems mentioned above."

43. *Ibid.,* par. 138 (p. 47).

44. For the instance in par. 134, see note 42 above. In par. 140, we are told that the universal authority deals only with things that are to be considered too difficult to be brought to a happy solution by the rulers of the individual states *(difficiliores sunt habendae quam ut a moderatoribus singularium civitatum feliciter expediantur).* The English version says here, "the public authorities of the individual States *are not in a position to tackle them with any* hope of resolving them satisfactorily."

45. Pius XII's Christmas message of 1944 was devoted to the distinction between a *people* and a *mass.* An application of the norms discussed there was made in Pius' address to the World Federalists, when he wrote: "No organization of the world could live if it were not harmonized with the whole complex of natural relations, with that normal organic order which rules the particular relations between man and man and between different peoples. If it does not do that, then, no matter what its structure may be it will not be able to stand up and endure" (Yzermans I, p. 143). It will be seen that these latter words imply the distinction between society and state that is expressly drawn in Pope John's last letter. Pius XII's 1942 Christmas message (on order) and 1957 message (on harmony) enforced the same truths, that political order is "not merely external linking up of parts which are numerically distinct," but "is, rather, and must be, a tendency and an ever more perfect approach to an internal union; and this does not exclude differences founded in fact and sanctioned by the will of God or by supernatural standards" (Yzermans II, p. 53, and compare pp. 153, 185). His attack on the technological, mechanical, mathematical treatment of society (in the Christmas messages of 1952 and 1953) is the other side of this preoccupation with the real sources of moral unity in any polity.

On the basis of these more general truths about the nature of political unity Pius constructed his teaching on "coexistence," which was the subject of his 1954 Christmas message: "There are many who volunteer to lay the bases of human unity. Since, however, the bases, this bridge, must be of a spiritual nature, those sceptics and cynics are certainly not qualified for the task who, in accordance with doctrines of a more or less disguised materialism, reduce even the loftiest trust and the highest spiritual values to the level of physical reactions or consider them mere ideologies. Nor are those apt for the task who do not recognize absolute truths nor admit moral obligations in the sphere of social life. These latter have already in the past—often unknowingly, by their abuse of freedom and by their destructive and unreasonable criticism—prepared an atmosphere favorable to dictatorship and oppression; and now they push forward again to obstruct the work of social and political pacification initiated under Christian inspiration" (Yzermans II, pp. 195).

Mr. Clancy, in a debate, offered to explain Pius' thought on co-existence, when he said, "I think that we do share something with the Communists that is even more basic than ideology, and that is the human condition; we share a common necessity to survive, I think, as Pius said, perhaps the only kind of co-existence we have is co-existence in fear, which is better than no co-existence at all, the alternative to co-existence being, obviously, no existence." (*Public Forum* transcript, May 25, 1960, p. 23.) Yet Pius said precisely the opposite—that if fear takes away men's realistic appraisal of the bases of true community, then all their efforts at order will be self-subverting: "Hence also it becomes clear that pacifist efforts or propaganda originating from those who deny all belief in God—if indeed not undertaken as an artful expedient to obtain the tactical effect of creating excitement and confusion—is always very dubious and incapable of lessening or eliminating the anguished sense of fear" (Yzermans II, p. 188). Of this "false realism" Pius said, in the 1956 Christmas message, "We must with deepest sadness mourn the help given by some Catholics, both ecclesiastical and lay, to the tactics of obfuscation, calculated to bring about a result that they themselves did not intend. How can they fail to see that such is the aim of all that insincere activity which hides under the names of 'talks' and 'meetings'? Why enter into a discussion, for that matter, without a common language? How is it possible to meet if the paths are divergent, that is, if one party rejects or denies the common absolute values, thereby making all 'coexistence in truth' unattainable? Out of respect for the name of Christian, compliance with such tactics should cease, for, as the Apostle warns, it is inconsistent to wish to sit at the table of God and at that of His enemies" (Yzermans II, pp. 223-4).

46. *Pacem in Terris*, par. 7 (Gibbons, p. 7).

47. *Ibid.*, par. 163 (p. 56).

48. *Ibid.*, par. 154 (p. 52).

49. *Ibid.*, par. 164 (p. 56), emphasis added.

50. Yzermans II, p. 226.

51. *Cf.* Yzermans I, p. 143, II, pp. 226-7, 29, 208-10, *Pacem in Terris*, pars. 109-29.

52. *We Hold These Truths*, p. 234.

53. Yzermans II, pp. 224-5. And see I, p. 215.

54. *The Pope Speaks* 3, pp. 443-6.

55. Yzermans II, p. 194.

56. *Cf.* Father Murray's argument to this effect: "The Soviet Union as a power imperialism must be confronted by power, steadily and at every point" (*We Hold These Truths*, p. 245).

57. Thus when difficulties involved in the co-operation with Communists were presented in terms of the Popes' own teachings, Mr. William Clancy dismissed them as the subterfuges of bad faith: "To paraphrase Augustine, give us international organizations, Lord, but not now" (*Public Forum* transcript, May 25, 1960, p. 21).

58. Pope Pius XII, Allocution, March 23, 1952 (Yzermans I, p. 197).

PART FOUR

LIBERTY AND
MORAL LAW

LIBERTY, like love, both looses and binds. This paradox is usually applied only to the perfect freedom found in God, "to serve whom is to reign." But, in varying degrees, down through the whole range of achieved freedoms, the mystery is constant. A stone is determined by the forces immediately at work on it. A dog is less determined, since phantasms lingering with him from an earlier situation can divert him from external influences impinging on him; and to the extent that this happens, he has escaped the dependence on instant force that a stone suffers. Ring a dinner bell, and the dog will surrender a bone, lured by his memory of a steak. Man is more free than the dog since he can carry a world in his head; mentally he can attend a scene unrelated to that his eyes are relaying to him at the moment. In this way, he becomes a self-mover (Aristotle's definition of a free thing), selecting from a large store of ideas, objects, memories. The amount of freedom man can effectively exercise depends, among other things, on the size of this store, on the number of alternatives he can make present to himself. For this reason, an adult is freer than a baby, a civilized man is freer than a savage, a sane man than a psychotic. A man expanding his freedom (and freedom is essentially expansive) is not the "man without ties," with nothing to do, with time on his hands, with no calls upon him. The paucity of inner alternatives offered to the bored lounger on a street corner is a hedge upon his freedom more severe than the duties of a man who responds to a progressively refined body of objects eliciting choice.

Yet here the paradoxes begin; and, once begun, never end. To respond to higher and higher enticements is to incur loyalties, admirations, respect, duty, responsibility. Freedom binds. Further-more, to acquire a store of alternatives involves a minimal (and then an ascending) degree of mental discipline, an effort, an asceti-cism of observation and discernment. And, at an even deeper level, the very thing that frees man—his intellect—is, in a crucial sense, not free. Given clear evidence of a fact, the mind is not free to reject it, except by ceasing to be itself, by a suspension of function. Fur-thermore, though the mind offers to the will a repertory of objects for choice, giving it a liberating goal, the will is somehow already in motion, making one call this or that object into the mind. Man moves himself, but in a mystery, intellect and will interacting. And, last paradox of all, let one find an object of his desire, not by way of compulsion, of an obsession blinding him to relative values and the whole of things, but by an effort of the sharpened awareness, at-tuned to reality—let *that* happen, and the mystery of liberty *be-comes* the mystery of love. One finds one's freedom in attentiveness, devotion, service of another. One loves, honors, and *obeys*. Freedom is freedom to choose what one will serve.

This mystery has been present in the background, looking over my shoulder, as it were, throughout the discussion conducted in this book. The nice sorting out of duties, the careful discernment of another's mind, the effort to enter into it, even to anticipate its mo-tions, yet not by ceasing to be oneself, not by severing other ties with reality—all of the things a Catholic must do when dealing with the authoritative pronouncements of the Church, things which can sound mechanical or slavish or ignoble—all of these things are natural for one who loves. And all of it is, or would be, ignoble, were it *not* the expression of a love for the Church, and, channeled through the Church, for God. Catholic duty in this mat-ter is the ritualization of a love for Christ; more precisely, taking place in his body the Church, it *is* his love for the Father. I have not talked of these matters, of course, since this is a book concerned only with the dry, juridical structure of a system, not with the far more exciting matter of the motive for embracing the system at all. The discussion will seem incomplete to those who do not share, or can-not imagine, the motive for a Catholic's perpetual fiddling with those scales that weigh the various obligations incumbent on the faithful. Those who share the motive for these gaugings and adjust-ings, who walk the line of paradox, know that this delicate process is no more an empty legalism than is the delicate network of cour-tesies, demands, concessions that make up the ritual of married life. Belonging to the Church is not a matter of private mysticism, just as marriage is not a single poetic ecstacy. In both cases, love is ex-pressed and deepened by a discipline of love, a combination of habit and spontaneity, of yielding and asserting, of giving and tak-ing—in short, of freedom perfected in community. And even those who look at this process from the outside, but with sympathy, may come to respect the Catholic's motives, as dealing with realities, from his practical assessment of the limits of obligation, of the task of achieving maturity and independence *within* a freely accepted discipline of charity.

I shall not, in this final section, plunge into theological depths by attempting to say *why* one accepts the pleasant burden of Catholi-cism; but I would like to move a short way over in that direction— to move, say, from discussing what one *can* and *cannot* do as a Cath-olic to the listing of what seem, to a Catholic, the liberating side-effects or advantages of this discipline. There is not only freedom in the Church; the Church contributes to freedom in many direc-tions. I shall not try to deal with the paradox of freedom—that service is rule—in its central mystery, in the love of God that is man's greatest liberation, but in one of its lesser manifestations, where it touches on politics: it is one of freedom's paradoxes that the Church's law, informing conscience, is a liberating thing in it-self. Catholics not only love freedom, but love a *freeing* thing.

The riddle of liberty lies in the relation between achieved con-tacts with reality (offering alternatives for choice yet also creating ties), and spontaneous action along the gamut of these contacts. To define liberty in isolation from the *mind* that frees by *knowing*, by making the commitment involved in an apprehension of things as true or good, is to avoid difficulties only by settling for unlivable simplicities. Freedom, for instance, has been defined as "release from restraints." Release of *what* from restraints? Is a stone free if we remove it from the push and pull of surrounding objects? Is a baby free if we take him from his mother, a savage if we take him suddenly from his tribe, or man if he is released from the burden of intelligence? Is frontal lobotomy the ultimate in liberation? If one says that freedom is the release of *man* from restraints, one comes closer to the problem; but then one must decide what *restrains* man, and what *sustains* him. Do not free man of oxygen, or the company of his fellows, or the irritation of thinking. As Chesterton remarked, one can free a tiger of his bars; but if you try to free him of his stripes, you destroy him.

And so the merely *procedural* definition of freedom, the attempt to define by saying "do this" (remove restraints), fails in its secret aim—which was to avoid facing the complexity of the problem. This is the mental evasion that has become so common in our world of process and quantification: men say, let us have more of good, whatever good is; and, rather than define what good is, they opt for more of everything, hoping good will somehow get increased also. But it will not work. One must decide what good is if one wants to have more of it. In the same way, one must come to know the *quality* of human liberty before one can evaluate maxims on how to increase it *quantitatively* (e.g., the more restraints removed, the freer we are). Freedom is a word that demands completion—free of what, free for what? Freedom, for a man, is freedom to act as a man. And so one must face the whole problem of *what man is* if one hopes to discuss the freedom proper to him. One can free man of error, of responsibility, of danger, by brutalizing or imprisoning him. This action would fit the merely mechanical definition—restraints *are* removed—but it will not embody the complete concept of freedom.

Nor is it possible, at this point, to take the jump that tempts theocratic politicians—to say that freedom is the freedom *to do good*. Either this is tautology (*all* choices are made under the aspect of good, of something desired) or it is an evasion of the problem exactly parallel to the libertarian's procedure: if "freedom to do good" is taken in a procedural way—the more objectively good acts that, by any means, get done, the more freedom there is—then one is denying the *central* good at issue here, the structure of man's nature, which makes him *responsible* for his own actions, good or bad. The ruler who would prevent evil thoughts by a censorship process meant to keep men children is trying to "free" the tiger of his stripes, to take away man's noblest (if most dangerous) gifts—the judging intellect, the executing will. The theocrat tries to undo the creative work of that God in whose name he violates the human person. Man, to the extent that he is man, must become increasingly responsible for his own actions. All education, social pressure, and political restraint should work in this direction. The attempt to define freedom procedurally as freedom to do *what one ought* fails as drastically as the definition that says it is the freedom to do *anything*. The stone does what it ought. But if man is to follow his nature, he must exercise his ability to choose, to be responsible for his preferences, to have dominion over his acts.

And so we return to the fact that freedom is rule. It cannot be treated as mere lack. The irony of the "liberal" definition of freedom is that it tries to ennoble the individual by defining his most precious quality in a passive way—as the removal of restraints *from* him, the making of an environment permeable by him. Freedom is not a quantitative process, and certainly not the result of that process. It is the quality of a certain *act* with certain *objects*; it is a spontaneity toward alternatives. In the political order, the work of the state is to throw man back, as far as possible, on himself as the ruler of his inner forum. The free man, said St. Thomas, is the master of his own movements, *dominus actuum suorum*.[1] So antimonarchical was "liberal" thought, so frightened of "rule" as a "necessary evil," that this essential aspect of freedom was blotted out in subsequent discussion of the problem. Tyrants are not bad because they *rule,* because power is bad or the state is bad. They are *usurpers,* who rule where another has right. They are kings who trespass against the monarchy that every man exercises over himself. Their sin is not in being kings, but in denying the fact that monarchy is a fellowship. The tyrant is a regicide; and the "regicides" who have overthrown kings were sometimes the truest defenders of monarchy.

If the discussion of freedom is to get back on the right track, then, we must stop discussing it as the lack of rule, and see the way in which it is dominion over the self, and the origin of all right rule in the state. The "laboratory" approach to freedom and order as opposites to be combined in a palatable mixture is an outgrowth of nineteenth-century scientism at its worst. To start a more fruitful discussion of the matter, one must reflect on the ways in which freedom is an exercise of *rule*. "Freedom of conscience" must rest on the truth that, as Newman says, "Conscience is an authority."[2]

I.

Man achieves his escape from the stone's passivity by an internal leverage of the mind on the will, the will on the mind. The will can grasp only what the mind has grasped before it. Man apprehends only what he has comprehended. He is mobilized toward several objects by the mind's ability to range out through reality, making things its own, presenting this or that object as preferable to others within reach. Man is not determined toward any one thing in that wide field of reality, because his mind is able to know things under many aspects, abstracting, assessing, comparing; *this* is preferable to *that* in terms of one value; all things are available to the will's assent because the mind can consider them all under the aspect of good.[3] Freedom is man's mastery of things; it is not sufficient that he be free of their mastery; he must have the power of absorbing them.

The libertarian and the theocrat both deny this mastery. The libertarian does not look to a specifically human act in all its complexity, its mastery of the real order. His concept of freedom, therefore, gives one no norms for distinguishing between different restraints (all of which are all and equally bad, simply because they *are* restraints). This makes it impossible to assess freedom realistically, to treat limitations on it with a practical set of priorities. At an even deeper level, this "impartiality" toward man's acts, so long as they be unrestrained, rests on or leads to the ultimate destruction of freedom's mastery—moral relativism. Relativism makes it impossible for the mind to prefer this to that by any fixed standard; the will thus remains equally disposed to all things, not put in motion toward one. The range of choices dwindles, the will begins to act in a random way. This is sometimes given desperate justification as an "absolute freedom," that of the "gratuitous act," the will choosing for no other reason than that it chooses. Of this voluntarism Chesterton wrote:

Exactly as free thought involves the doubting of thought itself, so the acceptation of mere "willing" really paralyzes the will. . . . You cannot praise an action because it shows will; for to say that is merely to say that it is an action. By this praise of will you cannot really choose one course as better than another. And yet choosing one course as better than another is the very definition of the will you are praising. The worship of will is the negation of will. To admire mere choice is to refuse to choose. If Mr. Bernard Shaw comes up to me and says, "Will something," that is tantamount to saying "I do not mind what you will," and that is tantamount to saying, "I have no will in the matter." You cannot admire will in general, because the essence of will is that it is particular.[4]

That last sentence could be recast, in the terms we have been using, to read "You cannot praise freedom as the lack of rule, because freedom is the basic form of rule." To want everything indifferently is the logical other side of the formula "to have no restraints"; and it is a condition, not of freedom, but of paralysis. As George Herbert put it, in *The Porch*, "who follows all things, forfeiteth his will."

The theocrat denies the mastery involved in freedom, not by saying one should will anything, but by saying one should get one thing, whether one wills it or no. He is so impressed by the good of an action's object that he becomes careless of the good involved in the action itself. He tries to make man do good, but not be responsible for good. He denies man his proper sovereignty, so awed is he by the sovereignty of God and God's law. Yet God is the one who made man sovereign over his own acts. The theocrat, professing reverence for God, actually tries to "correct" God's work.

II.

There is a second way in which freedom is an exercise of rule, not over other things but over oneself. Self-possession is the condition of the will's thrust toward other things. Man's self-possession arises from the nature of knowledge; man comes to know himself, in the act of knowing other things, precisely as a being whose activity is to know (and so control) other things. This self-possession involved in every act of knowledge was pointed out by Thomas Aquinas: "No judging power moves itself to judge unless it reflects on its own action; for if it moves itself to judge, it must know its own judgment;

and this only an intellect can do."[5] Here, too, we see how man fulfills Aristotle's definition of the free thing as a self-mover: man has a relation *of* himself *to* himself, as knower and known, as grasper and grasped, as mover and moved, that is impossible to beings without intellect: "The self-possession of knowledge, the ability of the intelligence to reflect upon itself and possess its own act as well as the thing understood by that act, leaves the soul distinct from its own being."[6]

In the light of the intellect's simultaneous possession of other things and of itself, the will is put in act toward things that are congenial, fitting, connatural to the self that is comprehended in this complex action. And so the minimal self-possession necessary for freedom—the faculty of reflective intellect—tends of itself, and aside from other forces acting on it, to become more responsive to realities complementary to one's own, able to identify and appropriate them with greater ease.

The libertarian and the theocratic definitions of freedom both tend to prevent the self-encounter that gives man sovereignty over himself. The libertarian does this by overlooking the fact that there are knowable things about man that serve as norms for his appropriation of things outside him. He would try to *appropriate* without knowing what is proper to the person. The condition of man's being free is his knowing what man is. The theocrat, by neglecting the importance of freedom in the choice of a good outside man, does not see that man must come to recognize the good in himself as a basis for his choice of goods outside him.

III.

Freedom manifests itself as dominion in a third way—in the free man's relations with his fellows. A grasp of oneself as responsible, as a moral agent, involves a recognition of the freedom and responsibility of others. To deny the one is to deny the other; and so man must rule his own actions in such a way that he does not deny the freedom of others, or he is perverting the structure of moral responsibility that is the mainspring of his *own* action. A free man at war with freedom in others is, like the tyrant, guilty of usurpation; he is a king at war with monarchical principle. There is no question, here, of the "social contract" theory that takes a mercantile, quid-pro-quo attitude toward relations between men, each of whom gives up some quantity of his ideal "freedom" in order to save the rest of it, letting the state possess that quantum of power that has been surrendered by the aggregate of individuals. Freedom is not an hypostatized "given" that can be bartered with in this way. It is precisely the action of man as a moral agent, which takes place only in relation with other men, whose human rights are also the basis of his own action. The libertarian, defining freedom as absence of restraint, thinks of it as present 100% only in the individual suspended in a vacuum; for him, contact with others always represents a diminution of freedom, an alloying of it with other considerations (such as the need for self-protection against this menacing contact with others). The state is, for such a man, the necessary evil that regulates the alloying process. The theocrat, on the other hand, does not let man encounter the mystery of freedom in himself as a correlate of his respect for it in other men. For him, the man who misuses his freedom does not retain the awesome status of a moral agent; since only the "right act" is important, not the free act, he will tend always to reduce man to the level of his performance, without the proper honor for his very existence as the image of God. Thus man loses the rights that belong to him *as man* if he does not act according to the theocrat's definition of *the virtuous man*.

An adequate view of freedom as dominion would have to begin, I believe, with the consideration of these three sides of the mystery.[7] And in all three areas the Church is the champion of freedom. At the basis of her effectiveness in these areas is the fact that the philosophy of freedom as a form of *rule* has been preserved and developed primarily in her teaching—most obviously in Leo XIII's *Libertas Praestantissimum*. That encyclical takes its origin from the passage in *Ecclesiasticus* (15.14), "God made man from the beginning, and left him in the hand of his own counsel," and expounds the verse in St. Thomas' terms: "He is master of his action who can choose one thing out of many."[8] Then Pope Leo enters into the paradoxes of freedom, noting that "natural freedom," available to all men by virtue of the mind that fashions alternatives for the will, acquaints man with himself precisely as *responsible* for his acts. And this responsibility is to be faced, if man is to live justly, as a moral responsibility. For man to come to know himself is to know himself as a moral agent, subject to the dictates of reason—that is, of moral law. And so he enters the realm of "moral freedom," a higher freedom achieved by means of, but reaching beyond, natural freedom. If liberty is the freedom to choose what one will serve, man's final liberation is to serve God, who alone is worthy of man's high gifts, who alone does not disappoint his servants. To serve lesser things is, in varying degrees, to cripple oneself, to lose, a little, one's human perfections, including liberty itself; to be "a slave to sin" (John 8.34). To be free is to be able to go after what one wants; but wanting anything is a form of esteem, of service. To serve fame, or wealth, or sex, to serve even reason, or human love, or mankind, is to subject man to something that is his equal or inferior. Only when God is served in and through these things is man the master of everything else under God, so that, as St. Paul writes, "the spiritual man judges all things, and he himself is judged by no man" (I Cor. 2.15). Pope Leo's doctrine is not theocratic, though his comments on Church-State relations are somewhat history-bound in their formulations, formulations whose true meaning was finally explicated in Pope John's last and greatest encyclical.

But to see the full import of the Church's theory, all we need do is turn again to the three forms of mastery already mentioned.

I.

First, with regard to the mind's mastery over things, as a condition of man's sovereignty over his own acts, the Church has held, simply and unswervingly, that there *are* things to be mastered. This is a much greater achievement and service than it might sound. There is a tendency in man, out of sheer weariness or disillusionment or thwarted ideals, to lapse into relativism, Manicheism, or solipsism—the belief that the world is formless, or not worth knowing, or not *there* to be known. These moods have swept over Christian civilization, as they do over all cultures (and, as moods, at least momentarily, over every individual). A circumambient pessimism touched the work of St. Augustine; it was an atmosphere to which he was partially attuned; but he fought it, and had to fight it, as a Christian thinker. As an ex-Manichean neo-Platonist of the declining Empire, he distrusted matter. But as a Christian, who believed in the Creation and the Incarnation, he had to distrust his distrust. To the Platonist, who thinks that matter only *seems* rather than *is,* the Church has given the answer it gave to the Docetists: Christ's body *was,* it did not merely *seem* to be. And on this great doctrine of matter, the toughest part of our civilization is founded. Other civilizations have succumbed to the temptation to immaterialism, and the temptation is always with us—just now taking odd new shapes in the wake of Einstein and Heisenberg, as in the profound antimaterialism of de Chardin. But the West has said its Credo to the world; and said it as part of the Creed it recited in Church.[9]

Not only is there a world, in Catholic dogma; all that is is *good,* created by God, meant to serve man. Not only can the mind know reality, and place it at the disposal of the will. The will can be in motion toward it as worth having, as good. The world is not only worth having, but, at the cost of Christ's blood, worth saving. It is a literally precious thing, bought at a high price. For the Christian, there is everything to live for, since it is what God died for. And here again the paralyzing moods of other high cultures, the moods that empty freedom of reality, have been opposed with all the energies of the Christian faith.

The Church has kept man aware that the world exists—and so sheltered freedom by giving it an arena of action. But it has also taught that the world is only the world—and so freed man of his servitude to all the forces of this world. By her teaching that all things are made for man, but man for God, the Church has preserved man from intimidation by the forces that seem to make the individual act of will a useless thing—whether internal forces, like pride and sexual desire, or the external might of ideologies and empires. The helplessness felt under these preponderating earthly forces is countered by the Christian belief in another City. The concrete impact of the Church in this area is best seen by looking at her influence on the development of political philosophy in the West. Government as it existed in primitive times, or in the non-Christian

East, or in classical antiquity, confused, when it did not positively equate, the functions of priest and king. State worship was the cohesive force of such societies. Religion was only separated from politics when and if the former became an insignificant force in human affairs. This means that the state possessed, by positive cooperation of other powers, or by their defection, the whole of institutional authority over man. From it there was no appeal. But Christianity changed all this by a radical freeing of the soul from political dominance. Although the Christian recognizes a legitimate sphere of political authority, his final allegiance is to a more lasting city. Lord Acton, the great student of liberty's development, put the consequences of this profound change in these terms:

Christianity introduced no new forms of government, but a new spirit, which totally transformed the old ones. The difference between a Christian and a rationalist democracy is as great, politically, as that between a monarchy and a republic. The Government of Athens more nearly resembled that of Persia than of any Christian republic . . . in the Jewish as in the Gentile world, political and religious obligations were made to coincide; in both, therefore— in the theocracy of the Jews as in the politics of the Greeks—the State was absolute. Now it is the great object of the Church, by keeping the two spheres permanently distinct—by rendering to Caesar the things that are Caesar's, and to God the things that are God's—to make absolutism, of whatever kind, impossible.[10]

Ever since Augustine began the investigation of these new complexities in his philosophy of the Two Cities, the keynote of the Church's politics has been a division and balance of authority, earthly and spiritual. By making the soul of man responsible to God and his *priestly* representative, the Church gave an effective definition and hedge to the powers of the *State*, removed man's conscience from the direct dominion of any earthly institution, fenced the rights of religion about from secularization. This is the theme of John Courtney Murrays' essay "Are There Two or One?" in *We Hold These Truths*: the Church destroyed the monolithic concept of society as subject in its entirety to a single institution:

What appeared within history was not an "idea" or an "essence" but an existence, a Thing, a visible institution that occupied ground in this world at the same time that it asserted an astounding new freedom on a title not of this world. . . . And this comprehensive right, asserted within the political community, requires as its complement that all the intrapolitical sacrednesses (*res sacrae in temporalibus*) be assured of their proper immunity from politicization.[11]

The freedom of the Church was a pledge of man's freedom in a thousand other areas, of the sacredness of conscience. And the general theme of Father Murray's book is that the American freedoms were worked out on the basis of that division of authorities first achieved by Christianity, in the civilization to which it contributed.[12] Only when the Church had taught men that the world is only the world were they able to maintain, effectively, that the State is only the State. It is in this sense that Father Murray wrote:

If one wished to sum up Leo's [Leo XIII's] concept of government in its relation to the socio-economic order, one might as well use the phrase "as much freedom as possible, as much government as necessary."[13]

II.

The aspect of the Church's teaching considered under the last heading—as committed to man's mastery of things—excludes the "libertarian" view of freedom, which does not recognize an objective moral order. But, in defending freedom as man's mastery of himself,[14] the Church is also at odds with the theocratic perversion of liberty. And this is a point that is perhaps less understood than the former one. Even if it be granted that the Church, by separating the priest from the king, freed man from the vast, superincumbent power of the state, it might be argued that this act introduced a deeper bondage, since the priest, forswearing external coercion, tries to influence the soul directly, to insinuate his own norms there—to act, almost, as a surrogate conscience. Even the Old Law was, according to Saint Paul, comparatively external, a matter of observances. But the Church enters the soul's tribunal, where no other institution can go. Here is the threat of violation men fear in her.

The extent of the New Law brought by Christ is indicated in his own words, "You have heard that it was said to the ancients,

'Thou shalt not commit adultery.' But I say to you that everyone who so much as looks with lust at a woman has already committed adultery with her in his heart" (Matt. 5.27). But, in a paradoxical fashion that perfectly fits the reversals in the nature of freedom, this command is itself the pledge of Christian freedom. It throws the responsibility for man's acts back on their source. It forswears the kind of external conformity that can be imposed on man. To appeal to conscience is to treat man as free, as the origin and judge of his own acts: "For who among men knows the things of a man save the spirit of the man which is in him?" (I Cor. 2.11.) Exterior acts can be imposed, without regard for the integrity of the willing process. Yet the integrity of the willing process is precisely the object of Christian morality. As St. Thomas remarks, "If virtue were at odds with man's nature, it would not be an act of the man himself, but of some alien force subtracting from or going beyond the man's own identity."[15] The Christian ethic makes man responsible to himself for the fate of his soul. This encounter with God in the depths of the soul is the essence of the New Law, which is the law of the Spirit, superseding the letter.

It is no wonder, then, that liberty is emphasized so heavily in Holy Scripture, whose teaching is that "The truth shall make you free" (John 8:32). Law is hardly ever mentioned without a counterbalancing mention of that *liberty* which is at the heart of the Christian law. This "circumcision" is "a matter of the heart in the spirit, not in the letter" (Rom. 2.29); it is "the perfect law of liberty" (James 1.25), "the law of the Spirit" (Rom. 8.2), and "Where the Spirit of the Lord is, there is freedom" (II Cor. 3.17), so that "the spiritual man judges all things, and he himself is judged by no man" (I Cor. 2.15).

Although there are external laws and rules of discipline in the Church, St. Thomas made it clear that the Church's action is supplementary and subordinate to the Spirit's action in the soul, and is only valid insofar as it turns to this for its sanction.[16] To attack the internal law of the Spirit is to destroy the basis for all of the Church's external provisions; as Newman says, "did the Pope speak against Conscience in the true sense of the word, he would commit a suicidal act. He would be cutting the ground from under his feet."[17] And so the saints, urged by the internal law of love, have often opposed deviations from that law by the men who hold authority in the Church:

The witness of freedom of speech in the Church has been borne by Irenaeus against Pope Victor, Jerome against Pope Damasus, Columban against Boniface IV, Bernard of Clairvaux against Eugene III, Bridget of Sweden against Gregory XI, Philip Neri against Clement III; and by so many other saints like Catherine of Siena, Thomas More, Robert Bellarmine. . . . It was Gregory the Great who said, "But if scandal is taken at the truth, it is better to allow scandal to arise than to neglect the truth" (In Ezech. Hom. 7). And Thomas Aquinas stressed the necessity for free criticism, *correctio fraterna*, even to ecclesiastical superiors (*S.T.* II-II, q. 33, a. 1-4).[18]

The Church upholds man's freedom, not only from the state's unjust pretensions, but from those of ecclesiastical authorities.

One of the teachings of the Church that does not seem to correspond with this doctrine of freedom is the dictum that "error has no rights."[19] Error is not, in itself, a positive thing, but a *denial* of truth. It is evil, and evil is opposed to existence, having no positive principle of its own; it is a disorder, perverting what has existence in its own right. Only what exists has the right to man's esteem, as a product and partial image of the supreme Existence. So much is the traditional teaching of the Church. But to say "error has no rights" is not to say "erring men have no rights." For erring men do exist, and are, as men, the highest earthly existents and images of God. They obviously do have rights.[20] In fact, in the ordinary political use of the term "rights," *only* men have rights, so that the dictum "error has no rights" does not enter into discourse at this popular level.

Furthermore, men hold even the most mistaken views under some aspect of good or truth, so that in the erroneous view, *as it is held by men*, there is some admixture of truth; the existent opinion itself can therefore be honored insofar as it is true.[21] Fortunately, we no longer have to go to the theologians to get explanations of this matter,[22] since the Pope himself cleared away all misunderstanding when he wrote, in *Pacem in Terris,*

One must never confuse error and the person who errs, not even when there is question of error or inadequate knowledge of truth in the moral or religious field. The person who errs is always and above all a human being, and he retains in every case his dignity as a human person; and he must be always regarded and treated in accordance with that lofty dignity. Besides, in every human being, there is a need that is congenital to his nature and never becomes extinguished, compelling him to break through the web of error and open his mind to the knowledge of truth. And God will never fail to act on his interior being, with the result that a person, who at a given moment of his life lacks the clarity of faith or even adheres to erroneous doctrines, can at a future date learn and believe the truth.[23]

That is, there is always hope that the erring man will see the truth so long as his intellect is kept operative and independent. Freedom is the condition and means of man's reaching the goal of man.

On the second point, that erroneous views, as embodied in man's real history, can contain positive elements of truth, the same document asserts:

Erroneous movements, in so far as they conform to the dictates of right reason and are interpreters of the lawful aspirations of the human person, contain elements that are positive and deserving of approval.[24]

A mistake related to the one just treated (which takes "error" as if it were a *person* who could be *denied* rights) is the misuse of Leo XIII's teaching that the state must serve God.[25] It is true that all man's actions and works, including his social and political acts, must be performed to serve God if they are to be properly ordinated. But the state does not serve God *as a person serves him*, any more than error can lose *personal* rights. It has no soul to save. "America" will not go to heaven or hell.[26] To say that the state must serve God means that it must do this *as a state*; not by praying itself, but by respecting the freedom of worship among its citizens.[27] If a community's freedom of worship finds expression in national rites, then the state must protect this exercise of freedom. If, on the other hand, freedom of worship is protected or made possible by its channeling through extra-political expressions, then the state must protect these arrangements. The test is, always, freedom. In a pluralistic society, one religion cannot seek a status that would deny the rights of another religion, for

Every human being has the right to honor God according to the dictates of an upright conscience and therefore the right to worship God privately and publicly.[28]

Furthermore, even the use of religion to gain partial political advantage would be wrong, on two counts, as subjecting a higher good to a lower, and as a perversion of justice in the political sphere itself, since

It should not happen that certain individuals or social groups derive special advantage from the fact that their rights have received preferential protection.[29]

Churchmen have not always been true to the Church's own teaching, in this matter as in all others, but these are the basic principles to which the Church returns, the teaching it maintains, the freedom it has for centuries helped to establish and proclaim. And there is an especially unfortunate consequence of departure from this truth by Catholic rulers, since theocracy can so easily disguise itself as simple theism. The motives of theocratic usurpations are so loftily phrased, so reminiscent of familiar maxims (e.g., "error has no rights"), that they have a certain authoritative ring about them. But in truth the theocratic attack on liberty is the most terrible one of all. All aggressions against the proper self-rule of a rational man are, as I said, usurpations, violations of the internal kingdom of man. But the theocrat, who disregards the proper autonomy of conscience, usurps not only the rule of man, but that of the Spirit. The New Law is one of Grace, of the creator acting on man's nature in such a way as to open for him new realms of supernatural activity and achievement. Only the author of man can act at this level without violating the nobility of his own work. The Church itself must serve the Spirit that "blows where it will" (John 3.8). The theocratic ruler would anticipate and contain and dictate to the Spirit, would replace other men's conscience with his own or with the State's, would shut off the area of mystery in which divine Grace alone can operate without violating human freedom. Such a ruler "takes God's name in vain" in the deepest sense, assumes God's own work, and, in proposing the State as the instrument for this work, asks men to commit idolatry, treating a creature as God.

III.

In the third area of freedom's mastery, the control of oneself as confronted with the legitimate freedom of others, the Church is also an effective ally. She has never adopted the "social contract" theory of community as an egotism making concessions to an unfortunate necessity. In her teaching, the State has always been a natural society, deserving obedience out of fealty to the author of nature. A radical individualism, treating the state as a "necessary evil," has no place in her history or doctrine. This has been pointed out by Reinhold Niebuhr:

It has always been one of the virtues of Catholicism that it has a firm hold on the social substance of human existence and was never tempted to the extreme individualism of many versions of Protestant and secular faith. It also skipped the whole period of classical economy and never doubted that political authority should exercise dominance over the economic sphere in the interest of justice.[30]

Leo XIII's great letters, *Diuturnum Illud* and *Immortale Dei* state the Catholic doctrine of human rights within the human polity— that they are not conceded, not to be bargained for, not created by human compact, but that they are given in natural law as part of the very structure of reality arising from God's will.

But at a deeper level even than the Church's stress upon the "spiritual reality" of the political society is her devotion to community itself as this is perfected in the Mystical Body. The faith is always a *community* in belief, what St. Paul called the faith we, each of us, hold with one another (τῆς ἐν ἀλλήλοις πίστεως, Rom. 1.12). From its origins, this faith cut across class divisions, so that "there is neither Jew nor Greek; there is neither male nor female. For you are all one in Christ Jesus" (Gal. 3.27-8). "For in one Spirit we were all baptized, into one body, whether Jews or Gentiles, whether slaves or free; and we were all given to drink of one Spirit" (I Cor. 12.13). The Church first ameliorated and then eliminated slavery, that "permanent institution" of antiquity; and this not by direct political action, but by the natural pressure of the unity that had become a reality in her own life, and which acted as a leaven on all other forms of community.[31] And even today, the world instinctively discerns that world unity must come from religion into politics, rather than *vice versa*—an instinct that was apparent in the glad reception of Pope John XXIII's efforts "that all may be one."

In theory, then, and in the three areas of man's practical mastery, the Church is a friend to freedom. Because of this, she has a special relevance to each period of history. And perhaps her message for our time, a time of unprecedented freedom, is her reminder that liberty does not entail an indifferentism to fixed truths. This is especially applicable in the realm of politics, where democratic theory is often presented as an adaptability to whatever a majority of voters might decide is true. This is simply an application of the libertarian, procedural theory of freedom. Mill's concept of free speech as a mechanism producing large quantities of usable truth, which was modeled on the free market that produces wealth, has itself become the model of democratic society. By these standards, the most morally plastic man is the ideal politician, one who approaches the deliberative process without previous commitment, ready to reflect whatever that process registers. The processes for accomplishing the goal of good government are themselves made the goal. Yet one might as well go to a microphone in order to discover from it what speech to make as seek in the polling system the moral attitude one should take toward problems of the political order. The devices men have found for protecting the rights of conscience cannot accomplish their aim if men do not *have* consciences formed by the responsible scrutiny of reality. As Father Murray has written,

The totalitarianizing tendency [is] inherent in the contemporary idolatry of the democratic process. . . . What is urged is a monism, not so much of the political order itself, as of a political technique. The proposition is that all the issues of human life—intellectual, religious, and moral issues as well as formally political issues—are to be regarded as, or resolved into, political issues and are to be settled by the single omnicompetent political technique of majority vote.[32]

And Pope Pius XII reminded the world that only men of conscience, committed to deeper norms than the ballot sheet, will "prevent the ballot-box, which can be the meeting ground for irresponsibility, ignorance and passions, from passing a sentence of ruin on the true and genuine state."[33]

The Church helps protect democracy from this perversion of its techniques precisely because her moral law is formed, her appeal to conscience is prior to any claim the State can make upon man, her teaching forces Catholics to take an independent political stand on matters that affect their conscience. The moral nature of the presidential office was seen in a new and pressing light when John F. Kennedy ran for that office, precisely because the Church makes so explicit the duty of conscience. Here was a man who, because of his committed moral position, stated before he took office that, if there was conflict between his faith and his oath of office, he would have to surrender the office. The significance of this statement was expressed in a letter to the New York *Times*:

The President of the United States was never a mere administrator of the national or Congressional will; but in this past thirty years he has become the principal and continuing initiator of policy. A faithful Catholic President would not be morally free to initiate policies clearly condemned by the Church. And under certain circumstances he would not be free to execute national policies even if the responsibility for their initiation lay elsewhere.

Is this an alarming state of affairs? I for one say it is far from being that; it is most reassuring to men of all faiths that a President should have moral moorings that can ride out the passionate and anarchistic tidal waves that sometimes wreck whole nations.

I should remind those who are fond of constructing the abstract conflict and then holding it up for the public to gaze at in horror that all civilized men acknowledge laws that are prior to political laws. That much, at least, was posited at Nuremberg, whatever the merits of the legal arguments, and a fresh affirmation is being made for us by the government of Israel, as it prepares the case against Adolf Eichmann. Mr. Eichmann did not have the right to follow Hitler's orders when those orders were to go out and commit genocide; and it made no difference whatever that in Hitler the supreme political authority was vested. Beware the man who says he is not governed by a higher law than that formulated by his constituents.

What needs, then, to be understood, I think, is that by renouncing political mandate in the event of conflict, a Catholic President would almost certainly be taking the more enlightened course; the same course which, most probably, properly instructed Protestants and Jews would also take under similar circumstances.

For Catholics it is a certitude, for others it should be the operative presumption, that the Catholic Church will over the years maintain a more reliable moral equilibrium than can be presumed by any single nation (let the vainglorious among us remember what happened in our time to Russia, to Germany, to Japan, to Italy); and that therefore, on that unknown, unforeseeable day when nation X might well find itself fighting a hot moral war with the Vatican, the chances are that the Vatican will be right.[34]

Unless such individual integrity is the aim of the democratic process, then "freedom of conscience" is an empty slogan; for what is this freedom, but the right of conscience to recognize moral claims upon it? Professor Herberg has reminded us that recognition of these obligations is not only right in itself, but solidly in the American tradition of constitutional government:

What is totalitarianism ultimately but a regime that sees itself as its own highest majesty, and refuses to recognize a majesty beyond itself? Totalitarianism is thus a thoroughly secularized system on which is built a thoroughly self-absolutizing state. Against such totalitarianism, we have our tradition of the constitutional limited-power state which does recognize a majesty beyond itself (the "higher law") in everything it says and does . . . the divine majesty enters life not only in personal existence but also in social, cultural, and political life as well, calling men to responsibility and setting limits to the pretensions of men and states and cultures.[35]

The advantage that citizens have in dealing with a Catholic politician, like President Kennedy, is that his moral position is clearly defined, in essentials, and can be assessed from the outset. Some others, with less explicit moral views, might have to be "taken on trust" in a way that a Catholic need not be. Deep philosophical opposition to Communism, for instance, is a given principle in a Catholic's faith (though the Catholic does not necessarily have the best skills for opposing Communism in the realm of prudential action, where debate and the learning process go on continually). This is, for those of other faiths, part of the "usefulness of anathema" considered earlier in this book. The dogmatic structure of the Church is there for all to see. Its adaptability to any legitimate temporal conditions is also visible—that "bearing towards the Civil Power . . . various as the Church is invariable"[36]—in its long history, its fortunes under all kinds of regimes. Its temporal policy, insofar as the Church needs to formulate one for the coherence of the body of faithful living in the most varied circumstances, is also enunciated in the continuing teaching of the encyclicals and papal addresses. Wholehearted support of pluralism, for instance, is not merely a clear inference from the Church's doctrine and history, but a publicly stated attitude of the magisterium. Here, too, going out beyond the circle of a specifically Catholic community, the encyclicals are "letters of unity," proclaiming the moral law and revealed truth, inviting others to come and learn from both, or at least to ascertain exactly where the Church stands in this moment of history. This much, at least, is there for all to see. Only Catholics are fortunate enough to see that the Church stands, as well, *above* history.

NOTES TO PART FOUR

1. *C.G.* II, 47.3.
2. Essay on Keble.
3. *S.T.* I, q. 83 a. 1, *resp., C.G.* II, 47.5, 48.6.
4. *Orthodoxy*, Doubleday Image edition (1959), p. 39. *Ibid.*, pp. 107-8: "We may say broadly that free thought is the best of all the safeguards against freedom. . . . As long as the vision of heaven is always changing, the vision of earth will be exactly the same. No ideal will remain long enough to be realized, or even partly realized. The modern young man will never change his environment; for he will always change his mind."
5. *C.G.* II, 48.3.
6. Frederick D. Wilhelmsen, *The Metaphysics of Love* (Sheed and Ward, 1962), p. 24. *Cf. S.T.* I, q. 83, a. 1 ad 3.
7. An entirely different approach to liberty as a form of rule is taken by St. Augustine in *De Libero Arbitrio* I, 7-13. The argument, like most of Augustine's, is clever, difficult, and profound, too many-sided for me to attempt sound statement or criticism of it; but in its total reliance on the concept of dominion it could be of great service in an age that has neglected this essential aspect of liberty.
8. *Libertas*, par. 5. St. Thomas also used the *Ecclesiasticus* passage as the basic text for a discussion of freedom (*S.T.* I, q. 83, a. 1).
9. *Libertas*, par. 4.
10. *History of Freedom and Other Essays*, Macmillan, 1907, p. 205. *Ibid.*, pp. 16-7: "If I may employ an expressive anachronism, the vice of the classic State was that it was both Church and State in one. Morality was undistinguished from religion and politics, there was only one legislator and one authority. . . . The passengers existed for the sake of the ship."

11. *We Hold These Truths*, pp. 204, 203. The importance of the Church as an *institution*, rather than religion as an *idea*, for the practice of freedom is also stressed by Acton. *Cf.* "The Protestant Theory of Persecution," now in the Meridian *Essays on Freedom and Power*, p. 114: "The modern theory, which has swept away every authority except that of the State, and has made the sovereign power irresistible by multiplying those who share it, is the enemy of that common freedom in which religious freedom is included. It condemns, as a State within a State, every inner group and community, class or corporation, administering its own affairs; and, by proclaiming the abolition of privileges, it emancipates the subjects of every such authority in order to transfer them exclusively to its own. It recognizes liberty only in the individual, because it is only in the individual that liberty can be separated from authority, and the right of conditional obedience deprived of the security of a limited command. Under its sway, therefore, every man may profess his own religion more or less freely; but his religion is not free to administer its own laws. In other words, religious profession is free, but Church government is controlled. And where ecclesiastical authority is restricted, religious liberty is virtually denied. For religious liberty is not the negative right of being without any particular religion, just as self-government is not anarchy. It is the right of religious communities to the practice of their own duties, the enjoyment of their own constituion, and the protection of the law, which equally secures to all the possession of their own independence." For an example of the "atomistic liberty" Acton is attacking, *cf.* Rousseau, *Social Contract* 2.3 (Gateway edition, Kendall translation): "Where, however, blocs are formed, lesser associations at the expense of the broader one, the will of each of these associations comes to be general with respect to its members and particular with respect to the state. . . . If, then, we are to have a clear declaration of the general will, we must see to it that there are no partial societies within the state, so that each citizen forms his own opinions." A corrective to these errors will be found in the encyclicals' teaching on "intermediate organizations."

12. *Cf.* Will Herberg, *National Review*, August 13, 1963: "Note well that this restriction of the state to the civil ('secular') order is not a peculiarly American 'separationist' notion derived from the First Amendment; it is, as I have said, deeply rooted in our Western tradition, and rests upon the primary distinction between State and Church, which was at least as clear to Augustine and Thomas Aquinas as to the justices of the Supreme Court."

13. *Theol. Stud.* 14, p. 559.

14. *Cf.* Pius XII, Allocution, March 23, 1952 (Yzermans, I, p. 203): "True liberty . . . is the self-decision to will what is good and to accomplish it; it is the mastery of one's own faculties."

15. *S.T.* I-II, q. 108, a. 2, ad 2.

16. *S.T.* I-II, q. 108, a. 2 *resp.*, ad 1, ad 2. *Cf. Mystici Corporis*, par. 65: "There can, then, be no real opposition or conflict between the invisible mission of the Holy Spirit and the juridical commission of Ruler and Teacher received from Christ, since they mutually complement and perfect each other—as do the body and soul in man—and proceed from our one Redeemer."

17. "Letter," p. 132.

18. Hans Küng, "The Church and Freedom," *Commonweal*, June 21, 1963, p. 351.

19. *Cf. Libertas*, pars, 23-4.

20. In *Libertas* (par. 6), Pope Leo called "the pursuit of what has a false appearance of good . . . a proof of freedom, just as a disease is a proof of our vitality." And so one can as well deny human rights to an erring man as kill everyone who catches a cold. The cold is proof that life still exists (corpses do not catch colds); and human life is sacred. The same is true of liberty.

21. St. Augustine saw the same two-fold good in even the limited aspirations of earthly society—since it is a striving after *things* under the aspect of their goodness, and it is the striving of *men*, who are themselves precious existents: "The things this society desires are good in themselves, and it is itself a great good, as made up of human beings" (*City of God*, 15.4).

292 POLITICS AND CATHOLIC FREEDOM

22. But see, for instance, John Courtney Murray, S.J., in *Proc. Cath. Theol. Soc. of Am.* 3 (1948), p. 33.

23. *Pacem in Terris,* par. 158 (Gibbons, pp. 53-4).

24. *Ibid.,* par. 59 (Gibbons, p. 54).

25. *Libertas,* par. 21.

26. *Cf.* John Courtney Murray, S.J., "The Problem of the Religion of the State" and "For the Freedom and Transcendence of the Church," *Am. Eccles. Rev.* 124 (1951), pp. 327-52; and 126 (1952), pp. 525-63.

27. On the Church's recognition of the rights of conscience and freedom of worship, see the documents cited by Msgr. Journet, *op. cit.,* pp. 228-31.

28. *Pacem in Terris,* par. 14 (Gibbons, p. 9).

29. *Ibid.,* par. 65 (Gibbons, p. 26).

30. *Christianity and Crisis,* Aug. 7, 1961.

31. *Cf.* Leo XIII, *In Plurimis,* pars. 8 and 9, *Libertas,* par. 12.

32. *We Hold These Truths,* p. 234.

33. Allocution, March 7, 1957 (*The Pope Speaks,* 4.1, p. 98). *Cf.* William F. Buckley, Jr., *Up From Liberalism* (McDowell, Obolensky 1959), p. 119: "Even though democracy is a mere procedure, all the hopes of an epoch were vested in it. Intellectuals have tended to look upon democracy as an extension of the scientific method applied to social problems. In an age of relativism, one tends to look for flexible devices for measuring *this* morning's truth. Such a device is democracy; and indeed, democracy becomes epistemology: democracy will render reliable political truths just as surely as the marketplace sets negotiable economic values."

34. William F. Buckley, Jr., Letter, New York *Times,* October 17, 1960. *Cf.* Newman, "Letter," pp. 123-4.

35. Will Herberg, "Religious Symbols in Public Life," *National Review,* August 28, 1962. *Cf.* Herberg, *National Review,* July 30, 1963, p. 61: "Therefore the 'established order'—the state, above all—ought to include within itself signs, symbols, and ceremonials constantly reminding itself and the people that it *is* subject to a majesty beyond all earthly majesties."

36. Newman, "Letter," p. 120.

BIBLIOGRAPHICAL NOTE

THIS is, so far as I know, the first complete book in English to deal with the problem of establishing norms for the interpretation of papal encyclicals in political discourse. I learn that everyone who has looked into this matter at all is surprised to find how exiguous is the bibliography that can be consulted with profit. Theologians, it appears, must construct their norms of interpretation from the general principles enunciated in the treatises *De Ecclesia*—treatises which are themselves undergoing the most drastic revision and rethinking. Meanwhile the layman must, for the most part, content himself with things like the exhortations which, prefixed to commentaries on the individual encyclicals, are meant to commandeer attention for what follows. These exhortations vaguely (sometimes with vague menace) inform the Catholic that he must be obedient to papal authority—which is a safe, but not particularly helpful, observation.

Rather than discuss what there is of this dreary and scattered literature, I put down at once the two articles that make a realistic beginning on the kind of analysis we need. Both are by Alfred de Soras, S.J., and both appeared in *Revue de l'action populaire*: "La portée des documents pontificaux en matière politique, économique et sociale" (February, 1961) and "La facture littéraire des documents pontificaux en matière politique, économique et sociale" (March, 1961). As for the early history of encyclicals, I was not able to procure a copy of the major work, Bencini's *De Litteris Encyclicis* (1728). I relied, instead, on Dom Paul Nau's summary of Bencini's findings, in Nau's *Une source doctrinale: les encycliques* (Paris, 1952), which is the most important and useful modern book on the papal letters.

As for the text of the encyclicals and other papal documents, I turned to the originals, published in the *Acta Apostolicae Sedis*, only where appeal to the text was made, or made necessary, by commentators whose work appeared in the general press—e.g., Mr.

Clancy on *Humani Generis,* Mr. Cort on *Quadragesimo Anno,*
Father Davis on *Pacem in Terris*—since this is a book concerned
with the political use of encyclicals by and for the layman, which
normally means use in the vernacular. But this itself suggests a
problem—the fact that so little of the papal literature is available
in English. Since 1954, it is true, we have had the useful collection
published quarterly in *The Pope Speaks.* But even this does not
give us as wide a selection as the French, for instance, can find in
La documentation catholique. It is especially regrettable that so
much of our American journal's space (and, presumably, money)
is devoted to the inclusion of pictures of the Pope, taken from every
angle. It should leave this to *Life* magazine, and give us more of
the Pope's own words. Nonetheless, we should be grateful for the
good work that this quarterly is doing. Its translations are of quite
high quality. It seemed to be embarking on a very useful custom,
of giving the Latin original also for more important documents,
when, in number 7.4, the Latin text of *Mater et Magistra* was
printed along with Father H. E. Winstone's translation for the
Catholic Truth Society. Unfortunately, the practice was abandoned in the case of *Pacem in Terris.* But the journal did give us
the first English version of *Pacem*—again by Father Winstone—
from the Latin original, a service which should not have been
needed at this late date, but which is all the more welcome for that
reason. (I use their translation of *Mater et Magistra* in the text of
this book, but the *Pacem* issue came too late for me to use. In
citing that encyclical, I had to use the Paulist Press edition, for
which William J. Gibbons, S.J., assisted by others, corrected the
text that had been released to the English-speaking press. The
nature of the translation itself, and of the "corrections" in the
Paulist edition, made it necessary, in this case, to refer to the original
throughout; which reminds me that—though discussion of *Pacem*
had for some time filled the pages of both the secular and the religious press, and controversy had arisen over the accuracy of the
translation—I discovered that the only copy of the original text in
a large seminary's library still had its pages uncut, a sad commentary on the guidance priests will be giving to the discussion of encyclicals.)

One of the many services performed by Doubleday's Image Books series is the publication, in inexpensive form, of excellent English translations and notes for the major encyclicals of Leo XIII (*The Church Speaks to the Modern World,* edited by Etienne Gilson) and Pius XI (*The Church and the Reconstruction of the Modern World,* edited by Terence P. McLaughlin, C.S.B.). All page references to the pertinent documents in my book are to these handy editions. Vincent A. Yzermans has published many collections of papal statements, especially those of Pius XII. Two of his books I have used constantly: *All Things in Christ, Selected Encyclicals and Documents of Saint Pius X,* Newman Press, 1954, and *The Major Addresses of Pope Pius XII,* North Central Publishing Company, St. Paul, 1961. The last work is in two volumes, the second of which contains all the Christmas messages—those messages which Pope Pius made his principal vehicle for discussing social problems. It is a very valuable book, and should be (though it is not yet) in every library. For the other encyclicals of Pius XII, one must go to the NCWC publications in pamphlet form. Twenty-nine of these have been collected in an expensive binding, with an index, as *Selected Documents of His Holiness Pius XII, 1939-1958.* There are many collections of excerpts from the papal letters and speeches, often arranged according to subject matter. One of the more useful is *Papal Pronouncements on the Political Order* (Newman, 1952), by Francis J. Powers, C.S.V. Other books of selections or outlines are:

Chinigo, Michael, *The Pope Speaks,* Pantheon, 1957.

Freemantle, Anne, *The Papal Encyclicals in Their Historical Context,* Mentor, 1956.

Gonella, Guido, *The Papacy and World Peace,* Hollis and Carter, 1945.

Harte, Thomas J., C.S.S.R., *Papal Social Principles,* Peter Smith, 1960.

Hughes, Philip, *The Pope's New Order,* Macmillan, 1944.

Koenig, H. C., *Principles for Peace,* Bruce, 1943.

Kothen, Robert, *L'Enseignement social de l'église,* Louvain, 1949.

Naughton, James W., S.J., *Pius XII on World Problems,* The America Press, 1943.

Quinlan, Maurice, *Guide for Living* (Pius XII excerpts), Longmans, Green and Company, 1960.

For a list of encyclicals issued between 1878 and 1937, one can consult Sister M. Claudia Arlen, I.H.M., *A Guide to the Encyclicals of the Roman Pontiffs,* H. W. Wilson Company, 1939.

For the whole large subject of the magisterium, or teaching authority of the Church, there is no one major book to recommend; only one major author—Newman, whose feel for the Church as an irreducible reality within history has been a touchstone for all my thinking in this area, and for that of men far more learned than I am, theologians like Josef Rupert Geiselmann and Hans Küng. The bulk of Newman's work is out of print, difficult or impossible to purchase; but here, too, Doubleday's Image series has come to our rescue by making some of his books available in paperback (one hopes for more). I have used in my text, and cited by their pagination, the Image editions of the *Apologia Pro Vita Sua, Essay on the Development of Christian Doctrine, Idea of a University,* and *Grammar of Assent,* with valuable introductions by, respectively, Philip Hughes, George N. Shuster, Gustave Weigel, S.J., and Etienne Gilson. Newman's discussion of the political bearing of the Vatican (I) Decrees is of course, especially relevant; and for that I have used Alvan Ryan's edition of the "Letter to His Grace the Duke of Norfolk," in *Newman and Gladstone: The Vatican Decrees,* Notre Dame Press, 1962. Other citations from Newman are from the Longmans, Green *Works* or the recent Longmans edition of certain essays and sermons edited by Charles Frederick Harrold. I should probably mention, at this point, that the *Rambler* controversy treated in Part II of my book is the subject of many useful studies—first of all, in the biographies of its principal actors (Newman, Acton, Ward, Wiseman), but also in Douglas Woodruff's introduction to Acton's *Essays on Church and State* (London, 1952), John Coulson's introduction to Newman's *On Consulting the Faithful in Matters of Doctrine* (Sheed and Ward, 1961); and the importance of the conflict is well brought out by

Josef Altholz in *The Liberal Catholic Movement in England* (Montreal, 1961), and by Hugh A. MacDougall, O.M.I., in *The Acton-Newman Relations, The Dilemma of Christian Liberalism* (Fordham Press, 1962). For the discussion of Newman's concept of conscience in Part IV, I have been particularly helped by Adrian J. Boekraad, *The Personal Conquest of Truth According to John Henry Newman*, Louvain, 1955 (especially pp. 251-90), by Brother F. James Kaiser, F.S.C., *The Concept of Conscience According to J. H. Newman*, Catholic University Studies No. 106, 1958, and by Boekraad and Tristram, *The Argument from Conscience to the Existence of God According to J. H. Newman*, Louvain, 1961. One last, very appropriate Newman reference might be to the tenth lecture in his *Difficulties of Anglicans*, whose title—"Differences Among Catholics No Prejudice to the Unity of the Church"— could stand as the motto of this book.

Apart from the works of Newman, these were the writings I found in one way or another helpful in approaching the subject of the magisterium:

Bainvel, J-V., S.J., *De Magisterio Vivo et Traditione*, Paris, 1905.

Benard, Edmond, "The Doctrinal Value of the Ordinary Teaching of the Holy Father in View of *Humani Generis*," *Proceedings of the Catholic Theological Society of America*, 6 (1951).

Billot, Louis, S.J., *De Ecclesia Christi*, I (1927) and II (1929), Rome.

Butler, Basil C., *The Church and Infallibility*, Sheed and Ward, 1954.

Caudron, M., "Magistère et infaillibilité pontificale d'après le constitution *Dei Filius*," *Ephemerides Theologicae Lovanienses* 36 (1960).

Choupin, Lucien, S.J., *La valeur des décisions doctrinale et disciplinaires du Saint-Siège*,[2] Paris, 1912.

Cicognani, Amleto Giovanni, *Canon Law* I[2] (translated by O'Hara and Brennan), Newman, 1934.

Danielou, Jean, and Vorgrimler, Herbert, *Sentire Ecclesiam*, Freiburg, 1961.

Dewan, Wilfrid F., C.S.P., "Preparation of the Vatican Council

Schema on the Power and Nature of the Primacy," *Epheme-rides Theologicae Lovanienses* 36 (1960).

Fessler, Joseph, *The True and the False Infallibility of the Popes*[3] (translated by Ambrose St. John), London, 1875.

Franzelin, Johann B., S.J., *De Divina Traditione et Scriptura*, Rome, 1882.

Journet, Charles, *The Church of the Word Incarnate, I. The Apostolic Hierarchy* (translated by A. H. C. Downes), Sheed and Ward, 1954.

Journet, Charles, *The Primacy of Peter*, Newman, 1954.

Jung, Nicholas, *Le magistère de l'église*, Paris, 1935.

Labourdette, M., "Les enseignements de l'encyclique *Humani Generis*," *Revue thomiste* 50 (1950).

McNabb, Vincent, O.P., *Infallibility*, London, 1905.

Möhler, John Adam, *Symbolism* (translated by James Burton Robertson), London, 1906.

Pegues, Thomas M., O.P., "L'Autorité des encycliques pontifi-cales d'après Saint-Thomas," *Revuen thomiste* 12 (1904).

Rahner, Karl, S.J., "Lehramt," *Lexikon für Theologie und Kirche*.

Scheeben, M. J., *The Mysteries of Christianity* (translated by Cyril Vollert, S.J.), Herder, 1946.

Todd, John M. (editor), *Problems of Authority*, Helicon, 1962.

Vacant Jean-Michel-Alfred, *Le magistère ordinaire de l'église et ses organes*, Paris, 1887.

This is not the place to give a complete bibliography on other matters that enter into my discussion. On the whole problem of Church and State relations, for instance, I can do no more than refer to the principal authors—Lord Acton, Luigi Sturzo, Joseph Lecler, Waldemar Gurian, Heinrich Rommen, John Tracy Ellis, Gustave Weigel, S.J.—and conclude with an expression of my profound debt to, and admiration for, the most important recent work in this area, that of John Courtney Murray, S.J. A partial bibliography of Father Murray's and his critics' writings, compiled by Gustave Weigel, S.J., can be found in *Theology Digest* 1 (1953), pp. 173-5. The Murray articles I have used most extensively, and whose titles I give in the appropriate footnotes, will be found in the following journals: *Theological Studies* 6 (pp. 229-86), 9 (pp. 491-535), 10 (pp. 177-234), 13 (pp. 525-63), and 14 (pp. 1-30, 551-67); *American Ecclesiastical Review* 124 (pp. 327-61), 126 (pp. 28-48); and *Proceedings of the Catholic Theological Society of America* 3 (pp. 26-98).

Another relevant subject is the role of the layman in the Church, since it is the layman who must in large part carry out the papal social program. On this there is a valuable literature—by, among others, Karl Rahner, S.J., Yves Congar, O.P., Jacques Leclerq, and Daniel Callahan. The particular problems and achievements of the American layman have also been studied extensively. The two authors I am particularly indebted to on this subject are Walter J. Ong, S.J., and Will Herberg.

Since this book is concerned only with the proper method for reading encyclicals, with one's *mode* in applying any of them, and not with the content of particular encyclicals, I shall not venture into the bibliography on specific problems as these have been treated by the Popes. Although few things have been written on the way to read encyclicals generally, particular readings have been offered us in abundance, displaying every possible degree of skill and conscientiousness. Some, such as *The Church and Social Justice,* by Calvez and Perrin, are very useful. But even the presence of a few works of merit does not free us from the task of establishing the norms by which their merit is to be measured.

Most of the abbreviations used in the notes are self-explanatory. AAS stands for *Acta Apostolicae Sedis,* DC for *Documentation catholique,* ST for St. Thomas' *Summa Theologica,* CG for his *Summa Contra Gentiles.* To draw attention to the precise wording of documents, I italicize words and phrases in the quoted portions of encyclicals. This emphasis is always mine, not part of the document itself. I do not note this in each instance, though I frequently remind the reader of it, especially where there might be any confusion. The same applies to emphasized matter in the quoted comments of others on the papal texts.

I append a paragraph, in the last stages of printing, to express my regret I was not able to use some books which have appeared on the eve of this book's publication. They brighten the somewhat dismal situation described in this bibliographical note. The major event in this field is the publication of Father de Soras' *Documents d'église et options politiques,* (Paris: Editions du Centurion, 1962). The second half of the book is made up of the two articles I lean on so heavily in my book. The earlier sections are devoted to a criticism of the "integrist" group known as "La Cité Catholique." This right-wing movement cites papal documents in a simplistic way to force its political position on Catholics. Father de Soras criticizes certain examples of this abuse, as I have tried to do with the American version of the practice. The fact that opportunistic citation can be indulged in by either the right or the left should surprise no one; the abuse is widespread, and a reading of Father de Soras' book will acquaint one with a typical form it takes in other countries. Another, more popular book by de Soras has just appeared as Volume 106 in the *Twentieth Century Encyclopedia of Catholicism* (Hawthorn Books). It is called *International Morality,* and it is perhaps the briefest and the best book on this subject. This, too, gives a brief summary of his articles (Chapter three), and then it takes up questions resembling those I deal with in the last chapter of Part Two. I think a comparison of my chapter with Chapter five of his book may interest the reader. Although de Soras and I would, of course, disagree on practical conclusions and specific policies (which neither of us arrive at), our agreement on the relevant principles, and on the problems that arise in the historical "minor," is striking, at least to me. And, to me, very encouraging. If agreement can be reached on these matters, if two or more independent analyses coincide because basic principles of procedure were followed (in this case, principles I had learned from de Soras' earlier work), then discourse can be re-opened in many areas where it is at present closed.

I was given a great deal of help in assembling and assessing the literature on the encyclicals by Richard Costigan, S.J.

ACKNOWLEDGMENTS

T HIS book began as a contribution to a book of essays by Catholics—as an essay dealing with the practical problems involved in the interpretation of papal encyclicals. I meant to circumscribe my material by considering only such problems as arose out of the controversy over *National Review's* treatment of *Mater et Magistra*. I have adhered to that plan, but with increasing dismay as I saw the problems increase under my gaze. The modest essay has become a far larger, but perhaps even more modest, book—one meant to dispel some of the illusions I lived with and lost as I watched my little problem enlarge itself and reopen all the problems of freedom and authority that haunt papal statements.

The essay absorbed, too, the book for which it was planned. As I worked on my portion of the whole, I found myself faced with many of the problems that were to be assigned to others. The large interconnections sketched by the editor became, by his generosity and assistance, part of my essay's network. The essay was a parasite which lived off the book, which finally (again, by the editor's generosity) supplanted it.

By the time I realized how far I had wandered into this strange country, it was too late to return. The problems themselves fascinated me, and many friends encouraged me to linger here, where they had come before me and discovered many things before I arrived, things they gladly surrendered to my newcomer's eyes. Most of the help came from the man who was to have been the book's editor, and is now almost its co-author, Mr. Neil McCaffrey. Others, it is true, clergymen and lay, Catholics and non-Catholics, offered helpful criticisms—especially Bishop John J. Wright, Msgr. Florence D. Cohalan, Rev. Stanley Parry, C.S.C., Rev. Vincent Miceli, S.J., Rev. Thomas A. O'Connor, S.J., Professor Will Herberg, Mr. Murray Kempton, and Mrs. Elsie Bown Meyer. All of these read the book in manuscript, and, by their comments, helped reshape it; without, of course, becoming responsible in any way for its shortcomings.

But I cannot let Neil McCaffrey off with the usual disclaimers. He *is* to blame for this book. Whatever praise or censure it meets with, he must share with me. Mr. McCaffrey has a disconcerting gift for making his Catholic friends *exercise* the freedom to which they have a right. He is a close student of Catholic life in this country, something of a nemesis to any of his acquaintances who lapse into complacency about it—and a hard taskmaster, who always has projects to suggest to people who prefer reading poetry or writing about less controversial matters. This book was his idea. The journalistic material on which it is based came from his vast files. (It is only fair to warn Catholic journalists that he has files on many other subjects treated by them, and other friends as dutifully responsive to his call as I.) In dealing with this material, he worked with me and against me, while insisting that I call my work what is only partly mine. The best is his. The idea is his. I hope I have not spoiled it.

To all those who helped so generously, then—and, most cordially, to Neil—the author's thanks:

οὔτε κασιγνήτοις ἐπιμέμψομαι, οἷσί περ ἀνήρ,
μαρναμένοισι πέποιθε, καὶ εἰ μέγα νεῖκος ὄρηται.

The selection from *Lay People in the Church,* by Yves Congar, O.P., is reprinted by permission of The Newman Press.